D1474686

The Philosopher-King

in Medieval and Renaissance Jewish Thought

Abraham Melamed

Edited and with a Foreword by
Lenn E. Goodman

State University of New York Press

Published by
State University of New York Press, Albany

For information, address State University of New York Press,
90 State Street, Suite 700, Albany, NY 12207

Production by Michael Haggett
Marketing by Patrick Durocher

Library of Congress Cataloging-in-Publication Data

Melamed, Abraham, 1944–
    The philosopher-king in medieval and Renaissance Jewish thought / Abraham Melamed
: edited and with a foreword by Lenn E. Goodman.
    p. cm. — (SUNY series in Jewish philosophy)
    Includes bibliographical references and index.
    ISBN 0-7914-5567-X (alk. paper)—ISBN 0-7914-5568-8 (pbk. : alk. paper)
    1. Philosopher-kings. 2. Philosophy, Jewish—History. 3. Plato—Contributions in
political science. 4. Political science—Philosophy—History. 5. Jews—Civilization—Greek
influences. I. Goodman, Lenn Evan, 1944– II. Title. III. Series.

B757.P45 M45 2003
296.3'82'09—dc21
                                                                    2002026880

10 9 8 7 6 5 4 3 2 1

The Philosopher-King

in Medieval
and Renaissance
Jewish Thought

SUNY series in Jewish Philosophy

Kenneth Seeskin, editor

For my parents,
Bluma and Isaac Melamed
of blessed memory

Contents

Foreword   ix

Preface   xi

1   Philosopher, King, Prophet   1

2   The Sources   13

3   First Influences   23

4   The Class System   61

5   Transmission   75

6   Adaptation   93

7   Application   111

8   Christian Applications and the Machiavellian Revolution   141

9   Rejection   167

Afterword   185

Appendix: The Hebrew Versions of the Philosopher King's Virtues   189

Notes   199

Bibliography   247

Index   265

Foreword

The publication of Abraham Melamed's *The Philosopher King in Medieval and Renaissance Jewish Political Thought* brings to fruition a project with which I was involved since the early 1990s, when my old friend Menachem Kellner of Haifa University brought this important study to my attention. The work was written in Hebrew, and the process of its translation, editing, and final preparation for the press has involved great efforts on all sides. Throughout that process of reading, rereading, reviewing, Englishing, and ordering this major contribution, I was a believer. Melamed's text surveys primary texts in their original languages to follow the Jewish medieval history of the idea of the philosopher king from its roots in Greek philosophy to the Arabic commentaries and Hebrew writings of creative thinkers who made the idea at home in their own political and philosophical environments and put it to work within the context of their philosophical and political thinking. As a result, this book affords readers a Cook's tour of Jewish political philosophy during a period when most scholars have been led to suppose that all such life forms were extinct.

Comparative in method and interpretive in perspective, Melamed's study makes use of materials that are seldom read, let alone studied, by modern authors. Some survive in manuscript or are little known and cited by prior researchers. With his translations and transcriptions from the original Hebrew and Italian texts of these primary sources, Melamed has made their thought accessible to a wide range of modern readers and thinkers. In doing so, he has added a bright new chapter to the history of political theory and enriched our understanding of Jewish intellectual life and political ideals in one of the richest periods of Jewish intellectual history, the period that extends from the Middle Ages and into the Renaissance. Warm appreciation is due to Menachem Kellner, for championing this book, and to James Peltz and Kenneth Seeskin for welcoming it into the SUNY Series in Jewish Philosophy. I take modest pride in Abraham Melamed's achievement here. I am confident that readers will long profit from his substantive and probing researches.

Lenn E. Goodman

Preface

1

This book deals with the great encounter between the Jewish political tradition and Platonic political philosophy. This encounter is examined by means of the basic idea of Plato's political thought, the theory of the Philosopher King. The first stage took place in Hellenistic-Roman times, when Philo of Alexandria identified the principles of Plato's political philosophy in the Torah, and described the ideal figure of Moses in terms of the Philosopher King theory. In the Middle Ages the encounter between Jewish thought and the Platonic political tradition was renewed from the tenth century or thereabouts, following the penetration of that tradition into the Muslim cultural world, which, in turn, influenced Jewish thought. This book deals with the renewed encounter from its beginnings until its rejection and disappearance from Jewish culture in Western Europe on the eve of the Enlightenment.

The history of this intellectual motif, as this book will interpret it, shows clearly, in microcosm, the complex reciprocal influence exerted between Jewish culture and that of the majority cultures in which it functioned for centuries: Hellenistic-Roman, medieval Muslim and Latin-Christian from the late Middle Ages, through the Renaissance, up to the beginnings of the modern period. Every culture exists and develops through the reciprocal influences of others. This is even truer for minority cultures like the Jewish, one that persisted throughout its history in the midst of changing majority cultures. Jewish culture never existed in a vacuum. As in every other intellectual sphere, also, in this case, Jewish culture functioned within a complex framework of reciprocal influences. It can be properly understood only in the intellectual, cultural, and historical context in which it operates, which affects it and on which it exerts its own reciprocal influence.

An examination of the stages through which Platonic political philosophy first penetrated medieval Jewish thought affords a good example of this complex process. First of all, Jewish thought like every other culture, was not affected by outside influences in a random fashion. Effective influences were those that fitted its needs and served its purposes. One of the central findings to be discussed in this book is the fact that Jewish thought absorbed Platonic and not Aristotelian political philosophy—*The Republic* and not the *Politics*. The opposite might have been anticipated, given that in all other areas of philosophy and science, Jewish thought based itself massively on the Aristotelian tradition. As will be shown later on, this did not happen by chance, but rather because the Platonic political world view fitted in better with the political theology of Islam and of Judaism, both in essence holistic, than did Aristotle's *Politics*, which was better suited to the dualistic political theology of medieval Christianity. Hence, it is no coincidence that Christianity based itself on the *Politics* and not on *The Republic*, in marked contrast with both Islam and Judaism. Neither is there any coincidence in the rejection of the Platonic political tradition and its disappearance from Jewish culture just before the Enlightenment. That was a direct result of the internal needs of the culture when it came under modern influences and went through gradual secularization processes that undermined the holistic framework of traditional Rabbinic Judaism.

Second, in keeping with the general process of cultural transfer, we do not find that outside influences are simply adopted and copied, but rather they are extensively adapted and transposed to meet the needs and characteristics of the receiving culture. It is a gradual process, beginning with the translation of relevant texts, and ending with their adaptation and application. In the first stage of the transmission of the Philosopher King theory, one finds simply a Hebrew translation of the relevant Platonic texts from the Arabic, along with medieval Islamic commentaries. We are well aware, of course, that no translation can be more than commentary filtered through a cultural prism. In the second stage, we find application, with extensive adaptation of both the translated works of Plato and their Muslim commentaries to meet the developing needs of Jewish culture.

Third, we have before us a clear example of the process of repeated reciprocal influence. Herein lies the important contribution of medieval Jewish political thought to the history of western political thought in general. In this instance, as in so many others, Jewish scholars functioned as transmitters of culture—texts and ideas—from the Greek—Muslim cultural world to the Latin-Christian of the later Middle Ages and the Renaissance. This was their most important contribution to the Platonic political tradition in the west, and to the history of western political thought as a whole; scholars to this day are barely aware of this influence. The main expression of this contribution lies in the transmission of the influence of Ibn Rushd's important commentary on Plato's *Republic*, first through the fourteenth-century Hebrew translation, which influenced Jewish political thinking in the later Middle Ages and the Renaissance. Then the Hebrew was translated—twice—into Latin for the consumption of Christian readers, and had considerable impact on the renewal of the Platonic political tradition during the Renaissance. The Hebrew translation of Ibn Rushd's commentary on *The Republic* is of great significance, since it constitues the only surviving evidence of this commentary: the Arabic original has disappeared. Up to this time, scholars dealt only with the renewal of the Platonic political tradition in the west during the Renaissance following the transmission of the Platonic dialogues, in the original Greek, from Byzantium to Italy in the first half of the fifteenth century, after the Ottoman conquest of Byzantium. They were unaware of the parallel transmission channel via Muslim culture, by means of Latin translations of Ibn Rushd's commentary on *The Republic* in Hebrew, and through contemporary Jewish scholars' contacts with the Platonic-Muslim political tradition, as absorbed into Jewish thought of the later medieval times. Ernest Barker once maintained that Plato's *Republic* disappeared completely from European culture for a thousand years, until rediscovered in the Renaissance. He was unaware of the totally opposite situation prevailing in Jewish and Muslim cultures: Aristotle's *Politics* had disappeared, while Plato's *Republic* with its Arabic commentaries in Hebrew translation continued to serve as a basic political textbook throughout the Middle Ages. James Hankins' important work, *Plato in the Italian Renaissance* (Leiden 1991) is obviously unaware of it, so completely ignores the parallel Jewish channel through which the Platonic political tradition entered Renaissance culture. My book, *Philosopher King*, is designed to make up for this lack, documenting in detail the Jewish contribution to the Platonic political tradition in the Middle Ages and the Renaissance.

2

The study of medieval Jewish political philosophy is still a comparatively neglected field, especially in comparison with the amount of research in other branches of medieval Jewish philosophy, such as ethics and metaphysics. This state of affairs is perhaps natural and even justified by the very fact that political philosophy is only "wisdom's little sister," as the Italian Jewish scholar of the fifteenth century, Moses of Rieti, phrased it nicely in his *Mikdash Meat*.

This assessment is basically still valid, despite Leo Strauss' heroic attempt to interpret the whole body of medieval Muslim and Jewish thought as Platonic political philosophy disguised in monotheistic theological garb.

Still, for the medieval mind, or for its Greek predecessor, political philosophy is no queen of the sciences but a by-product of the basic premises of ethics, metaphysics, and theology. Unqualified acceptance of Strauss' bold thesis might have provided a wonderful justification for the scholarly value of our field of study (that is, if justification is needed at all!). Alas, I do not think that an objective assessment of medieval thought can validate such an extreme claim. Political philosophy is still wisdom's little sister, but like most little sisters, it is a very special one indeed.

The study of medieval Jewish political philosophy was pioneered by Strauss, whose contribution to the field is, of course, invaluable to this day, even if one does not accept all his conclusions. In his footsteps came E. I. J. Rosenthal, S. Pines, R. Lerner, and L. V. Berman, whose fruitful work in this particular field was regrettably cut short by his untimely death. My research owes a special debt to all of them.

Still, the present state of research in medieval Jewish political philosophy does not yet permit the writing of a comprehensive history of the subject, as was attempted by E. I. J. Rosenthal in medieval Muslim political philosophy, and by R. W. Carlyle, E. Lewis, W. Ullmann, and others, in medieval Christian political philosophy. Much research must still be done on particular problems like the one I have undertaken to deal with in this work. Especially needed are the study and reinterpretation of primary sources, many of which are still in manuscript form, like Isaac Ibn Latif's *Sha'ar ha-Shamayim* and Yohanan Alemanno's *Hai ha-Olamim,* which are discussed in this study.

This study covers roughly the period from the tenth to the eighteenth century. It begins when the theory of the philosopher king reemerged in Jewish thought as an integral part of medieval Jewish philosophy. This resulted from the renewed encounter between Jewish theology and Greek philosophy and science, via Arabic intermediaries. The study traces the development of this theory in medieval Jewish philosophy. It follows the route by which this idea was transmitted from Arabic adaptations of the original Greek theory, transformed and re-adapted in the milieu of Jewish thought, as its scholarly centers gradually shifted from a Muslim to a Latin-Christian environment beginning in the late twelfth century. One of my major findings is that despite this development, Jewish political philosophy remained essentially anchored in the Platonic-Muslim philosophical milieu practically until the seventeenth century. The influence of Christian philosophy was, at best, marginal, much less than on any other branch of late medieval Jewish philosophy. This will be explained by cultural as well as theological and halakhic considerations. The Jewish attachment to an essentially Platonic-Muslim frame of reference was shattered only as a result of the reverberations of the fierce Machiavellian onslaught upon the whole medieval world view in the sixteenth and seventeenth centuries. Here we shall find the theory of the philosopher king finally rejected and sadly laid to rest.

Thus, my book starts with the very beginnings of medieval Jewish philosophy and ends with the very beginning of modern Jewish philosophy in the later seventeenth and the eighteenth centuries. Although I share the widely accepted opinion that Jewish philosophy was by and large "medieval" in its essence, at least until the late sixteenth century, a proviso must be added here.

From the late fifteenth century on, a clear and ever-growing influence of Renaissance culture is evident. Jewish thinkers like Yohanan Alemanno, Isaac Abravanel, and Simone Luzzatto would be grossly misunderstood if the Renaissance were not taken into account when we consider their thought. It is true that the Renaissance is not as strong in Jewish as in Christian thought, but it would be misleading to disregard its influence altogether, especially on Jewish political thought.

This is a study in the history of ideas; it follows the traditional methodology of this field, striving to follow a single idea in its context, to find out how and why this particular idea entered Jewish thought at a given time, was transmitted, adapted, further developed, and applied to Hebrew sources and Jewish history, until it was finally rejected and allowed to drop out of sight.

Often the distant origins of a work can be traced back to a doctoral dissertation. In my case it was *The Political Thought of Jewish Thinkers in the Italian Renaissance* (in Hebrew, Tel Aviv University, 1976), supervised by Professor J. G. Sermoneta. In this dissertation, the subject of the present book was a minor topic, one among many others. One of the then new findings was the elaborate political discussion in Yohanan Alemanno's magnum opus *Hai ha-Olamim.* This discussion caps a long-standing Jewish adaptation of the Platonic-Averroist theory of the philosopher king. As a doctoral student, I was conscious only of the Plato—Ibn Rushd—Alemanno connection. Many intermediary stages in the development of the theory were still unknown to me. Chronologically, I started almost at the end of the process. In the years that followed, I gradually traced back what I consider now to be almost the complete unfolding of this intellectual tradition in medieval and Renaissance Jewish thought. This study is the consummation of that effort.

For Arabic, Hebrew, Latin, and Italian texts, which are available in English translations, I have followed the appropriate translation in the body of the work, as indicated in the notes. On certain occasions, I found it advisable to make changes in existing translations. Any such instance is indicated in the notes. Medieval Hebrew texts not yet available in English translation, some still in manuscript form, were translated by me. Likewise with the passages from Simone Luzzatto's two Italian works. The appendix includes all the lists of the ideal ruler's virtues in the Hebrew original, for the sake of comparison. In the body of the text these lists appear separately in English translation. The system of transliteration employed generally follows that of the Encyclopaedia Judaica.

I wish to express my thanks, first of all, to my teacher, Professor J. B. Sermoneta, who introduced me to medieval Jewish texts and those of Italian Jewish thinkers of the Renaissance in particular. Professor Sermoneta died when I was in the final stages of writing this book. His guidance has been a lasting influence on my work. I would also like to thank Dr. R. Jospe, who was kind enough to read attentively an early draft of the whole manuscript and make many useful comments, which I took into careful consideration, and which helped to make this study a better product. Special gratitude goes to my friend and colleague Professor M. Kellner, without whose encouragement, assistance, and friendship throughout the whole long process of making this book never would have seen the light in its present form. Many thanks to Mr. M. Rave and Mr. A. Goldstein who diligently and tastefully translated the text into English. Finally, I wish to thank Professor L. E. Goodman, who followed closely the whole project, for the careful reading of the manuscript and the many improvements he suggested in style as well as content which were essential in making this book a better product.

Grateful acknowledgment is made to the Lucius N. Littauer Foundation and to the Wolfson Chair of Jewish Thought and Heritage at the University of Haifa for grants which made the completion of this book possible. My thanks also to the staff of the Research Authority at the University of Haifa and to the staff of the Institute of Microfilmed Hebrew Manuscripts, the Jewish National and University Library in Jerusalem, for their expert technical assistance and cooperation. Special thanks to Danielle Friedlander and Heather Kernoff, Chantal Asher, and Angela Greenson for their heroic struggle to decipher my elaborate notes. On the home front, I would like to thank my wife Paula, who, despite never totally understanding the point or content of the intellectual gymnastics involved in my work, always supported it, and my children, Noa, Yonatan, and Tamar, who let me disappear into my study to tend my intellectual offspring. Finally, I want to acknowledge my late parents, Bluma and Isaac Melamed, to whose memory this study is dedicated. They taught me the value of hard work and of pursuing my calling diligently; and they made it clear what it means to love books and cherish learning.

1

Philosopher, King, Prophet

1

Medieval Muslim thinkers based their political discussions on Plato's *Repub-lic* and *Laws*, not on Aristotle's *Politics*. They did so despite being acquainted with most of Aristotle's extant writings, except for the *Politics*, and being markedly influenced by the Aristotelian tradition.[1] The bias might have been the result of pure chance—the manuscript of the *Politics* simply did not reach them. Perhaps, as R. Walzer supposes, late Hellenistic philosophy simply pre-ferred Plato's *Republic* to Aristotle's *Politics* as a basic textbook on politics. The fact is that we do not have even one commentary on Aristotle's *Politics* dating from that time.[2] Muslim thinkers inherited the same manuscripts to which late Hellenistic philosophy inclined and adapted them to their own philo-sophical and theological world view. They also continued the accepted prac-tice in late Hellenistic philosophy of seeking to unify Plato's different texts and, what is relevant for us, his political writings, especially *The Republic* and the *Laws*, and to blur the differences among them. The Neoplatonic philoso-phers like Plotinus and Proclus, who held that the philosopher must shun human society and strive for divine perfection, leaned toward the *Parmenides* and the *Theaetetus*. Muslim philosophy, by contrast (with the exception of Ibn Bajja), emphasized the social obligation of the philosopher and favored *The Republic* and the *Laws*, read through Neoplatonic modifications and the influ-ence of Aristotle's *Nicomachaean Ethics*. These two Platonic dialogues became the foundation of Muslim political thought. E. I. J. Rosenthal justly titled the second part of his magnum opus on Muslim political thought, which treats political philosophy, "The Platonic Legacy."[3]

Whatever the reason for the Muslims' bias toward Plato's *Republic* over Aristotle's *Politics*, *The Republic* undoubtedly suited their theological and

1

philosophical world view better. In qualifications and definition of functions, the Platonic philosopher king nicely paralleled the lawgiver-prophet of the Muslim tradition. As Ibn Rushd remarks in his commentary on Plato's *Republic*, translated into Hebrew by Samuel ben Judah of Marseilles: "Consequently, these terms, that is, Philosopher, King and Lawgiver, are as it were synonymous; so also is 'Priest.'"[4] The superimposing of the Platonic philosopher king on the lawgiver-prophet of the Muslim tradition is clearly reflected in the medieval discussion on the virtues of the ideal ruler.

This identification was facilitated by the Farabian-Platonic world view, which established an exact parallel between philosophy and politics, with philosophy dealing with right beliefs and politics with right actions. Each of these two spheres reflects and is conditioned on the other. Without the attainment of perfection in one, perfection in the other is not possible. When philosophy is political, then, the philosopher may, indeed must be, the statesman. al-Farabi (following Aristotle) defines political wisdom (as Falaquera translates it in his *Beginning of Wisdom [Reshit Hokhmah]*) "the perfect kingly art," the most noble philosophical domain. Whoever attains knowledge of this sort, must apply it in right actions. Thus, if the sciences of religious law and of theology (*fiqh, kalam,* translated by Falaquera in the same place as "the art of jurisprudence" and "the art of dialectical theology") are made ancillary to the science of politics, the philosopher, who is also king, may at the same time also be lawgiver and prophet, and perhaps even priest.[5]

2

Medieval Jewish thought, like Muslim thought, followed Plato's *Republic*. Christian thinking, in contrast, founded its political philosophy on Aristotle's *Politics* from the time the work was translated into Latin in the thirteenth century. Even R. Klibansky, who emphasized the continuity of the Platonic tradition in medieval Christian culture, stressed that this influence was exerted through such dialogues as the *Timaeus* and the *Parmenides*. There is no vestige of *The Republic* in medieval Christian sources in the West. Thus, Ernest Barker, who completely ignored the Muslim and Jewish traditions and dealt with the Christian tradition alone, stated bluntly, "Compared with the *Politics*, *The Republic* has no history. For a thousand years it simply disappears." Jewish thought, however, was hardly aware of the *Politics*.[6] The first direct quotation from the work is found in *Sefer ha-Ikkarim (The Book of Principles)*, written by Joseph Albo toward the end of the Middle Ages, and this reference was mediated by the influence of Latin-Christian culture.[7] All other areas of Jewish philosophy, however, were based squarely on Aristotle.

Beyond the casual fate of manuscripts, did the theological differences between Judaism and Islam on the one hand and Christianity on the other dictate which text they chose to adopt? This study argues that the differences in the textual traditions do reflect qualitative theological differences. Albertus Magnus, for example, commissioned the translation of the *Politics* into Latin in the thirteenth century, clearly because he felt the relevance of the work to the political context of Christian theology. In all three religious cultures, the theology preceded the appearance of a particular work and its concomitant influence. The text, whether it simply chanced to find its way into the scholars' hands or was deliberately selected, was singled out for the purposes of commentary and the ongoing development of historic theological tenets.

Common to the three cultures was an underlying political philosophy that dealt with the principles and essence of every human society. This philosophy was based on writings from the world of classical pagan culture. The differences among these cultures lay in political theology, which assigned a particular political significance to the revelation of each faith. In their political theology there is a good measure of proximity between Judaism and Islam; Christianity, is qualitatively different.

Judaism and Islam were both fashioned in the desert, where law was absent. It was vital to present these revelations as law, an exclusive, divine law: there was no other. Christianity, on the other hand, developed within an existing civilization. It did not manifest itself as law, but as *religio*. It recognized the legitimacy of other laws and conceded the sphere of the law to the temporal authority. Christianity focused on beliefs and opinions. Thus, there is no distinction between law and faith in Judaism and Islam, but such a distinction is vital to Christianity.

Christianity conceived revelation as a source of religious dogma. Following the theory of the two swords, which sharply separated temporal from spiritual authority and was influenced by Roman law, medieval Christianity inclined, as did Aristotle in the *Politics*, to see the political sphere as separate and independent, concerned with human laws and temporal rule. This sphere was largely isolated from divine law and affairs of spiritual authority, which were deemed nonpolitical or supra-political.

By contrast, Judaism and Islam, as Strauss has pointed out, laid distinct stress on the political quality of the revelation as divine law. The founding prophet was also a lawgiver and political leader. Therefore, Judaism did not develop a systematic division between the powers, such as grew up in Christianity. In this context, the Platonic teaching, which so emphasized the spiritual dimensions of politics, and hence identified the philosopher as the perfect political leader, was extremely relevant. The prophet-lawgiver of the Jewish and Muslim traditions could easily—in theory, at least—be identified with the Platonic philosopher king. Christianity, however, generally identified, and differentiated, its founder as one who wholly detached himself from the political life to enter the pure, spiritual sphere. Thus, Moses and Muhammad may be depicted in the form of the Platonic philosopher king, an idea that sheds light on the nature of their activity. For the image of Jesus, the philosopher king was much less relevant. Medieval Christian thought, following Augustine's *Civitas Dei*, generally did not consider the possibility of actualizing the ideal community here and now: It was a matter for the hereafter. In this world, Christian thought sought no more than seemed attainable. In this sense the *Politics*, which set only temporal political goals, suited it better. Judaism and Islam, however, did pursue the ideal community in this world. For both, the *civitas temporalis*, too, could and must become—indeed—a perfect community. The Jewish state that would arise after the coming of the Messiah, like the ideal Platonic state, was expected to be such a state. Thus, Plato's dialogue had much appeal for Jewish thinkers as a basic political text.

In this respect, I cannot agree with R. Lerner and M. Mahdi's assertion that "Jewish political philosophy was, by and large, divided into Judaeo-Arabic and Judaeo-Latin branches." Our sources show us only one branch: Platonic with Islamic influences, which subsequently was somewhat touched by the Aristotelian-Latin philosophy. Jewish political philosophy continued to follow Plato's *Republic*, not Aristotle's *Politics*, despite the *Politics'* influence upon Christian political philosophy. Al-Farabi and Ibn Rushd, not Saint Thomas Aquinas, dominated Jewish political philosophy until the beginning of modern times.[8]

For all the differences in political theology among them, the three medieval religious traditions held the same broad philosophical position, influenced by the same classical writings, chiefly those of the other Aristotle, he of the *Nicomachaean Ethics* and the *Metaphysics*. All concurred that the supreme purpose of human existence was not in the area of practical intelligence, but in the sphere of theoretical intelligence—recognizing and loving the intelligible.

3

Jewish thought in the Middle Ages absorbed the Platonic political tradition through the agency of two Muslim sources, Al-Farabi and Ibn Rushd, who concerned themselves with the ideal state and employed abstract terms suitable for any existing society. Since the two philosophers deliberately eschewed narrowly Islamic terms, it was easy to apply their theories in the realm of Jewish thought. The philosopher king was supposed to hand down a law based on philosophical principles, but phrased in figurative language suited to the understanding of the common folk. In the Muslim context, this role is assigned to Muhammad, who received the Qur'an. In the Jewish context, it belongs to Moses, who gave the Torah.[9]

The first influences of the Platonic theory of the philosopher king in Judaism mediated through Islam may be found in Saadya Gaon and Judah Halevi. Maimonides certainly acquired his knowledge of the doctrine through Al-Farabi, but qualified the philosopher-king theory for halakhic and theological reasons. Many Jewish thinkers—among them Samuel Ibn Tibbon, translator and first commentator of the *Guide to the Perplexed*, Joseph Ibn Caspi, Efodi, and Joseph Shemtov Ibn Shem Tov—tended toward the governance of the solitary, along the lines of Ibn Bajja, and found little of interest in the philosopher-king theory. It fully penetrated Jewish thought only in the generation after Maimonides, beginning with Isaac Ibn Latif and Shemtov Ibn Falaquera in the first half of the thirteenth century. It was reflected chiefly in the philosophical current that followed Al-Farabi, Maimonides, and Ibn Rushd in emphasizing the political responsibility of the philosopher

The first stage of the transmission of this tradition into Jewish thought saw an almost literal translation of Al-Farabi and Ibn Rushd. Ibn Latif was the first to summarize several chapters of Al-Farabi's *The Virtuous State (Al-Madina al-Fadila)*, which he did in his essay, *Gate of the Heavens (Sha'ar ha-Shamayim)*. Falaquera presented an exposition of the philosopher-king's virtues in two works. In his encyclopedia of the sciences, *The Beginning of Wisdom (Reshit Hokhmah)*, his statements are based on Al-Farabi's *Philosophy of Plato and Aristotle*, while in the *Book of Degrees (Sefer ha-Ma'alot)*, the subject is discussed as presented in Al-Farabi's *The Virtuous State*.[10] In the fourteenth century, Samuel ben Judah of Marseilles translated into Hebrew Ibn Rushd's commentary on Plato's *Republic*. This translation acquires prime importance, since the Arabic original is lost. The Hebrew translation is our sole evidence for the existence of Ibn Rushd's commentary.[11]

Thus, the first detailed entry of the tradition into Jewish thought contains hardly any comment on the applicability of the subject to the problematics and sources of Jewish thought and no significant changes in the enumeration of the ideal ruler's qualities. On this foundation, at the second stage, we find the list of virtues applied to the Jewish political tradition in various ways. Some philosophers base themselves on Al-Farabi's version (whether using Ibn Latif's and Falaquera's translations or otherwise), while others rely on the translation of Ibn Rushd's commentary on *The Republic* by Samuel ben Judah of Marseilles.

The discourse on the virtues of the ideal ruler is adapted to the requirements of Jewish thought in two ways. The first way is by adding virtues to those indicated by Al-Farabi and Ibn Rushd and introducing modifications and additions to the familiar virtues that are meant to suit a philosopher King of Israel. For example, Isaac Polkar adds a thirteenth virtue to the twelve listed in Al-Farabi's text in order to match the traditional concept of the thirteen divine attributes that the perfect man is supposed to imitate. Yohanan Alemanno augments the qualities defined in Ibn Rushd's version with the four special virtues halakhically expected of the King of Israel.

The second way of adapting to Jewish thought is by applying in detail the virtues taken from one of the sources to the historical paradigm of the Jewish ruler. Usually these virtues are found in Moses; sometimes in Abraham, King Solomon, or others. Such accounts seek to prove that these leaders express the highest realization of the virtues of the ideal ruler in human history. A purely apologetic aspect is revealed here that accompanies Jewish thought from the Hellenistic period to the Enlightenment: an attempt to prove, in the circumstances of the diaspora, the cultural and even political primacy of Judaism. Polkar, for example, shows how every virtue listed by Al-Farabi is found in Moses. Alemanno seeks to prove that with one exception all the leaders of Jewry, even Moses, failed to attain the perfection of the philosopher king; the sole exception, surprisingly, is Abraham, whom Alemanno presents as the ideal philosopher-prophet-king.

In the third stage of the unfolding discussion, the philosopher-king's virtues are applied liberally to Hebrew sources to meet the developing needs of Jewish thought, without undue adherence to the classical models of Al-Farabi and Ibn Rushd. Cases of this kind appear only toward the end of the Middle Ages and during the Renaissance. The more time that passes, the wider the distance grows from the classical exemplars. Isaac Abravanel applies the concept to Moses, David, and Solomon; Alemanno also applies it to Solomon. In Joseph Albo's comparative analysis of the kingly attributes of Saul and David, the discourse is far removed from the classical model.

Simone Luzzatto and Benedict Spinoza reject the philosopher-king theory and bring its history in Jewish thought to an end. The rejection results from Machiavellian influence, direct and indirect. Machiavelli, who dislodged the Platonic political tradition as he did the medieval world view as a whole, presented the Hebrew patriarchs, as well as the leaders of Greece and Rome, in a new light: not as ideal founders and perfect leaders, but as flesh and blood rulers.

Yet long after Luzzatto and Spinoza laid the philosopher king to rest, Moses Mendelssohn still voiced an echo of nostalgia for the ideal of sole rulership by a prophet-statesman—even as he acquiesced to existing circumstances and fervently supported the division between religion and state. Nevertheless, he derives quite modern conclusions from the new situation. At this point our discussion ends.

Plato, then, founded the ideal of the philosopher king. Al-Farabi and Ibn Rushd used it as their foundation to construct the second story, involving Muslim theological philosophy. Jewish thinkers added the third story, applying the two foregoing levels to the needs of Jewish thought.

The first modern historian of ideas to consider this subject was L. Dukes, the mid-nineteenth-century scholar of Jewish *Wissenschaft*. He noted that the twelve virtues of the philosopher king listed in Falaquera's *Book of Degrees* seem to follow Al-Farabi's *The Virtuous State*. Leo Strauss traced the unfolding of this tradition, and he made the Plato-Al-Farabi-Falaquera connection.[12] Strauss, however, did not know of the earlier rendering by Ibn Latif, the parallel version of Ibn Rushd, or the ongoing development of the theme in Jewish thought of the late Middle Ages and Renaissance. The purpose of the present study is to continue, and perhaps complete, what was begun by Dukes and Strauss. As always, according to the old saying that has a long history of its own in medieval and Renaissance Jewish thought, we stand on the shoulders of the scholars who preceded us and, therefore, we can see further.[13]

.4

In Jewish tradition monarchy is usually identified as a halakhic norm; however, the biblical sources provide no unequivocal statement on the matter. The form of government established by Moses on the advice of Jethro (Exod. 18; Deut. 1) was not essentially monarchical. The regime was deemed by medieval and Renaissance commentators—some favorably, some negatively—to be an amalgam of the Aristotelian Polybian type: a combination of monarchy, aristocracy, and democracy, with a strong theocratic component.[14]

Nowhere in the Torah is kingship set forth as an imperative. Monarchy is presented in Deuteronomy 17 as a hypothetical possibility, not an obligation: "And thou shalt say, I will set a king over me" (v. 14). Indeed monarchy is portrayed as undesirable in principle. The wish to set up a king is depicted as a human urge, not the expression of the divine will. It reflects a desire to be "like all the nations that are round about me" (v. 14), a desire consistently portrayed in a negative light. Although the Torah permits the elevation of a king over Israel, such rule is subjected to strict limitations. The monarchy is made constitutional, and subordinate to the Torah, which is binding upon the king. The role of the king is defined as obedience to the laws of the Torah and concern for the public good, terms that greatly limit the king's status and powers. The biblical text is replete with strictures imposed on the king (negatives like "not" and "be not" appear ten times in the six verses devoted to the subject). Clearly great fears were associated with kingship.

A similar approach informs the account of the people's request to Samuel to place a king over them (1 Sam. 8). The request is described twice as the people's wish to be "like all the nations" (1 Sam. 6 and 20). Furthermore, it is portrayed as an open revolt against the rule of Heaven, a continuation of the sinful and idolatrous practices of the Children of Israel since the exodus. Monarchy is defined forcefully by Samuel as despotism

The entire history of relations between kings and prophets, from Saul and Samuel to the destruction of the First Temple, is marked by persistent struggles and the leveling of sharp criticism by the prophets against the institution of the monarchy. The biblical authors showed a marked suspicion of kings and derived no comfort from their schemes. Scripture fluctuates continually between the ideal desire of the direct kingdom of heaven, as evinced in Gideon's refusal to rule over Israel: "I will not rule over you, neither shall my son rule over you; the Lord shall rule over you" (Judg. 8:22–23)—and fears that the absence of strong, centralized, temporal rule may lead to anarchy, as expressed in the last verse of Judges: "In those days there was no king in Israel; every man did that which was right in his own eyes" (Judg. 21:25).

The Sages tended to favor the monarchy, for the independence of Jewry in its own land was traditionally linked with the House of David. The era of David and Solomon was the lost golden age of the ancient Hebrew state, which would revive with the coming of the annointed son of David. The messianic concept was invested in the idea of monarchical rule. The Sages, too, however, vacillated throughout the period from the Tanaim to the Amoraim and the later Midrash over the halakhic qualifications for kingship. Among the Tanaim, R. Judah in particular held that the Torah commanded the appointment of a king. But R. Nehora'i, for example, asserted that the call for a king was "a disgrace to Israel."[15] Despite all the disputes, the Mishnah, ultimately assumes that there is a king in Israel.

Although the Sages adopted monarchy as a halakhic norm, it was presented, as in Deuteronomy 17, as a constitutional authority. The halakhic norm presumed a division of political, legal, and ceremonial powers, thus restricting the monarchy and making it dependent on other sources of authority, as expressed in the principle of the Three Crowns *(ketarim):* Torah, Priesthood, and Kingship. Possession of the three crowns by one man according to certain sources was forbidden even to Moses; how much more so to ordinary kings.[16] In all events, the crown of kingship is explicitly subordinated to the crown of Torah.[17]

Acceptance of limited monarchy did not end the debate. Medieval Jewish thought—halakhic, philosophical, and exegetical—continued to be exercised by the problem of kingship. When Maimonides determined that monarchy was a halakhic obligation (*Hilkhot Melakhim*1.1: "Three commandments—to be carried out on entering the Land of Israel—were enjoined upon Israel: [one of these was] to appoint a king, as it is said, 'Thou shalt in anywise set him king over thee'"), he was taking a stand on an issue still fiercely in dispute. The question of monarchy had been a major bone of contention between the Geonim of Babylonia and the Exilarchs. The

Geonim—Saadya, Samuel ben Hofni, and Samuel ben Ali—all took exception to the claim that it was a halakhic imperative to establish a monarchy. Maimonides, in viewing this as a halakhic obligation, sided with the Exilarchs, the successors of the monarchy, in their historic debate with the Geonim of Babylonia. The argument against monarchy, that it was not a halakhic requirement at all, was advanced firmly by Saadya and, later, Abraham Ibn Ezra. More moderate critics conceded that there was a halakhic norm, but that it was limited to times of emergency and did not apply in normal circumstances.[18] All agreed that even in an emergency the monarchy was clearly limited and subject to the spiritual authority.

Maimonides' decisive stance was accepted by most of the medieval sages who treated the subject—Moses of Coucy, Menahem Hameiri, Nissim Gerondi among others. Many, though, harbored reservations: The critics included Bahya ben Asher; Nahmanides, whose stance was markedly ambivalent; Joseph Ibn Caspi; and, of course, Isaac Abravanel, who was outspoken in his halakhical and philosophical rejection of a monarchical regime.[19]

The ambivalence and skepticism regarding the institution of monarchy in medieval Jewish thought are all the more striking since medieval political thought, in general, and Islamic and Christian thought in particular, viewed monarchy as the optimal regime. In Muslim and Christian realms, monarchy was the accepted form of government. Despite the disastrous experiences of Nahmanides and Abravanel, it was frequently the monarchy that protected the Jews from the rage of the mobs in Christian Europe. The intellectual fashions and historical reality that led Islam and Christianity to favor the institution of monarchy influenced medieval Jewish thinkers profoundly. However, utopian desires for the direct kingdom of heaven and the well-founded Biblical suspicion of despotism left many in strong opposition to a monarchical regime and many others ambivalent toward it. The theory of the philosopher king was not only monarchist but absolutist in essence. Jewish thinkers who were influenced by this theory were forced to reconcile it with their halakhic position.

The core of Platonic political theory that influenced Jewish thinkers was monarchical. As the soul rules the body and the rational faculty rules the soul, so government should be in the hands of one who has attained perfection of the rational soul, the philosopher king. Medieval thought translated this principle into theological language appealing to the unity of God, His uniqueness, and His absolute rule over creation. Bahya Ibn Pakuda, for example, ensconces this principle at the heart of his claims regarding the unity of God in the first part of his *Duties of the Heart:* "Among the signs of God's governance of his creation we see that rule can neither succeed nor be constant unless it lies in the hands of one who alone holds sway in word and deed, like a king in his kingdom, like the soul in the body. Aristotle said in his discussions of unity that a plurality of rulers is not good—the real head is but one. The scriptures also say (Prov. 28:2): "For the transgression of a land many are the princes thereof."[20]

In medieval Jewish thought, we find many images of this sort in the theory of God and the theory of the soul. Thinkers like Abravanel, who rejected a monarchical regime in principle, also made much use of these images but refused to infer from the principle of divine rule the necessity for monarchical rule in human society. For them, the theological principle did not extend to government by a single human ruler; it actually called for the extension of the direct rule of God to the social order. Thinkers like Saadya who in principle affirmed a monarchical regime, albeit not necessarily for the people of Israel, or who affirmed it for the people of Israel, too, as did Maimonides, fully exploited Plato. The Platonic analogy ranged from the single rule in the cosmos and in the soul to the single wise rule in the perfect social order—for was it not a commandment for humanity to imitate God?

Support for a monarchical ideal did not necessarily mean complete acceptance of the Platonic theory, which identified the king with the philosopher, and, in the medieval theological context, added to this identity the prophet or even the priest. Maimonides, an avowed monarchist, had serious doubts about the Farabian-Platonic identification of the philosopher king with the prophet. Abravanel, a marked antimonarchist, had no reservations about this identification when he ascribed supreme human and political perfection to Moses and Solomon. The monarchist Maimonides restricted the Platonic theory with many qualifications because he supported the division of powers among the Three Crowns. The anti-monarchist Abravanel applied the theory in its entirety to Moses and Solomon on the assumption that they alone merited all the kingly epithets as a result of the direct and miraculous influence of the divine will. Other thinkers, such as Polkar and Alemanno, regarded monarchy as a halakhic norm; they fully accepted the Platonic theory of the philosopher king as adapted to the requirements of scriptural monotheism by the Muslim philosophers Al-Farabi and Ibn Rushd.

To sum up, despite the parallelism of the Platonic philosopher-king theory and the Jewish tradition of the lawgiver-prophet, the two concepts conflict with each other in two respects. First, the Jewish political tradition posited a division of functions and powers, on the lines of the Three Crowns, at least for the period following the founding of the state by the prophet-lawgiver. This tradition makes for a clear-cut distinction between the prophet-lawgiver and the king. The Platonic stance, by contrast, preferred the combination of powers in a single individual. Second, the Platonic theory was essentially monarchical. By contrast, the halakhic posture viewed the monarchical regime with a large measure of suspicion and therefore, favored a restricted monarchy as distinct from the absolutism of the Platonic theory.

Thus, medieval thought that came into contact with Platonic theory through the agency of Islam had to contend with this serious tension. As in other areas of theology—for example, the problem of creation—medieval Jewish philosophy was hard pressed to deal with the Greek philosophical tradition. The philosophers we shall study coped with the problem in a variety of ways.

2

The Sources

1

The historical starting point for a consideration of the philosopher king is the description of the ideal state in Plato's *Republic*. Following his mordant criticism of Athenian democracy and Sophist political notions, Plato presents an alternative based on his theory of Ideas.

The great debate between Socrates and the Sophists on the definition of justice generates the discussion. To achieve an objective definition, Plato takes the position that the state is the individual "writ large"; he passes from the difficult attempt to define justice on the individual level, the microcosm, to a definition of justice in society at large, the macrocosm. The assumption is that both definitions are based on the same principle ("We think of justice as a quality that may exist in a whole community as well as in an individual"),[1] and it will be easier to define justice first at large, in the macrocosm, and then to apply the principle behind this definition to just actions in each individual. The discourse leads Plato to develop a hypothetical—ahistorical—theory of the essential stages in the development of human society, in logical and psychological terms. Within this he develops a theory of the classes that emerge in the development of human society.

When he arrives at a definition of justice, "that each one should do his own proper work,"[2] Plato can apply it to the three-class structure of the ideal state, based on a precise division of functions and tasks. This structure constitutes a magnified image of the relationships among the three parts of the soul: appetite or desire, spirit, and reason. The common people, whose function is to supply the material needs of the ideal state, represent appetite or desire. The guardians, whose task is to protect this state internally and externally, represent spirit; the philosophers, whose role is to rule this state by virtue of the

13

perfection of their intellect, represent reason. As reason must rule the inferior parts of the human soul, so they who are gifted with rational perfection must rule organized human society.

The qualities of each of the classes in the ideal state reflect the qualities of the ideal state itself. They are the virtues that make it the ideal state ("obviously, then, it is wise, brave, temperate, and just").[3] Each class possesses its own special abilities and therefore its own special functions. Justice and temperance are virtues possessed by all the classes. Temperance, as applied universally, means the readiness of each member to accept a role and suppress his personal desires—because the role assigned is that for which the person is best suited and because one recognizes the needs of the society as a whole. It is thus obvious why these two virtues are attributed to all three classes. The guardians possess the added virtue of courage, which is necessary in their communal role.

The ruler-philosophers, as the highest class in the ideal state, necessarily possess all the virtues of the two lower classes: justice, temperance, and courage; however, they alone possess the virtue of wisdom. There is then, an exact match between the virtues of the philosopher king and those of the ideal state, the former being a miniature of the perfect virtues of the philosophical state and the latter being a reflection of the perfect virtues of the philosopher king.

Plato sets the description of the perfect virtues of the philosophical soul on three planes. The first relates to potential: the possessor of the philosophical soul is quick to learn and has a good memory. Only such an individual with "constant passion for knowledge," in Plato's phrase, is able to desire certain knowledge and to attain it. Certain knowledge is defined as knowledge of the Ideas ("something of that reality which endures forever and is not always passing into and out of existence").[4] The desire for perfection in knowledge necessarily leads one to perfection in the other virtues: whoever channels all his desires into a single direction will of necessity have a weaker appetite for other things. Such a person will necessarily possess balanced virtues ("temperate and free from the love of money, meanness, pretentiousness, and cowardice").[5] Plato summarizes the virtues of the possessor of the philosophical soul like this: "by nature quick to learn and to remember, magnanimous and gracious, and friend and kinsman of truth, justice, courage, and temperance."[6]

The philosophical soul, then, combines three basic qualities: the potential for attaining the truth, the desire for that attainment, and the perfection of moral as well as intellectual virtues. Since these are the qualities of philosophers, it follows that the philosophers will be best suited for leadership of the ideal state, once they realize their talents ("When time and education have brought such characters as these to maturity, would you entrust the care of your commonwealth to anyone else?").[7] Whoever has attained perfection of the moral virtues and of the intellect has both the ability and the obligation to govern the community. Thus, the philosopher becomes the ruler.

In the myth of the cave, following the ideal of his master, Socrates, as expressed in the *Apology*, Plato stresses the political commitment of the philosopher. The philosopher does not achieve knowledge of Ideas for the perfection of his own intellect alone, but also, and chiefly, for showing the community the light and bringing it to the highest perfection that it is capable of attaining. Whoever is able to define the just and the good objectively and absolutely must also realize these qualities in the life of action. Whoever has emerged from the cave and looked straight into the sunlight must go back down into the gloom and teach human society, which is imprisoned there by its prejudices.[8]

Society will not be saved unless the philosopher rules over it. With a measure of political realism (or perhaps total detachment from the political reality?), Plato presents an alternative to transforming philosophers into kings; namely, that rulers be turned into philosophers by being properly educated by philosophers. Plato would make such an attempt with the tyrant Dionysius of Syracuse, but in vain: "Unless either philosophers become kings in their countries or those who are now called kings and rulers come to be sufficiently inspired with a genuine desire for wisdom; unless, that is to say, political power and philosophy meet together . . . there can be no rest from troubles . . . for states, nor yet, as I believe, for all mankind."[9]

In the *Laws*, Plato briefly returns to the philosopher-king theory, but with a significant change. Discussing the establishment of a new state following the migration of citizens from an existing state, the Athenian stranger contends that the regime of the new state will be the best if it is governed by an absolute ruler. He repeats essentially the same list of virtues developed in *The Republic:* "Give me a state which is governed by a tyrant, and let the tyrant be young and have a good memory; let him be quick at learning, and of a courageous and noble nature; let him have that quality which . . . is the inseparable companion of all the other parts of virtue, if there is to be any good in them."[10]

The one virtue that was most important for the ruler-philosopher in *The Republic*, perfection of intellect, manifested in the desire for truth, is now absent. Plato, now old and the wiser for his bitter experience in Syracuse, retreats from the extreme position he had adopted in *The Republic*. He now advocates the rule of law, arguing that several types of regime may bring about the best government. The new preference for youth perhaps accords with associated virtues—facility in learning, courage, and so forth—but it is certainly not in accord with the requirement of the perfection of the intellect. In *The Republic* the ruler must be a mature man. The process of realizing his potential for attaining the truth is long and drawn out. The absolute ruler of the *Laws*, by contrast, need not be a philosopher at all.[11]

Elsewhere Plato links discussion of the supreme perfection of the philosopher with his theory of *imitatio Dei*. In the *Theaetetus* he notes that the purpose of human existence is "to become like God as far as this is possible; and to become like God is to become righteous and holy and wise."[12] Here it is important to emphasize the limitations of human knowledge. Human perfection does not mean simply perfection of the intellect; rather the latter is a means of attaining perfection in all the virtues. The supreme purpose of the philosopher, then, is not theory, but praxis: "to become righteous and holy and wise."

Many Jewish philosophers in the Middle Ages were influenced by Plato's theory of three classes and its parallels with the order of the soul and the order of the cosmos.[13] For obvious reasons, however, they could not accept community of property; and certainly not community of wives.[14] Nor did they usually connect the class theory with the question of the philosopher king. Jewish medieval thinkers used the treatment of the philosopher king in *The Republic*, not the qualitatively different version of the *Laws*. On the other hand, the emphasis on the divine foundations of government in the latter, was important.[15] It is entirely absent from *The Republic*, in which government is legitimated by the perfection of the human intellect. The medievals also explored the relationship between the virtues of the ideal ruler and the imitation of God, an analogy that reached them from Neoplatonic sources and was assiduously applied to monotheistic thought. The philosopher king became the lawgiver-prophet, who as far as humanly possible imitated the virtues of God and put this mimesis to work in his just rule over the community of men. Thus, the imitation theory came to acquire a strong political force, which was not central in Platonic thought but was characteristic of medieval Jewish and Islamic thought alike. For Plato, the philosopher king might rule in a utopian future. Jewish and Muslim theological thought transferred his reign to the past; a utopian past, at the founding of the nation. For the philosopher king was the prophetic founder of the religion.[16] He would reappear with the coming of the king-messiah.

2

Abu Nasr Al-Farabi, the "second teacher" after Aristotle, as he was called by the medieval philosophers, created the great synthesis between the Greek-Hellenistic philosophical tradition and Islam in all areas of philosophy, not least political thought. Following Plato, Al-Farabi emphasized the importance of politics in the philosopher's quest for knowledge of God, the universe, and man. Philosophy seeks knowledge of the Creator, and in his activity the philosopher must strive to be like the Creator as far as humanly possible. This expression of the Platonic theory of the imitation of God came to Islamic thought apparently by way of Plotinus. The aim of politics is to allow man to live a proper life in this world, so as to prepare himself for the world to come. Politics here acquires metaphysical, and thus theological, weight.

Accordingly, Al-Farabi's *The Virtuous State (Madina al-Fadila)* deals mostly with metaphysical and philosophical matters; only its last nine chapters treat political issues proper. It is not a specifically political composition like Aristotle's *Politics,* but a study with far-reaching philosophical implications like Plato's *Republic.* Politics does not appear in Al-Farabi except as a means of serving loftier purposes. The full title of the work, *The Book of the Principles of the Beliefs of the Citizens of the Virtuous State,* well illustrates this orientation. The virtuous state exists only to perfect the right beliefs of its citizens. This is also the case with Al-Farabi's political writings; for example, *al-Siyasa al-Madaniya (Civil government)* and *K. Tahsil al-Sa'ada (On Attaining Happiness),* to mention the two most important, are devoted mainly to metaphysical subjects and the theory of the soul, and political inquiry in each rests on metaphysical and psychological considerations.

Al-Farabi's political thought follows Plato, with modifications drawn from the *Nicomachaean Ethics;* there are intermediary influences from Hellenistic thought and adaptations to Islamic theological and historical circumstances. This amalgam is expressed in the various subjects that Al-Farabi considers in the sphere of political thought, as well as in the order of the inquiry: the theory of the political nature of man; the division of labor; class theory; the distinction among different states according to size and nature, based on the psychological analogy between the perfection of the individual and the perfection of the whole. Principally the adaptation is expressed in the theory of regimes, with the ideal state governed by the philosopher king.

Al-Farabi presents several classes of the ignorant state *(al-madina al-jahiliyya),* but adds to the original four types enumerated by Plato in the ninth book of *The Republic* to produce a total of seven kinds of ignorant state. The common denominator is that the seven maintain wrong opinions and strive for specious, material ends, because they are not led by rulers possessing true philosophical knowledge, but by various types of men imitating philosophers or prophets and exploiting their ability to influence the masses in order to acquire hegemony, wealth, and honor. The differences among the various kinds of ignorant state arise from the goals of their rulers. To this Platonic account, Al-Farabi adds the distinctively Islamic overtones of the *jahiliyya,* marking these states as pagan and barbarous.

In contrast, Al-Farabi sets forth the ideal state, in which the philosopher king governs. What makes this state unique is that it sustains right opinions, and thereby pursues the supreme spiritual purpose of human existence. Only the philosopher can know, define, and realize this supreme purpose, and therefore his rule is a necessary condition for the establishment of this state. This ideal ruler for Al-Farabi unites the Platonic philosopher king and the Islamic prophet-lawgiver.

Both Greek and Islamic thinkers held that an ordered human society could not exist without the rule of law. Only he who is able to establish a society and who understands its inner meaning and ultimate purpose is capable and worthy of ruling. The Greek concept, however, generally posited a human origin for the law. The Islamic posited that the source of a perfect law could only be divine: it came by revelation. Greek law related only to this world; Islamic law also concerned the hereafter. Thus, Platonic philosophy identified the philosopher as a human lawgiver of the perfect law. Al-Farabi identified the prophet as one who received the law by revelation and conveyed it to human society. The prophet, then, must also be simultaneously a philosopher, in order to comprehend the hidden meanings and higher purpose of the revealed law, and a king, in order to establish that law in human society.

In Al-Farabi's system, this combination of philosophical and prophetic qualities in a single man was essential to the ideal state. The virtues of the Platonic philosopher alone were insufficient. Prophetic qualities were irreplaceable. What marks the philosopher is the ability to communicate directly with the active intellect by way of the theoretical soul. What marks the prophet is the ability to maintain this connection through the imaginative soul. Each of these abilities contributes in its special way, and each is vital for the existence of the ideal state. The philosopher, for all the perfection of his intellect, is unable to rule without a developed, imaginative soul that will enable him to transmit philosophical truth to the people in metaphorical language suited to the level of their understanding. The imagination, however, is liable to misread reality without constant supervision by the theoretical soul, otherwise it may go out of control and make wildly erratic associations. Integration in a single man of the qualities of the prophet with those of the philosopher is therefore essential in order for the ideal state to be established and maintained. This superimposing of the perfection of the prophet's imaginative soul upon the perfection of the philosopher's theoretical soul constitutes the high point of Al-Farabi's synthesis of the ideal ruler of the Platonic tradition with the ideal ruler of Islamic theology.

Al-Farabi offers several listings of the virtues of the philosopher king in *al-Madina al-Fadila* and *K. Tahsil al-Sa'ada*. Usually they are twelve in number; in essence, Plato's list in *The Republic* with Islamic adaptations. This list will be a central focus in our examination of how Ibn Latif, Falaquera, and Polkar each adapted these twelve virtues into Hebrew.

As a faithful student of Plato and Aristotle and as a person who experienced the Abbasid caliphate, Al-Farabi knew how rare it would be to find a man who was perfect in all twelve virtues. As a practical matter, Al-Farabi was willing to be satisfied with finding someone with six virtues. The successor of the founder of the ideal state would not be gifted with prophetic qualities. He will be a philosopher king in a more restricted sense: one who knows the perfect law given by the first prophet-lawgiver and is able to apply it for the betterment of human existence.[17]

Ibn Rushd, who lived in the same generation as Maimonides, is known as the greatest medieval interpreter of Aristotle. In the sphere of political thought, however, he continued Al-Farabi's Platonic path. Ibn Rushd took exception to Ibn Bajja's divergence from the political commitment of the philosopher and idealization of the governance of the solitary. He regarded the *Nicomachaean Ethics* as the theoretical basis of practical wisdom. Since the *Politics* was not available to him, he used *The Republic* as his primer in politics, but he studied Plato not only as a Muslim but also as an interpreter of Aristotle. He found no qualitative difference between Plato and Aristotle, who to Ibn Rushd represented different aspects of the same system. His commentary on *The Republic* expands on the tenets of the *Ethics* and interprets the dialogue in terms of the contemporary political situation of the countries of Islam, particularly in North Africa. At times this original juxtaposition leads him to severe criticism of prevailing Islamic norms; for example, Islamic attitudes toward women, as compared to the egalitarian Platonic stance. The force with which Ibn Rushd applied Platonic concepts to Islamic culture is all the more striking in view of the fact that his commentary on the *Nicomachaean Ethics* is purely theoretical and given no topical application whatever.

Although Ibn Rushd was greatly influenced by Al-Farabi, two essential differences characterize their approaches to Plato. First, Al-Farabi used Platonic concepts to write original works that differed in many respects from the Platonic dialogues. Ibn Rushd wrote only his detailed commentary on *The Republic*. Second, Al-Farabi's interest in politics was theoretical. He concentrated on the virtues of the philosopher, prophet, lawgiver, king, *imam*—on his intellectual perfection and his supreme happiness. Al-Farabi was a metaphysician; he was not himself a statesman. He never openly applied Platonic political ideas to the Islamic states of his time, even by analogy. Ibn Rushd, by contrast, had both a theoretical and a practical interest in politics. The theoretical aspect related to the perfection of the citizens and rulers of the ideal state. The practical aspect related to the relevance of the Platonic ideas to the Islamic society in which he lived.

Scholars are divided over Ibn Rushd's position on the relationship between Plato's ideal state and the perfect Islamic state. Beyond the difficulties found in the analysis of specific texts, this debate brings us back to the distinction between an esoteric and an esoteric reading. Consistent with his views on Al-Farabi, E. I. J. Rosenthal holds that Ibn Rushd, too, was first a Muslim and only secondarily a student of Plato and Aristotle, meaning that philosophy was no more than the adopted sister of the *Sharia* and must serve its needs. Rosenthal argues that Ibn Rushd never held the double truth theory later attributed to him, but posited one divine truth attained by man through prophetic revelation. In this view, philosophy is for philosophers alone, whereas religion is for all, philosophers and common people alike. Accordingly, it is argued, Ibn Rushd also posited the supremacy of the perfect Islamic state of the first khalifs over the ideal Platonic state. The *Sharia* is not merely the Platonic *nomos* transplanted into Islamic surroundings. Rather, the revealed law, the *Sharia*, necessarily supersedes the Platonic *nomos*. It imparts to man perfect ways of conduct with certainty and immediacy. The human intellectual law, considering its limitations, is capable only of approaching this condition, and that after a long, painstaking process of trial and error. The *nomos* of the Platonic republic constitutes the perfect law only for the "secular" states that have no revealed law.

Ibn Rushd accepted the great synthesis of Al-Farabi between the prophet lawgiver of the Islamic tradition and the Platonic philosopher king, but diverged from "the second teacher" on one central issue. In Al-Farabi's system, the philosopher king must also be a prophet. Ibn Rushd left this question open. The addition of prophecy to the qualities of the philosopher king appears in his work only as a possibility, not a requirement. Rosenthal explains this divergence as arising from Ibn Rushd's conviction that prophecy ended with the death of Muhammad. The Islamic ideal state had existed in the past, and the present Islamic state was as close to it as any imperfect state could be. Why, then, did Ibn Rushd retain the obligation of the philosopher king to be a lawgiver? Was not the perfect revealed law already given? Rosenthal explains this position as a vestige of the emphasis placed by the *falasifa*, following their Greek masters, on the rule of law.[18]

S. Pines, on the other hand, finds this divergence by Ibn Rushd to be radically significant, and he extracts far-reaching conclusions from it. In Pines' opinion, it is superficial to present Ibn Rushd as obliged to choose between opposition to and defense of religion. Ibn Rushd's purpose is not to attack the Muslim creed, but to place it in the position it merits in accordance with philosophical criteria. Therefore, the ideal Platonic state is judged superior to the ideal Muslim state. From the fact that the ideal ruler did not have to be a prophet, it followed that the ideal state did not have to be a Muslim state or any kind of state founded on prophecy. At best, the early Khalifate was an imitation, in the Platonic sense of the term, of the ideal Platonic state. Correspondingly, the Islamic state could in time become an ideal state by Platonic criteria if it came to be governed by a series of philosophical rulers.

Pines concedes that in other compositions, such as *K. Fasl al-Maqal*, Ibn Rushd explicitly assumes the superiority of the revealed law over the philosophical law. He ascribes such remarks, however, to the difference between esoteric and exoteric texts. Ibn Rushd's true position, Pines believes, is well concealed in his esoteric interpretation of Plato's *Republic*. Here the superiority of the philosophical law over religious law is evident, thus projecting the superiority of the Platonic state over the imamate. Pines reads Ibn Rushd's commentary on *The Republic* in much the same way as he reads Maimonides' *Guide to the Perplexed*.[19] We shall soon see how meaningful this debate is for an understanding of Maimonides' and subsequent Jewish thinking about the philosopher king.

3

First Influences

1

The philosopher king first appears in Jewish thought in the Hellenistic period, in Philo of Alexandria, the first Jewish philosopher. As part of his reconciliation of the Torah with the Greek philosophical tradition, Philo identifies Moses as the prototype of the Platonic philosopher king, and is the first to connect philosopher, king, prophet, lawgiver, and even priest. In Philo's *Life of Moses*, we read:

> There are four adjuncts to the truly perfect ruler. He must have kingship, the faculty of legislation, priesthood and prophecy, so that in his capacity of legislator he may command what should be done and forbid what should not be done, as priest dispose not only things human but things divine, as prophet declare by inspiration what cannot be apprehended by reason. I have discussed the first three, and shown that Moses was the best of kings, of lawgivers and of high priests, and will now go on to show in conclusion that he was a prophet of the highest quality.[1]

Nevertheless, this description applies only to the figure of Moses. In general Philo adopts the stance of the Sages, which separates the Three Crowns: Torah, priesthood, and kingship—and regards the last of these as inferior to prophecy and priesthood. He obliges the king to honor the prophet and priest of his day.[2]

Philo's writings were hardly known in the Middle Ages, however, and he had no direct influence on the development of discourse on the subject. His influence begins only with the Renaissance.[3]

The philosopher-king theory reappears in Jewish thought only with the beginnings of contact with Muslim culture. As early as the time of Al-Farabi, we find brief, scattered references to the subject. For example, the tenth chapter of Saadia Gaon's *Book of Critically Selected Beliefs and Convictions* refers to a man's thirteen "loves," perfection in each of which results in the realization of his purpose. The number and themes of these "loves" parallel the thirteen attributes of God that the prophet-leader must imitate. Saadia illustrates the thirteenth and highest moral perfection, calmness of spirit, with a reference to kings: "Seest thou not that the kings are, of all men, those that rest the most? Were not rest, therefore, the greatest of all goods [he argues dialectically], they would not have chosen it for themselves." He attributes these virtues to the character of King Solomon, who is depicted, as usual, as the prototype of the wise king.[4] Saadia, as we have noted, may have reservations about treating kingship as an obligatory halakhic norm, but he does present monarchy as the ideal form of regime.

The same thesis is expressed far more strikingly in the *Kuzari* of Judah Halevi. Several scholars have pointed out the Platonic structure of this dialogue,[5] but its content, too, presents obvious elements of the Platonic political tradition. The Khazar himself is portrayed as a righteous king, possessed of sound intentions, who also seeks right action. The entire work may be seen as part of the literary topos of the education of rulers. It belongs to the Platonic political tradition that later developed in both Islamic and Christian political literature into the *Speculum Principium* genre, as we shall observe below.[6] In this respect, the *Kuzari* reflects the second alternative presented by Plato for the maintenance of the ideal state. The first is that the philosophers should become rulers; but if this proves unattainable, the next best thing is for the rulers to become philosophers through being wisely educated.

Like Dionysius of Syracuse, who summoned Plato to teach him the art of proper government—a relationship that ended with great mutual disappointment—and like Alexander the Great, who according to various traditions was a pupil not only of Aristotle, but even of Diogenes the Cynic, and who also, according to Talmudic tradition, sought learning from the Sages of the Negev, the Khazar also went to the philosopher and the wise men of religion in search of the right path. He eventually found the ideal teacher in the Jewish scholar. The Khazar approached each potential master not simply as a private individual seeking the way of truth, but as a ruler in search of the true path for the community over whom he reigned. He was not looking for correct views proper to a philosopher, but for correct action, relevant to a leader. He rejected the words of the philosopher as irrelevant, because the philosopher, like Ibn Bajja, argued for the withdrawal of the perfect man from human society and negated the Platonic connection between intellectual perfection and public commitment. The Jewish scholar was preferred, in part, because he placed more emphasis than the rest on rightful action. The Jewish scholar, who convinces the Khazar king of the truth and justice of the way of Judaism and teaches him its practical beliefs and commandments, transforms the ruler not only into a more perfect man, but necessarily, into a better king, too. In the literature of mirrors for princes *(Speculum Principium)*, the encounter between the king and the philosopher-educator often ends badly. The king may ignore the philosopher's advice, or the philosopher may have to flee for his life from a disillusioned king, as in the case of Plato and Dionysius. In the *Kuzari*, the momentous meeting between the king and the man of theory ends well: the king accepts the teaching of the scholar and leads all his people in its light.

At the beginning of the third essay of the *Kuzari*, the Jew ably expresses the conflict faced by Halevi and many other medieval Jewish philosophers: between the desire for solitude and the need for political commitment. The perfect man yearns for the seclusion ascribed to Enoch, Elijah, or Socrates; but Socrates, while loving his philosophical isolation, still longed for the company of his pupils, who stimulated his thinking. Even prophets, with all their activism and social responsibilities, retired from the world and dwelt in the wilderness. Yet, they did not remain in total isolation in the wilderness, but banded together with their ilk, the sons of prophets. When, however, prophecy departs from the land and wise men like Socrates are not to be found, seclusion is not abandonment of the world, but a descent to the condition of beasts. Such a condition places one not above, but below the level of humanity. The perfect man, insofar as he is perfect, has not only a personal need to satisfy material and social wants, but also a responsibility to the community. The quest for philosophical-prophetic solitude becomes an ideal never to be realized.[7] Therefore, when the Khazar asks the scholar to describe "the doings of one of your pious men at the present time," the Jew immediately describes the perfect ruler: "A pious man is, so to speak, the guardian of his country, who gives to its inhabitants provisions and all that they need. He is so just that he wrongs no one, nor does he grant anyone more than his due. Then, when he needs them, he finds them obedient to his call. He orders and they comply; he forbids and they abstain."[8] When the Khazar wonders about this equation of the pious man with the ruler, the scholar replies that "the pious man is nothing but a prince." He cites the well-known analogy of Proverbs 25:32: "He that ruleth his spirit [is better] than he that taketh a city." The text draws a parallel between the microcosm (the rule of the pious man over his spirit) and the macrocosm (the rule of the king over the state). Practice in ruling the spirit is a preparation for rightful rule over the state: "He is fit to rule, because if he were the prince of a country he would be as just as he is to his body and soul." He who attains perfection of the soul and controls his corporeal desires will also be fit to rule human society: "He arranges his community in the same manner as Moses arranged his people around Mount Sinai."[9]

Halevi gives a clearly Platonic interpretation to the passage from Proverbs, which acquires special weight by virtue of its attribution to King Solomon. If the state is the individual "writ large," as Plato describes it,[10] the just man should be the prince. The use of the Biblical analogy with a Platonic interpretation and in a political context was common in medieval Jewish thought. Other major examples of this manner of exegesis are provided by Bahya Ibn Pakuda and Abraham Ibn Ezra.[11]

The sole qualitative difference between Halevi's pious ruler and the Platonic philosopher king is that the latter's rule is based on perfection of the human intellect alone, whereas the pious ruler also follows revelation. The Torah by itself ensures just decisions in every aspect of human life: "The social and rational laws are those universally known. The divine Laws, however, which were added in order that they should exist among the people of the Living God, who guides them, were not known until they were explained in detail by him."[12] Herein lies the absolute advantage of the pious ruler whom the scholar put forward, over Plato's philosopher king. As posited by the scholar, the Khazar, who learns the ways of the pious ruler, is sure to become the ideal monarch.

2

In certain respects, the philosopher-king theory reached its zenith in Jewish philosophy with Maimonides. Yet he accepted this theory only in a limited and restricted way. Just as in his physics and metaphysics he attempted to interpret the Torah in Aristotelian terms, so in his political thought he wanted to show the fundamental accord between the Torah and the Platonic philosophy of Al-Farabi.

In his famous letter to Samuel Ibn Tibbon, the translator of the *Guide*, Maimonides asserts that the writings of Plato, although "profound and full of parables," need not necessarily be studied, because the books of his pupil Aristotle hold "the ultimate perfection of human knowledge" and contain everything a man should know. Whatever was said by philosophers before Aristotle, including Plato, becomes of secondary importance, if not superfluous. Yet Maimonides portrays Al-Farabi as the greatest philosopher since Aristotle: "Everything he wrote, and the *Book of Principles*, is pure flour. A human being can understand his sayings and be enlightened by them, since he was of abundant wisdom."[13] This encomium is telling, for Al-Farabi was the chief transmitter of the Platonic political tradition to medieval Muslim philosophy. Maimonides knew his work very well, including the most important of his political essays, *The Virtuous State (al-Madina al-Fadila)*. Thus, in Al-Farabi's recension, Maimonides carried the Platonic political tradition into the Jewish philosophy of the Middle Ages.[14] Halakhic and theological considerations, however, prevented him from wholly accepting the parallel between the Platonic philosopher king and the prophet-lawgiver of the monotheistic tradition.

As L. V. Berman showed, the entire architecture of the *Guide* may be likened to Plato's myth of the cave. The *Guide* opens with the mighty struggle against false apprehensions of the idea of God. This initial stage parallels the Platonic description of human society living in a cave sunk in the depths of false beliefs. The discourse on true beliefs in the second and third parts of the *Guide* may be compared to the emergence of the philosopher from the cave and his search for divine truth. The last part of the *Guide,* which moves from a discussion of true beliefs to a discussion of sound actions, the commandments, and the conclusion and climax of the essay, with the political theory of *imitatio Dei* at the end of the last chapter, is readily likened to the return of the philosopher to the cave to educate and improve the common people, still mired in superstitious beliefs.[15]

The *Guide* and, like it, the philosophical sections of Maimonides' halakhic writings are filled with the powerful images from the Platonic myth of the cave: ascent and descent, light and darkness. There is, in the introduction to the *Guide,* for instance, the famous parable of the lightning or, another leading example, the fable of the blind man, which is related in the one brief chapter directly treating messianism (III, 11). Indeed, the images of ascent and descent, and of light and darkness, are not only prevalent in any number of books of the Bible and Talmud, but they also are archetypal in human culture. There can be no doubt that the way in which Maimonides applies them, these images bear a clearly Platonic character. A clear example is found in the allegorical interpretation that Maimonides gives to Jacob's dream (*Guide* I:15). Although it has recently been shown that Maimonides used the midrash here,[16] he fuses the biblical parable in a marvelous way with the Platonic myth of the cave. In this sense, his interpretation of Jacob's dream of the ladder constitutes a miniature of the *Guide to the Perplexed.* The angels—these being the prophets—ascend the ladder in order to descend again; they do not remain on the rung of the ladder they are capable of reaching and thereby isolate themselves in divine perfection. The purpose of the ascent is to gain knowledge of God's attributes of action, to the extent that man is able to do so. The descent is to realize the principle of imitation of God and implement what has been learned of God's attributes of action by establishing just rule in human society: "Ascent comes before descent; for after the ascent and the attaining of certain rungs of the ladder that may be known comes the descent with whatever decree the prophet has been informed of—with a view to governing and teaching the people on earth."[17] The call of Moses is presented in exactly this way in the chapters of the *Guide* on prophecy (II:33). Moses ascended the mountain alone, and then descended to lead a human society: "And he, peace be on him, went to the foot of the mountain and communicated to the people what he had heard."[18] What he had heard and then related were not only the first two commandments, which belong to the intelligible category and may be known by human intellect alone, but also the remaining eight, which belong to generally accepted opinions; namely, laws ordering the social and political relationships of human beings. These relations are not a matter for unaided human intelligence. The perfect sociopolitical law must stem directly from revelation, or knowledge by the prophet of God's attributes of action and their application in the social framework.

While Maimonides' interpretation of Jacob's dream is based on the motifs of ascent and descent, the parallel fable of the blind man, found in the chapter on messianism (*Guide* III:11), is based on the motifs of light and darkness that are present in the myth of the cave: "Just as a blind man, because of his lack of sight, continuously stumbles, is injured and injures others, because he has nobody to guide him, the various sects of men—every individual according to the extent of his ignorance—does to himself and to others great evils from which the members of our kind suffer. If there were knowledge, whose relation to the human form is like that of the faculty of sight to the eye, they would refrain from doing any harm to themselves or to others."[19]

This theme is especially prominent in the closing lines of the last chapter of the *Guide* (III:54), which Maimonides composed out of a mosaic of verses from Isaiah's redemption prophecy; but it is replete with the Platonic motifs of light and darkness: "Then the eyes of the blind shall be opened, and the ears of the deaf shall be unstopped. The people that walked in darkness have seen a great light; they that dwelt in the land of the shadow of death, upon them hath the light shined." The blind man cannot find the right way himself. He needs proper direction "to guide him." This is the case with the mass of men within the cave; they are ruled by their false beliefs, they cannot rectify their opinions or their way without the benefit of proper leadership. It is here that we meet the philosopher-king theory. Like Halevi and many other medieval philosophers, Maimonides struggled with the question of the political commitment of the prophet-philosopher. On the one hand, the final chapter of the *Guide* presents the perfection of intellect, the fourth and highest perfection (until that stage!), as unique in being characterized by solitude. In antithesis to the third perfection, that of moral virtues, the fourth is identified as a pure, supra-political condition of the philosopher's seclusion: "But this last perfection is yours alone. There is no other with you in partnership at all."[20] We find the same attitude in the lengthy comment that Maimonides appends to the parable of the king and the palace (*Guide* III:51). The man who has attained the closest possible proximity to God is supposed to be in a state of absolute solitude: "You alone, no one else being associated in it with you in any way."[21] He strives to return as nearly as possible to the situation in which Adam existed so long as he upheld the divine command, before the fall.[22] Here we find the attraction of the prophet-philosopher in the direction of the governance of the solitary, according to Ibn Bajja.[23]

Yet Maimonides adds a proviso: "It consists in setting thought to work on the first intelligible and in devoting oneself exclusively to this as far as this is within one's capacity."[24] Does "one's capacity" refer to the greatest possible extent that one can know the first intelligible, if one considers man's epistemological limitations; or might it refer to the degree of seclusion from society of which a man, even the righteous sage, is capable? The two alternative answers may be interwoven: the extent of knowing the first intelligible is equivalent to the degree of seclusion. Because a man, even a righteous man, is not capable of attaining complete knowledge of the first intelligible, can he be completely isolated or isolated only to "one's capacity?" This reservation occurs repeatedly sometimes at critical points, in Maimonides' writings.[25]

Maimonides continues as follows: "Thus it is clear that after apprehension, total devotion to Him and the employment of intellectual thought in constantly loving Him should be aimed at. Mostly this is achieved in solitude or isolation. Hence every excellent man stays frequently in solitude and does not meet anyone unless it is necessary."[26] If this is so, the attainment of God will indeed be perfected in solitude and separation, but only "mostly"; that is, not always. Every righteous man must be secluded for the most part, which means that he cannot be secluded absolutely. He has no need to be together with anyone except for essential purposes; thus, these essential purposes do exist and, in order to fulfill them, there is need for being together with others. True, the perfect man should remove himself entirely from corporeal desires: "He will have detached his thought from, and abolished his desire for, bestial things,"[27] although it should be emphasized that his desire for these things, not his natural need for them in correct measure, must be eliminated. Desires and needs should not be confused. They are two different matters. Not even Moses rose completely above bodily needs, except for a short time, at the climax of his retreat: "he did neither eat bread nor drink water."[28] This need characterizes the other prophet-philosophers, all the more, since they are at a lower level of perfection than Moses.

The qualitative difference between the perfect man and the common man lies not in his needs but in his thoughts and desires. The common man desires only to satisfy bodily needs, which he changes from a means to an end and, therefore, tends to excess in regard to them. The perfect man takes care to satisfy his bodily needs in the correct measure, but turns his thoughts and desires "to acquiring the science of the secrets of what exists and knowledge of its causes . . . in the knowledge of the deity and in reflections on His works"[29] alone. The perfect man, too, still has to join the commonality: "He should rather regard all people according to their various states with respect to which they are indubitably either like domestic animals or like beasts of prey. If the perfect man who lives in solitude thinks of them at all, he does so only with a view to saving himself from the harm that may be caused by those among them who are harmful if he happens to associate with them, or to obtaining an advantage that may be obtained from them if he is forced to it by some of his needs."[30] Even the perfect man, the recluse, may find himself in a social framework, either by chance "if he happens to associate with them" (i.e., the multitude) or when he has some need of social services "if he is forced [into the situation] by some of his needs." Considering the bestial nature of the masses, the perfect man must, in the first case, beware of their harmfulness and, in the second case, aim at benefiting from whatever use they can be to him, particularly in satisfying bodily and emotional needs, but he must still be cautious of the harm they can do. It is true that Maimonides makes his statements conditional: "If he is forced to . . . ," "if he happens to . . . ," meaning that the perfect man does not necessarily have to exist in a social framework. The very fact that Maimonides presents this possibility immediately after characterizing the perfect man as one who sets himself apart proves how vital the social condition is even for the latter.

As a result, Maimonides consistently portrays the saintly man's isolation from society in a negative light. His ethics, decisively influenced by the Aristotelian theory of moderation, identifies isolation as a grave exaggeration in the direction of deficiency. This is shown in two places: *Eight Chapters* and *Hilkhot De'ot* in the *Book of Knowledge*. In chapter 4 of *Eight Chapters*, solitude, together with other forms of asceticism and self-mortification—fasting, vigils, abstention from meat and wine and from sexual intercourse—is described as a specific therapeutic technique that should be adopted, to the right extent; as suitable for people in a certain emotional state or in a particular society; and as effective for a limited period only: "at certain times . . . some individuals. . . ." Maimonides deliberately and continually repeats the term "certain" or "some." His intention is to restore the correct balance of moderation to those who have behaved excessively. He does so by means of a temporary and controlled excess in the opposite direction. Maimonides, though, utterly rejects the avoidance of satisfying our bodily and emotional needs in correct measure. He sharply criticizes as fools those who play at being righteous, but who have mistakenly confounded a temporary therapeutic technique with conduct that is consistently proper in a man who is spiritually healthy:

> What the virtuous men did at certain times and also what some individuals among them [always] did in inclining toward one extreme—
> for example, fasting, rising at night, abstaining from eating meat and drinking wine, keeping away from women, wearing garments of wool

and hair, dwelling on mountains, and secluding themselves in desolate places—they did only with a view to medical treatment, as we have indicated. Again, if they say that due to the corruption of the people of the city they would be corrupted through contact with them and through seeing their deeds and that social intercourse with them would bring about the corruption of their own moral habits, then they withdrew to desolate places where there are no evil men. As the prophet said, peace be upon him: "O that I were in the desert" (Jer. 9:1). When the ignorant saw these virtuous men perform such actions, but without knowing their intention, they thought those actions to be good and aimed at performing them, claiming to be like those virtuous men. They set about afflicting their bodies with every kind of affliction, thinking they were acquiring virtue and doing something good and would thereby come near to God—as if God were an enemy of the body and desired its ruin and destruction. They were not aware that those actions are bad and that one of the vices of the soul is thereby acquired.[31]

Maimonides justifies temporary seclusion from human society, on mountains and in deserts only when a man has a therapeutic need for temporary isolation, so as to balance the negative tendency of uncontrolled association with everyone; or when society is so corrupt that it may corrupt even the best of the righteous. The first case involves the personal problem of one who has a spiritual ailment; the second case, the general problem of corrupt society, which is liable to affect even the perfect man.

In *Hilkhot De'ot* Maimonides deals only with the general situation. He evaluates the various alternatives in such circumstances, there being a direct correlation between the degree of corruption of the society and the appropriate degree of isolation from it. The guiding principle is the obligation to choose the absolute minimum of isolation as required by the social situation. This principle is lucidly stated in Maimonides' interpretation of Hillel's precept, "Do not separate yourself from the community" (*Avot* 2:4): "One should not separate from the community except in the measure of their corruption."[32] A classification of the alternatives is stated, in *Hilkhot De'ot:*

It is natural to be influenced, in sentiments and conduct, by one's neighbours and associates, and observe the customs of one's fellow citizens. Hence a person ought constantly to associate with the righteous and frequent the company of the wise, so as to learn from their practices, and shun the wicked, who are benighted, so as not to be corrupted by their example. . . . So too, if one lives in a country where the customs are pernicious, and the inhabitants do not go in the right way, he should leave for a place where the people are righteous and follow the ways of the good. If all the countries of which he has personal knowledge, or concerning which he hears reports, follow a course that is not right—as is the case in our times—or if military campaigns or sickness debar him from leaving for a country with good customs, he should live by himself in seclusion, as it is said, "Let him sit alone and keep silence" (Lam. 3:28). And if the inhabitants are wicked reprobates who will not let him stay in the country unless he mixes with them and adopts their evil practices, let him withdraw to caves, thickets or deserts, and not habituate himself to the ways of sinners, as it is said, "O that I were in the wilderness, in a lodging place of wayfaring men" (Jer. 9:1).[33]

A man must be aware that it is his nature to be affected by social pressures, and be extremely careful. Just as it is right to keep the company of righteous sages in order to be positively influenced by them, it is equally essential to stay away from the company of evildoers.[34] Maimonides defines the "righteous state" in chapter 3 of *Hilkhot Teshuvah* as one in which "the merits of all its inhabitants exceed their iniquities."[35] In order for the upright man to remain in this state, he must be careful to keep clear of the wicked and to consort only with the righteous.

A more serious situation arises when one lives in a state defined as a "wicked state," which is the case "if their iniquities preponderate" over their good qualities.[36] In such circumstances, the alternative is to leave for a righteous state. A more extreme condition occurs when public circumstances, such as poor conditions of safety, or personal circumstances, such as illness, make departure from the evil state hazardous. When all states are evil, "as is the case in our times,"[37] a man should isolate himself from the evil of society: "He should live by himself in seclusion." Only in the most extreme case, when he is not left alone and attempts are made to force him to join in the corrupt activities of the evil state, is it justified to adopt the most extreme alternative: to live in caves and deserts in absolute isolation from human society.[38]

Clearly, then, Maimonides regarded complete isolation from human society as fundamentally undesirable, an act not to be adopted except in the most extreme conditions, when all other avenues have been exhausted. Indeed, in several places Maimonides even justifies associating with the wicked if this is the virtuous man's only means of being part of society, which is emotionally vital for him.[39]

Perhaps the most stringent rejection of isolation in Maimonides' writings is found in his interpretation of R. Joshua's list in Tractate *Avot,* 2:11, of the things that "remove man from the world." One of them is hatred of mankind. Maimonides explains this as:

the malady of melancholia which will bring a man to disdain what his eyes behold and loathe it. The company of beasts and solitude in deserts and in forests will be beneficial to him, and an area that is uninhabited will be preferable to him. This (type of withdrawal) on his part is not from the standpoint of "separateness" but (is to be attributed) to the evilness of his passion and his envy of others; these (traits) will undoubtedly put a man to death, for his body will become sick and he will die before his time.

Isolation is permissible, as long as it serves temporary therapeutic needs; Otherwise it is presented as a negative, essentially bestial condition. In its extreme form, then, isolation from human society is a mental disease, and one of the cases in which a man has no share in the world to come (*Hilkhot Teshuvah* 3, 6:11).

The foregoing references serve to emphasize Maimonides' repudiation of seclusion. In terms of both his needs and his obligations, a man, even a perfect man, must exist within the social framework as far as possible: "He shall dwell in a city and follow justice and equity; he shall not inhabit caves or mountains."[40] Three theoretical possibilities thus present themselves: First, to live in a wicked state; second to withdraw from it to the deserts and mountains; and third, to dwell in a virtuous state. The last is obviously the preferred choice. The perfect man must separate himself from the wicked state and even inhabit deserts and mountains if he has no alternative. But he must always strive to live in the most desirable setting, that of the virtuous state, "and follow justice and equity." (*Guide* III:51).

What is this "unless it is necessary" of which Maimonides speaks? Is it primarily the supply of the personal needs of the sages? In the introduction to the *Commentary on the Mishnah (Tractate Zera'im)*, Maimonides stressed the dependence of the sages on a social framework for satisfying their physical and emotional needs. The common people, who are unable to realize the supreme goal of human existence, exist to fulfill the needs of the sages: "Those people were created for two reasons. One purpose is for them to serve that [unique] individual. . . . Therefore the masses were created to provide company for the wise."[41] In order to be free to achieve intellectual perfection, the sages depend on the masses. Accordingly, the interest of the prophet-philosopher in improving human society is also a personal interest. A better human society will make it easier and less dangerous for him to exist.

The necessity of obtaining his physical and emotional needs is not the only constraint that prevents the prophet-philosopher from cutting himself off from human society. His moral, educational, and political obligations, also compel him, even against his natural inclination, to function in a social setting. In other words, the social existence of the prophet-philosopher results, in part and indeed chiefly, from his public duty. Like the Platonic philosopher who returns to the cave to educate the masses living in the gloom of their false beliefs, so must Maimonides' prophet-philosopher use the divine truth he has acquired through his intellect to educate and lead human society. The angels—these being the prophets—in Maimonides' interpretation, ascend the ladder so as to attain knowledge of God; but then they descend to apply their knowledge in the guidance of human beings: "For after the ascent comes the descent with whatever decree the prophet has been informed of—with a view to governing and teaching the people of the earth."[42] This was the case with Moses, who climbed Mount Sinai and then came down to tell the people what he had heard. What he had heard was not confined only to the intelligibles; it especially related to accepted opinion on the conduct of men.

His divine perfection indeed furnishes the prophet-philosopher with greater privileges than are given the masses, who are obliged to serve him and fulfill his needs. Prophetic perfection, however, also imposes the burden of guiding those same masses. Who ever has attained intellectual knowledge has the duty to employ it in leading the people. It is precisely the person who has succeeded in reaching the highest level of isolation who must engage in the highest level of public involvement.

Maimonides consistently presents prophecy as a political conception. The prophet-philosopher is characterized not only by intellectual perfection but also by his political leadership: "He will be aware and achieve knowledge only of matters that constitute true opinions and general directives for the well-being of men in their relations with one another."[43] Philosophers acquire the divine emanation only in their theoretical soul; leaders of states, lawgivers, magicians, and the like acquire it in their imaginative soul. The prophet-philosopher, however, acquires the emanation in his intelligent and in his imaginative soul together. Maimonides subdivides the class of prophet-philosophers. One subclass includes anyone who has received sufficient divine emanation in his imaginative and intelligent soul for himself alone. The second subclass includes whoever has acquired an excess of emanation. In the latter case, the prophet-philosopher necessarily becomes a special kind of political leader, a so-called public prophet. Hence, in *Hilkhot Yesodei ha-Torah* 7:7:

> The gift of prophecy may be vouchsafed to a prophet, intended for him alone. . . . Sometimes the prophet is sent on a special mission to a particular people or to inhabitants of a certain city or kingdom, to direct them aright, teach them what they are to do or restrain them from the evil they were pursuing.

The public prophet must realize and apply his added inspiration to the sphere of moral and political leadership of people. The excess emanation in the imaginative soul is essential to him not only to experience prophetic visions but also to reach the masses, people in whom the imaginative soul alone reigns and distorts their perception. The public prophet leads them by means of the imaginative fables. The philosopher who possesses perfection of the theoretical soul sufficient for himself alone and the prophet-philosopher who possesses perfection of the imaginative and intelligent soul sufficient for himself alone do not have the ability, desire, or duty to share their perfection with others. The public prophet, by contrast, has this ability: he can pass on to others the excess of divine emanation in his imaginative and theoretical soul, like surplus water spilling out of a container. He will, therefore, have both the desire and the duty to educate the masses. Philosophers and prophet philosophers of the first kind must limit themselves to the oral transmission of esoteric wisdom to the few. Public prophets, on the other hand, must commit their wisdom to writing, to give the masses access to it:

> And sometimes the measure of the overflow is such that it moves him to compose works and to teach. The same holds good for the second class. Sometimes the prophetic revelation that comes to a prophet only renders him perfect and has no other effect. And sometimes the prophetic revelation that comes to him compels him to address a call to the people, teach them, and let his own perfection overflow towards them. It has already become clear to you that, were it not for this additional perfection, science would not be set forth in books and prophets would not call upon the people to obtain knowledge of the truth. For a man endowed with knowledge does not set anything down for himself in order to teach himself what he already knows.... The nature of this matter makes it necessary for someone to whom this additional measure of overflow has come, to address a call to people, regardless of whether that call is listened to or not, and even if he as a result thereof is harmed.[44]

As a result of the pressure of the excess of divine emanation, the public prophet is obliged, actually compelled, to follow his political call, even against his will, even if he is not heeded, and even if he imperils himself by doing so.

This compulsion is clearly expressed in the two great chapters on the political *imitatio Dei* in the *Guide* (I:54, and III:54). Maimonides' theory of divine attributes ends with the conclusion that the only positive attributes of God that man is able to know are the attributes of action (I:52). This fact expresses the epistemological limitation of man, who is unable to perceive the essence of God by his intellect. Our knowledge of the attributes of action, however, also expresses the divine consideration of man's social needs. The prophet-philosopher is capable of knowing precisely the attributes that will help him to lead human society justly. The application of the attributes of action through the theory of *imitatio Dei* enable him to realize his moral and educational obligation. Knowledge of God's attributes of action is the most relevant area in the perfection of the theoretical intellect for the purpose of acquiring perfection of the practical intellect.

God refused to reveal His face at the cleft in the rock—that is, the attributes of His essence—to Moses; but He acceded to the prophet's request to inform him of His ways (Exod. 33:12–23). The ways in which God related to Moses, according to Maimonides' commentary, are the ways of His governance of the created world; that is, His attributes of action. He who "knows how He governs them [His created world] in general and in detail"[45] must apply this knowledge to the proper leadership of human society in general and of the individuals in it in particular. Human leadership must mirror God's governance of the worldly order, the ways in which His actions—kindness, mercy, ·retribution (*Guide* I:54), judgment and righteousness—(III:53–54), are implemented for their own sake. They are administered according to just principles and an objective awareness of the requirements of human reality, not tendentiously or for the sake of personal gain, insofar as this is humanly possible:

> It behooves the governor of a city, if he is a prophet, to acquire similarity to these attributes, so that these actions may proceed from him according to a determined measure and according to the deserts of the people who are affected by them and not merely because of his following a passion. He should not let loose the reins of anger nor let passion gain mastery over him, for all passions are evil; but, on the contrary, he should guard against them as far as this lies within the capacity of man. Sometimes, with regard to some people, he should be merciful and gracious, not out of mere compassion and pity, but in accordance with what is fitting.[46]

Not by chance, therefore, are the attributes of action identified with the thirteen attributed traditionally assigned to God:

> Scripture has restricted itself to mentioning only those thirteen characteristics, although [Moses] apprehended all his goodness—I mean to say all His actions—because these are the actions proceeding from Him, may He be exalted, in respect of giving existence to the Adamites and governing them. This was [Moses'] ultimate object in his demand, the conclusion of what he says being: That I may know Thee, to the end that I may find grace in Thy sight and consider that

this nation is Thy people—that is, a people for the government of which I need to perform actions that I must seek to make similar to Thy actions in governing them.[47]

The attributes revealed were the most relevant attributes of action from Moses' viewpoint for the purpose of leading his sinful people at that critical time following the Golden Calf:

> We have made clear why scripture, in enumerating His actions, has confined itself here to those mentioned above, and that those actions are needed for the governance of cities. For the utmost virtue of man is to become like unto Him, may He be exalted, as far as he is able; which means that we should make our actions like unto His.[48]

The person who achieves knowledge of God's attributes of action also bears special responsibility to act accordingly. The public identifies him as one who imitates the divine attributes of action, and the members of the public tend to emulate such a leader's ways. As the prophet-philosopher must imitate the divine way, so the masses must copy the leadership of the prophet-philosopher in human society. Moses was punished because he strayed from his duty to lead in accordance with the virtue of moderation when he showed his anger at the people in the episode of the waters of discord:

> God disapproved of a man like him becoming irascible in the presence of the community of Israel, when irascibility was not proper. For this individual something like that was a profanation of the Name, because they would imitate his every movement and speech and would wish thereby to attain the happiness of this world and the next.[49]

This was the solution given by Maimonides to the awkward fact that biblical documentation is abundant in relating the physical deeds of the Patriarchs, when he himself presents them as sages who achieved divine solitude. Maimonides resolves the contradiction, a superficial one in his view, by ascribing the Patriarchs' performance of much bodily activity, not to profit or pleasure, but to a sense of duty stemming from their own divine perfection to lead the community. This duty goes beyond supplying the material needs of the people; it is the chief means of bringing the Children of Israel to the supreme goal of worshipping God and knowing Him:

> For in those four, I mean the *Patriarchs* and *Moses our Master*, union with God—I mean apprehension of Him and love of Him—became

manifest, as the texts testify. Also the providence of God watching
over them and over their posterity was great. Withal they were occupied with governing people, increasing their fortune and endeavor-
ing to acquire property. Now this is to my mind a proof that they performed these actions with their limbs only, while their intellects were
constantly in His presence, may He be exalted. It also seems to me
that the fact that these four were in a permanent state of extreme
perfection in the eyes of God, and that His providence watched over
them continually even while they were engaged in increasing their
fortune—I mean while they tended their cattle, did agricultural
work, and governed their household—was necessarily brought about
by the circumstance that in all these actions their end was to come
near to Him, may He be exalted; and how near! For the end of their
efforts during their life was to bring into being a religious community that would know and worship God. *For I have known him, to the
end that he may command,* and so on. Thus it has become clear to you
that the end of all their efforts was to spread the doctrine of *the unity
of the Name in the world.* and to guide people to love Him, may He
be exalted. Therefore this rank befitted them, for these actions were
pure worship of great import.[50]

These words appear in the lengthy comment that Maimonides appended
to the parable of the palace. This comment, stressing as it does the solitude of
the prophet-philosopher—"when, however, you are alone with yourself and no
one else is there"[51]—actually contains repeated reservations about the possibility and the obligation to maintain this absolute solitude because of the personal
needs and the political duty of the perfect man. Ultimately, the application of
the intellectual perfection of the perfect man to the behavior of the masses with
the aim of true worship of God is the philosopher's own true worship.

The last chapter of the *Guide* (III:54) closes with the theory of *imitatio
Dei*. After describing the four perfections in accordance with the Aristotelian
tradition—the foremost being intellectual perfection, characterized by a state
of solitude—Maimonides adds, under obvious Farabian influence, a fifth,
supreme perfection. This is the practical imitation of God's attributes of
action. This addition, however, changes everything. Here is how he interprets
Jeremiah's words:

But he says that one should glory in the apprehension of Myself and
in the knowledge of My attributes, by which he means His actions,
as we have made clear with reference to its dictum: *Show me now Thy
ways* and so on. In this verse he makes it clear to us that those actions
that ought to be known and imitated are *loving-kindness, justice,* and

righteousness. He means that it is My purpose that there should come from you *loving-kindness, righteousness,* and *justice in the earth* in the way we have explained with regard to the *thirteen attributes:* namely, that the purpose should be assimilation to them and that this should be our way of life. Thus the end that he sets forth in this verse may be stated as follows: It is clear that the perfection of man that may truly be gloried in is the one acquired by him who has achieved, in a measure corresponding to his capacity, apprehension of Him, may He be exalted, and who knows His providence extending over His creatures as manifested in the act of bringing them into being and in their governance as it is. The way of life of such an individual, after he has achieved this apprehension, will always have in view *loving-kindness, righteousness,* and *justice,* through assimilation to His actions, may He be exalted, just as we have explained several times in this Treatise.[52]

It is necessary to apprehend God's attributes of action—*hesed* (kindness), *mishpat* (justice), and *sedaqah* (righteousness)—to the extent that is humanly possible. Then it is necessary to achieve these in action; in other words to pass from the theoretical sphere to praxis. The prophet-philosopher turns into a political leader. This is also the necessary result of Maimonides' theory of God. If man is to emulate God and God is described as essentially active, then the best way to emulate God is not the contemplative, but the active life, following His ways in directing human society and not withdrawing into contemplation. Maimonides presents the practical imitation of God as the supreme purpose of the perfect man at the climax of the *Guide.*

Maimonides opens the *Guide* with an explanation of the word "image" *(selem),* and concludes it with the theory of *imitatio Dei.* Man's being created in the image of God relates to the perfection of his theoretical intellect, while the theory of *imitatio Dei* refers to the application of intellectual perfection to political leadership. The work thus opens with theory and ends with praxis. Maimonides' other great treatise, *Mishneh Torah,* likewise begins, in *Hilkhot Yesodei ha-Torah* with the perfection of the intellectual soul and ends, in the *Book of Judges,* with "the conduct of kings and their wars." Maimonides' principal work in the philosophical sphere and his principal work in the halakhic sphere, therefore, begin with theory and end with practice; that is, with the political perfection of man. The parallelism reinforces the view that Maimonides the halakhist and Maimonides the philosopher are not in conflict but complement each other. In the halakhic and the philosophical context the supreme perfection of man is expressed in the political and social sphere.

The theory of *imitatio Dei* undergirds the use made by Maimonides and other philosophers of parables of the king (e.g., *Guide* I:56; III:51). Just as

God rules with kindness, justice, and righteousness in the created world so should the king in human society. The king in the state is made a simile for God's role and rule in the created world. Against this background Maimonides defined the name *Elohim* as an equivocal term of the derivative kind (*Guide* I:2), referring first of all to judges and leaders and, figuratively to angels and to God.[53] Hence, the possibility of regarding the king as a simile for God.

Maimonides' prophet-philosopher oscillates between two poles. On the one hand, there is his personal, elitist, even egotistical wish to detach himself from a corrupt human society and to ensconce himself in his intellectual ivory tower in a quest for divine perfection. On the other hand, the force of his educational obligation drives him to make use of his divinely imparted gifts to lead human society. Maimonides himself struggles here, as a philosopher and as a leader, between the two poles: the reclusive philosopher of the Ibn Bajja ideal and the philosopher bound up in the Platonic Farabian tradition.

Maimonides' prophet-philosopher contends with exactly the same problem as the Platonic philosopher in the myth of the cave. He settles it with the same kind of moral judgment. Socrates, as described in the *Apology*, is urged— in fact, forced—by the Oracle to accomplish his philosophical and political mission.[54] Maimonides portrays the prophet Jeremiah in the same way. Moses is a unique prophet-lawgiver, but Jeremiah is the prototype of the public prophet, whose task it is to rebuke the rulers and the sinful people.

As we have observed, Maimonides twice refers to Jeremiah's words. "O that I were in the wilderness, in a lodging place."[55] Despair at the corruption of society and its unwillingness to mend its ways seems to urge withdrawal. But the words of the prophet express only a wish—"O that I were"—one that is never fulfilled. Despite his personal desire to distance himself from a human society that is rotten, Jeremiah remains engaged, because of his prophetic duty. He continues to fight to correct the ways of this society.

The longing to break away appears in the first part of the *Book of Jeremiah*. The prophet's struggle is encapsulated in chapter 9, which begins with the exasperated wish, "O that I were in the wilderness" (v. 1) and culminates with the political imitation of God (v. 23). Like Socrates, who was indicted, jailed, and condemned to death, Jeremiah is cast into a pit in the Court of the Guard. Neither man abandoned his duty as a public prophet. Maimonides sees Jeremiah as compelled to fulfill his political mission—even if he does not wish to do so, even if he is not heeded, and even if he is harmed:

> The nature of this matter makes it necessary for someone to whom this additional measure of overflow has come, to address a call to people, regardless of whether that call is listened to or not, and even if he as a result thereof is harmed in his body. We even find that

prophets addressed a call to people until they were killed. This divine overflow moving them and by no means letting them rest and be quiet, even if they met with great misfortunes. For this reason you will find that Jeremiah, peace be on him, explicitly stated that because of the contempt he met with at the hand of the disobedient and unbelieving people who lived in his time, he wished to conceal his prophecy and not address to them a call to the truth, which they rejected, but he was not able to do it. He says: *Because the word of the Lord is made a reproach unto me, and a derision, all the day. And if I say: I will not make mention of Him, nor speak anymore in His name, then there is in my heart as it were a burning fire shut up in my bones and I weary myself to hold it in, but cannot.*[56]

Maimonides asserts that courage, the ability to withstand physical danger and social pressure, which is potentially found in all men, must be constantly active in the public prophet. In its absence, the prophet will be unable to sustain the public aspect of his task. Again, Maimonides presents Jeremiah as the model:

These two faculties must necessarily be very strong in prophets, I mean the faculty of courage and that of divination. And when the intellect overflows toward them, these two faculties become very greatly strengthened so that this may finally reach the point you know: namely, the lone individual, having only his staff, went boldly to the great king in order to save a religious community from the burden of slavery, and had no fear or dread, because it was said to him: *I will be with thee.* . . . Thus it was said to Jeremiah: *Be not afraid* and so on. *Be not dismayed at them,* and so on. *For, behold, I have made thee this day a fortified city.*[57]

Thus, the entire *Guide* fittingly ends with a philosophical explanation of Jeremiah's statement, "Let not the wise man glory in his wisdom," and so forth: The perfect man has no need to glory in his wealth, his courage, or his wisdom, but basks in the perfection of his intellect alone: "[so] that he understandeth and knoweth Me." The prophet does not halt here; he goes on to indicate the specific content and burden of the relevant knowledge. It does not relate to theoretical questions like the unity of God or His unique nature, but precisely, and deliberately to knowledge of God's attributes of action: "that I am the Lord who exercise loving-kindness, justice, and righteousness in the earth." Neither does the prophet stop here, but adds, "For in these things I delight, saith the Lord." Maimonides interprets these words in accordance with the theory of imitation: "It is My purpose that there should come from you loving-kindness, righteousness and justice on earth."[58] Jeremiah practices what he preaches. Despite his own desire to find an intellectual lodging place in the desert, far from the madding crowd, he will always decide, gritting his teeth and almost against his will, to fulfill his public duty, like Socrates and Maimonides after him.

Maimonides himself did not retire to a life of pure contemplation but continued to his last day in public activity. This fact in itself is highly significant, especially if one considers the strength of his declared wish for a life of solitude. Like his contemporary Ibn Rushd, he chose to engage in two specific public roles. Maimonides worked as a physician and as a communal leader and teacher of halakhah. According to the Platonic outlook, the unjust state is one that is sick in body and in soul. To treat the one a physician is required; to treat the other, a judge. In the ideal state, which is whole in body and soul, there will no longer be any need for these two professions. But Maimonides knowingly chose to fulfill precisely these two essential roles, in order to offer guidance to his fellow men.[59] As a teacher of halakhah, Maimonides identified with Moses' legislative mission. This is clear from the declared ambitious goal of the Maimonidean Code and the title he gave it, *Mishneh Torah*. As a philosopher, Maimonides identified with Jeremiah's inner struggle between a desire to retire into contemplation and the duty to fulfill his social obligation. In the end, he reached to the same resolution as the prophet.

Maimonides' messianic vision is also replete with motifs of the Platonic utopia. Right action is described, in Platonic language, as the outcome of intellectual perfection. Men do not commit evil out of ill will, but out of ignorance: "For through cognition of the truth, enmity and hatred are removed and the inflicting of harm by people against one another is abolished." Whoever knows good will naturally do good: "The cause of the abolition of these enmities, these discords, and these tyrannies will be the knowledge that men will then have concerning the true reality of the deity."[60] If men attain intellectual perfection—that is, knowledge of God's attributes of action—they will also know how to perform the right act. As Maimonides puts it concisely in the introduction to *Perek Helek*, "since the earth shall be full of the knowledge of the Lord and wars will cease."[61] There is a complete correlation between perfection of opinions and perfection of action. Intellectual perfection will bring about the establishment of the perfect human society.

For both halakhic and Aristotelian reasons, Maimonides rejected Platonic communalism, with its common ownership of property and abolition of the family. The idea that in the messianic era, too, "the world follows its customary pattern" held not only for the natural order but also for what Maimonides defines as the natural social order. Class differences will continue to exist after the advent of the Messiah: "In the days of the Messiah there will still be rich and poor, strong and weak."[62] Yet Maimonides also evidently accepts the Platonic analysis of class structure. In the introduction to his commentary on the Mishnah, as already indicated, he identified the raison d'être of the "common people" as service to the needs of the small minority of sages. This conception reflects an obviously Platonic distinction between artisans and sages, a division of labor that frees the wise for a life of contemplation. Indeed in *Hilkhot Melakhim,* Maimonides stresses that sages and prophets (the common people are not mentioned here at all!) yearn for the days of the Messiah, not to win power or material benefits "but to devote themselves to the Torah and its wisdom."[63] Likewise in the preface to *Perek Helek:* "The prophets and saints looked forward to the days of the Messiah and yearned for them because then the righteous will be gathered together in fellowship and because goodness and wisdom will prevail." Here, again, the masses are not mentioned. In *Hilkhot Teshuvah,* though, we find the entire people of Israel included in this longing: "Hence, all Israelites, their prophets and sages, longed for the advent of messianic times, so that they might have relief from the wicked tyranny . . . that they might have ease, devote themselves to getting wisdom." I believe that a scale of degrees in acquisition of the truth exists here among the different groups of the people, from the commoners of Israel to the sages, to the king-Messiah, at the apex of the system. For he is described as one who has attained the supreme perfection of wisdom. The same hierarchy is found in the preface to *Perek Helek,* as we shall see below. In this hierarchy of wisdom, one level is attributed to all the people of Israel, as Maimonides quotes from Jeremiah (31:34) in the preface to *Perek Helek:* "For they shall all know me, from the least of them unto the greatest of them." Here, too, we see a gradation in terms of "knowledge" *(yediah).*

The *Mishneh Torah* closes by emphasizing: "Hence Israelites will be very wise, they will know the things that are now concealed and will attain an understanding of their Creator to the utmost capacity of the human mind." "To the utmost capacity of the human mind" means not only what humankind is able to grasp, but also what different men are able to comprehend according to the extent of their capacities. If, as Maimonides specifically argues, the natural order will not change in the days of the Messiah, then relative human potential will not change, either. Just as class differences will persist among people, so will differences in their levels of wisdom. Furthermore, there is even some correlation between levels of wisdom and class distinctions. If so, the Platonic nature of the messianic period is very much in evidence in the Maimonidean conception.

Ultimately, the uniqueness of the messianic age, like that of the Platonic state, lies in the fact that sages will be perfectly free to engage in learning and will attain the highest level of wisdom possible for a man. The common people will accept the governance of the sages willingly, as they will be led by "the proper Guide." Here lies the real significance of the attribution of the perfection of wisdom to all the people of Israel in the messianic period. Perhaps for that reason, Maimonides in his messianic discussions cites the following from Isaiah twice: "For the earth shall be full of the knowledge of the Lord"(11:9). In other words, the Earth will be full of wisdom, the wisdom of the few sages. This will necessarily radiate over the masses of the people; but this does not mean that all the people of Israel as individuals will attain that measure of wisdom. Maimonides chooses his words very carefully; he speaks of "the knowledge that men will then have concerning the true reality of the deity"; he does not say, the knowledge possessed by *all* men. The interpretation of the verse from Isaiah that wisdom will be the heritage of all the people of Israel to the same degree in the messianic age contradicts Maimonides' well-known position that there are natural differences in intellectual potential, and that the natural order will not change with the coming of the Messiah.

At the head of the hierarchy stands the king-Messiah. The introduction to *Perek Helek* describes the king-Messiah in Platonic terms as one who possesses perfection of practical and rational intellect together: "the righteousness and the abundant justice of the Messianic king . . . the salutary influence of his unprecedented wisdom . . . his nearness to God."[64] More expansively than in *Hilkhot Teshuvah*, Maimonides here compares the king-Messiah as a king to King Solomon and as a prophet to Moses. As prophet, the king-Messiah will only approach the level of Moses; but as king, he will surpass Solomon, the wisest of men, who is the supreme exemplar of the philosopher king in the medieval tradition: "The king who will arise from the seed of David will possess more wisdom than Solomon."[65]

The comparison with Solomon is important not only in regard to intellectual perfection but also, inevitably, in connection with his political role. Like the reign of Solomon, the days of the Messiah will be a period of world peace. The world will continue in its accustomed way and class differences will persist in the messianic period, too, but social struggle will disappear. The just rule of the king-Messiah and the fact that the poor will easily satisfy all their own needs, owing to the improvement in climatic conditions with the advent of the Messiah, will bring it about that: "In that era there will be neither famine nor war, neither jealousy nor strife. Blessings will be abundant, comforts within the reach of all."[66]

Following the Farabian attitude, Maimonides threads clear Platonic strands into the theory of the philosopher-prophet, who must become a political leader (as expressed in the image of Moses). And he inserts these Platonic themes into the description of the messianic period and the image of the king-Messiah. For this reason various scholars have argued that an exact parallel exists between Maimonides' philosopher-prophet-leader and the Platonic philosopher king. As Rosenthal, for example, defines it:

This synthesis (i.e., philosopher / lawgiver / king / imam) represents Al-Farabi's outstanding contribution to political thought in Islam, and it may be added in Maimonides (who accepted the theory of prophecy and the prophet / philosopher / lawgiver as the ideal ruler) but not in Judaism generally.[67]

Maimonides, however, accepted the parallel only partially and critically. Following Al-Farabi, he indeed admits the parallel and posits that the ideal leader, being a prophet, must possess the thirteen virtues, thereby imitating the divine pattern of governance in the created world. In his view, though, the philosopher is not wholly identified with the prophet, and prophecy may be denied the philosopher through divine will. The philosopher receives divine emanation only in his rational soul, whereas the prophet receives it in his rational and imaginative souls alike. The philosopher is secluded with the intelligibles; but the philosopher who is also a prophet and leader is in the end unique in his political commitment. For its sake he requires perfection of his imaginative soul. The equating of the philosopher with the prophet is not automatic, then, but potential (*Guide* II:32).

For both philosophical and halakhic reasons, Maimonides never includes kingship in this parallelism. He draws a sharp distinction between the king's qualities and functions and those of the philosopher. The role of each is different, and each is exalted by divine emanation in a different part of his soul: the philosopher in his rational soul, and the king in his imaginative soul. The king and the prophet both possess a well-developed imaginative soul; hence, their political talents. In this respect, the prophet creates a seeming point of contact between the philosopher and the king (*Guide* II:37), but their political acumen and duties are essentially different. The prophet is either a lawgiver (in the case of Moses) or a critic and chastiser at the gate (the other prophets).

The political function of the king, by contrast, is entirely executive (*Guide* II:39–40). Moreover, kingship as an empirical phenomenon is illuminated by Maimonides in quite a negative light—as an expression of the material appetites of man. After all, a king receives divine emanation in his imaginative soul, and nowhere else. In Maimonides' psychology, the imaginative soul possesses a vital function, but one that is also somewhat problematic. Its influence is liable to be disastrous if it is not ruled by the rational soul. Maimonides, in fact, identifies the king with the problematic force in the human soul. Thus, the king is presented as an example of the desire for property, a desire that Maimonides places lowest on the scale of perfections, and one that is presented in the last chapter of the *Guide* as external to man, not as a part of his essence. By contrast, Maimonides attributes the fifth and supreme perfection, the actual imitation of God, to the philosopher-prophet, who is identified with the dominion of the rational soul.[68] It is true that Maimonides' parables of the king (*Guide* I:46; III:51; etc.), portray kingship as an ideal condition. Here, though, the king is presented as a metaphor for God, not as a representative example of empirical monarchy. Clearly the king is assigned a lower role and status than the prophet-leader. In the *Guide* Maimonides depicts the king as an executive who implements legislation and the directives of the prophet: "Among them there is the one to whom the regimen mentioned has been revealed by prophecy directly; he is the prophet or the bringer of the *nomos*. Among them are also those who have the faculty to compel people to accomplish, observe, and realize that which has been established by those two. They are the sovereign who adopts the *nomos* in question."[69] The prophet, concerned with the welfare of the body and the soul together, legislates divine law, whereas the king is no more than a legislator of human law *(torah nimusit)*, concerned with material and social perfection alone. Since the king takes as his basis the directions of divine law, it necessarily follows that he is subject to the authority of the prophet. Hence, Maimonides does not draw a Platonic kind of parallel between the king and the philosopher-prophet. He establishes a clear division of functions, with the unequivocal supremacy of the prophet as the legislative authority (in the case of Moses) or restraining authority (in the case of the other prophets) over the king. It may perhaps be said that Maimonides in this connection accepted Al-Farabi's position on the possibility of the division of rule among two or more men in circumstances in which the rare man who is perfect in all the virtues is not to be found.[70] The same holds for the halakhic context. In *Hilkhot Talmud Torah*, Maimonides presents the traditional Three Crowns, exemplifying the division, not identity, of roles and the clear-cut supremacy of the Crown of the Torah over the Crown of Kingship.[71] Maimonides, as already noted, does posit monarchy as a binding halakhic norm in *Hilkhot Melakhim*, contrary to the *pshat* of the Bible. However, the monarchy he presents here is strikingly limited. Everyone, including prophet and priest, owe allegiance to the king, and Maimonides describes at length the external symbols of the ruler's glory and status, which are essential for submission to his rule. In turn, though, the king also owes obedience to the prophet and the priest. Scrutinizing the text, we find that aside from much external ceremonial and recognition of the king's right to make use, up to a point, of his position to gain material benefits, his powers in substantive matters are limited indeed. Monarchy is explicitly depicted as a means of achieving certain goals. The status of anyone portrayed as an instrument necessarily depends on the function he is assigned. Thus, the appointment of the king is linked with Israel's obligation to fight Amalek and to build the Temple: "But whatever he does should be done by him for the sake of Heaven. His sole aim and thought should be to uplift the true religion, to fill the world with righteousness, to break the arms of the wicked, and to fight the battles of the Lord. The prime reason for appointing a king was that he execute judgment and wage war."[72]

The king is appointed by the prophet. This was true with the choice of the House of David in general, and the procedure will hold if a king is chosen from another lineage in Israel. The king requires the consent of his subjects. He must copy out the Torah, an act emphasizing his obligation to uphold its laws. In any clash between the decrees of the king and the commandments of the Torah, the latter takes undisputed precedence. It is obligatory in such an event to refuse to obey the king's command. As another example, the king is forbidden to embark on an elective war without the approval of the Sanhedrin. Maimonides follows the continuation of the biblical text in Deuteronomy 17, and this time in the spirit of the *pshat,* he stresses the many restrictions imposed on the king: not only the positive commandments peculiar to the monarch, but also a long list of negative commandments.

Thus, Maimonides is most circumspect toward monarchy in his philosophic works; in his halakhic writings, monarchy appears as a halakhic norm, but its powers are greatly limited. All this serves to emphasize that Maimonides could hardly accept the Platonic Farabian identity of philosopher, prophet, and king, philosophically or halakhically. The only person in history who answers to such a description is Moses, whom Maimonides presents as sui generis. Moses is described in the *Guide* as the first lawgiver and leader, but never as king (II:39), even though this description could accord with the tradition of "And there was a king in Jeshurun" (Deut. 33:5); in Maimonides' halakhic writings, we find only one allusion to Moses as king.[73]

The complete king-philosopher-prophet parallel holds for king-Messiah. Maimonides supposes that prophecy in general will also be restored with the coming of the Messiah (*Guide* II:36), "in its accustomed form," that is, as it was in the past. Once prophecy with its recognized philosophical and political features, resumes in messianic times, and exists parallel to kingship, the question will once more arise concerning the relationship between the king-Messiah, who is also a prophet, and the other prophets. Unfortunately, the answer to this question is not sufficiently clear in Maimonides' writings. It seems to follow, though, that even the full identity of the king-Messiah as king who is simultaneously philosopher and prophet must clearly be subject to some restraints if other philosopher prophets are to be active in the same era.

Maimonides never establishes a direct parallel between the king, on the one hand, and the philosopher, prophet, and lawgiver, on the other; indeed, such a parallel is not possible in his system. For that reason, Maimonides nowhere gives a precise list of the philosopher-king's virtues. In the theory of imitation of the thirteen divine attributes and their application to political leadership, he merely hints at such a list. Moreover, the thirteen virtues enumerated by Maimonides are all moral virtues (including courage, *gevurah,* mentioned in *Guide* II:38), while the tradition of the philosopher-king's virtues includes also physical and rational virtues. Although Maimonides mentions thirteen virtues, he himself states that these are merely examples of the divine attributes. Al-Farabi notes only twelve virtues,[74] and Averroes lists ten, as we shall see. The commentators on the *Guide* did not associate Maimonides' discussion of the thirteen divine attributes with the theory of the philosopher-king's virtues. Even Falaquera and Abravanel, who knew the theory and made direct use of it, ignore this discussion in their commentaries to *Guide* I:54.

It has been proposed that in writing the *Mishneh Torah*, Maimonides set himself up as the law giving philosopher-king of the Farabian variety; further, that the whole structure of *Hilkhot Yesodei ha-Torah* is based on Al-Farabi's *Virtuous State*.[75] But Al-Farabi explicitly sets forth the theory of the philosopher-king's virtues. Maimonides *Hilkhot Yesodei ha-Torah* ignores it entirely.

For all the Platonic and Farabian influence, Maimonides did not accept the philosopher-king theory in full. His theory of political *imitatio Dei* bears on our subject because of its possible influence on other thinkers who linked the Maimonidean *imitatio Dei* to the theory of the philosopher-king's virtues.

Thus, Rosenthal's claim[76] that the philosopher-king-prophet theory was accepted by Maimonides, but not by Jewish philosophy as a whole, is inaccurate. The situation in medieval Jewish thought was in fact the reverse. It was Maimonides who did not fully accept this tradition, while many Jewish philosophers after Maimonides, from Ibn Latif and Falaquera to Alemanno and Abravanel, absorbed the theory enthusiastically. The contribution to Jewish political thought that Rosenthal mentions was not made by Maimonides. It was added by later translators, commentators, and philosophers, who transmitted this tradition *in toto* from Muslim to Jewish philosophy.

3

Maimonides wrestled with two rival definitions of human perfection, the perfection of the rational soul of the reclusive philosopher, as against the perfection of the practical soul of the public philosopher: Adam versus Moses, Aristotle of the *Ethics* versus Plato of *The Republic*, Ibn Bajja versus Al-Farabi.[77] Maimonides, as we have observed, ultimately favored the Farabian Platonic orientation of the "public prophet." Jewish commentators from the thirteenth to the fifteenth centuries continued to struggle with the problem, and each resolved it according to his own personal and philosophical background and the historical circumstances in which he worked. Among these various philosophical resolutions, we can discern three trends. The first trend, which extended and also aggravated Maimonides' ambivalence, is well represented by Falaquera. The second, which leaned toward unequivocal political commitment, is best represented by Jacob Anatoli. A more moderate formulation of this position is found in Polkar and Alemanno. The third trend covers most commentators on the *Guide* who took issue with the Maimonidean position, tending toward governance of the solitary, as did the first translator and commentator of the Guide, Samuel Ibn Tibbon. This position was also held by Moses Narboni, Joseph Ibn Caspi, Joseph Ibn Shemtov, and Abravanel among others.

Falaquera manifests Maimonides' ambivalent tendency even to a somewhat greater degree.[78] In contrast to Maimonides, though, he did not in the end come to any resolution. On the one hand, Falaquera stressed the political role of the philosopher-prophet, as we find markedly in the *Book of Degrees (Sefer ha-Ma'alot)* and in his various translations-commentaries of Al-Farabi's writings, especially *Reshit Hokhmah (Beginning of Wisdom)*. Indeed, in these compositions, as we shall see, the philosopher-king theory reaches its fullest expression,[79] with Falaquera stressing the political commitment of the philosopher-prophet even more than Maimonides. Maimonides, as mentioned, nowhere offers a comprehensive listing of the philosopher-king's virtues, while Falaquera did so more than once. The *Epistle of the Debate (Iggeret ha-Vikkuah)* also underlines the philosopher's duty to educate the people, despite an awareness of the esoteric nature of philosophy and of the personal dangers involved in an open discussion of matters involving mystery, allegory, and riddle. This obligation necessarily stems from a definition of the aim of philosophy: "Its purpose . . . is to liken themselves [philosophers] to God, may He be exalted, as much as is within human power,"[80] a definition with a clearly Platonic-Farabian-Maimonidean character.

By contrast, in his commentary on the *Guide,* the *Guide to the Guide (Moreh ha-Moreh),* Falaquera manifests an orientation toward the separation of the philosopher-prophet from any public duty. While the *Book of Degrees* reveals the influence of Al-Farabi, the *Guide to the Guide* reveals Ibn Bajja's influence. This influence is especially expressed in the commentary on *Guide* III:51, and 54, two of the central chapters in which Maimonides struggled with the question of the seclusion as opposed to the social obligation of the philosopher-prophet. Maimonides states that ethical perfection in the social framework is no more than a means of attaining intellectual perfection and is not an end in itself. Falaquera stresses this point still more, asserting that a human being is no different from a beast in respect of ethical perfection. This assertion is wholly that of Ibn Bajja. Although Maimonides makes a similar assertion about physical perfection, he says nothing of the sort about ethical perfection.[81] Elsewhere Falaquera makes an even more extreme statement: not only is ethical perfection not essential to human beings, but it is actually an obstacle to attaining intellectual perfection.[82] Where Maimonides stresses the requirement of keeping to a balanced middle way, Falaquera reveals a marked leaning toward extreme abstinence.[83]

Falaquera, similarly overemphasizes what Maimonides deems man's true perfection: the intellectual perfection of the reclusive philosopher: "Be complete in your special perfection, and be complete in yourself, and you will not need the presence of others. On the contrary, every man and every existing thing is injurious to you."[84] He interprets the counsel of the Sages, "Acquire a friend," circumspectly: not for nothing were the Sages careful to use the singular "friend" rather than "friends"; they sought to limit to the minimum any social contact of the sage-recluse with all others. This interpretation is starkly opposed to Maimonides' broad exegesis of the phrase, which led him to a consideration of different legitimate types of friendship. The highest of those, of course, is the spiritual love between a pupil and his master.[85]

Following Maimonides, Falaquera recognized the sage's need for the fulfillment of elementary bodily and social needs; and, like him, tended to limit these needs to the essential minimum: "He should completely separate himself from other people if this is possible, and he would not associate with them but only in the necessary matters and in the necessary degree."[86] He terms "strangers" *(gerim)* those individuals, like the Patriarchs and other righteous men, whose intellectual fervor did not cease even when they were forced to engage in material affairs: "For although they are in their homeland and among their companions and neighbors, they are strangers *(gerim)* in their opinions, having traveled in their minds to other stations that are like a homeland to them."[87]

Paraphrasing Ibn Bajja, Falaquera then achieved a clear resolution of the tension between the political duty of the prophet-philosopher and his wish to isolate himself from human society. Even when the prophet-philosopher is forced to live in society and lead it, he does so only with his body; in his rational soul, he remains totally detached and alienated from human society.[88]

Accordingly, Falaquera devoted most of his commentary on the last chapter of the *Guide* to the distinction between the intellectual perfection of the reclusive sage and perfections inferior to it. He ignores almost entirely Maimonides' discourse at the end of the chapter on the political imitation of the Divine attributes. It seems that he entirely disagreed with the note that Maimonides added after the fourth perfection, and he concludes his commentary on the *Guide* once again with the theory of the intellectual isolation of the wise man: "A perfection belonging to him alone."[89] The *Guide* here tilts plainly toward Ibn Bajja.

Overall, it may be said that most of the late medieval philosophers and commentators tended to draw Maimonides' position toward the governance of the solitary. This understanding undoubtedly was the result of a combination of factors. Maimonides, a leader of the community and a man of halakhah, naturally had a social obligation of a high order, which affected his perception of the functions of the philosopher-prophet. Most of the thinkers who succeeded Maimonides, however, did not hold public positions. They developed their thinking as private individuals, a circumstance that probably influenced their leaning toward the separation of the philosopher from public duty. This trend was likely reinforced by the fact that the profession of philosophy, which reached its peak of legitimacy following Maimonides, went on the defensive with the troubles of the fifteenth century in Spain. Conservatives and Kabbalists ascribed these problems to the pursuit of philosophy, which in their view led to an estrangement from Torah. The solitary tendency also expressed an Averroist emphasis on separation between mass belief and philosophical knowledge. Maimonides presented a far more moderate stance, positing different stages on the way to knowledge of the one truth and also requiring the masses to maintain true basic opinions.[90] Christian Averroist influences led various commentators from the thirteenth century on to separate the pursuit of philosophy from political activity.

Few commentators interpreted Maimonides as unequivocally favoring the political commitment of the philosopher. A salient early example of the line of interpretation is found in the thirteenth-century collection of philosophical homilies, *Students' Goad (Malmad ha-Talmidim),* by Jacob Anatoli, who drew Maimonides forcefully in a Farabian or Averroist direction. Anatoli's father-in-law, Samuel Ibn Tibbon, harbored reservations, as we shall see, about Maimonides' accent on the political duty of the philosopher-prophet, but Anatoli accentuated this feature. Following the *Nicomachaean Ethics,* Maimonides declares that "man is political by nature."[91] Anatoli follows Aristotle when he states that "it is not natural for man to live in seclusion *(mitboded),* since he is political by nature *(medini ba-tevah)."*[92] Even more emphatically than Maimonides, Anatoli sees in seclusion a condition essentially opposed to human nature. The existence of a proper political order, *hanhagah yesharah,* "righteous governance," as Anatoli terms it, is a vital condition for the attainment not only of physical perfection, but also of perfection of the rational soul, "that man may understand and know and grasp the truths."[93] In a condition of isolation, it would be impossible to fulfill the purpose of human existence.

Not only does he emphasize the political nature of man in general, Anatoli, in consequence, also stresses the political duty of the Sages. Under Platonic influence, he presents a triple class structure, at the head of which stand the Sages. Following Maimonides, he identifies the philosopher with the prophet and underlines the leadership role of the Sages:

> The third class relates to the rational power and [includes only] the very few. This class is composed of those unique few who are wise, intellectually cognizing *in actu,* grasping the truths. . . . And it is essential that this class should obey the chosen one . . . and the second class should obey this one. . . . This is the only way by which the human species can be perfect.[94]

Anatoli lays stress on the political obligation of the Sages to the point of asserting that even when this ideal political structure is absent, and an inferior type of regime exists, the Sages must continue to live in the state and to obey its legitimate rulers. In this way they will provide a good example for the masses of how the law should be obeyed; in doing so, they will foster the proper political framework to allow a man to achieve perfection both of body and of intellect. Here Anatoli uses the exact rationale and phraseology of the *Guide* II:40:

> Even the wise men should obey the ones who are greater than they, or one chosen great man, even when his degree is but little higher than theirs, whether he is chosen by a prophet or by a wise man or by many [men]. It is most essential for human governance not to dispute the chosen one or the many chosen men. This is so because the individuals of this species, which means the human species, as a result of its being the last one to be composed, have many natural differences. They also need each other in order to supply the two kinds of essential needs, which are food and clothing. This is why they need a leader, and they should honor and fear him and not dispute him.[95]

Anatoli is perhaps the most outstanding and unreserved spokesman for the political duty of the philosopher-prophet. Several later philosophers display more moderate versions of this posture. Isaac Polkar, in the fourteenth century states in *Defense of the [Divine] Law (Ezer ha-Dat)* that although the personal perfection of the philosopher-prophet would oblige him to strive for a state of governance of the solitary, his social obligation necessarily leans toward leading the community:

> For this divine man, who possesses complete felicity *(hazlahah tamah)* and true perfection *(shlemut amiti)*, it would have been appropriate, as far as he himself is concerned, to be separated and isolated, living solitary and away *(mitboded u-mitiahed)* from the rest of humanity, for nobody is like him or to be compared with him. However, only because of divine providence, which always exists in the human species, and because of the virtue of generosity *(nedivut)* he possesses and his superior goodness, he will continually emanate on his fellow men whatever he has which is in surplus and overabundant. It is obligatory for him, then, to dwell and abide amongst them and to bear their burden as a leader.[96]

Polkar retreats from the position of Maimonides, who states that the personal needs of the philosopher-prophet make him dependent on the organized, human social framework. But, like Maimonides, Polkar comes to the conclusion that the sage must live a life of political commitment, on the basis of the obligation of *imitatio Dei.*

Yohanan Alemanno, in late-fifteenth-century Italy, continued the Aristotelian tradition grounded in the political nature of man. He was influenced by the emphasis in Renaissance thought on the *vita activa* as opposed to *vita contemplativa* (or *solitaria*). Yet, through the direct influence of Ibn Bajja and Ibn Tufayl, he had his reservations: "For man is political by nature *(medini batevah)* and human association *(kibbutz medini)* is indispensable for him, unless he belongs to the solitary men, *(mitbodedim)* who are extremely rare."[97] In Alemanno's view the solitary men are "extremely rare," both in numbers and in excellence. He identifies the solitary sage with the figure of Simeon Bar Yohai, who cast off the vanities of this world and secluded himself in a cave to study Torah. Alemanno though, held back from bar Yohai's extreme demand that all men separate themselves from material life and enclose themselves in absolute isolation. He identifies with the words of the divine voice, which said to Bar Yohai: "Return to your cave and leave the people alone who are busy with their work, so that you may occupy yourselves with wisdom and the Torah."[98] Most men cannot exist outside a social framework. A few sages in the mold of Bar Yohai are able to abandon society completely. In the Platonic myth, man must dare to leave the cave for the daylight so as to attain knowledge of the Ideas. Bar Yohai, in contrast, is obliged to return to the seclusion of the cave in order to attain divine happiness.

In a Renaissance application of medieval theory, Alemanno greatly expands on the figure of King Solomon as the prototype of the philosopher king. He directly connects the theory of man's political nature with the Renaissance theory of Platonic love.[99] In Polkar and Alemanno, then, we find two of the most interesting exemplars of the use of the philosopher-king theory in Jewish thought. For the most part, however, the commentators tended decidedly toward the governance of the solitary. Maimonides' first translator and commentator, Samuel Ibn Tibbon, had reservations about the tone of the conclusion of the last chapter of the *Guide*, which favors political activity by the philosopher prophet, on the basis of *imitatio Dei,* over the solitary perfection of the rational soul:

> Although the Rabbi, of blessed memory, gave this verse a good interpretation in the 54th chapter of the third part. . . . I would rather interpret differently some of his [Jeremiah's] words. . . . It is an innovation in its quality and truthfulness, I have no doubt. . . . And it is different from his [Maimonides'] interpretation. . . . It is that the basic sense of what he says—"For in these things I delight, saith the Lord"—is related to "understandeth and knoweth me." Here he gave

the reason why it is appropriate to glory in these two things, and not the above-mentioned three [i.e., loving-kindness, judgment and righteousness]. For these two, that is, "understandeth and knoweth me," are His ultimate delight and purpose for men.

The same return to the spiritual and contemplative reading of "understandeth and knoweth me" is also found in Ibn Tibbon's *Ma'amar Yikkavu ha-Mayyim*.[100]

That some commentators tended to slant Maimonides' words in the direction of governance of the solitary is plain in their treatment of his philosophical interpretation of Jacob's dream (*Guide* I:15). Maimonides argues that it is not accidental that the text reads "the angels of God ascending and descending on [the ladder]" (Gen. 28:12). The ascent toward knowledge of God to the extent of man's capacity comes before the descent, which has as its purpose, the application of the knowledge acquired, to be put to use in the leadership of human society. Just as in the Platonic myth of the cave, this physical descent is in reality a moral ascent: for the rightful leadership of human society, the prophet must apply the knowledge he has acquired, which is of God's attributes of action. (Thus, specific rungs of the ladder are spoken of, not its summit.) The prophet acquires precisely the type of theoretical knowledge that is most relevant for public leadership. The descent is not a severance, retreat, or deviation from intellectual perfection, but just the opposite—an application of intellectual perfection to the supreme moral purpose.

Most medieval commentators who treated this matter interpreted the argument as pointing to the governance of the solitary. It is true that Shemtov ben Joseph Ibn Shemtov connected it, correctly, to Maimonides' discourse on *imitatio Dei* theory in the *Guide* I:54, and so comes close to accepting the political emphasis that Maimonides placed on it. But Shemtov presents the process as optional:

> It is appropriate for anyone who desires to govern the people *(le-han-hig ha-briot)* to know how the Lord of the universe rules His creatures *(yanhig briotiv)*. As it is said, "Show me now Thy ways," etc., and then, "And consider that this nation is Thy people" (Ex. 32:13). The desire relates to his people because he wanted to know how the Lord rules His universe, and from him to learn how to govern his fellow men *(le-hanhig zulato)*.[101]

Maimonides, by contrast, does not treat this as an optional matter at all, but an obligation: the descent must follow the ascent. In chapter 54, he cites Moses, who stated: "A people for whose government I need to perform actions that I must seek to make similar to Thy actions in governing them." Jeremiah is actually forced against his will to lead the public. But Shemtov, like most of the other commentators, presents the descent on the ladder as a decline in the distinction of the prophet, not as moral elevation, as it is ultimately depicted by Maimonides.

Joseph Ibn Caspi, Efodi, and Isaac Abravanel, similarly, do not see descent as a goal of ascent or its supreme moral purpose. On the contrary, they regard the need to lead the masses very critically. They see it as the factor responsible for forcing the prophet to cease his contemplation, the occupation most proper for him, which naturally can be fully pursued only in isolation. Efodi, at least, like Maimonides and unlike Joseph Ibn Shemtov, regards the descent as an imperative, not the outcome of free choice by the prophet. Like Maimonides, he presents the leadership of the returning prophet as an application of the theoretical knowledge that the prophet has acquired. For all that, Efodi interprets the descent not merely as realization and application, but as severance from contemplation.[102] Caspi returns to the subject in his commentary on the Torah, *Mishneh Kesef*, in which he describes the sage as completely isolated from physical life, although he is forced at times to break away in order to lead the people:

> The third kind [person] I have listed has the absolute perfection, which is the perfection of the intellect. . . . This is why he would have the leisure to devote his time to the glorification of the Lord, blessed be He, to worship Him. And at certain times he would descend in order to govern and teach the people of the land *(am ha-aretz)*, as the Master said in interpreting the verse "And behold the angels of God ascending and descending on it," . . . Then he would train his powers to seek solitude *(le-hitboded)* in the intelligibles . . . and the purpose of this man is repose and rest and consolation from the troubles of this world and its distractions.[103]

Descent for the purpose of leading the people is not shown positively as the moral fulfillment of the prophet's intellectual perfection, but negatively as a deviation and decline from it. Joseph Ibn Caspi reduces the duty to lead the people to an act that the philosopher prophet is obliged to perform "at certain times"; normally he must "seek solitude in the intelligibles." Maimonides voiced no such reservation. In his system, whoever ascends must of necessity also descend, to lead the people. He applies the phrase "at certain times" to signify the possibility of righteous men's isolating themselves from human society, when normally they should be living in it.[104]

The commentators, in sum, shift the sense of Maimonides' interpretation of Jacob's dream in three ways: first, by transforming the descent to lead the people from an obligatory to an optional act; second, by describing the descent as severance from intellectual perfection, not its moral realization; and third, by claiming that the descent is made only "at certain times."

Most medieval commentators who used the Platonic class theory, as we shall see, drew a sharp distinction between rulers and sages, thereby making the combination of king and philosopher impossible. Even Anatoli, who followed Maimonides faithfully, allotted definite leadership roles to the sages, but clearly distinguished between sages and earthly rulers.[105] Other commentators—among them, Shem Tov Ibn Falaquera, Immanuel of Rome, Abraham Bibago, and Joseph Albo—weakened Jacob Anatoli's emphasis on the necessity for the lower classes to accept the rule of the sages. These commentators stressed contemplation as the exclusive occupation of sages: "And all his deeds were spiritual." Indeed, Albo made it a virtue to keep remote from positions of power and material prosperity.[106] Caspi and Isaac Abravanel presented a still more extreme definition of the class of sages, that specifically included the principle of isolation. Abravanel points out in all the versions of his discourse on the Platonic classes that the sages are theorists devoted to learning. Twice he accentuates the purely eremitic nature of their activity and terms the sages "the sect of wise men and the solitary *(mitbodedim)*."[107]

The seventeenth-century thinker Abraham Azulai, who in his commentary on tractate *Avot* made use of the class theory, brings matters to their ultimate extreme. If the sages must isolate themselves as much as possible, he argued, they cannot be included in the class structure of human society at all. They belong outside and beyond it: "Since the political association *(kibbutz medini)* is divided in every respect into three parts, nobody can exist out of them, except the solitaries *(mitbodedim)* engaging in wisdom, who are above it all; and they have no business with any man."[108]

Maimonides' earliest commentators noted that in a lengthy note he added to the Parable of the King's Palace in *Guide* III:51, he approaches Ibn Bajja's position closer than he does anywhere else. Efodi remarks at the beginning of his commentary on this chapter that the chapter "describes the governance of the solitary and the way he should conduct himself." Efodi contends that Maimonides bases himself here on Ibn Bajja.[109] This may be true of the note in the second part of the chapter; but it is certainly not true of the Parable of the Palace, which appears in its first part, where the political nature of man is highlighted.

We have already seen how Shemtov ben Joseph Ibn Shemtov treats Maimonides' interpretation of Jacob's ladder as a lessening of the political duty of the philosopher-prophet. At the end of his commentary on the *Guide*, Shemtov notes, in regard to its last chapters that "in these chapters, which lead to the governance of the solitary *(hanhagat ha-mitboded)*, the final human purpose *(tahalit ha-adam)* will be expounded."[110] What Efodi read into chapter 51, Shemtov now reads into all the last chapters. Like Falaquera before him Shemtov completely ignores Maimonides' shift at the very end of the last chapter toward political imitation of God's attributes of action as the supreme moral purpose of the philosopher-prophet. This tendency is especially marked in *The Dignity of God (Kevod Elohim)*, written by Shemtov's father, Joseph Ibn Shemtov, which is a free interpretation of the *Nicomachaean Ethics*.[111] The author observes that the realization of man's highest perfection is a function not of his political life but of solitude:

> since this bliss and contemplation are not necessarily a social condition *(hevrah)*, but a state of solitude *(hitbodedut)* and isolation *(hafradah)* from mankind and political affairs *(asakim medini'im)*. This is why wise men sought deserts and caves, and Rabbi Simeon bar Yohai and his sons dwelt twenty-two years in the cave and Elijah lived solitary in the mountains.[112]

The son of a renowned Kabbalist, Shemtov Ibn Shemtov, Shemtov ben Joseph certainly knew that Elijah and Bar Yohai were central figures for Jewish mysticism. Maimonides had regarded seclusion in caves and deserts as undesirable, a course that should be taken only in the most extreme cases, but Shemtov presents it as an ideal. Maimonides cites Jeremiah repeatedly as an example of one who seeks to isolate himself in a cave but is obliged to forego this desire and lead or guide the people. Shemtov, though, offers the example of sages who achieved this desire. He moves away from Maimonides and approaches Ibn Tufayl, whose stance is more extreme than that of Ibn Bajja himself.

Later Shemtov sets out the more moderate position of Averroës in his *Epistle of Conjunction,* arguing that man must isolate himself only if his is a wicked state. This is the very position that Maimonides presents in *Eight Chapters* and *Hilkhot De'ot.* In Shemtov's view, Plato himself held the same position, and one may interpret Maimonides' reservations in *Guide* III:51, in this way. The desire of the righteous man to seclude himself as much as possible, unless he has a vital need to be in contact with others is treated as a moral necessity.[113]

Shemtov adopted a position acceptable to Ibn Bajja himself: if the state is just, the philosopher can exist within it. Here he liberally cites Ibn Rushd's commentary to Plato's *Republic,* which stressed the political duty of the philosopher. But such a state does not exist; the possibility of its existing is so slight as to be of theoretical interest only: "After all his philosophizing, Ibn Rushd concluded at the end of the *Epistle of Conjunction* that this bliss is extremely difficult [to attain]. It can exist only in perfect generations and the precious states ruled by a wise king, where the associations would be excellent, helping each other. [This situation] is not to be found in contemporary states."[114] Shemtov concurs that human perfection is not attainable in the framework of the existing state. In contrast to Ibn Rushd, however, and following Ibn Bajja, he holds that it can be reached by means of isolation from the state.

This conclusion may perhaps express Shemtov's personal situation, since he was significantly involved in public matters and even held senior posts in the king's court. He wrote *The Dignity of God* after he had retired from these offices, and his yearning for a life of bliss may have reflected an idealization of the life of contemplation.[115] Perhaps in this idealization of the solitary prophet, too, the mystical tendencies of Shemtov's father finally surmounted the Maimonidean rationalism he had championed in his youth. The shift from Maimonides to Ibn Bajja is well expressed in the choice of texts he took as his basis. At the hub of *The Dignity of God* is the free interpretation, along the lines of Ibn Bajja, of the *Nicomachaean Ethics*, which sees in the life of the mind the highest purpose of human existence. Still he makes ample use of Ibn Rushd's reading of Plato's *Republic*.

The current of governance of the solitary in medieval Jewish thought reached its strongest course in the translations and commentaries of the Arabic *Hayy Ibn Yaqzan*, by Ibn Tufayl. This philosophical epistle expresses the philosopher's despair of finding fulfillment in human society. It idealizes retirement to a life of pure contemplation on a desert island. This is a kind of contemplative *Robinson Crusoe*. Daniel Defoe's novel is actually a literary revival of *Hayy Ibn Yaqzan*.[116] We have two Hebrew renditions of Ibn Sina's spiritual prototype of this work, one by an anonymous translator, and the other a poetical translation by Abraham Ibn Ezra. The identity of the Hebrew translator of Ibn Tufayl's work is not known; but in the mid-fourteenth century, Moses Narboni wrote a commentary to Ibn Tufayl's *Hayy Ibn Yaqzan* and added a translation-summary of Ibn Bajja's *The Governance of the Solitary (Tadbir al-Mutawahhid)*, which he rightly regarded as a suitable complement to his commentary. We have already observed the influence of this version on Shemtov and Alemanno.[117]

Ibn Tufayl's philosopher refuses to live even in a just state; he finds that solitude is the only way to cleave to the active intellect. Ibn Bajja, by contrast, held a more moderate position, for all its extremism. He recognized the possibility that the philosopher may attain perfection in the state, on condition that it is a just state. The philosopher, though, always reserves the option to isolate himself, inside or outside the state, when the state is very corrupt.

Narboni's treatment of Ibn Tufayl's text expresses well the conflict waged by medieval Jewish commentators over this matter. He regards Ibn Tufayl as a thinker who followed but far exceeded Ibn Bajja, to the point of total removing of the philosopher from human society. Thus, Narboni included his translation of and commentary to *The Governance of the Solitary* in his commentary to *Hayy Ibn Yaqzan* with the aim of achieving balance and moderation. He interpreted *Hayy Ibn Yaqzan* itself in a moderate way too, by introducing politics into the text, even if in the restricted sense imparted to it by Ibn Bajja.[118]

Narboni argues in the introduction to the translation that the very fact that Hayy Ibn Yaqzan secludes himself in the company of his pupil Absal and is not utterly alone is a clear intimation that isolation need not be complete. The aim of seclusion can still be achieved in the right company: "He hinted by this that the solitary would be one or more than one [man], for when they had ultimate felicity the company of one would not hurt the other, but would benefit him." Narboni finds support for his moderating interpretation of the nonexclusive reclusiveness of the philosopher in the text of Ibn Bajja: "He had already mitigated this [opinion] when he dealt with the governance of the solitary, who is part of a state. He ordered a quest for those states where there are more wise men, and he permitted association with them." Narboni defines the goal of the Ibn Bajja's entire composition as follows: "This book of ours would include the practices of the governance of the solitary *(hanhagat hamitboded)*, whether separate *(nivdal)* or political *(medini)*, either if his state is perfect *(medinah hashuvah)* or imperfect *(bilti hashuvah)*."[119] Thus, the Jewish philosopher who more than all others went in the direction of the governance of the solitary cannot overstep a certain boundary.[120]

Narboni prefers the more temperate solution, in the manner of Ibn Bajja: spiritual isolation within human society. Like Falaquera and Ibn Bajja himself, he describes philosophers as "strangers" *(gerim)* who live physically within human society but are completely apart from it spiritually:

> For although they live in their homeland and among their companions and neighbors, they are strangers in their opinions, having traveled in their minds to other stations that are like a homeland to them, according to the opinions of the first of their group. And this is the reason David gave when he said, "I am a stranger in the earth, hide not thy commandments from me." (Ps. 119:19)[121]

King David, the very fleshly ruler of the Books of Samuel here gives way to the ascetic David of the Book of Psalms.[122] Maimonides' description of the Patriarchs in his note in *Guide* III:51 is very close to that of David. For he, too, was influenced by Ibn Bajja. Maimonides, though, did not use the image of the "stranger"; and from his description it is difficult to say that the Patriarchs were completely detached from human society when their whole bent was to create a nation that would worship God.

Narboni's modified version of the solitary life is nicely expressed in the commentary he appended at the conclusion to his translation, which is reminiscent of the way Maimonides brought the *Guide* to a close, with the theory of the imitation of God's attributes of action in a gloss on Jeremiah.[123] Like Samuel Ibn Tibbon before him, Narboni does not actually ascribe to the theory of imitation the same political significance as Maimonides does, and he presents Jeremiah's famous words immediately after defining the supreme purpose of human beings, in the spirit of Ibn Bajja, as pure spiritual perfection.

This ending expresses not only his modification of Ibn Tufayl by way of Ibn Bajja, but even his modification of Ibn Bajja by way of Maimonides. On the other hand, he clearly draws Maimonides himself in the direction of Ibn Bajja, as we see in various places in his commentary on the *Guide*.[124] Here the circle closes. Narboni tempers Ibn Tufayl, makes Maimonides more extreme, and presses both of them in the direction of Ibn Bajja.

Clearly the more a philosopher is attracted to the concept of governance of the solitary, the less available to him is the philosopher-king theory. Indeed, we find this theory in full in Falaquera, Polkar, and Alemanno, all of whom posited different versions of the position stressing the political duty of the philosopher. We do not find it in Caspi and Narboni, who tended toward the governance of the solitary. This hypothesis, however, does not obtain in all cases. Maimonides, for reasons discussed above, eschewed the complete parallel between king and philosopher, even though he stressed the political duty of the philosopher-prophet. Joseph Ibn Shemtov, for all his orientation toward governance of the solitary, wrote a commentary-summary of Plato's *Republic*. Making ample use of Ibn Rushd's commentary on *The Republic* in his *Kevod Elohim*, Ibn Shemtov included a detailed discussion of the ten virtues of the ideal ruler when commenting on the rebellion of Korah. The rule of Moses is identified as the supreme realization, in the proper biblical context, of the philosopher king ideal.[125] Ibn Shemtov's version of the virtues of the ideal ruler is not identical with that of the platonic school. It is more traditionally Jewish in character. Still, despite his professed inclination toward the governance of the solitary, even Shemtov made a contribution to the discussion of the virtues of the ideal ruler. Finally, Abravanel, who had the same inclination, presents several versions of the philosopher-king theory on the assumption that this ideal was, in fact, realizable through miraculous intervention by the Divine will.

4

The Class System

Plato's philosopher king marks the summit of the class structure of his ideal state. Before examining the influence of the theory of the philosopher king on medieval and Renaissance Jewish political thought, we shall deal in this chapter with the effect of the Platonic class system on Jewish philosophy in these periods

The class system of the Platonic state, distinguishing the three classes—artisans, guardians, and philosopher-rulers—and constituting a macrocosm of the three parts of the soul and their interrelationship,[1] filtered into medieval Jewish thought primarily through the Arabic commentaries to the Platonic text.[2] In the late Middle Ages, this influence also may have flowed through the Three Estates theory, which was popular in contemporary European literature. This theory draws a distinction among the clergy or rulers, the knights, and the workers *(senatores, equites, plebs)*. Another distinction, which Ernest Barker traced back to Plato himself, was among *oratores, bellatores,* and *laboratores*.[3] The medieval Jewish commentators based their own versions of this class division on cosmological, theological, and psychological tenets, which they applied to the biblical texts and the teachings of the Sages.

A general expression of the class theory is found in Maimonides' introduction to his commentary on the *Mishnah*. Basing himself on the Platonic principle of the division of duties, Maimonides distinguishes between the *Am ha-Aretz* (the common people), who were created to work and supply the material and emotional needs of human society in general and of the few sages in particular, and the Sages, who are enabled by this division of labor to devote themselves to a life of contemplation and, thus, to realize the ultimate human perfection.[4] As with the philosopher-king theory, here, too, it can be seen that Maimonides was influenced but did not adopt Platonic ideas directly or fully.

61

The class theory of the Platonic state, like the philosopher-king theory, appears in Jewish thought after Maimonides as a product of the great enterprise of translation from Arabic to Hebrew in the thirteenth and fourteenth centuries. From the thirteenth to the sixteenth century, the two motifs find expression in such thinkers as Anatoli, Falaquera, Hameiri, Immanuel of Rome, Joseph Ibn Caspi, Albo, Bibago, Alemanno, Abravanel, and Azulai. In the great majority of cases, the Jewish commentators attach their consideration of the subject to an allegorical interpretation of the biblical mention of the three sons of Adam. Each is perceived as a prototype of a certain power in the soul, of one of three types of good according to the Aristotelian classification (*Nicomachaean Ethics* I:8), and of one of the three classes inhabiting the ideal state in the Platonic mold. We find the theory applied by some commentators, especially at a later stage—for example, by Abravanel and Azulai—to other biblical texts as well, and to various dicta of the Sages.

All the commentators who treated this subject made a three-class division—figuring the world on the putative structure of the soul. In this sense they followed the structure and rationale of the Platonic method. Most, however, differentiated the three classes differently than Plato did. Plato distinguished among artisans, guardians, and philosopher-rulers, whereas the Hebrew commentators usually make the distinction among workers, rulers, and sages. They discarded the guardian class, which was central in the Platonic system, and separated temporal leadership from the sage-philosopher class.

Consequently, most of these commentators avoided the philosopher king combination, the apex of the Platonic system. Thus, they used the external, technical structure of the Platonic class system but emptied it of its main content. Indeed, most Jewish commentators draw no particular connection between the Platonic class system, and the philosopher-king theory. Those commentators who applied the class system did not necessarily adopt the philosopher-king theory, and vice versa. Even those who used both ideas treated them quite separately. The application of Platonic political theory required a context, and the context for the Jewish commentators was not thematic but textual, the specific biblical or Midrashic text that was addressed.

Falaquera was the exception. His treatment of the three sons of Adam follows the accepted class division of most Hebrew commentators: sages, rulers, and laborers. Almost immediately, and almost as an afterthought, he reverts briefly to the full original Platonic structure: philosopher-rulers, guardians, and artisans. In fact, alone among the commentators listed above, Falaquera presents the philosopher-king theory in full, albeit completely in isolation.

Abravanel repeatedly used the original Platonic distinction among artisans, guardians, and sages. When we examine the way he defined each of these classes, however, we find that he continued in the tradition established by his Jewish forerunners: he, too, separated rulers from sages. Abravanel assigned temporal political leadership to the guardian class, while placing the philosopher-sages in the highest class. What was novel in his approach was that he reproduced the Platonic class structure exactly, including the guardian class, despite making a clear division between sages and rulers.

This divergence from the Platonic approach was undoubtedly influenced by the Aristotelian distinction of the animal, political, and divine states of man. Jewish commentators correspondingly distinguished between leaders and philosophers. Halakhic constraints were also important here, since they imposed a kind of "separation of powers" among the Three Crowns of Torah, priesthood, and kingship. Jewish tradition makes a distinction between the prophet-lawgiver and the king-executor.[5] The power of this tradition was so strong that Jewish commentators were unable to accept the absolute Platonic convergence of rulers and sages.

Samuel ben Judah of Marseilles makes clear reference to the class of guardians *(shomerim)* in his translation of Averroës' commentary on Plato's *Republic*.[6] Most commentators, with the exception of Abravanel and to some extent Falaquera, completely ignored this class, even though they retained the triple structure of the system. This fact may reflect the irrelevance for them of the military sphere.[7] No doubt, it stemmed largely from the traditional context in which they treated the subject. Most commentators used the theory in connection with the three sons of Adam, in which the class of guardians seemed irrelevant. The separation of rulers from sages was not only a halakhic necessity, but also a reflection of the requirements of interpretation.

Abravanel alone applied the original Platonic structure to interpret Jeremiah's differentiation of the wise man, the mighty man, and the rich man (Jer. 9:22) and the Sages' paraphrase of this distinction. Jeremiah's words had a long tradition of interpretation in medieval Jewish thought.[8] Here, though, there was room to include the guardian class, which could be relevant in the interpretation of the term "mighty man." Abravanel's unique interpretation marks the influence of the Italian Renaissance on his thought. Indeed, a renewed influence of Plato's *Republic* was a major theme in Renaissance political philosophy.

Jacob Anatoli was the first to use Plato's class system in regard to the three sons of Adam. The other commentators, except for Abravanel, offer no more than variations on this basic theme. In Anatoli's *The Students' Goad*, we find several applications of the system. Influenced by Aristotelian and Neoplatonic cosmology and psychology, Anatoli divided the human soul into three powers: the growing power, the vital power, and the rational power. This structure is manifested in the special status of man in the order of creation. In his growing power, man belongs with the flora and fauna; in his vital power, man belongs with the rest of the animals; but in his rational power, he belongs with the angels. Anatoli extends the triple structure of the cosmos and the soul to political organization. Rightful political order is a microcosm of the world order, "and this species is divided into three classes in accordance with these powers."[9]

The people equivalent to the growing power form the working class, which includes most human beings. Their purpose is to supply the material needs of human society: "The first class is related to the growing power only, in which all three classes share. This class includes the multitude, such as the tillers of the soil and those of their ilk, those who go down to the sea in ships, merchants and artisans—since all are needed for the nurture of man. Even the art of medicine, which is a form of wisdom in one respect, is connected with this class. And this class does not have any stratagem of leading mankind in the appropriate virtues, still less of teaching them wisdom. Thus, they should not glory in their humanity."[10]

The second class includes those who are compared to the vital power. Its degree of humanity is higher than that of the previous class. This class is comprised of men who are involved in the leadership of the state. Anatoli presents an obviously primitivist position here, like that set out at length in his gloss on the injunction in Proverbs "Go to the ant, thou sluggard."[11] This degree of humanity, though, which is expressed in man's leadership of the state, is not considered uniquely human, since other animals are also controlled by the vital power and "have a stratagem"; that is, they are able to work and sustain social cooperation: "The second class is related to the vital power, and it is less numerous than the first. This class includes virtuous people, counsellors and rulers of the people. Although their degree is higher than that of the first class, it is not appropriate for them [either] to glorify themselves and boast of the human rank they have achieved. For they have not achieved the final end of humanity. And other animals too employ stratagems for the preservation of their species and raising of their offspring. The apes are but little lower than they."[12]

The third class, likened to the soul's highest power, the rational, includes individuals who have realized the purpose of human existence and attained intellectual perfection. Only they are completely detached from the beasts. The two lower classes exist to create suitable material conditions for the highest class: "The third class is related to the rational power, and [it includes only the very] few. This class is composed of those rare few who are wise, intellectually aware *in actu,* grasping the truth. In this let him glory over the other classes. This is the purpose of human existence."[13]

The class of wise men is subdivided according to the level of wisdom that each of its members has attained. Whoever has reached a higher level of philosophical knowledge, no matter how little more, must lead those on a lower level. At this stage of the perfection of wisdom, any difference, even the slightest, is of great significance. The prophet and the priest stand at the head of this group of sages, for they, chosen by God, have succeeded in acquiring perfect knowledge of the Torah; that is, they have attained supreme philosophical knowledge: "The individuals of this class are also subdivided according to their degree. Whoever achieves more, even a little, will have a much higher degree than the others, since a little here is a lot. All the more so with whoever is chosen by God to be prophet or priest over the people, who ask to hear Torah from him. There is no doubt that his degree is much higher than the degree of all the other wise men, men of God."[14]

Thus, following Maimonides, Anatoli identifies the prophet with the philosopher and finds in the philosopher-prophet the ideal leader of human society. Also like Maimonides, he clearly distinguishes temporal leadership from the supreme spiritual leadership of the philosopher-prophet.[15]

The proper human society must be built as a hierarchy so as to imitate the natural order and the structure of the soul. Every group must obey the one above it: the workers, the leaders; and the leaders, the sages. The sages must obey the prophet or the philosopher-priest, who stands at the summit of the hierarchy: "It is essential that this class listen to that chosen one, and the second listen to this class, and the third class to the second; this and nothing else will bring about the perfection of mankind."[16]

Anatoli bases this structure on the Platonic definition of justice: "He should examine this arrangement and know what his own degree is in accordance with what is suited to him."[17] Social justice reflects cosmic justice. The triple structure of soul, society, and state is a microcosm of the triple cosmic order.[18]

In accordance with this division of the three powers of the soul and the classes paralleling them, Anatoli in several places glosses the figures of the three sons of Adam: Cain, who was a tiller of the soil and whose sons developed crafts, represents the class of artisans. Abel, a shepherd, represents the rulers. Seth, who was created in the likeness and image of his father, represents the sages. The birth order follows the temporal sequence of the needs of man: first, the supply of essential material requirements by the artisan class; second, political leadership by the ruling class; and third, intellectual perfection, attainable by the sages alone. There is an inverse correlation between the order in time of the fulfillment of these requirements (and the appearance of these classes) and their relative worth: "Cain came first among humankind, representing this class [the artisans]. This was so by nature, since he tilled the soil, and the account in the Torah relates the artisans to his descendents. . . . Abel came second among humankind, representing the second class [the leaders]. He was a shepherd who achieved a system of rule in life. . . . Seth came third, representing them [the wise. He was created] in the image and likeness of his father, of whom it was said that he was created in God's own image and likeness."[19]

This sort of homily has a lengthy history, dating as far back as Philo. It was to enjoy further development in subsequent generations. Anatoli's version is the first to offer a political-allegorical explanation relating to all three sons. Previous interpretations related to Cain and Abel alone: Cain as the animal man, who was also political; and Abel as the spiritual man.[20] Anatoli undoubtedly developed his own innovative interpretation against the background of the Platonic tradition, which, through Muslim agency, began to infiltrate Jewish cultural life in southern Europe from the start of the thirteenth century. The influence of the parallel Aristotelian distinction recognizing three aspects of man—the animal, the political, and the spiritual (*Politics* I:2, 9)—and the three kinds of good associated with them (*Ethics* I:8)—already existed. Aristotle's *Politics* had a far-reaching effect on Christian political thought from the thirteenth century on, and this influence may have reached Anatoli, too.[21]

The new influences excluded the possibility of identifying in Cain the animal man and the political man, the artisans and the rulers. They had to be separated. Instead of a distinction between perfection of the body and perfection of the soul, we find henceforth a triple distinction, animal, political, and spiritual: artisans, leaders, and philosophers. The political sphere is now to link the animal and spiritual stages of human existence. Cain, who founded a city and whose sons developed crafts, became identified as the animal man only, the prototype of the laborer class. Abel, who was a shepherd and thus had learned the art of leadership, became the political man, the prototype of the temporal leader and no longer the spiritual man. Seth was now brought into the tradition to represent the spiritual man, the prototype of the philosopher-sage.

Commentators from the thirteenth to the seventeenth century produced variations on Anatoli's theme with hardly any change. Foremost among these were Falaquera,[22] Immanuel of Rome,[23] Joseph Ibn Caspi,[24] Albo,[25] Bibago and Alemanno,[26] and finally Azulai in the seventeenth century. The use of this tradition by Immanuel of Rome, Albo, and Bibago was entirely stereotypical. Only in Falaquera and Ibn Caspi do we find some fresh aspects. Falaquera, in addition to the familiar homily of Adam's three sons, also treated the original Platonic structure. By distinguishing among "the rational power, which is like the species of the leaders *(ro'shim)* of the righteous states *(medinah yesharah)*, the irascible power for the species of the mighty men *(gibborim)*, and the vegetative power for the species of the artisans *(ba'alei ha-melahot)*." In this sense, he fully accepts the theory of the philosopher king; but Falaquera presents the theory as a quotation from Plato and does not signify that he accepts it as it stands. Indeed, he shows a preference for solitary existence in several places, and so his position remains ambivalent.[27] In Caspi, however, we find a distinct leaning in this direction. His description of the class of wise men as those who isolate themselves by virtue of their intellect and his explanation of Maimonides' interpretation of Jacob's dream demonstrate this well. The tendency toward isolation was to reach its climax in Abraham Azulai. He lays such emphasis on the dissociation of the wise from the material affairs of human society: "the solitary *(mitbodedim)* engaging in wisdom, who are above it all"— that, as we have seen, he removes the Sages from the class structure altogether.[28]

Abravanel's innovation is to expand the model to all human history, from Adam to Noah and the generation of the Tower of Babel. He reiterates the traditional differentiation of the animal, political, and divine states, to use Aristotelian terms. He parallels the differentiation of the laborers, leaders, and sages, to use Platonic terms.[29] Clearly, Abravanel takes not only the Aristotelian distinction as his basis, in the well-known version of the *Ethics*, but also Plato's *Republic*. He identifies Ham and his son Canaan as prototypes of the animal man and the laborer class. Accordingly, he offers an etymological explanation of the name Canaan as deriving from the Hebrew root for "submission." He takes Plato as his source in enunciating the duty of the laborer class, which is to obey and submit to the class of sages-rulers: "The philosopher [Plato], in his book on the governance of the state *(hanhagat ha-medinah)*, indicated that the wise men have by nature the desire for dominion *(shrarah)* and authority *(adnut)*; and the tillers of the soil, the desire for servitude. This is why he was named Canaan, which means submission *(hakna'ah)*, as I have explained, since the bestial life serves the pleasant life and submits to the rational life."[30]

In several other formulations, Abravanel makes a further step by seemingly reverting to the original Platonic classification: artisans, guardians, and the wise. Two formulations of this kind are based on a gloss of Jeremiah's words "Let not the wise man glory in his wisdom . . ." (Jer. 9:22–23), and Ben Zoma's midrashic interpretation of these words: "Who is wise? . . . Who is mighty? . . . Who is rich? . . ." *(Avot* 4:1). A third formulation, which is chronologically the first, is a commentary on the words of Rabbi Shim'on on the three who ate at one table *(Avot* 3:3). These two commentaries appear in *Inheritance of the Fathers (Nahalat Avot)*, which is Abravanel's exegesis of tractate *Avot*. A fourth formulation appears in a commentary to Numbers 6:22–27. These formulations are as follows:

INHERITANCE OF THE FATHERS (ON *AVOT* 3:3)

The meaning of the text in my view is that all men are divided into three parts in their political organization *(yeshuvam ha-medini)*. One part is the artisans, who include the tillers of the soil and the shepherds, craftsmen, merchants, and seafarers, since they all engage in labor. Another part is men of wisdom, who include wisemen, men of the law and magistrates, priests, levites, poets, and everyone else who deals with the art of knowledge. And yet another part is the mighty men and warriors. It includes the king and the officers and all those who are in their courts and castles, and the warriors. These three were called by the wise men of ethics, in their language: *laboratores, oratores, defensores.*[31]

INHERITANCE OF THE FATHERS (ON *AVOT* 4:1)

It may be said that these kinds of perfections which I have treated represent the three parts into which human beings are divided in civil society *(kibbutz medini)*: Those who have wisdom and knowledge and righteousness, which are one group. And the mighty men and the warriors, who are the second kind. They are called by the political [thinkers]: *oratori, difensori* and *lovoratori.*[32]

ON JEREMIAH 9:22–23

The prophet assumed that every people *(am)* and political community *(kibbutz anashim)* is divided, as political theorists *(medini'im)* state, into three parts. The first part comprises the wise men, thinkers, philosophers, and men of law, and all those who deal with books. The second consists of warriors and includes kings and officers and deputies and their subordinates, magistrates who rule the people with force, and every man who rules by might. And the third part consists of the tillers of the soil along with craftsmen and scribes, all of whom belong to this part. These three parts are called in their language: *oratori, difensori* and *lavoratori.*[33]

ON NUMBERS 6:22–27

The political thinkers *(medini'im)* said that the state is divided in general into three kinds of human beings. The first consists of tillers of the soil and the craftsmen and artisans who are called laborers. The second consists of the solitary and those who contemplate either the varieties of wisdom and the law or the prayers, who are called the contemplative. [The third] part consists of the warriors and the mighty men of the land. They are called warriors. The Roman [=Christian] wise men called them *lavoratori, oratori* and *difensori.*[34]

Abravanel ascribes the classification to the "political thinkers" or "wise men of ethics" (these being synonyms in medieval Hebrew terminology). It is clear, though, that the classification is Platonic. The familiar medieval tradition integrated the Aristotelian division of the three types of good with the Platonic division of the three classes. Abravanel here omits the Aristotelian division and applies the Platonic theory exclusively. And for the first time in medieval Jewish thought, apart from a brief mention by Falaquera, he includes guardians in the class division. His differentiation of workers, guardians, and sages closely follows the Platonic structure. This is most evident in the commentary on Ben Zoma, in which the guardians are warriors, while the sages are "those who have wisdom and knowledge and righteousness, which are one unit." In the three other formulations, too, the sage class includes those possessing wisdom, knowledge, and law. Here these characteristics are synonyms—"one unit." This sounds like a paraphrase of the identity established by Al-Farabi and Ibn Rushd of philosopher, prophet, and king, which we noted earlier, for example, in the Averroist formulation: "These terms, philosopher, king and lawgiver, are as it were synonymous; so also is priest."[35]

In none of Abravanel's four formulations is the king included in the class of sages. The king is not mentioned at all in the formulation of the commentary on Ben Zoma or on Numbers 6. Kings and ministers are included in the class of guardians in the commentaries on *Avot* 3:3 and Jeremiah. Abravanel keeps the king and the philosopher separate, as did the traditional medieval Hebrew texts and in contrast to the very essence of the Platonic system. All four formulations present the sages as theoreticians and men of letters, not practical men. This separation is stressed even more in the commentaries on Numbers 6 and Exodus 35, in which the sages become recluses, in the mode of Ibn Bajja and in striking contrast to Plato's stress on the political obligation of the philosopher.[36] We shall meet this tendency to separate the king and the philosopher in emphatic form when we deal with Abravanel's discourse on the ideal ruler. Abravanel, who was the first to introduce the Platonic class system into medieval Jewish thought, withdraws in the end to the traditional posture.

The sole remaining sign of the original Platonic position is Abravanel's addition in some versions of the term "jurists," *(shofetim)* or "masters of the law" *(ba'alei ha-mishpat)* to the list of people belonging to the highest class, of the sages. Even here, the reference seems to be to men who study the law in its abstract, theoretical sense, not practicing judges or, still less, the judge champions of the *Book of Judges*. Only a trace remains of the old Platonic idea of the philosopher who is also ruler and founding lawgiver. Since the monotheistic tradition posits that the prophet-lawgiver has already handed down the perfect divine law, there is no longer any possibility or need of full equivalence between philosopher and lawgiver. The philosophers and those who study the divine law belong to the supreme spiritual class; the king, to the second class, which is concerned with direct temporal rule and whose task is to implement these laws on Earth.

In addition to the influence of traditional medieval Jewish readings, Abravanel was significantly influenced by the reappearance of Platonic political theory in Renaissance Italy. The effect of Renaissance thought is expressed in various aspects of his philosophy, especially his political thought.[37] *The Republic* had been translated into Latin in the first half of the fifteenth century. A second translation of the text, with an accompanying commentary, was produced by Marsilio Ficino toward the end of the century. That the renewed interest in *The Republic* had a marked effect on contemporary political thought is evident in other Jewish philosophers of this period, such as Alemanno, as we shall see. The wide use of the Hebrew translation of Ibn Rushd's commentary on *The Republic* in this period also reflects this trend.[38]

The form in which Abravanel describes the class of guardians, the "warriors" in his phrase, in his commentary on Ben Zoma has a clearly humanist content. He defines the warriors' raison d'être as follows: "To become strong for their people and for the cities of their God, in order to stand up against their enemies."[39] In Jewish thought, the term "might" *(gevurah)* is understood both as purely physical force and as moral perfection: "Who is mighty? One who subdues his inclination" *(Avot* 4:4). Among the commentators who defined might as physical force were those, like Falaquera, who applied to this term the limiting sense of military prowess.[40] Abravanel continued this tradition but added to it. Might, in the form of military courage and not as mere physical force, had acquired the significance of a virtue in medieval thought. Now, however, this significance departed from the classical. In the Aristotelian sense, *gevurah* was defined as courage, the mean between cowardice and rashness; or as presented in Hebrew sources, as the victory of the soul over inclination. Now, in Abravanel, it becomes a civic virtue.

Abravanel's statement that the purpose of the warriors was "to become strong for their people and for the cities of their God in order to stand up against their enemies" is drawn from the speech by Yoav ben Zeruiah to his troops as they begin their expedition to fight the Ammonites (2 Samuel 10:12); however, it well expresses the renewal of the Roman concept of the social duty of the individual ("civic humanism") among fifteenth-century humanists. The words resonate with patriotic sentiment, urging the revival of Roman heroism among citizens loyal to the Italian city-state of the *quattrocento* and imbued with the Roman ideal of *dulce et decorum est pro patria mori.*[41] They recall *virtu',* a key term in the political thought of Machiavelli, who uses it to describe the fierce resolution of the fighting man.[42]

The setting, the exhortation of the commander before battle, was popular in the rhetorical and historiographic literature of the Italian Renaissance; it was very much alive in the political reality of the day. Whereas the humanists took their examples from the classical historians and philosophers, Abravanel's text was the classic source of the people of Israel, the Bible. Where his Italian contemporaries read and quoted the speeches of Scipio and Hannibal and Livy's history, Abravanel read and cited the speech of Yoav ben Zeruiah. We find the same in other Jewish thinkers of this period.[43]

All four of Abravanel's formulations provide in Hebrew transliteration the Hebrew names of the three classes: the Latin or Italian appellations *oratori, difensori,* and *lavoratori.*[44] In the commentary on Numbers 6, Abravanel attributes these terms to "the Roman scholars"; that is Christian scholars.[45] His distinction brings to mind the medieval Christian distinction among the *oratores, bellatores,* and *laboratores,* which Barker traced back to Plato. Abravanel knew this tradition, but his usage of these terms, in their foreign equivalents, is taken from the political literature of the Renaissance. The terms *difensori* and *lavoratori* are direct equivalents of "guardians" and "laborers" in the Hebrew versions. We have already seen that Abravanel applies the term "people" *(am)* to the workers as was common in Renaissance political literature but in contrast to the accepted usage of the term "people of the land" *(am ha-aretz)* in medieval Hebrew literature.[46]

A more complex process can be traced in Abravanel's use of the term *oratori.* His commentary on Numbers 6 defines this group as "those who contemplate either wisdom and the law or the prayers." This is the only place in which the *oratori* are defined not only as philosophers in the Platonic sense, but also as those who devote themselves to contemplation of the prayers, in parallel with the traditional medieval Christian classification. No wonder, then, that this is the only place in which Abravanel relates these terms explicitly to Christian scholars. He defines *oratori* in most cases as philosophers and jurists. His use of this term for the philosophers, however, is not merely a vestige of medieval Christian tradition. It largely reflects the new influence of Italian Renaissance thought, in which the orator replaces the philosopher. If the medieval Latin term *oratores* was invested with a religious Christian meaning, the Renaissance Italian *oratori* is imbued with a new, more secular intellectual meaning influenced by humanist rhetoric.

Abravanel departs here from the Platonic view, which saw a sharp contrast between rhetoric and philosophy; unlike the Sophists, it identified the perfect statesman, not with the rhetor, but with the philosopher. Humanist rhetoric reestablished the Sophist and Ciceronian identification of the statesman with the orator. Humanists like Leonardo Bruni and Ermolao Barbaro argued that there was no necessary conflict between philosophy and rhetoric; that indeed, there should be perfect harmony between them. Jewish thinkers like Judah Messer Leon held the same view. If the philosopher and the orator are one, then the perfect statesman, being an accomplished orator, is necessarily a philosopher.[47]

Abravanel's use of the foreign term *oratori* for the class of sages in the Platonic state is based mainly on this humanist position, which viewed, to paraphrase Ibn Rushd, philosopher, legislator, priest, and perfect orator as synonyms. Abravanel defined the sages as "wise men, thinkers, philosophers and legislators." By identifying them with the Italian *oratori*, he achieved the humanist integration of excellent orator and philosopher. But Abravanel, as was his habit, took a term from the general culture and altered its sense to suit his needs. He linked the philosopher and orator, but dropped the Platonic correlation between king and philosopher.

In the Platonic definition of justice, the virtuous state depends on each class fulfilling its role for the benefit of all. The desire to achieve selfish ends at the expense of the common good will necessarily lead to a wicked state. This is the rationale that Abravanel gives to Jeremiah's prophecy of the destruction of the kingdom of Judea:

> For the prophet Jeremiah warned the sons of Judea of their destruction and exile when he said that all their parts would be as nothing and as a thing of nought (Isa. 41:12). This [is the meaning of] let not the wise man glory in his wisdom (Jer 9:12). It means that if he had the wisdom of the Torah and of Prophecy it would have been appropriate for him to glory in them. But he should not at that time have gloried in wisdom which he acquired through his own contemplation and investigation. This kind of wisdom should be considered his shame and his disgrace. Neither let the mighty man glory in his might. This is the second part of the people, since their might would not rescue them at that juncture, but would abase them. And let not the rich man glory in his riches. This is the third part of the people, which includes all the people tilling the soil, and its palaces and goods, since their riches would be confiscated and used against them. (Eccl. 5:12)[48]

Wisdom may mean knowledge of the Torah, deriving from divine revelation, or scientific knowledge, arising from human inquiry. Might and riches may also have either the positive sense of moral perfection or the negative meaning of selfishness. Might and wealth in themselves have no weight in moral terms. Their moral value depends on the purpose to which they are put. They are a fitting source of pride only if they serve positive social goals. The sin of the sons of Judea was that the artisans, with their wealth, and the guardians, with their might, preferred narrow personal and class interests to the general good. The outcome was the destruction of the kingdom.

So far, Abravanel's argument matches the Platonic position. He equates the kingdom of Judea before its fall with the corrupt Athenian state described so vividly in the second book of *The Republic*. Abravanel, though, held back from the Platonic posture on the nature of the wisdom of the sages. As one who identified knowledge of the Torah as the true essence of wisdom, he could not accept the Platonic view, which identified wisdom with knowledge stemming from human contemplation. The error of the Platonic sages, as he saw it, was that they preferred human knowledge to knowledge whose origin was truly divine; in the political context, they preferred human authority to divine authority. Only one who accepts the authority of revelation will possess true wisdom and, as a result, will accept the just law that will lead to the establishment of the truly virtuous state. In keeping with the current of medieval Jewish thought, Abravanel argued for the superiority of the law of Moses even over the philosophical legislation of the Platonic state, since the latter, being human law, excellent as it may be, is necessarily inferior to a law whose source is divine.[49]

We find, then, that Abravanel applied two versions of the Platonic class system: the one traditional in medieval Jewish thought, which recognized sages, rulers, and artisans; the other, innovative, reverting to the Platonic original and recognizing sages, guardians, and artisans. Even in the fresh version, however, Abravanel eschewed the Platonic identification of king and philosopher and placed them in different classes. In this respect, he, like his predecessors, emptied the Platonic system of its core idea.

By the repeated application of the Platonic class system in various unlikely contexts, Abravanel brought matters almost to the point of absurdity, as was not unusual in his interpretive style. He applied the class theory to the three trees in the Garden of Eden, the three sons of Adam, the three sons of Noah, the structure of the Tabernacle, the blessing of the priests, the prophecy of Jeremiah, Ezekiel's parable of the ship, the words of Rabbi Shim'on about the three who ate at one table, and the words of Ben Zoma. In all these cases, he finds allegorical intimations of Plato's tripartite society, a microcosm of the tripartite soul and cosmic order.

We might expect the traditional version to appear in Abravanel's earlier writings and the innovative version to appear later, expressing the renewed influence of the Platonic source on the political thought of the Italian Renaissance at the end of the fifteenth century. In fact, the innovative version is presented earlier in Abravanel's writings: twice in the commentary on *Avot, Inheritance of the Fathers* (1496); once more, in the commentary on *Jeremiah* (1504); and again, in the commentaries on *Exodus* and *Numbers* (1504–05). The traditional version, in connection with the three sons of Adam and the three sons of Noah, is found in the commentary on *Genesis,* which was also written about 1505. The traditional version appears again, as we have noted, in Abravanel's responsa to Shaul ha-Cohen Ashkenazi, written even later, in 1507.[50]

All these commentaries were written in the last decade of Abravanel's life, beginning from 1496, by which time he was living in Italy. Apparently Abravanel was aware of the two versions from the start. He inherited the traditional version from medieval Jewish thought; while the innovative one, in all probability, arose under the influence of Renaissance thought. In the traditional commentary, Abravanel uses only Hebrew names to describe the three classes. In all the versions of the innovative commentary, however, he presents in Hebrew script the Latin or Italian names of the three classes.

Abravanel applied each of the versions according to the needs of his commentary. When he interpreted the stories of the sons of Adam and the sons of Noah in keeping with his predecessors, he used the traditional version. When making use of the Platonic class system to interpret the words of Jeremiah and to paraphrase Ben Zoma, he adopted the original Platonic classification. Inclusion of the class of guardians in the system was useful in explaining the term "mighty man" *(gibbor)*. It was redundant in discussing the three sons of Adam and the three sons of Noah. Abravanel's many predecessors had no need of the Platonic class system when they interpreted the words of Jeremiah. He, however, used the innovative version even for his gloss on texts whose explanation did not require this version at all (*Avot* 3:3; *Exod.* 25:10; *Num.* 6:22–23). His enthusiastic adoption of this new way of thinking was probably a natural result of the renewed influence of the Platonic original on the political thought of the Italian Renaissance.[51]

5

Transmission

The first stage in the transmission of the tradition of the philosopher-king's virtues to medieval Jewish thought was the almost literal translation into Hebrew of the Arabic versions. This step formed an integral part of the great endeavor of translating scientific and philosophical works from Arabic into Hebrew that was conducted from the twelfth to the fourteenth century. Several of the philosophers whom we shall discuss, especially Falaquera and Samuel ben Judah of Marseilles, played a central role in this enterprise. Al-Farabi, who was the first to transmit the Platonic theory to Muslim philosophy, was also the first to be translated into Hebrew.

Al-Farabi's discourse was put into Hebrew by two thirteenth-century Jewish philosophers, Isaac Ibn Latif and Shemtov Ibn Falaquera. Up to now scholars have assumed that the first summary-translation into Hebrew of Al-Farabi's political writings is found in Falaquera. The as yet unpublished manuscript of Ibn Latif's *Gate of Heaven (Sha'ar ha-Shamayim)*, however, contains an earlier rendering of the Arabic works into Hebrew. *Gate of Heaven* was written in 1238. Ibn Latif (c. 1210–1280) was an older contemporary of Falaquera (c. 1225–1295) and, by his own account concluded writing *Gate of Heaven* while still a young man.[1] Since Falaquera at the time was apparently still a youth, Ibn Latif's work clearly antedates the former's translation. Ibn Latif was the first to translate Al-Farabi's political discussion in *The Virtuous State* into Hebrew. Lengthy passages in the last chapters of the first book of *Gate of Heaven* are either a translated summary or at times, almost a *verbatim* translation of *The Virtuous State*. Ibn Latif admits as much in several places,[2] arguing that Al-Farabi's ideas are cogent and also consistent with the words of the prophets and the Sages.[3]

In accordance with Al-Farabi's distinction between the virtuous state and the various erring states, based on Plato's exposition in the ninth book of *The Republic*, Ibn Latif observed the parallel between the states and their leaders:

He said that the souls of the people of the ignorant state *(medinah
ivellet)* would stay deficient after they separate from their bodies, and
they would necessarily [still] need material sustenance, since they
had not yet acquired the truth of the ideas. . . . David, of blessed
memory, referred to this class of the people of the state when he said
that "the fool and the brutish together perish" (Ps. 49:11). . . . The
explanation is that the human soul would become so perfect that it
would no longer need matter for its sustenance. This means that it
would behave like the things separated from matter and would
remain so forever. Its degree, however, would be lower than that of
the active intellect, in a community that is perfect and virtuous *(kibbutz shalem ve-hasid)*. The state whose association is intended to
achieve the above-mentioned purpose . . . is what this philosopher
[Al-Farabi] called a virtuous state *(medinah hasidah)*. He said that
the virtuous state has its opposites, which are the ignorant state and
the wicked state *(medinah mirsha'at)*, and other contraries which
were mentioned by him. But we need not mention them here, since
they are not essentially different from these states. The ignorant state
is such that its inhabitants do not know the ultimate perfection and
are not even aware of it. They have not striven for it by themselves,
nor have they encountered anyone who would stimulate them to do
so. This is the reason why they do not believe in it or know it. They
believe only in God's material goods, which they consider to be the
best of all goods, like health and riches and long life and all the other
kinds of pleasures. And they go after *the stubbornness of their hearts*
(Jer. 3:17) and think that they are the ultimate perfection and that
this is the greatest good and its opposite is considered by them a
punishment. The philosopher included this to remind them that they
all share the opinions of this ignorant state. And these too are unnec-
essary for our purpose.[4]

The ignorant state is a reflection of the imperfect man. The virtuous state is
a reflection, or macrocosm, of the virtuous man, the philosopher, who is perfect
in all moral and rational virtues and who possesses the potential for prophecy:

Among its characteristics [i.e., those of prophecy] is an abhorrence of
the pleasures of this world. Money and gold and silver would be
despised by whoever abhors wickedness and anyone who does
wickedness, and who loves good and anyone who does what is good.
This soul gives a certain perfection to the rational [soul] and becomes
its form, as the rational [soul] is the form of the living [soul]. The
prophetic soul is the most beneficial and precious of all the powers of

the soul, and it is that which is ready to receive the supreme Divine emanation that makes a prophet of a man who is perfect in his reason and in his virtues, being ready to link with the active intellect.[5]

The purpose of the virtuous state is to reform human behavior and reinforce true opinions, insofar as this is possible given the basic limitations of human beings. He who possesses perfection of the intellect also has a political obligation. The righteous state

> reforms the souls that deviate from the path of righteousness and truth and leads men to the ways of truth, peace, and goodness and strives to establish for them laws and customs, to correct their deficiencies, and to allow them to live with one another. It promulgates decrees *(hukim)* and regulations *(nimusim)* and takes preventive measures to perfect the people, who are unable by nature to receive true and undistorted wisdom. For whoever is perfect in this way finds rational ideas imprinted in the soul and does not need premises or syllogisms in order to acquire wisdom.[6]

After describing the nature and purpose of the righteous state, Ibn Latif, directly following Al-Farabi, clarifies the virtues required of the philosopher, who must also serve the ideal ruler:

> I introduce you, dear reader, to the characteristics of the man who is completely perfect in the way that befits a member of the human species. These are twelve attributes, as recorded by the Ishmaelite philosopher Abu Nasr. I would condense them to ten attributes. These attributes have to be innate in him from the very beginning of his creation.[7]

Ibn Latif commonly uses the term *middot* (traits) to signify the virtues of the philosopher king. The expression suggests the philosopher's potential to be a prophet, modeled on the thirteen attributes of God. Ibn Latif uses synonymous terms too, such as *te'arim* (attributes) and *ma'alot* (virtues). Although he says that he has reduced the twelve virtues listed by Al-Farabi to ten, we shall see later that he telescopes this number still further.[8] Indeed, Al-Farabi himself sometimes presents shorter lists, of eight virtues, in *The Philosophy of Plato (Falsafat Aflatun)* and only six in *Aphorisms of the Statesman (Fusul al-madani)*.[9] Thus, Ibn Latif's reduction is not unusual. The number of virtues he suggests here equals the number set down in Ibn Rushd's commentary on Plato's *Republic;* in content, however, there are great differences from Ibn Rushd's list, and it is clear that Ibn Latif's source was Al-Farabi.

Ibn Latif paraphrases Al-Farabi as follows:

[1] First, his body should be strongly built and his limbs and organs perfect and strong, to make him fit for the actions that depend on them.

[2] Second, he should be resolute in setting his mind firmly to do what ought to be done, without fear; and he should be firm about forgiving wicked men.

[3] Third, he should by nature grasp easily whatever he hears, according to the true meaning of what is said to him and the intention of the one who says it.

[4] Fourth, it should be easy for him to learn and hard for him to forget, meaning that he should have a good memory and should not forget anything he has learned, understood, or heard.

[5] Fifth, he should be acute, so as to grasp deep things expressed by an obscure hint; he should catch and comprehend their true meaning.

[6] Sixth, he should be fond of learning, his intention being to understand and profit on his own and from others; and his nature should be adept so that the exertion of learning will not weaken him.

[7] Seventh, he should have fine diction, attuned to explaining perfectly to others whatever he understands.

[8] Eighth, he should by nature be of a humble spirit; and at the same time have self-respect and contempt for villainy and villains, so as not to shame or disgrace himself with any worldly pleasure. Rather, he should be content with his lot and have a magnanimous soul.

[9] Ninth, he should by nature love truth and hate falsehood.[10]

[10] Tenth, he should by nature be fond of justice and those who do it, and hate oppression and those who practice it, treat faithfully and receive whoever approaches him with justice and graciousness.[11]

Ibn Latif has omitted Al-Farabi's eighth and tenth virtues, relating to overcoming the appetites for food and drink, sexual intercourse, silver and gold, and subsuming them under the eighth virtue in his list.

Classifying Ibn Latif's virtues, we find a division into four types: physical perfection (1), potential for intellectual perfection (3–6), rhetorical ability (7), and ethical perfection (2, 8–10). As the virtues telescoped by Ibn Latif are ethical, these no longer form the largest group in his rendering of the virtues, as they do in Al-Farabi and as they will in Falaquera and others. Physical perfection does not appear at all in Plato, although it certainly suits the Platonic world view. Al-Farabi, however, included it in deference to the martial functions of the ideal Islamic ruler. Al-Farabi's perfect ruler had the task of educating his subjects in right opinions. He was the supreme teacher, as shown by his rhetorical perfection. Since there would always be those corrupt souls, who would refuse to accept his guidance, there was no alternative but to force right opinions on them. Here the Islamic concept of holy war, *jihad,* was introduced into the Platonic schema; however, Al-Farabi's Hebrew translators and commentators, from Ibn Latif on, ignored the military role completely. They retained the notion of physical perfection but ignored Al-Farabi's application of this virtue to the ideal ruler's military function. Although the idea of *jihad* seemed out of place to these commentators in their Diaspora setting, Jewish parallels may be found in the military role of the king-Messiah and in the description of war for a religious cause *(milhemet mitzvah).* Maimonides' treatment of this subject in *Hilkhot Melakhim* is a case in point. Nevertheless, all of the Jewish thinkers under review here deleted the military aspect of Al-Farabi's discourse on the philosopher king.[12]

The second and seventh of Ibn Latif's virtues reflect the political role of the philosopher king, who must apply his moral and rational perfection to leadership of the community. The second virtue concerns his courage. Here the word "courage," *gevurah,* is interpreted as a perfection of the soul, and it refers to the capacity of the philosopher king to contend with opposition to his policy. The seventh quality is rhetorical perfection, the ability to elucidate ideas and convince others to act virtuously. Al-Farabi emphasizes the philosopher king's need for rhetorical talent and, therefore, for a well-developed imaginative soul, so as to teach the people sound beliefs. Ibn Latif has overcome Plato's suspicion of rhetoric as sycophancy, suited to the Sophists, by hewing to Plato's advice that the philosopher king should lead the masses by "noble lies." For, unlike the Sophists, the philosopher king knows the truth; therefore he also knows when to hide it from the crowd and when to teach them by way of myths. Here the Hebrew translators and commentators wholly adopted Al-Farabi's modification, which reflected the influence of the image of the public prophet in Jewish and Muslim tradition.[13] Ibn Latif ignored Al-Farabi's cautionary comment that even the perfect man would find it difficult to perfect all twelve virtues, so that it might be necessary to make do with a subset.[14]

Thus, Ibn Latif, following Al-Farabi and with Maimonidean modifications, concludes:

The man in whom the ethical virtues are conjoined with the rational virtues considered previously, and who has acquired the characteristics of the soul referred to in the previous chapter, is truly the choicest of all men and completely perfect in the way proper to a member of the human species. He deserves a degree of excellence higher than any other: that the holy spirit [should] inspire him to prophesy, unless a Divine will *(hefetz Elohi)* prevents it, as I shall explain in the next chapter. So it is clear from this discussion that every prophet is a wise man and a philosopher. No philosopher, however, will become a prophet unless all the noble virtues mentioned above are united in him. These perfect the prophetic soul, which then becomes the form of the soul, as the philosophic soul is a form of the rational soul.[15]

In view of his moral and rational perfection, the philosopher king is worthy of prophecy, which he wins, unless God's will intervenes to disallow the fulfillment of his potential. In keeping with this Maimonidean proviso, Ibn Latif does not simply equate the philosopher king with the prophet. Perfection of the philosopher's moral virtues and reason constitutes a necessary, but not sufficient, condition for attaining prophecy. Thus, the ten virtues that Ibn Latif draws from Al-Farabi contain no direct reference to the prophetic aspect of the philosopher king's perfection, only to the intellectual, moral, and political aspects.

This situation is also reflected in Ibn Latif's citing of but one Hebrew source on the subject. At this stage of the theme's development in medieval Jewish thought, there exists only a translated summary from the Arabic source, with hardly any application to Hebrew sources. Hence, in his political discourse, Ibn Latif barely diverges from Al-Farabi, except for Maimonides' modification. His sole quotation from the Sages is this: "All the above-mentioned criteria were summed up by the Sages in three conditions, as they said: 'Prophecy descends only on the wise, the mighty, and the rich.' For these three comprehend in substance all the stipulations and conditions we have mentioned."[16]

Ibn Latif found a precise parallel in the Sages' words on the conditions allowing prophecy, with Al-Farabi's statements on the virtues of the philosopher king. After reducing Al-Farabi's list of twelve virtues to ten, he now reduces them to three, using the classification by the Sages: wise, mighty, and rich. The list, which appears in two places in the Babylonian Talmud (Shabat 92a, Nedarim 38a), had been used by medieval Jewish philosophers since Maimonides in connection with prophecy. Ibn Latif followed Maimonides' interpretation of the Sages' words exactly. Maimonides saw them as a reference to the perfection of the philosopher's moral and intellectual virtues, which were necessary, but not sufficient, conditions of prophecy. Maimonides interpreted might and riches, not as material attainments, but as virtues, and Ibn Latif did likewise. Of the philosophers who interpreted these statements by the Sages, Ibn Latif alone applied them directly to the virtues of the philosopher king. The others, including those like Falaquera who used the philosopher-king theory, never made such a connection. They considered the Sages' words only in the context of the conditions making prophecy possible.[17] The rulers and citizens of the virtuous state share many traits. They are persons whose rational soul will unite with the active intellect and win immortality:

> The rulers of the virtuous state are those people who have achieved such a degree of rational perfection that their virtue reaches the ultimate possible for a human being. Each of them in his generation would be suitable to rule over all the members of the species. These rulers, who succeed one another over time, all belong to the same soul. You and he are like one king forever. The same is true of any collection of virtuous souls, whether in one state or many. They are all one soul, and each one attains the ultimate goal in knowledge and practice.[18]

2

Falaquera, as mentioned, was more ambivalent than Maimonides on the question of the political duty of the philosopher. Unlike Maimonides, he makes no clear decision between isolation and social obligation. An eclectic philosopher and more a commentator and translator than an independent thinker, Falaquera tended to align himself with the arguments of the texts he translated or interpreted. Thus, his commentary on the last chapters of the *Guide* leans toward the solitary life, whereas his *Beginning of Wisdom (Reshit Hokhmah)* and *Book of Degrees (Sefer ha-Ma'alot)*, both largely based on Al-Farabi, show a distinct preference for the public prophet. His discourse on the philosopher-king theory is given full expression in these last two works.

In Falaquera's consideration of the class system, we found that parallel to the use of the amended version of the three powers of the soul, familiar in medieval Jewish thought, he also referred to Plato's original version: "The rational power relates to the class of the rulers of the virtuous state; the irascible power to the class of the mighty men; and the vegetative power, to the class of the artisans." He dwells on this matter at length in several other places.

Falaquera's writings discuss the philosopher-king theory principally in four places, always following Al-Farabi. One reference appears in the second part of the *Beginning of Wisdom* and is concerned with the division of the sciences. It directly follows Al-Farabi's *Ihsa' al-'ulum*. Falaquera's deliberations on political science are grounded in the distinction between two main types of regime, the "ignorant state" and the "virtuous state," the latter unique in being ruled by the philosopher king . It was necessary, Falaquera observed, to consider the "natural conditions" for the existence of the philosopher king. Owing

to the nature of the discussion, here, however, he did not present the theory
substantively: "It will be explained how whoever meets these natural conditions will be improved, and what should be eliminated from him so that he
may reach the kingly art and become a perfect king."[19] The second reference
appears in his translation of and commentary on Al-Farabi's *Philosophy of
Plato*, which is contained in the third part of the *Beginning of Wisdom*. Falaquera here briefly recaps a core theme of *The Republic:*

> This is why a different state must be founded, in which there will be
> true justice *(yosher amiti)* and goods that are truly good. This state
> will be one that will not lack anything needed to achieve ultimate
> felicity, and philosophers will constitute most of its members. In this
> state men will reach the desired perfection. All this is [explained] in
> his [Plato's] book *The Republic (sifro ba-hanhagah).*[20]

A comprehensive discussion of this subject is set forth in two other
places. One version is found at the beginning of the third part of *Beginning of
Wisdom*. It is an almost literal translation of the long introduction that Al-
Farabi prefixed to *The Philosophy of Plato and Aristotle*, which deals with the
supreme felicity of man *(tahsil al-sa'ada)*.[21] Falaquera first defines the individual terms that constitute the equation philosopher-lawgiver-king. The
philosopher is "whoever has attained theoretical wisdom and has the potential
to impart it to others, insofar as this is possible for him." Here we find the
combination of intellectual perfection and the responsibility to guide the
masses. The prophet-legislator is defined thus: "The 'legislator' *(menihah ha-
dat)* signifies [having] knowledge of the basis of practical ideas *(muskalim
ma'asi'im)* and the capability of bringing them to nations and the state." As for
"king," "The name 'king' signifies sovereignty *(memshalah)*and power *(yeholet)*,
and his art and perfection are of the greatest import." These separate definitions make the equation possible: "Therefore, the true king is the same as the
philosopher-legislator *(filosof mehadesh ha-datot)*, and he is the true philosopher." The philosopher king is identified here with the prophet only in the
context of the special political role of the latter as founding legislator, not necessarily in the context of prophecy as a whole. Falaquera translates Al-Farabi
literally, except for the Islamic term *imam*. He avoids translating *imam* as
"priest," *(cohen)* as Samuel ben Judah of Marseilles did in his translation of Ibn
Rushd's commentary on Plato's *Republic*.[22]

The starting point of this excursion into the virtues of the philosopher
king is the distinction between the true philosopher and the false philosopher.
The latter, a destructive counterfeit, "is the one who sets out to study the theoretical sciences without being naturally suited for them." He does not fulfill
Plato's first condition, possession of the potential to achieve rational perfec-

tion. His state will inevitably be an "ignorant state." The true philosopher must possess the requisite virtues: "These are the conditions prescribed by Plato in *The Republic*."[23]

Falaquera translates Al-Farabi's list of virtues as follows:

[1] He should excel in comprehending and discriminating what is accidental and what is essential. This is one of the main expressions of philosophical understanding.

[2] He should be able to endure the burden of study.

That is, he must possess the potential for study, have ease of understanding, and be capable of sustained studious effort. Al-Farabi's original, after Plato, adds to this the possession of an excellent memory. Falaquera does not note this here, but in a way he subsumes it in his second virtue.

[3] He should by natural disposition love justice and just people.

[4] He should not be gluttonous and should disdain the appetites and material possessions and the like.

[5] He should be naturally fond of being helpful and naturally learn magnanimity of soul as it is found among human beings.

[6] He should yield easily to goodness and be stubborn in yielding to evil and injustice.

[7] He should strongly favor the right and should be knowledgeable in the laws and customs that suit his innate disposition.

That is, he should be educated in accordance with his natural bent.

[8] He should adhere to perfections as understood by accepted opinion and should not forsake what are commonly recognized as noble deeds.[24]

This last requirement relates to the social obligation of the philosopher, while all the rest refer only to the conditions for his personal perfection, although they also reflect upon his social duties. The philosopher must respect accepted opinions in the society in which he lives (what Maimonides termed "generally accepted opinion"). These include the religion, which is the mass image of the knowledge comprehended by philosophers. Owing to his social obligation, the philosopher must transmit true opinions to the people on a level they can grasp and in terms of "generally accepted opinions" about belief and worship. He must respect these beliefs, even though he knows they are no more than images, because this is the way in which the masses worship God. This requirement is an obvious reflection of the realism of Plato, Al-Farabi, and Maimonides.

These eight virtues paraphrase Plato's list of eight in *The Republic*, and they contain all the conditions for perfection required of the philosopher king: the potential to achieve the truth (1, 2, 7) and to attain perfection in the virtues (3–6). The last alone (8) is Al-Farabi's addition, but it, too, nicely fits the Platonic world view. The virtues are presented in natural sequence: first the potential to achieve rational perfection, then moral perfection, and finally, intellectual perfection. As in Plato, most of the virtues involve moral perfection.

The philosopher who is perfect in all these ways must rule society and bring it to perfection. If he fails, the fault is that of the masses: "But the true philosopher is the one mentioned above. And if no use is made of him, it is not his fault but the fault of those who do not listen to him. Thus, the king is king by virtue of his art and perfection, regardless of whether or not anyone acknowledges him."[25]

Falaquera adhered to Al-Farabi's text without changing or "Judaizing" it. All he did, as was his custom, was to add an embellishment from the Sages, in this case citing tractate *Avot* (3:9): "Anyone who gives precedence to wisdom over fear of sin, his wisdom will not endure": Moral perfection must take precedence.[26]

In the *Book of Degrees*, Falaquera is generally more independent, but he still translates the philosopher king's virtues directly from Al-Farabi's *The Virtuous State:* "Abu Nasr Al-Farabi said that the man who is fit to be ruler of the virtuous nation must be perfect in all his virtues and must be a self-conscious and aware mind, and his imaginative faculty must by nature be truly perfect. . . ."[27] That is, the philosopher-ruler must be perfect in his rational soul and his imaginative soul alike. Falaquera goes on to cite Maimonides' well-known distinction (*Guide* II:37) among the philosopher, possessing perfection of the rational soul; the leaders of states, possessing perfection of the imaginative soul; and the prophets, possessing perfection of both the rational and the imaginative soul.[28] Like Ibn Latif, Falaquera follows Al-Farabi's theory of prophecy, with Maimonides' modification, which compels the philosopher king to meet all the preconditions for being a prophet but recognizes that he will not necessarily be a prophet.

The parallel between the philosopher king and the legislator relates specifically to the political function of the prophet as founding lawgiver, and not necessarily to prophecy as a whole. The fact that the philosopher king combines the special perfection of the king and the special perfection of the philosopher turns him into a philosopher king, but does not necessarily turn him into a prophet, even though the unique feature of prophecy is the merging of these two perfections. Prophecy is not a simple arithmetical summation of perfections; it is also the result of the "Divine will," in Ibn Latif's phrase.[29] Thus, Falaquera moves on, by way of a translation of Al-Farabi, to the conditions of prophecy itself, and he applies these directly to the figure of the philosopher king: "Abu Nasr said that the man we discussed above is the first ruler *(ha-rosh ha-rishon)* of the virtuous state, and he is the ruler of the virtuous nation *(umma hasidah)* and ruler of the whole of civilization *(yeshuv)*."[30] Optimally, prophecy enters into the equation, too.

Following this version of Al-Farabi, Falaquera lists twelve virtues of the philosopher king: "and it is impossible for anyone to reach this [kingly] degree, unless by nature he has twelve virtues, or most of them."[31] Like Ibn Latif, Falaquera chose the term *middot* to designate the virtues of the philosopher king. This term hints at the imitation of the thirteen attributes of God. Although Falaquera does not make this connection explicitly, it is presumed by his allowing for the possibility of the union in one person of king, philosopher, and prophet. In the *Beginning of Wisdom,* Falaquera lists only eight virtues. The *Book of Degrees* is more detailed and, in contrast to the other version, the virtues in it are numbered; but there is fundamental equivalence between the two versions.

The twelve virtues:

[1] One is that he should have limbs and organs that are healthy and strong, and that when he intends to perform an action with any of them, he accomplishes it with ease.

[2] He should be good at understanding everything said to him, and grasp it in his mind according to the true intent of what is said to him.

[3] He should remember whatever is said to him and whatever he comes to see and hear and whatever he apprehends, without forgetting.

[4] He should be very lucid; when he sees the slightest indication of something he should grasp its significance.

[5] He should have fine diction and be able to explain to perfection all that is in his inmost mind.

[6] He should be fond of learning, devoted to it, and grasp things easily, without finding the effort painful or feeling discomfort with the toil it entails.

[7] He should by nature be fond of truth and truthful men and hate falsehood and liars.

[8] He should not lust after food and drink or sexual intercourse, and should have a natural aversion to frivolity and a hatred of the pleasures which these pursuits afford.

[9] He should be of proud spirit, his soul being by nature above all things ugly and base and rising naturally to the highest things.

[10] Silver and gold and other wordly goals should be of little consequence in his view.

[11] He should by nature be fond of justice and hate oppression and those who practice it, giving his people and others their due, and urging people to act justly; he should lend his support to what he thinks fair and noble and just, and be obdurate if asked to do injustice.

[12] He should be resolute in setting his mind to everything that in his view ought to be done, and resolutely carry it out without fear.[32]

If we classify these virtues, we find, as in Ibn Latif, a logical division into four groups: physical perfection (1), potential for intellectual perfection (2–6), including rhetorical ability, the ability to influence others (5); and moral perfection (7–12). Here too, most of the virtues are moral. This version includes physical perfection, which is missing in the *Beginning of Wisdom*. Like Ibn Latif, Falaquera only mentions the need for physical perfection; he does not add Al-Farabi's explanation that this virtue is essential for the ideal ruler to fulfill his military functions when forced to go to war. In his Hebrew translation of *The Philosophy of Plato and Aristotle*, however, Falaquera thoroughly considers the military role of the philosopher king and provides relevant examples from the Torah. Here the king is described in Platonic terms, as the one who is allowed, and even obliged, to use force when all other means to correct the erring ways of humankind have failed. In religious terms, Falaquera translates Al-Farabi's *jihad* into the Jewish *Milhemet Mitzvah*.[33]

As for moral perfection, the two versions of the virtues basically match. Regarding the potential for rational perfection, the version in the *Book of Degrees* goes into greater detail, especially by the inclusion of rhetorical ability, which enables the philosopher king to transmit his ideas. This quality hints at his political function.[34] One virtue stressed by Al-Farabi in the previous version is missing here, however: the need of the philosopher-ruler to respect accepted opinions—that is, those religious beliefs suitable for the masses.

Even in the introduction to this discourse, Falaquera observes, following Al-Farabi, that the philosopher king must have most of the twelve virtues, but not necessarily all of them. From the outset he admitted that the philosopher king might not be able to achieve all of the virtues, since most human beings do not have so high a potential; even those few who do are hard pressed fully to realize their potential. Falaquera reverts to this theme after presenting the twelve virtues: "It would be extremely difficult to assemble all these in one man. This is the reason that only a single person in a generation and a few among the people may be found with this nature. If someone like this were found in the perfect state *(medinah shlemah)*, and he had most of these virtues, he would become the ruler, guide and true king."[35] Al-Farabi, too, regarded the twelve virtues that he set out as an ideal toward which the perfect man must strive. He was willing to accept the attainment of perfection in just six or seven of the virtues. Falaquera does not comment on Al-Farabi's ranking of rulers according to their attainment of the twelve virtues.[36]

People who accept the leadership of the philosopher king will necessarily follow the straight path: "Abu Nasr said that the people who follow this ruler *(rosh)* are the virtuous *(hasidim)*, the good and those who have acquired felicity *(mazlihim)*."[37] Therefore, their state will necessarily be an ideal state. Falaquera describes this state exactly according to the criteria of the Platonic state:

The philosopher said [that] the actions of the virtuous nation are all perfect and true, and this is its unique quality. For people will not eat harmful foods and will not need to know how to treat sicknesses, which are caused by over-eating. For they do not eat any food which is unsuitable. Thus it is one of the advantages of the virtuous nation that there will be no need in it for a physician or a judge . . . and it is known that every person in the virtuous state has already acquired whatever perfection he is suited for and that its beliefs are all true and contain no falsehood . . .[38]

3

The second channel along which the tradition of the philosopher king passed into medieval Jewish thought is the Hebrew translation of Ibn Rushd's commentary on Plato's *Republic*. The commentary was written at the end of the twelfth century and translated into Hebrew by Samuel ben Judah of Marseilles in the early fourteenth century.[39] Even more markedly than in the cases of Ibn Latif and Falaquera, we find here a direct rendering of the Arabic original, with no application to the Hebrew setting. Unlike Ibn Latif and Falaquera, Samuel ben Judah saw himself as only a translator, with no pretensions to originality. His translation is so literal that in places it is quite obscure.

At the beginning of the second treatise of Ibn Rushd's commentary, the discourse moves from the virtues of the guardians to those of the philosopher class in the ideal state. Like Al-Farabi, Ibn Rushd begins by defining the philosopher and the king separately. The philosopher is one who possesses both rational perfection—theoretical and practical—and moral perfection. The king is one who governs states. He will possess perfection in this art if all the virtues of the philosopher are present in him. In this way the king and the philosopher merge. Consequently, these terms—philosopher, king, lawgiver— are, as it were, synonymous; so, also, is "priest" *(imam).*[40]

More emphatically than the Hebrew paraphrases of Al-Farabi by Ibn Latif and Falaquera, the Hebrew Ibn Rushd presents prophecy only as a desirable possibility for the philosopher king. It augments his perfection, but it is not necessary for his political role. It is "an enhancement, not a requirement."

Ibn Latif and Falaquera subjected Al-Farabi to Maimonidean modification, but Samuel ben Judah does not tamper with the text of Ibn Rushd. We have already reviewed the debate between Rosenthal and Pines on the interpretation of Ibn Rushd's equating philosopher, lawgiver, and king and its far-reaching significance for a grasp of his true position. If we accept Pines' radical explanation, it means that Ibn Rushd, in contrast to Al-Farabi, did not identify the Islamic state with the Platonic state. He regarded the latter as the true ideal state, and the Islamic state as a successful imitation of it, at best.

If the philosopher king need not be a prophet, the question arises why Ibn Rushd still stressed his role as a lawgiver and considered the term "legislator" to be synonymous with philosopher king. Indeed, the lawgiving role of the philosopher king is emphasized at the beginning of the third treatise, where Ibn Rushd deals with the different kinds of regime.[41] Has not the ideal law already been enunciated by the philosopher or the prophet? Rosenthal glosses the mention of a legislative role as a means of highlighting the requirement that the philosopher king must be an expert in the law handed down by the first lawgiver.

Ibn Rushd defines the virtues required of the philosopher king, as "the natural qualifications in a king." This is his list:

[1] One of them, the most important, is that he be disposed by nature for study of the speculative sciences. This will be the case if he naturally grasps what a thing is in its essence, and distinguishes it from that which it is by accident.

[2] The second is that he should remember and not forget. For he who does not have these two qualities cannot possibly be taught anything. He will be under constant strain until he forsakes reading and study.

[3] The third is that he should love study, choose it, and desire to inquire into all parts of science. For he who ardently desires something aspires, as he says, to all its kinds. For example, a man who is fond of wine craves all kinds of wine, and the same applies to one who is fond of women.

[4] The fourth is that he should love truth and hate falsehood. The reason is that he who loves the knowledge of reality as such loves truth. For he who loves truth cannot love falsehood. So, he who is of this type will not love falsehood.

[5] The fifth is that he should loathe sensual desires. For if one desires something exceedingly, it will deflect his soul from the other appetites. So it is with these [people], because they already incline with all their souls toward knowledge.

[6] The sixth is that he should not love money, for money is a passion and passions are not proper for such men.

[7] The seventh is that he should be high-minded. For he who desires comprehensive knowledge of all that is and does not want to limit his knowledge of things to the confines of a primitive sense perception is high-minded indeed. Therefore, his reason is detached from earthly life.

[8] The eighth is that he should be courageous, because he who has no courage cannot reject the non-demonstrative arguments with which he grew up, especially one who has grown up in these states.

[9] The ninth is that he should be so disposed that he move of his own accord toward everything he considers good and beautiful, like justice and other such virtues. This occurs when his appetitive soul relies firmly on opinion and cognition.

[10] To these must be added that he should be a good orator, his tongue responsive to whatever is in his mind when he engages in philosophical argument. He should also quickly light upon the middle term.[42]

Two main groups of virtues may be discerned here: those relating to the potential to achieve rational perfection (1–3, 7) and those relating to moral perfection (4–6, 8–9). Most relate to moral perfection. The Hebrew translation of Ibn Rushd's list generally matches the versions of Ibn Latif and Falaquera. Courage (8), is given the same explanation here as that given by Ibn Latif: it enables the philosopher to withstand the wrong opinions of the wicked state in which he has grown up and to maintain true opinions, which are not accepted there. Thus, courage here takes the sense of moral strength and intellectual honesty.[43] As for rational perfection, the Hebrew translation of Ibn Rushd provides the same definition as Falaquera's, which followed Al-Farabi: this is the ability to discriminate the essential from the accidental. It is the chief virtue of the philosopher. Like the Platonic original, the philosopher is in search of "the knowledge of reality as such" (fourth virtue) or "knowledge of all things" (seventh virtue).

The addition of the tenth virtue is important. Ibn Latif and Falaquera cite the need for a developed rhetorical talent. Ibn Rushd spells this out in greater detail, laying stress on the social obligation of the philosopher. The commentary links this rhetorical skill with the ability to find the middle road. To be able to apply his intellectual perfection to the leadership of the people, the ideal ruler must possess a developed rhetorical capacity.

Samuel ben Judah's translation, like Falaquera's translation of Al-Farabi, concludes in this vein:

> The man suited to rule over this state is he in whom these conditions have been conjoined from the beginning of his life and who has also had the good fortune to grow up under the constitution which he will describe. How rare then, is such a man. This is the reason, too, that it is so difficult for such a state to come into being.[44]

Ibn Rushd composed a further variation on the theme at the beginning of the third treatise. Here the inquiry concerns Plato's classification of states in the ninth book of *The Republic*. The first type is the state with the ideal constitution, headed by the philosopher king. Ibn Rushd briefly specifies five conditions to be met by this king:

> For if there is placed over this regime *(hanhagah)* one in whom five prerequisites are combined—namely, wisdom, perfect intelligence, persuasiveness, good imagination, capacity for waging holy war, and no physical impediment to the performance of actions in connection with holy war—then he is absolutely king and his government will be a truly royal government.[45]

If we compare the philosopher-king's virtues ("prerequisites"—*tena'im*—in the Hebrew) as presented here with those of the previous version, we find one major difference: here there is no reference to moral perfection. Only five prerequisites are listed, half the number in the first version. The significance of the first four conditions(wisdom, potential for intellectual perfection, persuasive powers, and developed imaginative capacity) is clear.

Since the Hebrew text is obscure in places and the Arabic source is lost, Rosenthal compared the Hebrew version to equivalent passages in Al-Farabi in order to try to clarify the original sense. In his view, the text is directly based on Al-Farabi's discourse on the virtues of the king in *Fusul al-Madani*. Indeed, the addition of the need for a developed imaginative capacity, a condition which does not appear in Ibn Rushd's first version and which does not accord with his argument that the philosopher king need not be a prophet, points to the influence of Al-Farabi. It is the same with the cryptic fifth condition, which Rosenthal interprets as the ability to conduct a holy war *(jihad)*, for which the philosopher king requires physical perfection.[46] Ibn Latif and Falaquera in the *Book of Degrees* both place physical perfection first in their list of virtues, although those writers did not specify a military context.

Thus, Ibn Rushd's short version differs in several respects from his first. Only three of the prerequisites here have parallels in the first version: wisdom, intellectual perfection, and persuasive powers. Two are added that do not appear in the first version: perfection of the imaginative soul and physical perfection. Missing are all the conditions relating to moral perfection. As Dunlop and Rosenthal explained, Al-Farabi posits a more Islamic version of the theory, and Ibn Rushd here integrates it into his discourse on Plato. Following Al-Farabi, Ibn Rushd then goes on to consider the possibility that not all the virtues are to be found in one man. If they are distributed among different men, we can still have "leadership of the best" *(rash'iut ha-tovim, aristocracy)*—but then we no longer have a philosopher king.

The Jewish philosophers who followed Ibn Rushd's version used the first, longer version and ignored the short one. This was only natural, considering its more Islamic and less moral nature.[47]

6

Adaptation

Let us turn now to the second stage in the transmission of the philosopher-king theory to medieval Jewish thought. Here we observe the adaptation of translated texts to the context of the Hebrew sources and Jewish philosophy. This process is manifested in the two channels through which the theory passed into Jewish thought: the commentaries of Al-Farabi and Ibn Rushd on Plato's *Republic*. In chronological order, we first meet Isaac Polkar, in the fourteenth century. He applied the virtues of the king as presented in one of Al-Farabi's versions. Then later, at the end of the fifteenth century, comes Yohanan Alemanno, who wrote in a completely new atmosphere, taking the translation of Ibn Rushd's commentary as his text.

Each exegete adapted the virtues of the philosopher king to the Jewish context in his own way. Polkar made two adaptations. First, he added a thirteenth virtue to the twelve he copied from Al-Farabi; his aim was to match the virtues of the philosopher king with the thirteen attributes of God that the perfect man must emulate. Then he applied each of the attributes to Moses, to show that the prophet of Israel was the supreme embodiment of the philosopher king in human history. Alemanno, by contrast, added four virtues to those he copied from Ibn Rushd—four that he considered unique to the king in Israel according to the halakhah. He then tested how far various leaders of Israel had realized the virtues of the philosopher king.

1

Polkar's *Defense of the Law (Ezer ha-Dat)*[1] endeavored to demonstrate the superiority of the law of Israel through the use of medieval political concepts, chiefly based on Maimonides' *Guide*. The first two chapters of the first treatise describe man's need for social order, in language reminiscent of *Guide* II:40, and set out a natural conception of the ideal state. Polkar then argues for the uniqueness of the Torah of Moses as the ideal law for the perfect human society.

"Since the law *(dat)* of the Jews is the most righteous and veracious of all constitutions *(datot)*," it necessarily follows that the giver of this law is the most perfect of lawgivers: "It is also clear that this praiseworthy nation is the one over which the most perfect ruler and leader possible was appointed; he is king by nature. He is the one who teaches and leads them in these ways, which are the substance and essence of the law *(torah)*."² It is noteworthy that Polkar presents rule by the perfect individual as deriving from the law of nature. To prove all this, he sets out the virtues of the philosopher king and applies them to the figure of Moses.

Polkar does not actually name his immediate source, but cites "the wise philosophers" in general. It is clear from a comparison of the texts, however, that he copied Al-Farabi's *The Virtuous State*. Polkar's vague citation may reflect the fact that the theory of the philosopher-king's virtues was not exclusively Al-Farabi's. Indeed Al-Farabi himself noted that he had taken the idea from Plato. Although Polkar often cites his Hebrew and Arabic sources precisely, he generalizes wherever referring to ideas commonly accepted by other philosophers.³ Polkar used the same source as had Ibn Latif and Falaquera, in the *Book in Degrees*, but he did not take the passages from either of them. His text is different in many respects. He apparently translated and summarized Al-Farabi's writing on his own or used a Hebrew translation not yet known to us.

Unlike Ibn Latif and Falaquera, who engaged in a complex philosophical discourse that closely adhered to Al-Farabi's text, and who were influenced by Maimonides, Polkar presents a short treatment of the subject, in a more popular style. He opens with the generalization that "the wise philosophers have explained that twelve qualifications should be found in the man who is worthy of being appointed to govern and rule over the virtuous and praiseworthy nation."⁴ Again, unlike Ibn Latif and Falaquera, who chose the term "attributes" *(middot)*, Polkar chooses the expression "prerequisites" *(tena'im)*, which also appears in Samuel ben Judah's translation of Ibn Rushd. As we shall see, however, he replaces "prerequisite" *(tna'i)* with "attribute" *(middah)*, also meaning virtue, at a critical point, a shift that was to have great significance.

Polkar's prerequisites for a ruler, are these:

One, that he should be healthy in body and his limbs and organs perfect, to make him fit for the actions that depend on them.

Second, that he should by nature understand whatever he encounters; that he should comprehend things themselves and also whatever he hears, according to the speaker's intention.

Third, that he should always retain whatever he knows, understands, and hears, without forgetting anything.

Fourth, that he should know and understand things unknown, from the hints and sketches conveyed to him, so as to bring them to light; and he is the one who can discriminate one thing from another.

Fifth, that he should have fine diction, so as to be able to give the right interpretation and properly explain his observations and find the right words to express all that is in his inmost mind, so that he will be able to understand and to teach others.

Sixth, that he should be willing and eager to teach, so that others may profit from his wisdom; he is not lazy or jealous and does not shirk the toil of learning

Seventh, that he should by nature be fond of truth and truthful men, and hate falsehood and those who believe in falsehood.

Eighth, that he should not crave the various bodily pleasures that would give him no benefit, like meat gluttons, wine guzzlers and adulterers, nor amuse himself by watching various comic spectacles or listening to music and nonsensical tales.

Ninth, that he should be proud and noble of spirit, rejecting every-thing ugly and base, but simply rising naturally above all others.

Tenth, that riches and wealth should be contemptible and vile in his eyes, and likewise all material accidents like dominion and vengeance.

Eleventh, that he should by nature be fond of justice and righteous-ness, and hate injustice and oppression, aiming to deliver the poor from the powerful with his love and passion for justice, but not by means of malice and cruelty.

Twelfth, that all his actions should be done with courage, without fear and quailing, but with a strong and determined spirit.[5]

This version departs widely from the texts of Ibn Latif and Falaquera, although its content closely parallels theirs. Like them, Polkar does not spec-ify the military application of physical perfection. This is also expressed in the way he demonstrates this perfection in Moses. I have found only one signifi-cant addition in Polkar's presentation. In the sixth item, which in both Al-Farabi's original and in Ibn Latif and Falaquera relates only to the philoso-pher's ability to learn, Polkar adds the ability "to teach so others profit from his wisdom," a reference to the role of the philosopher king in political edu-cation. It also basically repeats the fifth stipulation.

So far, Polkar has closely followed Al-Farabi's version; but now he begins the application of the discourse to the Jewish tradition. First, he points out that it is proper to add an additional stipulation to the twelve listed by Al-Farabi. The addition of a thirteenth virtue obviously alludes to the number of attributes of God in Jewish tradition. Indeed, although Polkar had used the neutral term "prerequisites" *(tena'im)*, and not the more freighted term "attributes" *(middot)*, as Ibn Latif and Falaquera did, he now deliberately changes terminology. We find the same change later, when we observe how Polkar finds the thirteen prerequisites in Moses. The thirteenth becomes an attribute: "I say that in order to perfect this man to the utmost, and to uplift him to a degree than which there is none higher, an additional attribute must be found in him to complete the thirteen necessary for the perfect man."[6] This number is linked to the philosopher-king's virtues by the theory of *imitatio Dei*. The philosopher king, being a prophet, must imitate the attributes of God insofar as he is able, so as to reach the ultimate human perfection and lead men accordingly.[7]

Rosenthal argues that a thirteenth virtue can, in fact, be found in Al-Farabi's list in *The Virtuous State*, in addition to the twelve he enumerates.[8] However, both in Falaquera's version in The *Book in Degrees* and in Polkar's version presented here, only twelve virtues are set out. Polkar expressly states that the thirteenth is his original contribution. He ascribes the first twelve to "the wise philosophers," but declares that the thirteenth, which alone he designates as an attribute *(middah)*, is his own addition.

Polkar defines the thirteenth virtue thus: "It is that all his actions come from the human *(enoshi)* part of him, and not from the bestial *(behemi)*."[9] He goes on to clarify these concepts: which actions are bestial, which are mixed—bestial and human, and which are purely human actions. This last concept is reflected in the transition of the hylic intellect from potential to actual and in the unity of the rational soul with the active intellect. He whose actions are of this kind is the philosopher-king-prophet: "The existence of such a man, who is the goal and ultimate aim of the human species, is the result of the intellect's having emanated upon his rational faculty. By the splendor of this intellect he will become a wise man and a philosopher, and from what has emanated upon his imaginative faculty he will become a prophet and visionary."[10] Following Al-Farabi, Polkar establishes here a direct link between the philosopher king and the prophet. This philosopher-king-prophet is one who has attained the perfection of his rational and imaginative soul together, through the emanation of the active intellect. Unlike Ibn Latif and Falaquera, Polkar seems to disregard the Maimonidean modification of Al-Farabi's theory of prophecy; rather, he identifies the philosopher with the prophet.

We have already observed that Polkar, like many Jewish philosophers in the late Middle Ages, struggled between a leaning toward solitary existence and an emphasis on the political obligation of the philosopher. He attempted a kind of compromise, which differed in several details from that of Maimonides. Polkar finds no personal need for human company on the part of the philosopher-prophet. In this regard, he clearly supports the theory of solitary existence set out by Ibn Bajja: "Since this divine man has gained ultimate felicity *(ha-hazlahah ha-tamah)* and true perfection, it is appropriate for him, as far as his personal well-being is concerned, to be separate and withdrawn, dwelling alone *(mithoded)* and keeping apart *(mitiahed)* from the rest of mankind, since no one is like him and nobody can reach his degree."[11] Polkar does not offer the usual argument that it is better for such a man to be apart from the corrupting influence of human society. There is logic in his avoidance of this claim; for if the philosopher-prophet satisfies all thirteen conditions, there is no danger of any negative influence upon him. The argument Polkar advances, which suits his method, is that the perfect man has no need to become involved with human society, since he has nothing in common with others. This is opposed to Maimonides' stance, which held that the philosopher-prophet can meet his material and emotional needs only within human society—although it is preferable for him to keep the connection to the essential minimum. Maimonides justified temporary departure from society only in cases in which the society was utterly corrupt and liable to exert an evil influence even on the perfect man, or to harm him.[12]

But although Polkar holds it proper for the perfect man to isolate himself from human society from the standpoint of his own needs, he urges nonetheless that such a man bears an obligation to the people from the standpoint of his divine mission. Whoever has received an emanation of divine providence must share it with others and guide them. Polkar disagrees with Maimonides in regards to the personal needs of the philosopher-prophet, but he is in close accord with him regarding educational duty. Polkar's argument reflects that offered by Maimonides (*Guide* II:36) in being based on the theory of the imitation of God:

> Only because of the general Divine Providence which always exists in the human species and because of the virtue of generosity he possesses, and his superior goodness, whatever he has that is in surplus and over-abundant, he will continually emanate on his fellow men. It is obligatory for him, then, to dwell and reside amongst them *and to bear their cumbrance* (Deut. 1:12), in order to lead them and make their path straight, each according to his particular degree and potential, like a shepherd amongst the flock, so that the nation he dwells in needs no other judge or physician.[13]

Polkar pointedly uses the unusual biblical expression "to bear their cumbrance,"[14] which refers to the purposes of Moses' rule. Further on, he presents

Moses as the prototype of the philosopher-king-prophet. The ideal ruler is likened to a shepherd, as was common in medieval political allegory.[15] He naturally turns the state into an ideal state, and its citizens into perfect citizens, each to the degree attainable. In such a situation, as held in the Platonic tradition,[16] there will no longer be any need for a judge (to heal the sickness of the soul) or a physician (to heal the sickness of the body).

Polkar presents the philosopher king as one who is obliged not only to lead those of his own times, but also to guide future generations by committing his code of laws to writing: he is the first lawgiver of his own and subsequent generations. His goal is to guide future generations to live in perfection: "When he is of old age, it will also be obligatory for him, as an expression of his munificence, to put into writing in a book, for the understanding and direction of all those who succeed him—who would not know him or be acquainted with him—the path in which they should walk, and his commandments *(mizvotiv)* and laws *(hukotiv)*, by which they should act and live."[17] These words suit the Farabian outlook, which presents the ideal ruler as the premier lawgiver and the succeeding rulers as experts in the law given by him. There seems to be a hint here of the Torah's dictum (Deut. 17:18–19) that the king write a copy of the Torah. The Torah, though, states explicitly that the king will write the book for his personal use, "that he may learn to fear the Lord his God," which is also Maimonides' interpretation in *Hilkhot Melakhim* (3:1). Polkar, by contrast, gives the words a clearly Farabian sense in relating the writing of the book of laws to the direction of future rulers.

After listing the virtues of the philosopher king, Polkar introduces his major innovation: the application of these thirteen virtues to Moses, who is portrayed as the master of the prophets and prototype of the ideal man and ruler—in Platonic terms, the prototype of the philosopher king:

> Having described to you the virtues of this man who is worthy to be made governor and ruler over the virtuous and honorable nation, and shown the extent of his understanding, I shall inform you in truth that our master Moses is the one who attained these virtues and ascended toward God, which means toward the ultimate goal, which is the highest degree. I shall inform you, first of all, that in him the thirteen prerequisites which I mentioned, were and were seen, all perfect and right.[18]

Polkar now finds all thirteen virtues ("prerequisites") exemplified in the life of Moses:

> First I say, he should be strong and healthy in body. For it is known that he was heroic in killing the Egyptian who smote the Israelite

and in rescuing Jethro's daughters from the shepherds, and rolling away the stone, and when he was a hundred and twenty years old his eye was not dim nor were his natural powers abated.

Also, for the second prerequisite, the immensity of Moses' knowledge and the perfection of his apprehension are manifest and known among all nations, and the Torah specifies that there hath not since arisen a prophet in Israel like unto Moses. (Deut. 34:10)

The third prerequisite: it is well known that he remembered to include in Deuteronomy all the events and details that had occurred to him, and forgot nothing, despite the tribulations which had befallen him in caring for the interests of the people.

In the fourth prerequisite he was perfect. We know this by two credible witnesses: one, that when he saw the bush that burned with fire and was not consumed, he comprehended the matter down to the last detail, understood it and knew that God's angel was in the core of the burning bush . . . [additional examples].

In the fifth prerequisite: he demonstrated his powerful language and eloquent style in the song of the sea and in the portion *Ha'azinu,* and all his other rebukes and reproofs.

The sixth prerequisite is known and recognized by the fact that he was not jealous of Eldad and Medad who were prophesying, but said, "Would that all the Lord's people were prophets" (Num. 11:29). The same is demonstrated in how he taught the elders and Joshua and inspired them, as well as Aaron and Hur.

The seventh and eleventh prerequisites are well known by whoever witnesses the righteousness of his justice and the perfection of his decrees and laws. Also, because it is said of him, "He is trusted in all my house." (Num. 12:7)

The eighth and also the tenth prerequisites: It is well known that he abandoned and despised all bodily pleasures and preferred the spiritual. For he sent his wife away when he began to prophesy. And he abstained from food for forty days and survived, which is beyond the power of a living being.

Also, it is true that the ninth prerequisite relates to the fact that boasting and vainglory are practically nonexistent in Moses, as the verse indicates: "Now the man Moses was very meek" (Num. 12:3). It is known that meekness is intermediate between pride and humility, and that Moses was inclined in his virtues toward humility so as to achieve communion with Him, as the Sages, of blessed memory, said: "Be exceedingly humble in spirit" (*Avot,* 4:4). Except that for a man like him, who was appointed king and governor of a great people, it is impossible not to be occasionally obstinate and wrathful, to awe and intimidate whoever rejects his moral instructions. The twelfth prerequisite is also included in this virtue.

The thirteenth attribute. It is appropriate for us, and we also have the obligation to believe that the above-mentioned perfection and faultlessness and the achievement of the ultimate purpose are all found in Moses, since his solitary soul, which departed from its matter and despised it, changed the normal course of nature and performed the well-known miracles, as when the disembodied forms change material things and do anything they please with them. Also by his prophesying whenever he wished, as the verse says: "Stay ye, that I may hear what the Lord will command concerning you" (Num. 9:8). All this is a consequence of his permanent communion with the spiritual realm and his becoming a perfectly divine man, since the material accidents did not delay, distress or interfere with him, and none of his powers contemplated then any material instrument, for how could the action of a bodily power be of any importance or relevance for one who abstained from eating and drinking for forty days and forty nights?[19]

In applying the thirteen prerequisites to Moses, Polkar combined numbers seven and eleven, eight and ten, nine and twelve. These qualities, mostly concerned with moral perfection, are largely parallel. He could thus conjoin his proof-texts from the Torah. The fifth prerequisite, assigning rhetorical perfection to Moses contradicts the biblical statement that Moses was "slow of speech and of a slow tongue" (Exod. 4:10). Nissim Gerondi accepts the biblical statement as fact and uses it to prove the miraculous nature of Moses' prophecy; that is, Moses was able to lead the people of Israel despite this handicap. Polkar, however, ignores the biblical statement and presents Moses as possessing rhetorical perfection, albeit in his language, not in his oratorial delivery. In making this attribution, he wished to adapt Moses' characteristics to the virtues of Al-Farabi's philosopher king—which, of course, only serves to demonstrate, yet again, the political and educational character that Polkar ascribed to Moses' prophecy.

The discussion of the ninth and twelfth prerequisites is firmly based on Maimonides' ethics, the Aristotelian theory of the middle way, and Maimonides' argument that the truly perfect, saintly man will diverge slightly from the middle course toward deficiency in order to be on the safe side and ensure that he is not swept toward excess. In Maimonidean terms, then, Moses is presented both as a philosopher, keeping to the middle course, and as a saint, rising to a higher level than the philosopher in the human hierarchy.[20]

When Polkar copied Al-Farabi's twelve prerequisites for a philosopher king, he placed the emphasis on the king's being a philosopher; but when he applies the image to Moses, Polkar imparts to it an even higher level, that of the saintly prophet. Following Maimonides, Polkar asserts that Moses, in his role as king, sometimes had to act in anger and sternness, in order to correct and guide the recalcitrant people. As Maimonides asserts (*Guide* 1:54), the perfect leader, who imitates divine ways, may occasionally act with anger and resentment. This does not necessarily mean that he departs from the middle way, but that an objective assessment of the circumstances brings him to the conclusion that this is the best course of action for a leader. According to Maimonides (*Eight Chapters*, 4), Moses sinned when he was angry with the people at Meribah, not because he showed anger, but because such behavior was not justified in the circumstances.[21]

This stance is most strikingly expressed in Polkar's thirteenth virtue. By adding it, thereby elevating Moses' above the material life, Polkar perfected the parallelism of the philosopher king's virtues with the thirteen attributes of God. The perfect man seeks to imitate God's attributes as much as he can and to lead the people in their light.

A novel element is introduced into the description of the thirteenth virtue when attributed to Moses: the ability of the philosopher king to perform miracles. Here, Polkar departs from the Maimonidean rationalist tradition, which tended to play down miracles and attempted to subsume them as far as possible in the general framework of creation. Maimonides argues that the king-Messiah will not perform miracles but will act only within the bounds of nature.[22] Polkar was the only philosopher studied here to include miracle working among the virtues of the philosopher king. Even Abravanel, as we shall see, eschewed it.

Yet, with all his stress on the philosophic role and prophetic powers of the ideal, Polkar concludes his discussion by depicting Moses as a ruler, not simply as a philosopher or a prophet: "Here I have proven to you, as intended, that our king Moses was the one appropriate and fit to become prince and chief of the holy people."[23] This representation of Moses is consistent with the text "And there was a king in Jeshurun" (Deut. 33:5), but it also accords with the overall position that king, philosopher, and prophet are synonymous terms.

2

Yohanan Alemanno's inquiry into the virtues of the philosopher king in *Eternal Life (Hai ha-Olamin),* most of which was written in Florence at the end of the fifteenth century, reflects the fresh atmosphere of the Italian Renaissance at its height. Alemanno lived in Medicean Florence at the time when the Platonic Academy was established there by Ficino and Pico della Mirandola. This environment strongly influenced his work in general and his perception of the philosopher king in particular.[24] The Republic, as we have seen, was the basic text of medieval Muslim and Jewish political thought, whereas Christian political philosophy preferred Aristotle's Politics. The Europeans returned to Plato with the Renaissance and the revival of original classical works, particularly the rediscovery of The Republic. Ficino was the first to publish commentaries both on The Republic and on the Laws. Members of the Platonic Academy of Florence identified Plato's philosopher king with the ideal ruler and patron of their milieu, Lorenzo di Medici.[25]

The return to Plato's Republic as a primary source of political inquiry was reflected among Jewish scholars too. The translation of Ibn Rushd's commentary by Samuel ben Judah of Marseilles was recopied at least five times during the fifteenth century and twice translated into Latin. One of the two translations, that of Eliah del Medigo was lost; it was rediscovered only a few years ago. The other translation, by Jacob Mantinus, which is better known, was eventually included in the large Venice edition of the Aristotelian Opera Omnia with Ibn Rushd's commentaries. This edition was published in the mid-sixteenth century.[26]

The reliance of Jewish scholars on the classic Hebrew source ran parallel to the tendency of Christian scholars to return to the classical Greek sources. With their translations, del Medigo, Mantinus, and others helped restore Plato to the humanist tradition—although, for these Jewish scholars, it was the Plato they inherited from the Muslim thought of the Middle Ages.

Alemanno, following Ibn Rushd rather than al-Farabi, merged smoothly into this current. What mattered to him was the return to Plato rather than Ibn Rushd's commentary, which Alemanno even disclaimed. He pretended to base his excursion into the virtues of the philosopher king on Plato, although he was generally careful, in other cases, to cite the Arabic sources, including Ibn Rushd himself, meticulously.[27] In the Middle Ages, Falaquera and Samuel ben Judah self-consciously cited the Arabic sources; Polkar generally referred to "the wise philosophers." Only Alemanno, the Renaissance man, boasted of using Plato directly, omitting Al-Farabi and Ibn Rushd.

Alemanno's lengthy dialogue, Eternal Life, deals with the stages of human perfection, from that of the body to that of the soul, and its ultimate goal, mystical union with God. He included within this framework a long political discourse based on the assumption that man, as a social creature, cannot attain perfection of body or soul except in the ideal state ruled by the philosopher king. In keeping with tradition, Alemanno presents this figure as the antithesis of the tyrant. The philosopher king is the man who has realized all the stages of human perfection, as described at length in *Eternal Life*.[28]

Alemanno distinguishes the "perfections" *(shlemuyot)* from the prerequisites *(tena'im)*, or sometimes the "attributes" *(te'arim)* of the philosopher king. The perfections belong to the philosopher king after he has realized his potential. The prerequisites (or attributes) represent that potential. There are three perfections and fourteen prerequisites. The first ten prerequisites are based directly on the Platonic tradition; and for these, Alemanno uses the phrase "Plato described it." In regard to the perfections, he states that "this was Plato's intention," since the discourse is based on the Platonic tradition without actually appearing textually in this specific form.

Alemanno designates the three perfections in these terms:

This was the intention of the divine Plato,[29] that the king should be perfect in all three kinds of perfections which are truly perfect. They are as follows: *[a]* the perfection of the intellectual virtue governing practical affairs of nations and the states; *[b]* the perfection of contemplation of what comes afterwards, which is the object of his existence; *[c]* the perfection of the knowledge of the Torah, which provides everlasting good in this world and in the world to come.[30]

This tripartite distinction partly appears in Ibn Rushd's introduction to the discourse on the virtues of the philosopher king at the beginning of the second treatise of his commentary. Alemanno's propositions are no more than an abbreviated paraphrase of Ibn Rushd's presentation, particularly in regard to the first perfection: "It is therefore evident that he will not succeed in this unless he is wise in practical science and possesses, along with it, intellectual virtue, through which those things are mastered that are explained in the practical science dealing with nations and city-states."[31] The third perfection is extended to the Torah of Israel. Alemanno takes Ibn Rushd's general statements on the philosopher king, who is also the first lawgiver *(meniah ha-torah)* and thus even a prophet, and applies them to his third perfection, a knowledge of the Torah. In other words, he adds a specialized perfection for the philosopher king in Israel, perfection in Torah, to the Platonic and Averroist perfections, perfection of the practical and of the rational intellect.

Paraphrasing Ibn Rushd but attributing the statements directly to Plato, Alemanno concludes: "That is why he said in his book on governance *(sifro ba-hanhagah)* that the terms king, philosopher, and lawgiver *(meniah ha-dat)* or priest *(cohen)* are synonymous,"[32] He adds: "This is also what the Torah indicates when it says 'he shall write him a copy of this law in a book . . . and he shall read therein all the days of his life' (Deut.17:19). For a king cannot become perfect in political and intellectual virtue unless he is also perfect in the divinely revealed Torah."[33]

In Alemanno's view, then, Plato did not attain the peak of philosophical perfection, because he did not know the Torah. His ideal constitution was inferior to that promulgated by Moses, since it was based on human and not divine intellect: "Plato described him by ten attributes, which include all the intellectual and practical perfections. The attributes of the Torah, however, were unknown to him."[34]

When Alemanno uses the terms "prerequisites" *(tena'im)* and "attributes" *(te'arim)*, the former directly follows the Hebrew translation of Ibn Rushd's commentary. There is an inner logic in Alemanno's use of the former expression as these are the prerequisites for attaining the three perfections. On the other hand, the use of "attributes" may reflect the influence of the theory of *imitatio Dei,* although Alemanno does not develop this idea here or connect it to the theory of the virtues of the philosopher king.

Alemanno first sets out the general conditions that appear in Ibn Rushd's commentary:

> The first, which is by nature the most important, is that he should be apt by nature to the theoretical sciences, which means that he should in his nature recognize what a thing is in its essence and distinguish it from what it is by accident.

> The second, that he should remember things and not forget them. For he who lacks these two qualities cannot possibly be taught anything, since he will always be under constant strain until he forsakes reading and study.

> The third is that he should love study, favor it, and desire to inquire into all parts of science. For he who ardently desires something aspires to all its varieties, as a man who is fond of wine craves all kinds of wine, and a man who desires women desires them all.

> The fourth is that he should love truth and hate falsehood. For he who loves the knowledge of reality as such loves truth.

At this point, Alemanno distinguishes these four prerequisites from the six others: "These four perfections relate to the theoretical intellect, while those that follow relate to the practical intellect." The first four prerequisites lead to the attainment of the second perfection in his list, that of the theoretical intellect—the ultimate human perfection. The six remaining prerequisites relate to the attainment of the first perfection in the list, the perfection of the practical intellect:

The fifth, that he should loathe sensual desires. For if one desires something excessively, then he will deflect his soul from other appetites. So it is with these, because they already incline with all their souls towards study.

The sixth, that he should not love money, for money is an object of desire, and desires are not proper for these men.

The seventh, that he should be high-minded. For he who desires knowledge of everything, of all that is, and does not want to limit his knowledge of things to that which elementary perception obliges him, is perfect in his actions and very high-minded indeed, so that nothing can be compared to his cognitive soul.

The eighth, that he should be courageous, because he who has no courage cannot reject the non-demonstrative arguments with which he grew up—especially one who has grown up in these states.

The ninth, that he should be so disposed that he move of his own accord towards everything which he considers good and beautiful, like justice and other such virtues. This is so when his appetitive soul has firm trust in ideas and knowledge.

The tenth, that he should be a good orator, his tongue leading him to express whatever is in his mind. He should also, at the same time, quickly light upon the middle road.[35]

Up to now Alemanno has set out the ten conditions for achieving the first two perfections, that of the rational intellect (1–4) and that of the practical intellect (5–10). The conditions are almost identical in numbering, order, content, and formulation to Samuel ben Judah's translation of Ibn Rushd. Alemanno simply subdivides them according to the first two perfections, each group constituting a condition for attaining a particular perfection.

Alemanno then proceeds to introduce his own addition, which connects the prerequisites to the Jewish tradition. He adds four special prerequisites for the philosopher king in Israel: those necessary for attaining the third perfection, that of Torah:

Whatever perfection and potential he has that is not derived from human nature, but which emanates from Him, is constituted by these:

That he should write a copy of Deuteronomy and always read it, and carry it on his arm like phylacteries.

That he should listen to the words of the priest who reads in the Urim and Thummim, as the verse says, (Num. 27:21) "and he should

stand before Elazar the Priest," since all the matters of the nation are
revealed to the king from what the priest says, after he judges in
accordance with the Urim and Thummim.

That he should listen to the prophet of his time. Saul was dethroned
only because he did not obey what the prophet Samuel said to him.

That he should be fond of the Divine Practices like the sacrifices and
prayers and building temples for the Lord God of Israel, as David
and Solomon and the righteous kings did, and many more activities
like these, as political, theoretical and prophetic wisdom may direct.[36]

Here Alemanno passes from the Platonic-Averroist philosopher king to
the King of Israel acting according to the laws of the Torah; in other words,
from the abstract philosophical plane to that of practical politics. Beyond perfection in theoretical and practical wisdom, the King of Israel must be perfect
in the Torah of Moses and fulfill all its commandments, especially those
specifically directed to the king. Only he who has satisfied these four conditions will attain the third perfection, that of Torah and prophecy, which even
Plato did not attain. Only the King of Israel is the truly ideal ruler. The extra
virtues of Torah fit well with the biblical tradition of the king's rights and
duties (Deut. 17:14–20) and with the halakhic discussion as reflected, for
example, in Maimonides' *Hilkhot Melakhim*.

Whereas Polkar attempted to combine the philosophical tradition of the
virtues of the philosopher king with the Jewish tradition by integrating philosophical and theological ideas, Alemanno did so by integrating philosophical
and halakhic concepts. This delicate undertaking drew him into contradiction.
Halakhically, the king is placed under the authority of the Torah; he must
respect and obey those who represent it, the prophet and high priest of his day.
The halakhic position expressly separates kingship, priesthood, and
prophecy;[37] whereas the philosophical position followed by Alemanno makes
the king himself simultaneously a philosopher, lawgiver, prophet, and even a
priest. How, then, can he obey the words of the priest and prophet of his day?
The version of Ibn Rushd that Alemanno takes as his basis does not in fact
obligate the philosopher king to be a prophet. By adopting this position, Alemanno could have escaped contradiction; however, he deliberately abandons it
and takes Al-Farabi's position without Maimonides' modification, and this
complicates matters for him.

Alemanno twice comments that the philosopher king is necessarily a
prophet. His perfection in learning the Torah is identified with the presence
of prophecy ("the Divine prophetic Torah"). The inner contradiction grows
still worse when, by mechanically following the misleading literal translation
of Ibn Rushd's commentary by Samuel ben Judah of Marseilles, Alemanno

imparts to the King of Israel not only prophecy but also priesthood. The problem arises from taking the word *imam* too concretely. Perhaps Alemanno should have dropped it, as Falaquera wisely did. Alemanno, however, attempts to evade the problem created by the proximity to the Muslim position by attributing the theory directly to Plato, who as a pagan was certainly unaware of biblical prophecy, biblical priesthood, and the giving of the law. Alemanno adds these features as a kind of Jewish-monotheistic tier to the pagan Platonic theory. But the pieces do not fit, as becomes evident when it appears that the philosopher king must obey the prophet-priest of his day himself.

Had Alemanno portrayed Moses alone as the perfect philosopher king, as Polkar did, the elements would have harmonized well. Moses was perceived in the halakhic tradition, and in medieval philosophy, to represent a combination that was unique in history, that of sage, king, first lawgiver, prophet, and priest. Alemanno, however, becomes enmeshed in contradiction when he applies these attributes not just to Moses and King Solomon, but also to the perfect King of Israel in general, a person who is not necessarily a priest, usually is not a philosopher or prophet, and is a lawgiver only in the limited sense of knowing the laws of the Torah. Alemanno avoids these difficulties elsewhere, as we shall see, when he ascribes the virtues of the philosopher king specifically to King Solomon, without making a direct connection to the halakhic tradition of the king's status.

Having described the fourteen qualifications of the philosopher-king-prophet in Israel, Alemanno now examines the extent to which the monarchy in Israel conformed to this ideal standard. His findings are extremely critical:

> When, however, the kings are examined in light of [the accounts] the ancients and of the Torah, almost none of them is found perfect in all of these attributes. Not only were the wicked kings of Israel and Judah not perfect, even the righteous among them were lacking, and even when they were not lacking they were not perfect to the ultimate degree. You can observe how King David sinned in terms of Bath Sheba, as illustrated by the episode of Uriah and Bath Sheba, as is thoroughly explained in his book. And also Saul and Solomon. None of them achieved their ultimate perfection, and most of them sinned against Him. And not only these students, but even the master of prophets and master of kings was found lacking, at the water of Meribah, and the leadership was taken away from him and given to Joshua his disciple. And he too did not achieve perfection, since he was remiss in transferring the land to the tribes, and this was the reason Israel learned from the gentiles that Joshua spared.[38]

The wicked kings of Judah and Israel obviously did not meet the standard; but, even kings who are thought to be just were guilty of sins and did not achieve all three perfections necessary in a philosopher king. Joshua, Saul, and David were all found wanting in "kingly perfection." The reference to Saul's sinning appeared in Alemanno's discussion of the third virtue of Torah, the obligation of the king to obey the prophet of his day. King Solomon, too, whom Alemanno portrays elsewhere as the prototype of the philosopher king, appears here as one who did not attain all the kingly perfections—despite the fact that in enunciating the fourth virtue of the Torah, Alemanno speaks favorably of "David and Solomon and the righteous kings" who loved the divine ways. Even Moses, presented here as the "master of prophets" and "master of kings," failed in his leadership at a critical juncture. Alemanno here follows Maimonides' *Eight Chapters*, 4. Unlike Polkar before him and his contemporary Abravanel, he does not present Moses as the one philosopher king perfect in all the virtues.

Alemanno's critical assessment of the great kings of Israel appears generally consistent with Maimonides' exposition in *Eight Chapters*, 7, on the moral vices of the prophets of Israel, some of whom, such as Moses, Samuel, David, and Solomon, functioned as rulers. From the start, Maimonides posited that absolute ethical perfection is not possible in this life; but he stipulated that these leaders achieved at least the major part of ethical perfection. Alemanno presents all the rulers of Israel in a highly critical fashion, without referring to mitigating circumstances. No one else adopted so critical a stance.

After criticizing the kings of Israel, Alemanno focuses on the one person who was capable of fulfilling all fourteen stipulations:

> In the end, the first and foremost among the rulers and kings who led in the righteous way was Abraham, who was the foremost in the perfection of governing *(shlemut ha-hanhagah)*. He is the one who led the whole world towards right beliefs, which by our day can be found everywhere. And all this he did in the same great loving-kindness and compassion by which he planted a tamarisk tree in Beer Sheba, and gave great benefits to all the people of the world in his days and afterwards, forever.[39]

In contrast to the received medieval tradition, which portrays Abraham as a philosopher and prophet, but not a king, Alemanno presents the Patriarch as the ideal king. In the aggadic sources, kingship was indeed attributed to Abraham, but Samuel b. Nahman in the fourth century argued that Abraham refused to accept kingship, on the grounds that there was forever only one true king. Other traditions held that Abraham agreed to undertake the kingship.[40] Neither the medieval philosophical nor the halakhic tradition voices this claim, however. Maimonides distinguished between Abraham, who tried to direct people as individuals to the right path by philosophical proofs, and exemplary acts of kindness rather than divine ordinances, and Moses, who was a "public prophet," undertaking a mission of a distinctly political nature. Abraham is clearly portrayed as a Socratic philosopher, Moses as a Platonic philosopher king.[41] Alemanno was apparently influenced by the tradition of the Sages, in holding that Abraham acted as a king in all matters. The application of the terms "in great loving-kindness and compassion" to Abraham's political leadership clearly hints at the Maimonidean theory of the political imitation of the Divine attributes. Alemanno presents Abraham as the first of the kings of Israel in time and the first in perfection, the prototype for any future philosopher king. As Abraham's antithesis, Alemanno holds up Nimrod, "who was the first one to rule the people not for the glory of God."[42] Thus, in keeping with Platonic tradition, the philosopher king stands opposite the prototype of the tyrant, here personified by Nimrod, Abraham's midrashic adversary.

7

Application

1

The third stage finds the theory of the philosopher king applied freely to the Hebrew sources and the developing needs of Jewish thought without any direct reference to Al-Farabi's or Ibn Rushd's versions. Examples are found in Joseph Albo, Abraham Shalom, Alemanno, and Don Isaac Abravanel, all of whom were active during the fifteenth century. With the passing of time, the approach gradually grew more distant from the classical sources. Inquiry became focused not on the virtues of the philosopher king in general, but on the immediate context of the perfect virtues of a particular ideal ruler—Moses, David, or Solomon.

Moses alone is considered a prophet-legislator (and even prophet-priest, according to certain traditions). In the case of the kings of Israel generally, but chiefly David and Solomon, the Farabian approach focuses on the philosopher king of subsequent generations: he who knows and applies the perfect law promulgated by the prophet-legislator. Therefore, only in the case of Moses is it possible to speak of absolute monarchy. All other cases assume a limited monarchy under the authority of the Torah and sharing the functions of government with other powers.

These definitions display a distinctly apologetic tone. They attempt to prove, in the unhappy circumstances of the Diaspora, that the great historical kings of Israel exemplified the ideal of the philosopher king consummately. These rulers alone, therefore, created and maintained the ideal state.

This, of course, is a purely mythical view of Jewish history. The kings of Israel are portrayed not as they were in reality, but as paragons and ideal rulers. This mythical view permeated accounts of the kingship of Solomon in particular. It was rather more difficult to disregard the sins of David, who was punished for them by being prevented from building the Temple. One of the usual ways of solving the David problem, both in Jewish and Christian thought, was to emphasize the figure of the righteous composer of the book of Psalms and to avoid the descriptions of the temporal leader found in the books of Samuel. It was even possible to point to the shortcomings in the political leadership of Moses, specifically his anger at the waters of Meribah and his consequent debarment from the promised land. The image of Solomon's kingship as the zenith of the ancient Jewish state was so powerful, however, and so well-reinforced in medieval culture—Jewish, Christian, and Muslim alike—that the royal blemishes were overlooked. Even the shrewd Machiavelli accepted the myth of the blissful kingship of Solomon and, as was common, laid the blame for the dissolution of the kingdom at the door of Rehoboam, although the biblical text is distinctly ambivalent on the subject. Neither the plethora of Solomon's gentile wives, and the resulting increase in idolatry, nor the mutterings of the people against the burden of taxes could compete with the image of the perfect philosopher king created by the dream at Gibeon and the rendezvous with the Queen of Sheba. These events, along with the attribution of the three Wisdom books to this king, cast a potent spell on the historical imagination.

No sins could outweigh the fact that Solomon won the honor of building the first Temple. In the end, for all his sins and all the admonitions he received, Solomon died peacefully in his bed after a reign of forty years. It was not he who was punished, but his progeny. (By contrast, Moses and David were punished personally for their sins.) None of his political injustices could sully the name of the Kingdom of Solomon, whose ruler was the wisest of men. Under his reign Israel and Judah, not yet divided, dwelt in safety, each man under his own vine and under his fig tree, as the idyllic description of 1 Kings 5 has it. In that chapter even Plato might have identified the ideal state he longed for.

The astute yet ambivalent view of the Sages regarding Solomon gave way almost entirely to a mythical, stereotypical vision. Distance in time and the pressing need for apologia intensified this effect. For this reason, only one of the philosophers we shall consider shows the slightest historical realism about Solomon. The more problematic passages in 1 Kings and the Sages' critical remarks about Solomon are practically ignored, and, when any of these matters are referred to, a thousand and one explanations are sought to justify Solomon's doings. Maimonides, wishing to describe the degree of wisdom of the king-Messiah in the introduction to *Perek Helek*, compares him to Solomon. Nowhere does Maimonides mention Solomon's sins, although he does consider the prohibitions imposed upon the king in *Hilkhot Melakhim*. The *Eight Chapters*, chapter 7, does note that Solomon harbored moral vices—exaggerated appetites as reflected in his large number of wives (see

Guide II:28). For that reason Solomon earned a lower rank in prophecy than Moses, who himself erred. Both figures are excused under the premise that no person, being created of matter, can attain more than a majority of the moral perfections. Solomon is clearly portrayed here as having more than most. Perhaps following this exposition by Maimonides, Alemanno was bold enough to include not only Solomon but also Moses himself among those kings who sinned and did not attain kingly perfection. Subsequently, though, Solomon was presented by Alemanno, as was usual in his time, as the prototype of the philosopher king, perfect in all the virtues.

Against this background, let us now turn to the inquiry into the subject. Our examples are not necessarily in chronological order but are arranged by degree of proximity to the classical form of the discourse on the question.

2

Abravanel applied the theory of the philosopher king to three rulers of Israel: Moses, David, and Solomon. The discussion of Moses as the ideal philosopher king appears in his commentary on the portion Jethro (Exod. 18). The main question that Abravanel raises here is, why was the Torah given to Moses and not to Adam, Noah, or one of the patriarchs? Of the three reasons adduced, the second relates to the perfection of Moses. The Torah was given when it was, precisely because only then did there exist "the messenger *(shaliah)* and intermediary *(emtzai)* who was the most appropriate to be crowned with all the crowns of the virtues *(ma'alot)* and perfections *(shlemuiot)* over all mankind. There was no one in the human species like Moses our master."[1]

This characterization of Moses as the supreme realization of human potential, unique in history, is expressed in the ten virtues ascribed to him, which are found in no other man. In citing ten virtues Abravanel follows the Averroist model. But in listing physical perfection first among these virtues he recalls the Farabian model. This duality shows how detached Abravanel's exposition was from the classical models. Polkar first enumerated twelve virtues according to Al-Farabi (and added a thirteenth) and only then adapted the perfection of Moses to them. Abravanel named the ten virtues of Moses directly, including all the components found in Al-Farabi's version—bodily, moral, and intellectual perfection. These appear, however, in greatly diminished fashion, while the new components, relating to Moses' perfection in prophecy and his role in the leadership of the people of Israel, assume a central place.

Accordingly, Polkar preferred to designate Moses "king," despite his being a prophet and philosopher as well, while Abravanel chose the title "prophet and messenger." Moses' prophetic role, not his kingship, acquires the central place, in keeping with Abravanel's skepticism regarding the institution of monarchy.[2] This emphasis on Moses' prophetic role does not necessarily deviate from the classical model, which views king, philosopher, and prophet synonymously. But in the classical tradition, moral and intellectual perfection necessarily lead to prophetic perfection, and the prophet is simply a fulfilled or advanced philosopher. Abravanel had serious doubts about this tradition, which was absorbed into Jewish thought through Maimonides, albeit with some reservations. In Abravanel's view, the philosopher and the prophet are two different beings entirely, and there is no necessary connection between them.[3] Moses was not a prophet because he was a philosopher, as the Farabian tradition would assume. On the contrary, Moses was unique in his theoretical knowledge precisely because he was unique in his degree of prophecy. It was not his philosophical perfection that brought him to prophecy; it was his prophetic perfection that gave him rational perfection and made him the most perfect of men, in whom the Aristotelian goal of the human species was realized exclusively.

The structure of Abravanel's inquiry into each of Moses' ten virtues is reminiscent of Polkar's discourse, although Abravanel, as usual, is far wordier. Abravanel first notes a virtue and then presents examples and proofs of it from the Torah (some of which are found in Polkar), as follows:

1. "The first one, in his body, his disposition and his nature, his limbs and organs." Moses' bodily perfection (the balance of the four humors) is manifested in many examples that Abravanel produces from various periods of Moses' life, beginning with the circumstances surrounding his birth, proceeding to his youth, continuing to the climactic period of the giving of the Torah on Mount Sinai, and ending with his death. Regarding Moses' birth, Abravanel quotes the verse "And when she saw him that he was a goodly child" (Exod. 2:2), and the midrash that Moses was born circumcised, meaning "separated from the material things and the lust for the material things." Abravanel finds expression of Moses' bodily perfection in the episode of the giving of the Torah, in that Moses was able to survive for a length of time without bodily activity. Moses, according to Abravanel, thus rose to the point where he behaved as heavenly bodies do. For this reason the skin of his face shone. As for his declining days, the proof of his perfection is his longevity and good health: "His eye was not dim nor his natural force abated" (Deut. 34:7). There was also the special circumstance of his death: unlike other men, who are born of earth and returned to it, Moses' grave is unknown.

2. "The second was his moral virtue, by which [I mean] he was easily satisfied and distanced himself from material things." Moses' moral perfection

is expressed in this virtue alone. His sojourn on the mountain for so long a time without performing any bodily activity, neither eating nor sleeping, accustomed him to requiring little throughout his life. This condition is reflected in his celibacy after becoming a prophet, and in the fact that although he grew up in a palace he was not proud or discriminatory. He defended both his oppressed brothers in Egypt and Jethro's daughters. He was without jealousy or the lust for glory—"Now the man Moses was very meek, above all the men that were upon the face of the earth" (Num. 12:3)—a feature that in Abravanel's opinion was well illustrated by Moses' behavior in regard to the prophesying of Eldad and Medad.

3. "The third virtue and perfection was in his knowledge and wisdom, which he acquired through his prophecy. He acquired [knowledge of] the nature of all things, the highest and the lowest. He comprehended and knew the first, all-inclusive creation. . . ." Compared with the other prophets, whose prophecy was expressed in foretelling the future and reproving the people, Moses' prophecy was on an entirely different plane, that of intellectual perfection and, to the extent humanly possible, unity with the active intellect.

4. "The fourth virtue and perfection [was] that he was always ready to prophesy, while all the other prophets were not." This was a function of his moral perfection and his complete ascendancy over material life, to the point where nothing remained to hinder his continuous receptivity to revelation.

5. "The fifth virtue and perfection found in Moses our master, of blessed memory, was that he saved, rescued, and delivered Israel from Egyptian exile, and won their wars. Such actions cannot be found in any other prophet." Here Moses' prophetic perfection combines with his political and military leadership of the people of Israel. Other prophets foretold the exile and the redemption, but Moses actually redeemed Israel, both by miraculous acts, signs, and wonders and by active political and military leadership. According to the list of virtues cited by Al-Farabi, physical perfection is meant to foster the military functions of the philosopher king, which is the reason Moses is depicted as possessing bodily perfection.

6. "The sixth perfection was that all the virtues of the nation and its leaders were combined in Moses our master, of blessed memory." Abravanel briefly describes the operational structure of the Israelite government, in which Moses officiated at different periods in all the political and juridical frameworks. At first he sat in the minor courts; according to the text, "Moses sat to judge the people . . . from the morning unto the evening" (Exod. 18:13). After accepting Jethro's counsel, Moses served as head of the great court and as head of the Sanhedrin; according to the text, "The

hard causes they brought to Moses" (ibid. 18:26). Moses also reigned as king; according to the text, "And there was a king in Jeshurun" (Deut. 33:5). The Midrash (*Va-Yikrah Rabba*, 25) has it that Moses was also a priest who officiated in the high priesthood, and in contrast to his brother Aaron, the high priest, Moses could enter the Holy of Holies at all times, not just on Yom Kippur. Finally, Moses was the master of the prophets. Thus, ". . . all the appointments and all the virtues of the nation came together in him. Among the other prophets, none was [also] king and judge, but for the prophet Samuel."

On the surface, the Farabian perception of the philosopher-king-prophet-priest conjunction is again expressed here. However, according to the hierarchical order in which Abravanel cites the different positions held by Moses, it is clear that there is no strict union of the roles. Moses officiated in different roles at different times, not concurrently. Moreover, the roles have different weights and are presented according to a distinct hierarchy, from the less to the more important, from the material to the spiritual: judge, head of Sanhedrin, king, priest, and prophet. As Moses grew older, he rose not only in degree of perfection, but also in the importance of the roles he assumed. This process reflects the course of Moses' "professional" training for the leadership of the people of Israel in the critical period of its political and spiritual crystallization. In this respect Abravanel follows the halakhic stance in principle, distinguishing clearly between the Three Crowns of Torah, priesthood, and kingship. He consistently avoids attributing these three functions simultaneously to any one figure, not even to Moses—despite the fact that both in halakhic and philosophical thought it was common to do so—on account of the unique nature of Moses' virtue.[4] In taking this view, Abravanel forges a kind of intermediate position. From his viewpoint, Moses did indeed hold all three posts, yet the sharp distinction that he draws between kingship and prophecy does not permit the simultaneous exercise of these roles.

7. "The seventh virtue and perfection is the truthfulness and justice informing Moses' prophecy. This was not the case with the other prophets." The prophecy of the other prophets was expressed in fables and riddles, and therefore the language they used necessarily contained imaginative elements with equivocal meanings. Moses' prophecy, by contrast, was always straightforward in style, its meaning plain, and therefore there was never any danger of spurious images in it.

8. "The eighth virtue and perfection was in [the nature of] the prophecy of Moses our master, who did not use the imaginative faculty in order to prophesy. . . . [T]he prophetic spirit and emanation which reached him applied to his intellect only, in the highest possible degree, without any

association with the imaginative [faculty] as it was with the other prophets." Unlike these others, Moses alone acquired the emanation of the divine overflow into his intellectual soul, and therefore could speak truly without imaginative ornamentation.

9. "The ninth virtue and perfection was that Moses our master was the cause, the source, and the fountain from which the prophecy of all the other prophets originated." Just as the active intellect receives its emanation from the first cause without any intermediaries, and emanates on the disembodied intellects, so Moses received the prophetic emanation directly from the first cause, and from it inspired the other prophets. Their prophecies could not have existed without the constant emanation of prophecy from Moses.

10. "The tenth virtue and perfection, is the Lord's. It is that Moses our master did not receive his prophecy from the active intellect nor through the mediation of one of the disembodied [intellects], as was the case with the other prophets. Rather, the immediate emanating power which caused his prophecy was the First Cause, blessed be He, without any mediating power . . ." Abravanel provides a wealth of instances from the Torah of the direct contact between God and Moses, the likes of which no prophet who came after him experienced.[5]

Moses' ten virtues fall into several groups: physical perfection (no. 1), moral perfection (no. 2), and prophetic perfection (nos. 3–10). Several virtues in the last group have bearing on other spheres: the third is relevant to intellectual perfection, the fifth to military leadership, the sixth to juridical and political acumen. The remainder (nos. 4, 7–10), or half the total, relate solely to Moses' prophetic perfection.

The overwhelming emphasis on Moses' prophetic perfection clearly conforms with Abravanel's perception of prophecy. Unlike Maimonides, he regards prophecy as a distinctly suprarational, apolitical manifestation. For this reason, he tends to reduce to a minimum the implications of Moses' prophetic perfection for philosophical and political perfection. As we have seen, Moses' juridical and political roles are not conceived as parallel to his prophetic role, but are demonstrably separate from, and inferior to, it.[6]

Abravanel concludes the discourse as follows:

Thus it became clear from all this, how many good and perfect virtues were found in Moses our master. This is the reason that it was appropriate that the Torah be given by him and through him and be named after him, as it is said: "Moses commanded us a law" [Deut. 33:4] and "we should remember Moses' law" [Mal. 3:22]. And this is the second reason that the Torah was given at this particular time.[7]

3

Abravanel applies the tradition of the philosopher king's virtues to Solomon in his commentary on King Solomon's dream at Gibeon and God's message to him—"I have given thee a wise and an understanding heart, so that there hath been none like thee before thee, neither after thee shall any arise like unto thee" (1 Kings 3:12).[8] In the case of Moses, Abravanel took as his starting point the traditional idea of Moses as master of the prophets. With Solomon the traditional idea is that this king was the wisest of men—that is, the greatest among the philosophers. Abravanel cites the long-standing tradition of Solomon's stature as the greatest of the sages in the Jewish, Muslim, and Christian cultures.[9]

As is usual in his biblical commentaries, Abravanel opens with a question, here about the meaning of the verse in Kings quoted above. The verse is difficult, in his view, from the standpoint of Solomon's status relative both to the philosophers who preceded and succeeded him, and to other prophets. Regarding the philosophers, it cannot be assumed that there will be no one wiser than Solomon in the future, because human knowledge undergoes continual development. Regarding the prophets, the divine message is problematic because it suggests that Solomon's prophecy was superior to that of Moses, an obvious contradiction to the text of the Torah. To clarify the quality of Solomon's wisdom and to solve the problem about his standing as a prophet, Abravanel examines three issues: first, how Solomon's mode of apprehension differs from that of the other philosophers; second, how the content of his knowledge differs from theirs; and third, how his wisdom differs from that of other prophets.[10]

As to Solomon's mode of apprehension, Abravanel argues that Solomon, like Moses, differed from others in the manner of cognition. In the struggle for knowledge, most people must pass through all the natural stages from sense perception to grasping the intelligibles. Specifically, they must contend with five natural obstacles facing anyone undergoing this process. The first obstacle is labor: the need for effort in order to attain the truth. The second is the time factor: the process is prolonged and consumes much time; therefore wisdom is associated with old age. The third obstacle is grossness: the more material and gross the objects of knowledge, the easier they are to attain; the more abstract they are, the harder they are to attain. The fourth is the limitations of our apprehension, that is, the innate limitations that preclude our knowing the causes of things in their entirety. The fifth is the tendency to err in our conclusions, owing to the natural limitations of human knowledge, which is dependent on sense perceptions.[11] These five obstacles prevent the average human being from attaining knowledge naturally. Solomon's intellectual perfection, however, like that of Moses, was not the outcome of a natural process but the product of a miraculous event—the direct flow of the divine emanation into the intellectual soul. Solomon's quest for knowledge was not blocked by these five obstacles. He attained intellectual perfection immediately and absolutely.[12] This, in Abravanel's opinion, solves the problem of how it is possible for Solomon to be wiser than all who preceded him and all who will follow him. Cognition is indeed a cumulative process of acquiring knowledge, but only for someone who undergoes it naturally. This is not the case for someone who gains knowledge through a miracle.

Second, the content of Solomon's wisdom differs from that of all other sages. A difference in the cognitive process necessarily dictates a difference in the content of the knowledge. Abravanel isolates five areas of knowledge. The first is of the gross material world of momentary, perishable things. The second is knowledge of the intermediate world of heavenly bodies. The third is knowledge of the superior, spiritual world of the separate intellects. The fourth is knowledge of the practical intellect. The fifth is knowledge of the divine Torah.[13] This division of sciences follows Al-Farabi's model as presented in its Hebrew version in Falaquera's *The Beginning of Wisdom*. These five areas coalesce into three areas of perfect knowledge: theoretical knowledge (physics and mathematics, 1–3); practical knowledge (ethics, economics, and politics, 4); and knowledge of the Torah, its commandments, its mysteries, the act of Creation, and the act of the chariot (5).

Solomon's perfection in theoretical knowledge is manifested in his being a philosopher and stems, in Abravanel's view, from this king's prophetic perfection. His perfection in practical knowledge relates to his perfection as a king, while his knowledge of the divine Torah is based on his prophetic perfection. Once again, we find an expression of Abravanel's desire to distinguish prophecy from politics, even when the two spheres of activity are combined in one person. Usually, he notes, one man cannot be perfect in both the practical and the theoretical spheres, on account of the five obstacles listed above.[14] Solomon, however, having attained perfection in wisdom in a supernatural way, was unique in combining theoretical and practical perfection.

Solomon's perfection in practical intellect is presented in accordance with the tripartite Aristotelian division: ethics (governance of self), economics (governance of the household), and politics (governance of the state):

This is [manifest in] the way he conducted himself intelligently and virtuously in his traits and his actions—whether in the wisdom of ethics, or in the way one leads his household, the wife and the children and the servants, which is the knowledge of the governance of the house, or the way in which he led the affairs of kings in righteousness and judgment and good order, which is knowledge of the governance of the state.[15]

Solomon's moral perfection *(hanhagat 'atsmo)* is reflected, according to Abravanel, in his authorship of the book of Proverbs, which expresses the tenets of ethics. All the nations of the Earth that came to hear the wisdom of Solomon came to learn ethics from him. His perfection in economics *(hanhagat ha-bayit)* is reflected in the way he managed the economics of the state. He was able to support the requirements of the king's house and the various levels of the administration by means of the taxes he collected from the inhabitants of the land. These taxes were collected fairly and in consideration of the needs of his subjects to provide for their own wants. Abravanel presents Solomon as the antithesis of despotic kings whose wealth is founded on plunder. As a just king, Solomon gains his riches by sophisticated management of the affairs of state and by the creation of additional sources of revenue besides direct taxation. These sources, such as the development of international maritime trade (the dispatch of ships to carry gold from Tarshish and Ofir), enabled Solomon to enlarge his treasury without increasing the burden of taxation on his subjects.

Abravanel lays stress on Solomon's wealth, his amassing of silver and gold vessels, and the maintenance of a vast number of horses and riders. This accumulation, though, contravenes the message of the Torah (Deut. 17:15–17), and Abravanel is forced to rationalize it by contending that although it was not for the purpose of war, since the era was one of peace, it constituted a legitimate expression of the glory and majesty of the king: "In the multitude of the people is the king's glory" (Prov. 14:28).[16] Abravanel seems to draw upon his close acquaintance with the economic policies of the rulers of his day and his experience as a political and economic adviser to rulers in Spain, Portugal, and Italy.[17]

Solomon's perfection in politics *(hanhagat ha-medinah)* includes all things "unique to the king as king." The first is his perfection as a judge, which is essential for his political perfection, as the verse says, "And as for princes, they shall rule in justice" (Isaiah 32:1).[18] In this context, Abravanel draws the familiar Platonic medical analogy, presenting Solomon as a physician to the soul. Solomon's profound psychological insight is compared to the wise physician's understanding of the invisible operation of the internal organs. This perfection is clearly manifested in Solomon's role as a judge. Second, Solomon's political perfection is reflected in the eminent position that his kingdom held internationally, characterized by prevailing peace, "since this is the final purpose of the governance of a kingdom." A third manifestation of Solomon's political perfection are his economic accomplishments: his enormous personal wealth and the wealth of his courtiers. Fourth and last Solomon's magnificent architectural enterprises are crowned by the building of the Temple.

Thus, all the perfections—of philosophy, of Torah, and of politics—meet in Solomon as philosopher king. As noted by Al-Farabi and later Falaquera, these attributes are rarely found together in one person:

Since it is impossible to find the perfection of these modes of governance *(hanhagot)* conjoined and complete in one human being, He, blessed be He, said to him: "I have given thee a wise and an understanding heart; so that there hath been none like thee before thee, neither after thee shall any arise like unto thee." "Wisdom" relates to theoretical knowledge and "understanding," to practical [knowledge].[19]

To solve the third problem, of how Solomon's wisdom was distinct from that of the other prophets, Abravanel first lists seven categories of prophecy, according to content as follows:

Those whose emanation would lead them and cause them to be perfected for their own sake only, and not in order to convey the message of the Lord, blessed be He.

Those whose emanation would suffice to allow them to teach men and lead them.

And those whose emanation would suffice to allow them to reproach those who sin in their soul.

And those whose emanation would suffice to allow them to tell what would happen in the end of days.

And those whose emanation would suffice to allow them to work miracles and wonders.

And those whose emanation would suffice to allow them to praise and extol the Lord, blessed be He.

And there was also he whose emanation would suffice or allow him to apprehend a great measure in wisdom and science and the knowledge of things as they really are, and his interest in other things is diminished.[20]

Each prophet received divine emanation in a way that marked him for one specific degree of prophecy. Moses' prophecy, however, was different from that of all the other prophets in that it arose from direct contact with the divinity, with no material barriers. The patriarchs represented the first degree of prophecy (see *Guide* II:39; III:51); Jeremiah and Isaac, the third; Balaam and Daniel, the fourth; Elisha, the fifth; and David, the sixth. Moses does not belong in any of these areas. His prophecy was unique. Abravanel offers no examples of the second category, even though it, more than any other, relates to the political obligations of the prophet. Perhaps the omission was deliberate, an attempt to emphasize his position that prophecy is essentially supra-political.

Solomon alone among all the prophets exemplified the seventh degree. The divine emanation distinguished him in wisdom. Applying the verse in the dream at Gibeon, "I have given thee a wise and understanding heart," Abravanel writes: "And this was the case with Solomon, upon whom the prophetic spirit descended in order to perfect him in wisdom and understanding as much as possible, and not in anything else."[21]

Solomon's uniqueness manifested itself in the specialized areas of wisdom in which he alone excelled: physics, astronomy, astrology, and particularly political theory. These areas, however, were not essential, or even relevant, to his prophecy: "Even if we agree that the prophets' degree of wisdom was correlated to their degree of prophecy, still it is not appropriate to relate it to the particular areas of knowledge in which Solomon perfected himself, the sciences of economics *(yediat ha-bayit)* and politics *(Yediat ha-medinah)*, since these were remote from the concerns of prophecy."[22] But Solomon's perfection in the discipline of politics *was* relevant to his perfection as king. Here the equation philosopher-king-prophet indeed holds.

Abravanel's basic world view, is essentially antimonarchist. He believes that monarchy by its nature is bound to decline into tyranny (see his commentary on Deut. 17 and 1 Samuel 8). Therefore, he prefers a mixed "republican" regime with a theocratic stamp and tends to separate prophecy from politics.[23] Although he seems to be making use of the original Platonic structure in his discourse on the class system, as we have noted, Abravanel ultimately draws a sharp distinction between ruler and philosopher, and places them in different classes. How then can he apply the philosopher-king-prophet theory, which entails the fusion of prophecy and politics? This hybridization is possible only when the king is identified as a being who has attained both rational and moral perfection through the direct effect of divine emanation. Supernatural perfection ensures that the philosopher king will never descend to tyranny. Only a miraculous process can create the perfect man and, hence, the ideal ruler. In the merely normal course of nature, however, monarchy will necessarily turn into tyranny. Thus, the division of powers is preferable in natural conditions, as is a mixed "republican" government under the supervision of the prophetic power. The combined identity of philosopher, king, and prophet is feasible only with the aid of supernatural intervention.[24]

4

A second example of the free application of the idea of the philosopher king to King Solomon is to be found in the introduction that Alemanno added to *The Passion of Solomon (Heshek Shelomo)*, an allegorical interpretation of the

Song of Songs with mystical overtones. Since the biblical book is attributed to Solomon, Alemanno devotes a lengthy introduction, "The Song of Solomon's Ascents" *(Shir ha-ma'alot li-Shelomo)*, to an extensive inquiry into Solomon's virtues—seventeen in all, the largest number of virtues ascribed to a philosopher king.[25] Alemanno presents King Solomon as the prototype of the ideal philosopher king, an image that was revived at Marsilio Ficino's academy. Alemanno is the only philosopher to present two separate discussions of the philosopher-king's virtues, each belonging to a different stage of the discourse on the subject. In his *Hai ha-Olamim (Eternal Life)* his argument, as we have seen, follows Ibn Rushd's approach, and actually criticizes Solomon, portraying the patriarch Abraham, rather than Solomon, as the philosopher king. In *The Passion of Solomon*, by contrast, he pointedly applies the theory of the philosopher king to King Solomon, his aim being to prove to the humanists of his day that the Jews anticipated Plato with this concept,[26] and that their history contains the perfect manifestation of this figure. If scholars such as Ficino found the highest manifestation of the image of the philosopher king in a contemporary ruler, Lorenzo di Medici, Alemanno found it in the Golden Age of Israel in antiquity, in the wisest of men.[27] Alemanno described the stages of human ascent toward perfection in general in *Eternal Life*, while The "The Song of Solomon's Ascents" finds the peak of this perfection in King Solomon, as follows:

> For there I intended to describe a man of sound views, fulfilled in his own world, surrounded with all wonderful and desirable things, with all the most refined virtues of men of character, and crowned by all the many powerful forms of wisdom, who yet cared for none of these, nor sought them as his first perfection, since his soul desired only to cleave unto the revered and awesome Lord, as we find in King Solomon, who desired this ultimate bliss more than any riches, honor, authority, wisdom or science.[28]

In discussing the king's virtues, Alemanno relates most of them only to the political, and not the philosophical context. They include "the kingly virtues *(middot malhiyot)* appropriate to the rulers of states."[29] He also makes it plain that he is referring to the philosopher king parallelism—"the perfection which is appropriate to kings and wise men and rulers of the land."[30] Further, he links his exposition directly to the theory of the ideal Platonic state, "the philosophical state *(ha-medinah ha-filosofit)* whose people are all wise, all understanding, all knowledgeable of the law *(mishpat)*."[31]

This political emphasis is clearly reflected in the way Alemanno interprets Solomon's dream at Gibeon. If Abravanel took "a wise and understanding heart" as a reference to the general perfection of wisdom, theoretical, and practical, Alemanno imparts to this wisdom a limited political sense as perfection of the practical intellect alone—the ability to lead the people and to judge them justly. According to his interpretation, Solomon did not request intellectual perfection, since he realized that this was impossible. At a young age he had said: "And I am but a little child; I know not how to go out or come in" (1 Kings 3, 7). Nor did he seek material perfection, "since it is good for man as man but not as king." These were to be eschewed all the more since he reigned over the chosen people, who were wiser than all other peoples and knew well that there was a perfection superior to material perfection. The perfection he desired (as king) was legal perfection, even when it concerned the chosen people, who had already received the ideal law. The association of a large number of people living together would inevitably generate internal tensions, making it necessary for the ruler to be an expert in the law and to possess highly developed juridical skills so as to rule properly: "The [very fact of] association *(kibbutz)* causes many disputes and quarrels among them. . . . This is why I understood that if I did not know how to deal with wisdom, insight, and understanding and every intellectual skill with these judgments *(mishpatim)* and laws *(hukim)* and decrees *(torot)*, I would not be able to perform as king."[32] Applying Al-Farabi's terminology, we see Solomon depicted here as a philosopher king of the second generation. He is not the giver of the law but the one who understands the ideal law given by Moses and is capable of administering it perfectly.[33]

Alemanno selects the term "degrees" *(ma'alot)* to designate the virtues of Solomon as philosopher king. This term may convey a double connotation here: the sense of promotion in rank—he who wishes to reach the supreme perfection must rise through the ranks of the various perfections until he attains it; and the usual sense of virtue. Both possibilities exist without mutual contradiction.[34]

Alemanno, as already mentioned, posits the largest number of virtues for a ruler encountered in the literature so far—seventeen. Twelve of them match the classical division of categories of good—external, physical, and spiritual—and the secondary categories stemming from them.[35] Generally, the exposition parallels the medieval discussion of the virtues of the philosopher king. However, in applying the virtues of the philosopher king to Solomon, Alemanno does not adhere precisely either to Ibn Rushd's model, which he has used elsewhere, or to Al-Farabi's model, with which he was most probably acquainted, too.[36] On the basis of the classical tradition of the classification of the virtues in general, and of the philosopher king's virtues in particular, Alemanno constructs his own variation on the theme. It is the only case in which an entire work—almost three hundred printed pages!—is structurally based on the theory of the virtues of the philosopher king.

Alemanno added a fourth area to the classical triple division of physical, external, and spiritual categories of good. He defines four classes of virtues:

internal physical good, external physical good, internal spiritual good, and external spiritual good. Each of these in turn has four subclasses, making a total of sixteen types. At the apex of the pyramid of virtues is the "human spirit": whoever attains this gains immortality of the soul. Providing no more than a token explanation for determining these seventeen virtues, Alemanno mentions that in numerology, seventeen is an acronym for the Hebrew word "good" *(tov)*, which describes each of the virtues.[37]

Internal physical good concerns perfection of the body and includes four subclasses: beauty, health, strength, and long life. External physical good includes: wealth, honor, noble ancestry, and companions and supporters. Internal spiritual good is the perfection of practical and theoretical intelligence and includes: intelligence, self-control, fortitude, and justice (each of these having a further subdivision of its own). External spiritual good, with its four subclasses, has a clearly mystical Kabbalistic character of suprarational perfection that leads to adherence to God and immortality of the soul.

After enumerating all seventeen classes of virtue, Alemanno moves on to a detailed discussion applying each virtue to King Solomon. As noted above, many of the subclasses, particularly those relating to physical perfection (internal physical good), property (external physical good), and perfection of the practical and theoretical intelligence (internal spiritual good), are applied not only to Solomon's perfections as a man, but also to his perfections as a king. This expression of the philosopher-king equation is then linked to a description of prophecy as the highest stage of human excellence (external spiritual good),[38] creating the classical definition of philosopher-king-prophet: the man who is perfect in all the virtues is also the perfect ruler.

5

Alemanno and Abravanel display strong influences of the Platonic tradition as freely applied to the Hebrew sources. By contrast, the last two examples we shall discuss, Shalom and Albo, discuss the ideal ruler's virtues in a distinctively Jewish context, with only faint echoes of the classic philosophic tradition. Their approach aims to articulate a traditional Jewish view of the ideal ruler's virtues. Its emergence in fifteenth-century Spain reflects the influence of the milieu in which Jewish philosophy, being attacked by Jewish conservatives as the putative cause of all the tribulations that Spanish Jewry was undergoing, became defensive. Many thinkers adopted a less rationalistic approach in the face of these attacks, as reflected in their treatment of the theory of the ideal ruler.

Abraham Shalom's *Abode of Peace (Neveh Shalom)*, written toward the end of the fifteenth century, is a collection of philosophical homilies based on passages from the first tractate of the Talmud, *Berachot*. Shalom's aim is to illuminate the philosophical and allegorical significance inherent in the writings of the sages, based on the Maimonidean rationalist tradition.[39]

Shalom's major excursion into political theory and his specific consideration of the ideal ruler's virtues in *Abode of Peace* are included in an extensive allegorical commentary on the precept of Rabbi Yohanan: "A man should always exert himself and run to meet an Israelite King; and not only a King of Israel but also a King of any other nation."[40] As was his custom, Shalom uses a statement by the sages as the starting point for a lengthy homiletic and philosophical discourse, which occasionally flows from one subject to another in associative fashion.[41]

Shalom takes as his starting point the assumption, drawn directly from Maimonides, that man is a political animal by nature—"humans are forced by nature to be political *(medini ba-tevah)* and to associate with their kind."[42] For this purpose, an orderly social framework must exist, but it cannot exist without rightful government, "for 'when a wicked man reigns a people sighs' [Prov. 29:1] because his deficiency will spread to the whole nation. When a perfect king arises, however, he will lead the land with justice."[43] Shalom assumes that the proper form of government is monarchy. Yet, when Rabbi Yohanan says: "A man should always exert himself and run to meet an Israelite king," the intention is not, according to Shalom, that he should become personally involved with kings—Shemaya had said: "Do not make yourself known to the government" *(Avot* 1:10)—but rather that he should ascertain if a king is good or bad. The reference, Shalom believed, was not only to the kings of Israel, but also to the kings of the gentile nations as well.

Shalom does not present the criteria of kingly perfection as objective absolutes. Rather, they are dependent on the nature of the people and the laws of the state over which a king reigns. A good king, Shalom stresses, is not an absolute but a constitutional monarch. The king must obey the authority of the law:

> The difference between one people *(am)* and another necessitates a difference between one king and another. For the perfection *(shlemut)* of the king is dependent upon the perfection of the law *(dat)*. Thus, the king's degree is correlated with that of the law. This is so, since it is appropriate for the king to obey the law. And the law is what greatly differentiates peoples, since every people follows the path of its own law and God.[44]

For Shalom, this assumption is the basis of an attempt to prove the superiority of a King of Israel over kings of the other nations of the world. Since the former is ruler over the chosen among the nations, the people who received the divine law, he will necessarily be different from any other king:

And since Israel is the chosen people, and they received the Divine law *(torah elohit)*, it is appropriate that their king be the most perfect possible among the kings of all nations. For his perfection is dependent upon the Torah, and the Torah is perfect. Consequently, the king will also be perfect.[45]

Most of the thinkers we have dealt with set forth a set of criteria of the Platonic kind for the ideal king and tested different kings by this measure. Invariably, their conclusion was that only the kings of Israel met this ideal standard, although not all of them did so to the same degree. Shalom, by contrast, established from the outset different criteria for the kings of the world, who ruled according to varying legal systems. The criteria for the kings of Israel differ from those for the kings of the gentile nations. The result, however, is still the same: the superiority of the great historical kings of Israel:

Thus, whoever knows the difference between the kings of Israel and the gentile kings also knows the difference between the king of the soul's faculties and the king of the body's faculties. And this is of utmost importance, since the perfection of man and his ultimate bliss are dependent upon this. This is why it was commanded to watch the [performance of the] kings, since from this the governance of their soul and the governance of their body would be differentiated from each other, and one would honor [only] the true king.[46]

Shalom's discussion of the virtues of the ideal ruler relates only to the King of Israel. He sets out two parallel lists of virtues. The first contains four virtues, elicited from an allegorical interpretation of a statement by Jeremiah. The second specifies twelve virtues on the basis of the first list which are then applied to what the Torah says about the conditions for kingship (Deut. 17). In both cases, Shalom designates the virtues as "attributes" *(te'arim)* and explicitly relates his presentation to the theory of *imitatio Dei*, although, surprisingly, he signifies only twelve attributes, not thirteen as Polkar did.

The first list is based on Jeremiah's statement, "In those days, and at that time, I will cause a shoot of righteousness to grow up unto David; and he shall execute justice and righteousness in the land" (Jer. 33:15).

Shalom elaborates:

As he said, "I will cause a shoot of righteousness to grow up unto David," etc. [In this] He mentioned four attributes.

One, [that he should be] perfect in his virtues and opinions. For this he is called righteous, implying that whoever perfected his body and soul is called righteous.

Second, that he should be fit to reign, which means that a true king reign, not one unfit for the task, as it is said about Saul: "It repenteth Me that I set up Saul to be king" (1 Sam. 15:11). The reason He gave for this is, "For he is turned back from following Me" (ibid.), and another man would reign and his "would be the manner of the king." (1 Sam. 8:11)

Third, that he be influenced by the intellectual emanation, so that God would make his heart wise to do justice. The reason for this is that even a perfect and wise king might panic, not understand some matter and what he should do [about it], since it is so complicated, as happened to Solomon with those harlots. In such a case he needs Divine assistance, which would enlighten him and teach him knowledge so that he would truly act justly. And if he were not fit to [receive] this emanation and perfection, the name of the Lord would be desecrated, since he knew not what to do.

The fourth is that he exonerate the righteous and condemn the wicked, i.e., that he do justice. Since the purpose of his ruling is to imitate Him, blessed be He, "who exerciseth mercy, justice and righteousness in the earth" (Jer. 9:23). This is the reason why the King of Israel should always be from [the house of] David.[47]

The first virtue concerns moral perfection and the intelligence of the king in general. This follows the Maimonidean order of priorities: first moral perfection and then intellectual perfection based upon it. First physical perfection and, as a result, perfection of the soul. Whoever achieves both of these will be called righteous. The second virtue concerns suitability for kingship generally. As was customary, Shalom presents Saul as an example of the mistaken elevation to kingship of someone not suitable, indicating that an unsuitable king should be removed. The third and fourth virtues detail what was stated broadly in the first virtue in regard to the moral and intellectual perfection of the king. The third virtue relates to the influence of the divine emanation on the rational soul of a man who has already attained wisdom and who is also fit to receive such an emanation at the moment of need. Without this additional assistance, he would not be able to dispense justice in difficult cases. The example given is that of Solomon, who received divine enlightenment in order to hand down a just ruling in the case of the two women in dispute over a living child.

The fourth virtue refers to the moral perfection of the king, which enables him to govern fairly and do justice. Here Shalom applies the Maimonidean theory of the imitation of the Divine attributes, which represents the highest level of perfection of the philosopher-prophet, as leader of the community. Typically in this tradition, Shalom utilizes Jeremiah's statement and the classic commentary on it, which appears in the last chapter of the *Guide*. Shalom pointedly uses the term "attributes" *(te'arim)* when describing the virtues appropriate to the perfect King of Israel.[48] Prophecy, however, is not included in the attributes of the perfect king. The king whom Shalom portrays is not the prophet-first lawgiver but the wise king of future generations operating within the framework of perfect legislation. In view of these requirements, the perfect king is selected not only from among the chosen people, but also from its most perfect tribe, and within that, from the progeny of David, who is the most perfect of kings.

Next, Shalom establishes, on the basis of the four virtues, a more detailed classification involving twelve attributes:

You ought to know that the attributes appropriate to the perfect kings of Israel are twelve:

First, that he be energetic in the performance of God's commandments and the preservation of the Law.

Second, that he love righteousness and justice.

Third, that he love the wise.

Fourth, that he be modest and not haughty and that material abundance should not cause him to be rebellious.

Fifth, that he should be wise.

Sixth, that he set aside regular periods for Torah study.

Seventh, that he be merciful and not cruel.

Eighth, that he reward or punish each man according to his deeds.

Ninth, that he be brave.

Tenth, that he detest wrongly prized possessions and luxuries.

Eleventh, that he root out wickedness and the wicked and hate them.

Twelfth, that he fulfill the commandments of the Torah.[49]

The number of attributes fixed upon by Shalom corresponds with the Farabian tradition. Of the twelve, at least half are concerned with moral perfection. Two attributes (3 and 5) concern intellectual perfection, albeit in a general way and not in the usual terminology of the Platonic tradition.

Shalom emphasizes that wisdom is vital for the perfect king, but he refers expressly to practical, not theoretical, wisdom, in contrast to what is usual in the Platonic tradition:

And it is appropriate for you to know that being a wise man is necessary and constitutive for a king and vital to his rule, since his wisdom will establish his rule and he will be able to give the advice which is good for him and will distinguish between whoever gives him good or bad advice, and he will be successful in whatever he does and know when to be stern and when merciful and how he should lead his people and who will be suitable to be appointed to rule over his house, whom to remove and whom to bring close. And whoever is devoid of wisdom will not know these things. For how can he who cannot govern himself govern his fellow men, and how could he who cannot distinguish good from evil choose between them?[50]

Like Abravanel, Alemanno, and Erasmus, as we shall see, Shalom offers Solomon's dream as an example of the king's need for wisdom. However, like Alemanno, Shalom, too, ascribes only a limited meaning to Solomon's request to receive wisdom. In his view, the wisdom Solomon asked for and received was only practical wisdom, vital to his tasks of governance. The antithesis provided by Shalom is Rehoboam, an ignorant king, who was incapable of selecting the right advisers and of receiving good advice from them.[51]

Shalom seems to have had some notion of the classical tradition of discourse in medieval Jewish thought,[52] but he presents this tradition in a definitively Jewish context, albeit less halakhicly than Alemanno's addition to the ten Platonic attributes expounded by Ibn Rushd. Unlike most of his forerunners, Shalom presents the twelve attributes as relating to the perfect King of Israel alone, not to the philosopher king generally.

Indeed, Shalom links the twelve attributes he has established to an allegorical interpretation of the judgment of the king in Deuteronomy 17, as follows:

And these are the attributes alluded to in the portion *Ki tissa*, as follows:[53]

He starts with the first attribute saying, "Thou shalt in any wise set him king over thee, whom the Lord thy God shall choose" (v. 15). The man chosen by God is the holy one, who is careful to fulfill divine commands, whose soul hates wickedness and the lovers of oppression.

And the second is alluded to when he said "that he may learn to fear the Lord" (v. 19), since true veneration is doing justice and loving-kindness.

The third is alluded to when he said "before the priests" (v. 18), which means that he was commanded to study the Torah and copy it in their presence and according to their specifications. He was ordered to love them, since he should respect those who fear the Lord.

The fourth was hinted at when he said "that his heart be not lifted up above his brethren." (v. 20)

The fifth was hinted at when he said, "And it shall be with him, and he shall read therein" (v. 19), since the reading of the Torah and contemplating it would render a man wise.

The sixth was hinted at when he said: "And it shall be with him" (v. 19), which means that he should designate the appropriate time for studying the Torah, and this is the way by which it would be with him, not that he neglect its contemplation or contemplate it occasionally, because in such a case it would not be with him.

The seventh was hinted at when he said, "One from among thy brethren shalt thou set king over thee" (v. 15). The reason for this is that the sons of Israel are merciful, as the Sages described it, by three characteristics they possess: diffidence, mercy, and beneficence.

The eighth was hinted by him when he said "that his heart turn not away" (v. 17), since the king who does not reward or punish every man according to his behavior becomes like him who had lost his heart and deviated from the just path of kingship, since he does not [properly] supervise his subordinates. And this is a major cause of corruption of humanity and of injustice that cannot be eliminated.

The ninth is alluded to when he said, "He shall not multiply horses to himself, etc." (v. 16), since the courageous man is he who stands at the mean between a coward and one who recklessly endangers himself. This is why he said that one should not choose one of the extremes by returning the people to Egypt so that he might "multiply horses" (v. 16), which the Torah forbids him to do. Rather, he ought stoutly to subdue his desire and not multiply horses to himself, since doing so endangers him. This would be the opposite of courage, since virtuous men in general, and the king in particular, ought not to endanger themselves unnecessarily. Thus, when three brave men brought water from the cistern of Bethlehem to David, "he would not drink thereof" and said, "Be it far from me that I should do this; shall I drink the blood of the men that went in jeopardy of their lives?" Therefore he would not drink it. He did this in order to show that no one should unnecessarily endanger himself, nor desire any benefit from that which is derived from danger undergone illegitimately: "only one who would destroy himself does such a thing." (Prov. 6:32). "Even the most stout-hearted men" (Amos 2:16) would not be praised for this.

The tenth is alluded to when he said, "Neither shall he multiply wives to himself" (v. 17), since sexual intercourse is a major source of ritual impurity, and as Aristotle said, the sense of touch is a disgrace to us as human beings. You also know the prophet's statement, "Harlotry, wine and new wine take away the heart" (Hosea 4:11). That is why he stated nearby (v. 17) "that his heart turn not away," since committing adultery causes the heart to turn away and the mind to become foolish.

The eleventh is indicated by his saying "and silver, etc." (v. 17), which means that he should love justice and hate iniquity and not be tempted to amass silver, as it is said, "And lavished upon her silver and gold, which they used for Ba'al" (Hosea 2:10). It is known that he who was misled by his heart to amass silver, will not avoid evil ways, to wit, by being avid for bribes, something which is despicable in any perfected person, and surely for a king.

The twelfth is indicated by his saying "To keep all the words of this law" (v. 19), since the perfect king brings about obedience to the Torah, being the "cornerstone and pillar" (Zechariah 10:4) of the fulfillment of the commandments, since the people obey him and commit themselves to fulfilling it.[54]

After listing the attributes of the king, Shalom, like Polkar, cites a prooftext from the Bible for each on the basis of the biblical text. Selecting one of the two major scriptural passages dealing with monarchy, Deuteronomy 17:14–20, he expounds the text as was common in the halakhic tradition, through an exegesis of the obligation to raise up a king. However, he ignores the plain sense of this text, which is that monarchy is only an option, and an undesirable one at that. Shalom is the only commentator to use this text as the basis for his discussion of the attributes of the king. Whereas the biblical source constitutes a warning and a check on the misuse of the king's powers, Shalom reverses this meaning and presents the passage as a description of the attributes required of the good king.

Additionally, he does not adhere to the scriptural order of the qualities of the king; he changes it to suit his predetermined classification of the twelve attributes. In contrast to the Platonic tradition, the good king is presented here as a king who is subject to the rule of law. Since Shalom does not rely directly on the philosophical attributes, he avoids the contradictions faced by Alemanno, who attempted to fuse the halakhic and philosophical requirements. That the king is obliged to honor the priests and Levites of his day does not diminish his own status. Indeed, Shalom nowhere actually portrays the perfect king as a prophet, even though he uses the word attributes *(te'arim)* for his qualifications, with all the connotations that this particular term carries. None of these attributes, however, relates to prophecy. In terms of the Farabian tradition, the issue in question is not the philosopher-king-prophet and lawgiver of the first generation, but the wise king of future generations. The latter knows the ideal law handed down by the first lawgiver and acts wisely in accordance with it.

The prohibition against the multiplication of horses is interpreted allegorically in the ninth attribute, on the basis of the theory of the middle way, while the prohibition against many wives is explained in the tenth attribute on the grounds of the Aristotelian aversion to the sense of touch, which is perceived as the most bestial of man's senses. In both cases Shalom cites Maimonides explicitly as his source.[55] Even though Shalom applies the discussion of the king's virtues to a biblical text not usually used in this connection, it is clear that he was well-versed in the classical tradition. He returns again and again to the dichotomy between the hatred of evil and the love of justice that is so characteristic of the Platonic tradition.

After establishing the twelve objective principles for evaluating the qualities of the King of Israel, Shalom goes on to assess the extent to which various kings embodied the twelve attributes. David, Solomon, Josiah ("[the last] was endowed with all of these attributes, [and] it was said of him: 'And like unto him was there no king before him, that turned to the Lord' [2 Kings 23:25]"),[56] and Joash are defined by Shalom as kings who most completely realized the twelve attributes. However, following Jewish tradition, Shalom depicts Saul, Rehoboam, and Ahab as prototypes of the tyrannical King of Israel.[57] Typically of this genre of political literature, Shalom ends his discussion by presenting the classic antithesis between the good king and the despot as embodied historically.

Just as he depicts the perfect King of Israel as the model ruler, Shalom elsewhere describes Jerusalem as the ideal state. Applying his typically schematic approach, he isolates five characteristics to measure its perfection, basing himself on an allegorical interpretation of Psalm 122:

> And he said: "Jerusalem the built," etc. (Ps. 122:3). He meant by this Jerusalem when it was perfectly built. This is why he said "the built" with the definite article, to point out its perfection. Jerusalem was likened to a notable city, with all its perfections united together, and this is why he said, "as a city that is compacted together" (v. 3). The perfection of a notable city depends upon five things:

> That its inhabitants be perfect and also numerous. This is because the population of a city is like the form of a body, and as an excellent form gives a body excellent existence, so the perfect nation *(umah shlemah)* gives a city perfect existence. This is why he said, "Whither the tribes went up, even the tribes of the Lord." (v. 4)

That they be endowed with wisdom and a perfect law (Torah), since the law directs the people to their ultimate perfection, and perfects their condition after [they acquire] wisdom, which is the true cause of political association. This is why he said, "as a testimony unto Israel" (v. 4), and about the Torah it was said, "The testimony of the Lord is sure, making wise the simple" (Ps. 19:8). The perfection of its existence is in the Land of Israel, as we indicated above.

That the purpose of whatever they do be to worship the Creator, blessed be He; by this they purify themselves from the sickness of the [desire for] material things. Thus, he said, "To give thanks to the Name of the Lord" (v. 4), which indicates their true end, which is the ultimate perfection *(hazlahah aharonah),* and not imaginary perfections *(hazlahot medumot)* such as wealth.

That they be excellently governed *(hanhagah meulah);* and that their dealings be righteous and just, as he said: "For there were set thrones for judgment" (v. 5).

That its leaders be "men of truth, who fear God and hate unjust gain" (Exod. 18:21), and are from "a blessed fountain" (Prov. 5:18). Thus, he said, "The thrones of the house of David" (v. 5), since David was perfect in the human perfection which was ascribed to perfect leaders *(manhigim shlemim).*[58]

The first three characteristics relate to the moral and rational perfections required of the citizens of the perfect city. Here and elsewhere Shalom relates his exposition to the traditional ascription of a unique climate to the Land of Israel generally and to Jerusalem in particular, which was understood as a necessary condition for the perfection of their inhabitants.[59] The last two characteristics relate to the moral and rational perfections—especially practical intelligence—of the leaders of that ideal city. More broadly, the existence of the ideal state is the outcome of the moral and rational perfection of its citizens in general and its leaders in particular.

6

Our final example of the application of the idea of the philosopher king is Joseph Albo's *Book of Principles (Sefer ha-Ikkarim),* a work that is the most remote from the philosophical model of the philosopher king's virtues. We have, therefore, left it to the end, even though Albo predated Abravanel, Alemanno, and Shalom. Albo was well-acquainted with the Platonic tradition in medieval Jewish thought, clearly highlighting the Platonic motif of the philosopher king in the chapters dealing with politics in the first part of the *Book of Principles* (1:5–7). Unlike his predecessors, however, Albo deals with the virtues of the ideal king independently of this motif and he does so not in the philosophical context but almost exclusively in the halakhic context. Thus, the setting of his inquiry is almost wholly detached from the medieval theory of the philosopher king.

Albo treats the question of repentance and its conditions in a discussion of the third principle of his system of dogmas, namely, "reward and punishment." One of the central problems that exercises him here is why David's repentance was accepted after the Bathsheba affair, whereas Saul's confession of guilt and repentance after refusing to eliminate Amalek as commanded were not accepted. David, despite sinning, was rewarded by having the kingdom vouchsafed to him and his sons; Saul, in contrast, was punished by having the kingdom removed from him and his sons. The explanation that Albo offers for these conflicting outcomes is based on the distinction between two kinds of commandments, particular and general. A particular commandment is one that a certain person is individually ordered to perform, either on account of the specific situation in which he finds himself or in connection with the function he fills. This commandment does not necessarily apply to the entire people of Israel. A general commandment is one that applies to every person in Israel without distinction as to status, situation, or political role. In this regard, the status of the king is identical to that of the simplest of men.[60]

David, in Albo's argument, transgressed a general commandment in the incident with Bathsheba, and therefore his punishment was identical to that which anyone would receive in such a case. Like Machiavelli after him, but for completely different reasons, Albo clearly distinguishes between David the sinner in the private sphere and David the ideal ruler in the public sphere. Saul, however, sinned against a particular commandment linked to his role as king, when he disobeyed the divine injunction to destroy Amalek. Therefore, he did not deserve the kingdom. "Saul committed a misdeed in relation to the kingly art, hence it was fitting that he should lose that art, whereas David did not sin in relation to the kingly art; his sin was different and had nothing to do with the kingly art, hence he was forgiven."[61]

Saul's failure to fulfill his royal function was not limited to the matter of annihilating Amalek, for he had previously been told, "But now thy kingdom shall not continue" (1 Sam. 13:14). To understand the reasons that the kingdom was taken from Saul, Albo suggests that it would be worthwhile to clarify "the virtues requisite in a king."[62] Albo, like Falaquera, preferred the term "virtues" *(middot)*, although at times he also used the word "attributes" *(te'arim)*. Despite his use of these expressions, however, his discussion is devoid of any connection between the virtues of the king and the theory of imitation of God.

Albo points out "that there are six virtues a king, as such, must have." These six derive from the definition of his role as king according to the halakhic position dictating the kind of virtues required of him: "The purpose of appointing a king is to fight the enemy and to judge the people justly. When Israel demanded a king, they said 'that our king may judge us, and go out before us, and fight our battles' (1 Sam. 8:20). Hence, he must have the qualities necessary for this purpose."[63] This definition conforms with Maimonides' halakhic exposition in *Hilkhot Melakhim* (5,10). Like Maimonides, Albo cites the people's request to Samuel that he set a king over them (1 Sam. 8:20), and in contrast to the antimonarchical position, he treats these statements in a positive light as a legitimate definition of the purpose of kingship. It is no accident that he does not cite the beginning of the verse—"that we also may be like all the nations," on which the antimonarchists relied.

The definition of the king's role imposes certain duties and necessarily delimits his status. He must fulfill certain functions; he is forbidden to evade them or to act contrary to them. The main functions of the king—sitting in judgment and conducting warfare—are enumerated here. It is not by chance that Maimonides combines the halakhah of kings with the halakhah of war, for these constitute the chief tasks of the king: defense both from within (judgment) and from without (warfare).

The virtues of the king are thus determined according to these two central duties. The virtues of judges, as Albo notes, are clarified in the Torah, which speaks of the singling out of "able men, such as fear God, men of truth, hating unjust gain" (Exod. 18:21). When the attributes vital for the military functions of the king are combined with these virtues, according to Albo, they add up to six qualities, as follows:

One is that the king must be cruel to strangers but merciful to his own people and willing to give his life to save them.

The second is to be good to those who are good to him, to his servants and those who fight his battles, for if he does not, who will risk his life for the king's glory and who will take his part against those who are treacherous?

The third is that he should hate unlawful gain and not be covetous.

The fourth is that he should be a man of valor, strong and mighty to "break the jaws of the unrighteous" (Job 29:17). He must not defer to the faces of the poor, nor honor the faces of the great (Lev. 19:15), nor fear to do justice.

The fifth is that he should speak the truth. No wrong must be found upon his lips, and he should perform a righteous judgment, for the

man who lies or speaks falsehood does so either from fear or because
he cannot obtain his desire without it, but the judge must not be
afraid of any man . . . let alone the king. . . .

And the sixth is that he should fear God and tremble at His words.
He should be submissive to those who serve God, and observe those
commandments which he was given when he became king or after
he became king. And in regard to the other commandments too, he
must not consider himself superior to his brethren and think he is
free of the commandments any more than they. . . . For if the people
see the king disregarding the law and the teachers thereof, they will
all come to ignore it, and the whole Torah will fall.[64]

The first two virtues relate to the king's functions as commander. The
next three (3–5) concern his moral perfection and have implications for his
function as judge. The last virtue refers to his obligation to obey the laws of
the Torah, both as judge and as commander.

Because the virtues of the king described by Albo are based on the
halakhic definition of kingship, they are more limited in number and in
scope than if they had been based on the more detailed philosophical definition. Moreover, they diverge greatly in content and composition. Albo
makes no attempt to integrate the philosophical position with the halakhic
one, as do Polkar, Abravanel, and Alemanno, each in his own way. The only
real parallel between his presentation and the philosophical position is his
classification and numbering of the king's virtues in orderly fashion.
Notably, the very same virtues appear in Maimonides' *Hilkhot Melakhim*, but
there even the structure is in no way reminiscent of the philosophical tradition. In Albo, all that remains is the external form of that tradition, without
its Platonic content. The ruler, therefore, is presented as a king alone, not as
a philosopher or prophet.

Of the king's qualities that appear in the philosopher-king tradition,
only those relating to moral perfection (3–5) appear here. All the virtues concerning intellectual perfection are absent; the image of the philosopher king
is not expressed at all. Wholly missing, too, is the ruler's prophetic aspect,
which was central to the philosophical tradition, even though it would have
been quite possible to ascribe prophecy, if only of a temporary nature, to
David and even to Saul. For that reason, the last item, concerning the duty
of the king to obey the Torah and "those who serve God," including the
prophet of his day, conforms to the halakhic position. It does not contradict
other virtues that Albo attributes to the king, in contrast to Alemanno's version in *Eternal Life*. The classic equivalence between philosopher king and
prophet is absent altogether.

The sixth virtue is of great importance from the halakhic viewpoint. The king is subject to the rule of law both in his status as king (particular commandments) and as an Israelite (general commandments). He is obliged to fulfill the commandments in both these respects. His ruling authority does not release him from obedience to the law; on the contrary, it obligates him just like anyone else in Israel from the standpoint of the general commandments, and more than anyone else from the standpoint of the particular commandments pertaining to the king. In this connection, the king has a distinct educational role in his very subjection to the law: both as king and as an Israelite, he sets an example as to how people should obey the law and maintain public order. This position is well-known in the philosophical tradition, but here its context is purely halakhic.

At this point, having characterized which virtues a king must have in general, Albo examines the extent to which they were reflected in Saul as compared with David. Like Polkar before him, Albo first noted the virtues of the king generally, and only afterward applied them to a specific ruler. His innovation is that he carried out a comparative analysis of two rulers, Saul and David, to determine who met these criteria. It is clear from the outset that Saul did not satisfy the criteria: "Now if we examine Saul's virtues, we find that he was lacking in all of them."[65]

Saul failed in regard to the first virtue, the obligation of a king to be "cruel to strangers and merciful to his own people," because he did the opposite: he was merciful to enemies when he spared Agag, king of Amalek, and he was cruel to his own people when he put Nob, the city of the priests, to the sword. David, by contrast, acted in accordance with the virtue. He destroyed Moab but was compassionate with his people and sought mercy for them when the destroying angel appeared.

As for the second virtue, the duty to be good to those who were good to him, Saul did not deal kindly with David after the youth had killed Goliath. David, however, acted rightly when before his death he ordered that the sons of Barzillai the Gileadite be well treated.

Regarding the third virtue, that the king should hate unlawful gain and not be covetous, it is said of Saul, "But thou didst fly upon the spoil" (1 Sam. 15:19), whereas David was generous and distributed booty.

The fourth virtue is that the king should be a man of valor and not fear to do justice. Saul, fearing the people's reaction, avoided doing justice. Of David, it is written: "And David executed justice and righteousness unto all his people" (2 Sam. 8:15).

As for the fifth virtue, that he should speak the truth: Saul lied to Samuel and tried to conceal his crime while David at once admitted his transgression in the episode of Bath Sheba, when confronted by Nathan.

Regarding the sixth virtue, the obligation to obey those who serve God and the laws of the Torah, Saul disobeyed Samuel and the particular commandments he was given, whereas David obeyed Samuel and Nathan in everything he was commanded.[66]

The obvious conclusion is that Saul did not meet any of the criteria defining the proper behavior of a king, and that David met all of them, even though he had sinned against various general obligations.

Returning to the dichotomy between the just king and the despot, where Alemanno identified the prototype of the just king as Abraham and of the despot as Nimrod, Albo finds them in the figures of and David and Saul respectively. Saul is portrayed as a ruler lacking in all six virtues proper for a king. He therefore necessarily became a tyrant, exploiting his power and status for evil. David is the exemplar of all six virtues, and for that reason necessarily became a just king who functioned within the framework of the law and served the people whom he ruled well. The antimonarchical proponents made full use of Saul's failure as proof that a monarchy by nature is bound to degenerate into tyranny, just as Samuel had prophesied. By contrast, Albo, like Maimonides, saw this failure as a manifestation of the failure of a particular king and not of the monarchical system as such. Albo, therefore, presents David as a prototype of the ideal king as against the figure of the transgressor Saul, concluding:

We find that David was perfect in all these qualities, while Saul lacked them all. This was why God saw to it that the kingdom did not remain with Saul and why Saul left no descendants worthy of the kingship. Even Abner, the chief of his army, died in order that the kingdom might be firmly established in the hands of David and his children, as a lesson and example to kings who came after him, that they should not in their pride disobey God's will, for the kingdom is His. Hence a human king should not slight those who serve God and observe His Torah, for He alone is the King of Glory.[67]

8

Christian Applications and the Machiavellian Revolution

Christian and Muslim philosophers in the Middle Ages and the Renaissance commonly applied the philosopher-king theory to the leaders of the ancient Hebrew people. They described Judaism and its scriptures as a necessary prelude to the next stage in the development of monotheistic belief—namely, the rise of the founder-prophet of the tradition—and thus identified the great biblical kings of Israel as prototypes of the ideal ruler. Medieval literature, both philosophical and popular, is replete with references to the wisdom of Solomon and his ideal way of ruling.[1]

Investigation of this subject appeared in Christian thought not in its classic Platonic structure but independently, as part of the tradition of the *Speculum Principium*. Plato held that the rule of philosophers would guarantee the best society. He regarded the possibility of turning kings into philosophers as a second-best option and was greatly disappointed by his failure to transform Dionysius of Syracuse into a philosopher king.[2] By contrast, medieval Christian thinkers deemed Plato's second-best option the only realistic one. The philosopher would then have no ambition to rule, only the desire to influence and educate whoever was intended to rule. This ideology formed the basis for the development of the political literature of the *Speculum Principium*. In its discourse on the virtues of the ideal ruler, this tradition emphasized refined manners, handsome appearance, responsibility, loyalty, concern for others, and so forth, in addition to profound Christian faith. It makes few references to these virtues in their purely philosophical context.[3]

Two principal compositions of the tradition illustrate how the *Speculum Principium* presented the ancient Hebrew patriarchs as classic examples of the ideal ruler. The first, Saint Thomas Aquinas' *De Regimine Principum*, written in the mid-thirteenth century, is one of the earliest examples of the tradition; the second is the last great expression of this tradition before its demise, *Institutio Principis Christiani (The Education of the Christian Prince)* by Erasmus of Rotterdam, written at the beginning of the sixteenth century but still steeped in the medieval tradition. The Erasmian example will provide an appropriate basis for comparison with the revolution in the image of the ideal prince wrought by Machiavelli at that very time.

1

Aquinas was not directly acquainted with the Platonic tradition of the philosopher king. His political writing closely followed Aristotle's *Nicomachaean Ethics* and the *Politics*, which were translated into Latin in his time and which exerted a decisive influence on late-medieval Christian political thought. While Muslim and Jewish political philosophy was founded on the Platonic model, pre-Renaissance Christian political thought adopted the Aristotelian pattern as its basis.[4]

Of all the ancient Hebrew leaders, Aquinas devoted the most attention to King Solomon, positing him as the supreme exemplar of the wise ruler. Aquinas frequently cites Solomon's words *(illud Sapientis)* as both proof and illustration in his political writings.[5] For example, he quotes Solomon in support of Aristotle's claim that slavery is found in nature: "And the fool shall be servant to the wise of heart" (Prov. 11:29).[6] He notes regarding Aristotle's comment: "Solomon was of like opinion" *(concordat sententia Salomonis).*[7] As the antithesis to Solomon, the model philosopher king, Aquinas offers Ahab, "who sinned greatly" *(qui multum peccaverat).* Here was the Hebrew model of the tyrant.[8] Characteristically, Aquinas does not refer to the obvious philosophical framework for this assertion, Plato's theory of the philosopher king; instead, he applies Aristotle's position on slavery to prove a monarchic theory that was in no way acceptable to Aristotle.

Aquinas uses the models of Moses and David less frequently. Examining Jethro's advice to Moses, Aquinas characterizes Moses' rule not as a purely monarchical regime, but as a mixed government composed of the three most desirable regimes: monarchy, aristocracy, and democracy. This is the ideal form of government—"The best form of constitution which results from a judicious admixture" *(optima politia bene commixta).*[9]

Significantly, all of Aquinas' quotations from Solomon are taken from the books of wisdom, principally Proverbs and, somewhat less frequently, Ecclesiastes. There is no citation from or reference to 1 Kings, which describes Solomon's actual reign. This is the case with David as well. All the passages concerning him are taken from the Psalms, with no reference to or quotation from the Books of Samuel describing David's actual rule.[10] Aquinas thus presents Solomon, and to a lesser extent David, as utopian personifications of the ideal king, not as flesh and blood rulers coping with real political problems.

2

We encounter this approach even more explicitly in the well-known work by Erasmus of Rotterdam, *The Education of the Christian Prince (Institutio Principis Christiani)*, written for the purpose of training the future Emperor Charles V, and published in 1516. Although Erasmus was writing at the height of the Renaissance, some three centuries after Aquinas, his essay, reflecting his political thinking, retained a distinctly medieval character. Moreover, despite the considerable influence of the "pagan" sources of Renaissance thought, Erasmus' profound Christian belief was overriding. Machiavelli, who published *The Prince* in the same year that *The Education of the Christian Prince* appeared, revolutionized the image of the ideal ruler. Erasmus, rooted in the pious northern Christian Renaissance, preserved the traditional image of the medieval prince, whose virtues were perfect. Further, while Machiavelli, Thomas More, Luther, and others wrote in the vernacular so as to reach as large a readership as possible, Erasmus retained the language of medieval culture, Latin, the number of whose readers was constantly dwindling. His work is the last notable example of the well-worn tradition of treatises on the education of the ideal prince, a tradition that had become obsolete even before the work was published.

Erasmus acquiesced in the notion of a traditional monarchical regime although he favored a limited monarchy subject to law, as his definition of the role of the ruler concerned with the public good necessitated a limitation of his powers. Erasmus was not happy with the contemporary reality, in which sovereignty was determined by the principle of heredity. He would have liked kings to be selected according to their qualifications. But he accepted the situation and tried to make the best of it. If it were not possible to select the ruler, an effort should be made at least to educate him properly. Here lies the enormous importance of the prince's teacher and guide, who therefore had to be chosen with the greatest care.

Erasmus accepted the medieval theory of the imitation of God, that is, a good prince must imitate the beneficence of God, for "the prince is a sort of likeness of God" *(princeps Dei simulacrum quoddam est)*. As such, the prince must undoubtedly be a realist but also a philosopher and a true Christian. If he is not a philosopher, he will not be a successful ruler. But the good philosopher and the true Christian are identical. As is usual in this genre of political literature, the antithesis of the good prince is the tyrant, who uses his position to oppress and exploit the people.[11]

Also in the spirit of this longstanding tradition, Erasmus depends heavily on ancient sources. As a Renaissance man, he makes extensive use—far more than did Aquinas—of the revived classics: Plutarch, Seneca, Cicero, and Plato's *Republic*, which had been unearthed and brought into Christian thought by the humanists of the Italian Renaissance. To this was added the ongoing, massive use of Aristotle's *Politics*.[12] Like Aquinas and the other philosophers of this tradition, Erasmus persisted in regarding the Bible, especially the wisdom literature attributed to Solomon, as the chief source of the definition of the perfect prince. These biblical texts head the list of books recommended by Erasmus for the prince's education, followed by Plutarch, Seneca, Aristotle, Cicero, and others of the classical tradition.[13]

Like Aquinas, Erasmus bases himself primarily on the image of King Solomon, and in a far more limited way on King David. Moses is not mentioned at all. For the philosophers of the *Speculum Principium*, the image of Solomon as the wise king served as a proper, unproblematic model of the perfect prince. In contrast, the image of Moses, which appeared as the prototype of the philosopher king in medieval Hebrew literature, caused them difficulty. First, Moses appeared as the giver of the divine law to the people of Israel, the law that Christianity was to annul. Moses was, thus, too Jewish for them. Solomon, however, presented no such theological difficulty. Second, the regime that Moses established could be defined as mixed, particularly on the basis of Jethro's advice. In any case, it was not a monarchical regime in the usual sense. Furthermore, the identification of Moses as a prophet complicated matters. By contrast, Solomon's rule was monarchical in every way. This explains why Aquinas hardly referred to Moses in this context, while Erasmus ignored him entirely. Only Machiavelli, no longer subject to theological constraints, and viewing Scripture from a purely political perspective, was able to identify Moses as the ideal ruler, clearly superior to David and Solomon.

Erasmus, as noted, quotes mainly from the wisdom literature ascribed to Solomon.[14] He hardly cites anything from 1 Kings, which describes how Solomon actually behaved. In the two places when he does refer to this book, it is to interpret Solomon's dream at Gibeon. The King Solomon of the dream and of the wisdom literature, then, is the figure who appears as the archetype of the good prince, not the flesh and blood Solomon who contended with actual political issues.

Erasmus found it difficult to handle the harsh and cruel political reality depicted in the historical books of the Bible. When he advises his prince to learn lessons only from the deeds of the best rulers in the past, he warns that even then the prince must do so critically, choosing only the very best *(in optimo fit optimum)* and not imitating all their actions. He proceeds to give the examples of David and Solomon, both of them kings who pleased God *(regibus a Deo laudatis)* but who committed acts that would best have been avoided.[15] Erasmus stresses that although David was a good king, whose actions were to be imitated, he was punished by being prevented from building the Temple, because he engaged in warfare and shed blood. Moreover, just as it is wrong to imitate the best of princes uncritically, it is also wrong to accept everything written in the Scriptures at face value. Erasmus suggests that the prince read the descriptions of the bloody wars and acts of vengeance of the Hebrews allegorically *(ad allegoriam esse vocanda)*, lest these accounts have a highly undesirable effect. The Jews in the biblical age were permitted such brutal acts because of the barbaric norms prevailing then, but Christians had attained a higher level of behavior, which was binding on them.[16]

Erasmus voiced his projection of Solomon as the prototype of the philosopher king mainly in two parallel interpretations of Solomon's dream at Gibeon. The first, a brief exposition, appears in the introduction to the *Institutio*, while the second, longer interpretation appears in the body of the text. We have seen how Jewish philosophers of the generation preceding Erasmus, particularly Alemanno and Abravanel, interpreted Solomon's dream at Gibeon as embodying the prototype of the philosopher king. Alemanno assigned political significance to the wisdom that Solomon requested, viewing it as essential to the king as a political leader rather than a philosopher.[17] Abravanel, by contrast, interpreted Solomon's dream as a request for comprehensive wisdom, theoretical as well as practical.[18]

Erasmus adopts a kind of intermediate position. Solomon desired wisdom in general, but with the goal of ruling justly.[19] The starting point of the opening epistle in his *Institutio* is that wisdom is not only a lofty quality in itself, but also a necessary condition for the rule of law. Of all forms of wisdom, this practical type is divine and is the goal toward which the good prince must strive. It is the wisdom that Solomon requested in his dream. "That kind of wisdom is indeed to be sought by princes, which Solomon as a youth of good parts, spurning all else, alone desired, and which he wished to be his constant companion on the throne."[20] Erasmus quotes Proverbs (8:15): "Through me princes rule, and the powerful pass judgment,"[21] and glosses:

> Whenever kings call this wisdom into council and exclude those basest of advisers—ambition, wrath, cupidity, and flattery—the state flourishes in every way and, realizing that its prosperity comes from the wisdom of the prince, rejoices rightly in itself with these words: "All good things together come to me with her [wisdom]." (Eccl. 7:11)

Erasmus next cites Plato's well-known statement in *The Republic* that the state will be blessed when philosophers rule or kings become philosophers.[22] Solomon, then, is portrayed as the prototype of the Platonic philosopher king of the second type, who has inherited his power but has become a philosopher. Like Plato, Erasmus regards this as the lesser good. Characteristically, where Aquinas draws a parallel between Solomon and Aristotle, Erasmus draws one between Solomon and Plato.

Erasmus restates his position in the body of the text. In his discourse on the training of the good prince and on his desirable qualities, Erasmus reiterates, as an example, his interpretation of Solomon's dream at Gibeon:

> Solomon was praised by all because at a time when he was free to ask whatever he wanted and would have instantly received whatever he asked for, he did not ask for great wealth nor world empire nor the destruction of his enemies nor great honor and fame nor worldly pleasures, but he asked for wisdom. And not just an indifferent sort of wisdom either, but such as he could use to govern with credit the kingdom which had been entrusted to him.[23]

Scripture mentions three things that Solomon chose not to request: long life, wealth, and the destruction of his enemies. Erasmus lists five: great wealth, world empire, the destruction of enemies, honor and fame, and worldly pleasures—only two of which were identical with the list in the Bible (wealth and the destruction of enemies). This list of desires that the good prince should eschew incorporates two not found in the biblical source: world empire, and honor and fame. Erasmus may have been quoting from memory, and therefore erred,[24] or perhaps he was deliberately elaborating on the text to suit the needs of the future emperor, Charles V. What follows relates directly to that prince:

> We pray that our prince will have good fortune, and victories, and glory, and long life, and riches. If we really are devoted to our prince, why do we not ask for that one thing which Solomon asked for? And do not think his request was ill-advised. He was praised by God because of it.[25]

Erasmus, a declared pacifist,[26] emphasizes the characterization of Solomon as a king who desired peace. Consequently, according to Erasmus, Solomon chose not to request three of the five items which concern war: world empire, the destruction of his enemies, and honor and fame. True, when Erasmus applied these matters directly to his own prince, he relented somewhat and included victory and fame among the king's legitimate desires. Undoubtedly, this stems from the political considerations inherent in this kind of composition, written for the purpose of educating the prince but still requiring his and his advisers' approval.

The emphasis on Solomon's character as a king desirous of peace recurs later, in Erasmus' long pacifist discourse on the need of the good prince to preserve peace at almost any price and to reject war as a legitimate political tool. His central argument is purely theological: original Christian dogma manifestly proscribed war and bloodshed. Erasmus points out that the Jews were allowed to wage war only with divine approval. Jesus, by contrast, forbade taking up arms altogether. Yet Christians, warred even more than the ancient Hebrews. The divine prohibition against warfare was demonstrated by Erasmus as we saw above, through King David, who despite pleasing God on account of his virtues *(David aliis virtuibus Deo fuit gratissimus)*, was nevertheless forbidden to build the Temple because he had shed blood. God preferred Solomon, the man of peace *(Salomonem pacificum)*, for that task. Erasmus sums up on a critical note:

If these things were done among the Jews, what should be done among us Christians? They had a shadow of Solomon *(Salomones umbram)*, we have the real Solomon *(veram Salomonem)*, the prince of peace, Christ, who conciliates all things in heaven and earth.[27]

This status of Solomon as the prototype of the Prince of Peace complements the characterization of him as philosopher king. We have already observed in Alemanno and Abravanel a parallel portrayal of Solomon as the king who is the defender of peace, a quality that has its basis in the verse "And Judah and Israel dwelt safely, every man under his vine and under his fig tree, from Dan even to Beer-Sheba, all the days of Solomon" (1 Kings 5:5).[28] Machiavelli, as we shall see, also emphasized this aspect of Solomon's reign, except that he did not regard it as proof of political perfection. On the contrary, Solomon's attainments were actually less than those of the great conquerors and founders, Moses and David, in the Italian philosopher's view.

Erasmus, in his second interpretation of Solomon's dream at Gibeon, reiterates still more forcefully the argument that the wisdom that Solomon sought and received was not merely wisdom, that is, knowledge of philosophy in general, it was practical wisdom, the wisdom that could assist him in justly ruling the kingdom he had been given.

To back this up, Erasmus presents the dream dreamt by Midas, who was universally condemned for desiring nothing but gold, as the antithesis of Solomon's dream. Solomon the Hebrew is held up as the prototype of the good prince, while Midas the pagan is displayed as the prototype of the despotic ruler.[29] As is usual in this genre of political literature, Erasmus conducts a lengthy inquiry into the dichotomy between the good prince and the tyrant, following the model of the fifth book of Aristotle's *Politics*. He highlights the contrast by comparing two biblical texts: the image of the tyrant portrayed in Samuel's reply to the people after they request a king (1 Sam. 8), and the image of the good king in the description in Deuteronomy 17 of the commandments binding on a king.

Erasmus, however, has a problem with the first of these models. Samuel does not speak explicitly about tyranny but about the "law of kingship" generally. It is clear from the plain text that Samuel views kings as being generally tyrannical. Abravanel, who rejected monarchy in principle, referred to this *pshat* in his assertion that monarchy was by nature bound to degenerate into tyranny.[30] By contrast, Erasmus, who favored constitutional monarchy, was obviously unable to accept an automatic identification of monarchy with tyranny. He does admit that on the face of it, the passage in Scripture on the law of kingship is identical with the "law of tyranny" *(ius tyrannicum)*. He finds this surprising, because "there is no greater benefit than a good king" *(nihil sit salutarius bono rege)*,[31] and the identification of king with tyrant is liable to undermine the people's desire for a monarchy. He explains that there were indeed tyrannical kings in ancient states, hence, the identification of monarchy with tyranny. Samuel, by contrast, was a good king, who ruled the people justly. The people, however, mistakenly identified monarchy with tyranny, wished to be like all the nations, and called on him to become a tyrant. Therefore, Samuel harangued them with a lively description of the tyrant-king they sought, in order to dissuade them, although to no avail.

Samuel's speech was widely adopted in medieval and Renaissance political literature as a basic text in political thought. It was used in two contexts: the contest between spiritual and temporal authority—the prophet Samuel representing the demand of the former (i.e., the church) for supremacy in the political arena; and the theory of regimes, in which the debate turned on the identification of monarchy with tyranny. Those who viewed them as identical, such as Abravanel, preferred a republican or direct theocratic regime, while those who distinguished between them, such as Erasmus, favored a constitutional monarchy. Erasmus focuses here only on the second context, and, unlike the consensus then, presents Samuel not as a prophet representing spiritual as opposed to temporal authority, but as a king.

Erasmus draws a parallel between the Scripture's animal imagery of the tyrant—"Her princes in the midst thereof are like wolves ravening after prey, to shed blood" (Ezekiel 22:27), and "As a roaring lion, and a raging bear, so is a wicked ruler over the poor people" (Proverbs 28:15)—and Plato's simile in *The Republic* of princes guarding the state like dogs protecting the flock against wolves. When the guardians themselves turn into wolves, or, as Plato says elsewhere, into a preying lion, the entire flock is lost. Paul applied the same imagery to Nero.[32]

The good prince must, of course, conform to the description of the good king in Deuteronomy 17, not the description of the unrestrained tyrant in 1

Samuel 8. As a good Christian, though, Erasmus feels himself bound to add a reservation: the good Hebrew prince in Deuteronomy 17 acted in accordance with the law of Moses, which provided him with no more than the most basic rules of justice. By contrast, the Christian prince, who enjoys the guidance of the words of the apostles, must attain the supreme perfection of the good prince. If the King of Israel is commanded not "to be exalted over his people," how much more so is the Christian prince obliged to treat his subjects not as slaves but as brothers, just as Jesus Christ himself treated them.[33]

3

Machiavelli's *The Prince (Il Principe)*, Erasmus' *Institutio*, and Thomas More's *Utopia* all appeared in the same year, 1516, the *annus mirabilis* of early modern political thought. The study of Machiavelli's revolutionary image of the Hebrew patriarchs as good princes is especially illuminating, inasmuch as the vast body of scholarship on Machiavelli contains so little on this subject. Examining Machiavelli's stance will also make it possible to understand Simone Luzzato's and Benedict Spinoza's total rejection of the medieval theory of the philosopher king and their reevaluation of the Hebrew patriarchs. Without Machiavelli, we cannot properly grasp the last stage of the development of the philosopher king idea in Jewish thought.

In a true Renaissance spirit, Machiavelli regarded the lives of the ancients as models to be emulated. He was convinced that if he understood the secret of their political success he would also learn the right lessons, be able to apply them to his own period, and bring about the political revival of Italy.[34] His study of Livy's history was intended to further this goal.[35]

While the chief lessons that Machiavelli learns are derived from classical history, in some places he cites examples from the history of other ancient peoples, among them the Persians, the Carthaginians, and the Jews. At times he presents the Bible as a treasure trove of historical and political lessons. "Whoever reads the Bible attentively" *(che legge la Bibia sensatamente),* he states, "will derive useful lessons from it."[36] We find more than once that Machiavelli himself does not read the Bible quite as diligently as he advises, but approaches it in a distinctly tendentious way. He is not always precise in his quotations, and he finds exactly what he is looking for, which is not necessarily what is really there. Erasmus, we have seen, counseled his good prince to read biblical passages describing harsh political reality as allegory, lest his virtues be tarnished. Machiavelli, by contrast, advises his shrewd prince to learn a useful political lesson from precisely these same passages. Both Aquinas and Erasmus distinguish between two Davids: the temporal leader of the Books of Samuel, about whom they have serious reservations,

and the agonizing spiritual writer of the Book of Psalms, whom they ideal-
ize. Likewise, they prefer Solomon, the philosopher of the Books of Proverbs
and Ecclesiastes to the temporal leader of 1 Kings. By contrast, Machiavelli,
like Albo (but for different reasons altogether), distinguishes between David
the sinner in the private sphere and the ideal ruler of the public sphere; both
thinkers admire the latter. The varied biblical texts that all these writers chose
to use clearly illuminate their political inclinations.

Machiavelli's two major political works, *The Prince* and *The Discourses,*
directly discuss the ancient Hebrew state, the circumstances of its founding,
its laws, its institutions, and its three great leaders, Moses, David, and
Solomon in ten different places. Moses is mentioned six times; David three.
One of these discussions contains a direct reference to Solomon and his son
Rehoboam,[37] who elsewhere are referred to only indirectly.

In his article on the meaning of the key word *virtu'* in Machiavelli, Neal
Wood lists fifty-three historical personalities whom Machiavelli designates as
possessing the trait. Machiavelli transformed the meaning of the classical
term, *virtus*—a fine moral quality, to *virtu'*—a talent for political and military
leadership implying outright arrogance. In Machievelli's discourse, *virtu'* is a
changeable term, its meaning varying according to context.[38] Of the fifty-
three figures listed, the great majority—forty-seven—belong to antiquity.
That only six moderns are included in the list of possessors of *virtu'* reflects
Machiavelli's admiration for the political greatness of the ancients generally
(antiquitas virtus). Of these forty-seven, about half are Romans, corresponding to Machiavelli's well-known belief that the Romans were more virtuous
than any other people. The others include several Greeks, the Persian Cyrus,
the Carthaginian Hannibal, Moses—the first lawgiver of the Hebrews, and
David—the great Hebrew king. Most of the leaders noted by Machiavelli
belong to the period before the Punic Wars, the age that he regarded as the
zenith of political perfection in ancient times, which preceded the decline that
set in with the rise of the Roman Empire. Almost all the figures on the *virtu'*
list are from the eastern and central Mediterranean basin. Moses and David
fit nicely into this chronological and geographical framework. Notably,
Solomon does not appear on the list, even though Machiavelli considered him
a model of political leadership. Solomon, in his view, is not the lawgiver or
founder of a state, or even a military commander, but merely a successful and
fortunate heir to an existing state.

Four of the fifty-three possessors of *virtu'* are singled out as special. These
are leaders who founded states and acquired power not fortuitously but
through their ability alone: *"per propria virtu' e non per fortuna."*[39] They are, in
order: Moses, Cyrus, Romulus, and Theseus.[40] Discussing states founded on
the basis of the *virtu'* of a single leader, Machiavelli observes that these four
founders were "the greatest" *(il piu eccelenti);*[41] later, he again refers to "their

own great qualities" *(la eccelente virtu' loro)*.[42] They are the only ones to elicit the superlative *"eccelente,"* which Machiavelli adds to the description of their *virtu'*. In the last chapter of *The Prince* he defines these men, and principally Moses, as "rare and marvelous" *(uomini . . . rari e maravigliosi)*.[43] Although Machiavelli states that there are others like them, he names only these four. Regarding Moses, he has certain reservations, which we shall examine below, yet in spite of this, or possibly because of it, he still includes him among the select four—indeed in first place. Interestingly, although the list of possessors of *virtu'* is composed mainly of Romans and Greeks, only two of these are among the special four—Romulus and Theseus.

All four are founders of a state, military commanders, and lawgivers, whose success stemmed from their special talents, with barely any reliance on good luck *(fortuna)*. Moses appears at the top of the list of founders of states. Later in the same chapter, Machiavelli provides a detailed description of the special circumstances in which these founder-leaders operated, and here he changes the order of the four, yet Moses retains first place. The order becomes: Moses, Romulus, Cyrus, and Theseus.[44] Further on, the order is again altered—Moses, Cyrus, Theseus, and Romulus.[45] In the last chapter of *The Prince,* Moses still appears first in the list of founder-leaders, preceding Cyrus and Theseus,[46] while in *The Discourses,* he precedes Lycurgus, Solon, and the rest.[47]

Chronologically, Moses predates all the others. Moses was also the first whose acts resulted directly from a divine call and not merely from human initiative.[48] Machiavelli's attitude to this is ambivalent and it is not entirely certain that he regards it as an advantage. Conceivably, Moses appears first despite his divine call, not because of it. Apparently, Machiavelli consistently placed Moses first not only for the reasons listed above but also, and primarily, because he saw the Israelite as the outstanding example of leader, founder of a state, military commander, and lawgiver.

In *The Discourses* only Moses and Romulus are specifically assigned *virtu'*. There, Machiavelli cites Moses for "the talents of the founder and the success of his work, which is more or less remarkable . . ." *(la virtu' della edificatore . . . la quale e piu o meno maravigliosa . . .)*.[49] This serves to underline Moses' uniqueness in Machiavelli's eyes. Moses is the monotheistic prototype of the possessors of *virtu'*, while Romulus appears as the pagan prototype.

Moses' special status stands out in comparison with the other leaders, who have *virtu'* in general, and with the other leaders of the Hebrew nation specifically. It is no accident that Moses is discussed six times in Machiavelli's writings; that David, who also appears in the list of possessors of *virtu'*, is discussed three times; and Solomon, who is not on the list, appears only once. There is a direct correlation between Machiavelli's degree of esteem for these personalities and the number of times he presents them as examplars of successful political leadership.

Machiavelli, in the beginning of *The Prince,* distinguishes between states whose leadership is passed on by heredity and new states.[50] All the examples concerning Moses relate, naturally, to the second alternative. New states, according to the first chapter of *The Discourses,* are created in one of two ways: by natives or by outsiders. Moses is portrayed as the leader of a free people forced to leave their place of residence on account of bad conditions or disaster, and to settle elsewhere, that is, outsiders. Outsiders either settle in existing cities they have conquered or build new cities. The Hebrews, under the leadership of Moses, are presented as outsiders who settled in existing cities in the land they conquered:

> The founders of cities are independent when they are people who, under the leadership of some prince or by themselves, have been constrained *[sono constretti]* to fly from pestilence, war, or famine that was desolating their native country *[paese loro]* and seek a new home *[nuove terre].* These either inhabit the cities of the country of which they take possession, as Moses did. . . .[51]

Machiavelli later details the migratory process and again identifies Moses with it:

> These tribes migrated from their own countries *[paesi loro],* as we have said above, driven by hunger or war or some other scourge, which they had experienced at home and which obliged them *[e son constretti]* to seek new dwelling-places *[nuove terre]* elsewhere. Sometimes they come in overwhelming numbers, making violent eruptions *[con violenza]* into other countries, killing the inhabitants and taking possession of their goods, establishing new kingdoms *[nuovo regno]* and changing the very names of the countries. This was done by Moses. . . .[52]

This description, of course, is contrary to both the letter and the spirit of the Bible. Machiavelli depicts the exodus as an example of a general historical phenomenon, and Moses as the conqueror of the Land of Israel. He ignores, or is perhaps unaware of the fact that according to Scripture, Moses did not even enter the Land of Israel, and the lead in conquering the land went to Joshua. Only Machiavelli's characterization of the Jews as "a free people" suggests the biblical context of the exodus from Egypt.

Machiavelli associates one of the key concepts in his political thought with the exodus: "necessity" *(necessita'),* which forces people to act, to defend themselves, and to improve their condition. Since his view of human nature was fundamentally pessimistic, Machiavelli assumed that people act because of objective constraints rather than out of free choice. The human being by nature is slovenly and lazy, impelled only by the pressure of circumstances to take action to survive or improve his conditions.[53] This, Machiavelli believes, is what happened in the exodus.

In two places in *The Prince* Machiavelli does refer to the exodus not only in the context of general historical circumstances applicable to any people forced to wander and seek a new land, but also in the true biblical context of the enslavement of the people of Israel and the yearning for freedom. Here, too, however, he applies the general principle of necessity: "It was thus necessary *[necessario]* that Moses should find the people of Israel slaves in Egypt and oppressed by the Egyptians, so that they were disposed to follow him in order to escape from their servitude."[54] And in the last chapter of the work: "It was necessary *[era necessario]*, in order that the power *[virtu']* of Moses should be displayed, that the people of Israel should be slaves in Egypt. . . ."[55] The different context in which the example of the exodus appears in each of these cases accounts for the different portrayals of the event.

The most comprehensive treatment of Moses is found in chapter 6 of *The Prince*, which deals with new states established by virtue of the talents and courage of the leader rather than through good fortune. The difficulty in establishing a new state and guaranteeing its existence requires a special kind of political and military leadership and/or a large measure of luck. The more the leader's accomplishments depend on his abilities and the less on good fortune, the more capable and successful he will be in establishing a state that will endure. The *virtu'* of such a first lawgiver is so powerful that his ability to grasp the opportunities *(occasione)* that come his way is superlative; he possesses an unlimited creative ability to move things from potential to actual.

The relationship between the ruler and the ruled is likened by Machiavelli to the relationship between matter and form: the leader-lawgiver imparts meaning to the amorphous raw material.[56] The founder-leader becomes a Demiurge in the Platonic sense, the Creator, the fashioner out of primeval matter, the one who is able to realize all possibilities through creative action. Such a characterization places the leader on a level far above that of ordinary humanity.

Machiavelli constantly stresses the importance of the leader's freedom of action and absolute independence. Leadership in a time of crisis—and the creation of a state is such a time—can only be provided by a man acting alone. For this reason all founders must destroy their potential rivals and act alone. Machiavelli, in *The Discourses* (I:9), reiterates that the founder must do this "by himself" *(da uno)*,[57] as a god acting on his own volition. This is the basic rule *(regola generale)* on which the successful establishment of a new state depends. The same requirement applies to military leadership,[58] as well as to a political plot: the fewer the accomplices the more successful it will be. The ideal situation is that of the lone conspirator who involves others only at the last moment.[59]

Machiavelli opens *The Discourses* with a distinction between states established by free people and those established by people dependent on others. States that have an independent beginning, free of others, stand a better chance of success. Whoever is dependent on others will always find it difficult to free himself from their control.[60] Machiavelli also prefers a citizens' army to a mercenary force, with its crippling dependence on others.[61] He consistently presents Moses' state as the prototype of an independent state of free people established by a leader with unlimited ability to take action.

It is ironic that Machiavelli, otherwise the supremely realistic statesman, relies on semimythological figures to support his theory. The best examplars of political leadership are not real men like Cesare Borgia or the very Medici prince to whom *The Prince* is dedicated—but imagined figures from the remote past. These are the true heroes of *The Prince*. The supreme model is not that of a founder who operated in a concrete historical setting; it is "the founder" as an abstract concept.[62] The greatest of such founders are those who created states or religions, followed by military commanders who enlarged their states, followed in turn by the thinkers.[63]

Moses consistently heads the list of founders, and so possesses all the characteristics of such figures. The first of these is his absolute autonomy. In the first reference to the select founders in chapter 6 of *The Prince*, Machiavelli mentions that they were self-made men, to the extent possible for man. They were the exclusive generators of their success, *"per propria virtu' loro,"* which owed nothing to others or to chance except for the opportunity *(occasione)* to act. Their own talent, initiative, and strength enabled them to succeed and not waste the opportunities that presented themselves. Furthermore, they restricted assistance by external factors to the essential minimum.[64]

The first historical example of such circumstances that Machiavelli cites is that of Israel in Egypt. What is the *occasione*, the special circumstance in which Moses acted? It was not a favorable opportunity with conditions conducive to action by a founder-leader, but just the opposite: the extant conditions were actually intolerable. Yet, harsher the circumstances of the community led by the founder, the greater his opportunities. A great man thrives on difficulties, and the thornier they are the better he flourishes. When fortune *(fortuna)* seeks to shine on a man, it first presents him with a serious challenge. Moreover, difficult conditions, the fortune of the virtuous leader, inform his private life as well as the people he leads. His personal life history is a microcosm of the history of the people. The description of the difficult life situation of a man with leadership potential is applied by Machiavelli to Moses indirectly; that of the situation of the people he led is applied to him directly: "It was thus necessary that Moses should find the people of Israel slaves in Egypt and oppressed by the Egyptians, so that they were disposed to follow him in order to escape from their servitude."[65]

Following a presentation of the circumstances in which Cyrus, Romulus, and Theseus acted, Machiavelli develops his cyclical theory of history and uses it to describe the conditions necessary for the establishment of a new state. Such a development occurs at or near the nadir of a serious decline, engendering a reawakening and a renewed ascent. When a people sinks to its lowest point, it has nowhere to go but up. Unlike the living body, the body politic can recover and be restored to the freshness of youth.[66] We find this concept in the last chapter of *The Prince*, as well. When Machiavelli argues that now, the hour of Italy's greatest decline, is precisely the time for its salvation, his model is the kingdoms of antiquity, primarily that of the Hebrews. It was the slavery of the Children of Israel in Egypt that stimulated them to rebel and follow Moses: "And if, as I said, it was necessary in order that the power *[virtu']* of Moses should be displayed that the people Israel should be slaves in Egypt . . . , so at the present time, in order that the might of the Italian genius might be recognized, it was necessary *[era necessario]* that Italy should be reduced to her present condition, and that she should be more enslaved than the Hebrews."[67]

In the same way, difficult conditions shape the potential leaders' personal biography. At the beginning of his essay on the life of Castruccio Castracani, Machiavelli observes that it is not by chance that all the founders and lawgivers *(tutti coloro . . . che hanno . . . operato grandissime cose)* were born and reared in conditions of poverty and misery. The specific instance he chooses is that of the fourteenth-century Italian statesman, whom he presents as an individual example of a general principle *(regola generale)*. This principle holds equally true in the cases of baby Moses in the ark amid the bulrushes, and Romulus suckled by the she-wolf.[68] The need to contend with difficult personal *occasione* is precisely what prepares and tempers the leader to measure up successfully to the most difficult public *occasione*.

While Machiavelli did not invent the stories about the difficult beginnings of the great founders of states, he made very good use of these long-standing myths, well aware that the stories were mythological. He knew that even the greatest of the leaders were not the sons of gods, as the mythological tradition portrayed them, but in actuality came from a humble background. It is unlikely that he believed the tales of their special links with higher powers. In his view, the founders themselves created these myths, which were intended to strengthen and legitimize their rule after they had realized their vision.[69] The myths, nevertheless, did reflect their unique abilities.

Machiavelli also knew that not only did the personal origins of the founders undergo a process of mythicization, but also the beginnings of new states did so as well. He regards this as a sophisticated, deliberate act on the part of the first founder: for the "statesman-fox,"[70] mythicization is a means of legitimation. The victors always try to eliminate the past and conceal the bloodstained beginnings of their state. Machiavelli presents the Hebrew state established by Moses as a clear example of this process. After nations win control of new territories, they

> establish a new kingdom *[un regno nuovo]* and change the very names of their countries. This was done by Moses and equally by those Barbarian tribes that took possession of the Roman Empire. In fact, the new names *[nomi nuovi]* which we find in Italy and in other countries have no other origin than in the fact of being so called by their new occupiers *[nuovi occupatori]*.

It may be noted the word "new" *(nuove)* is used often in this passage and elsewhere. This reflects Machiavelli's stress on the founding ruler's need to create a new order from the ground up, so as to entrench his domination. Machiavelli proceeds to adduce many examples from Italy and other European countries. He also adds: "Moses also changed the name of the part of Syria which he occupied, Judea."[71] Here, again, Machiavelli mistakenly portrays Moses as the person who conquered the Land of Israel. The nation that fled from the Jews and, according to Machiavelli, reached Africa, acted similarly, he believes. What they could not do to the Hebrews who invaded the Land of Israel, they did to others in Africa.[72]

A second characteristic that marked the great founders of states was, according to Machiavelli, the ability to act vigorously and decisively and not recoil even from acts of cruelty and bloodshed, if this served their purposes. A leader of this kind would dare to commit acts considered unacceptable and even immoral: his success would ultimately justify his actions. We have already noted that Machiavelli described the conquest and occupation of a new country as manifest acts of violence *(con violenza)*. This is precisely how the Hebrews' invasion and conquest of the Land of Israel is presented.[73] After providing a detailed description of Romulus' mode of operation to exemplify this form of behavior in *The Discourses* (I:9), Machiavelli remarks that "the above views might be corroborated by any number of examples, such as those of Moses, Lycurgus, Solon, and other founders of monarchies and republics."[74] *The Discourses* (III:30) provides yet another detailed reference to the example of Moses. In this chapter Machiavelli develops the argument that a leader seeking to establish his authority must first eliminate the envy of others towards him *(invidia)*. There are various ways of doing this, including, as a last alternative, the physical liquidation of all potential rivals—a course of action that arises from the need for sole and undisputed leadership. The specific example that Machiavelli adduces is that of Moses. After descending from Mount Sinai with the tablets of the law, his first act was one of mass violence—his order to the Levites to slaughter the three thousand worshippers of the golden calf:

And whoever reads the Bible attentively will find that Moses, for the purpose of insuring the observance of his laws and institutions *[le sue leggi e che suoi ordini]* was obliged *[stato forzato]* to have a great many persons put to death who opposed his designs under the instigation of no other feelings than those of envy and jealousy *[invidia]*.[75]

According to the biblical source, this was less a case of jealousy of Moses' leadership than the people's loss of direction. Yet, undoubtedly, there was public criticism of Moses' actions and leadership, some of it probably due to envy. Hence, Machiavelli's use of Scripture in this context is not entirely misplaced. Significantly, Machiavelli refers here to the only instance in the biblical narrative in which the rebellious mass is not punished directly by God. Moreover, the text does not contain any direct instruction from God himself to punish the calf worshippers. The defiant mob is punished at Moses' initiative entirely. Furthermore, those who execute Moses' orders, the Levites, have no noticeable political or religious status at this stage. Authority is wholly in the hands of the leader. This example well suits Machiavelli's tendency to stress the independent status and initiative of the founder and initial lawgiver.[76] Machiavelli emphasizes that Moses carried out this act from a sense of responsibility, an awareness of the objective pressure of reality *(stato forzato)*, and in accordance with the demands of necessity, not out of some personal caprice. Machiavelli's next example, his contemporary, the politician-monk Savonarola, had a clear grasp of the need to use violence to achieve his goals but failed because he lacked the authority and the power to do so.[77] Moses, by contrast, not only understood the need for violence in certain circumstances, but he also had the power and authority to act, which he did efficiently and successfully.

Christian theologians since Augustine had used the examples of Cain who killed Abel and established a city, and Romulus, who killed his brother and established a city, to express the essentially negative character of all temporal power. For Machiavelli, they embodied the facts of life. Augustine would have made a clear distinction between Moses, who killed the three thousand worshippers of the golden calf and established a nation, yet was the emissary of God, and Cain and Romulus, who were motivated by material considerations. Machiavelli viewed the behavior of all three as motivated by the same real and legitimate political interests.[78]

For this reason, Machiavelli portrays the ideal founder-leader not only as a political person but also as a military commander. The leader's statesmanship will be to no avail unless backed by military force. In this connection, Machiavelli coined his famous epithet, "armed prophets" *(profeti armati)*. In order to conquer territory, establish a state on it, and convince the people to accept its laws and institutions, an armed force was necessary. Moses, Cyrus, Theseus, and Romulus would not have been able to sustain their charters for so long had they not been armed.[79] Machiavelli finds it highly symbolic that Moses' first act after descending from the mountain with the tablets of the law was to order the slaying of the calf worshippers. That he was a prophet who was armed and capable of inflicting violence was vital for the realization of his goals, which initially included turning the wild mob into a law-abiding nation.

Moses, despite being the prototype of the founder-leader, commander, and initial lawgiver, nevertheless causes a difficult problem for Machiavelli. Following the first reference to Moses at the head of the list of possessors of special *virtù* (chapter 6 of *The Prince*), Machiavelli immediately adds a stipulation:

> And although one should not speak of Moses, he having merely carried out what was ordered him by God, still he deserves admiration, if only for that grace which made him worthy to speak with God. But regarding Cyrus and others who have acquired or founded kingdoms, they will all be found worthy of admiration; and if their particular actions and methods are examined they will not appear very different from those of Moses, although he had so great a Master.[80]

Machiavelli seems to find it hard to accept the phenomenon of Moses, whose power is shown to derive directly from divine inspiration. From this passage, at least on the surface, it would even appear that the attainments of the other great leaders surpassed those of Moses: they achieved what he did without divine support. This would be in keeping with Machiavelli's emphasis on the independent initiative of the founder-leader. Indeed, Machiavelli states that the example of Moses is not relevant *(di Moise non si debbe ragionare)*. Immediately afterward in the same chapter, however, he again presents Moses as the example of the ideal leader. He does this repeatedly, placing Moses first on the list, as though the above-quoted stipulation did not exist. In fact, this is the only place where it appears. Everywhere else, both in *The Prince* and in *The Discourses*, Moses invariably appears first on the list of founders, with no mention of any special difference between him and them.[81]

Some Machiavelli scholars have argued, nevertheless, that the passage was intended to belittle Moses.[82] This is not the case. First, Machiavelli relates to Moses in this way only once. Everywhere else, he deals with Moses with great esteem, as with all the other founders. Second, when Machiavelli means to show scorn, he does so openly.[83] When he says that Moses is to be honored on account of the grace he won through his direct contact with God, the words ring true. Those who detect a note of contempt here are apparently influenced by Machiavelli's well-known criticism of established religion and its devastating effect on the life of action. Machiavelli, however, clearly distinguished between ancient religion *(la religione antica)*, which "consecrated only highly praiseworthy men of action whose deeds in this world got them a great name, such as commanders of armies and chiefs of states," and the established church of his day *(la nostra religione)*, which favored men who abstained from what it called the "vanities of this world" and thereby left the political arena open to "butchers" and "rogues."[84] For Machiavelli, Moses represented the ancient religion, which valued statesmen and the life of action. His was the prototype of a religion that hailed glorious men of action *(uomini pieni di mondana gloria)* like himself. Machiavelli viewed such a religion as a vital political tool, incomparably effective for creating and preserving the social and political cohesion of the state.

The passage on Moses' divine mission, then, may be read as expressing true religious sentiment, if no special effort is made to detect irony in it. Machiavelli speaks of Moses with the utmost sincerity, almost with the feeling of a believer: Moses "implemented the commands of God. . . . He is to be honored and esteemed if only for this grace alone, which made him worthy of speaking with God" *(debbe essere ammirato solum per quelle grazia che lo facheva degno di parlare con Dio)*.[85] In the last chapter of *The Prince*, too, Machiavelli suggests that the future liberator of Italy adopt the miracles performed for Moses and the people of Israel in the desert as a model. These miracles prove, he believes, that God, directly and by supernatural means, helps whoever takes his fate in his own hands. God helps only those who help themselves:

Besides this, unexamined wonders have been seen here performed by God. The sea has been opened, a cloud has shown you the way, the rock has given forth water, manna has rained, and everything has contributed to your greatness. The remainder must be done by you. God will not do everything, in order not to deprive us of free will *[libero arbitro]* and the portion of the glory *[fama]* that falls to our lot.[86]

Even if we do not overlook the obviously rhetorical nature of the closing chapter of *The Prince*, the various statements about Moses form a coherent picture. Moses is presented as having obtained direct divine support as a reinforcement of his superior abilities and initiative. If pagan *fortuna* comes to the aid of the wise and energetic man of action, Divine Providence does so too. In the final analysis, Machiavelli does not revert to paganism, as some have contended, nor does he cut himself off from medieval monotheistic theology.

All this is surprising only on the surface. Machiavelli, in fact, presents the acts of the founders in almost religious terms. He compares them to God, to the Demiurge, or to whoever imposes form upon of primeval chaotic matter. This is the case in respect to all the pagan founders. Machiavelli, in chapter 6, terms the founders "armed prophets" *(profeti armati)*, yet the fact that they are armed is not logically, theologically, or historically contradictory to their portrayal as prophets, for they are not depicted as prophets in the simple sense of the term. Machiavelli attempts to identify the prophet with the founder and initial lawgiver, and even with the military commander. This idea is not at root nonreligious. It had a long history in the religious and political thought of the Middle Ages. Since all founders sought to accomplish an act that was beyond normal human capability, their activity is described as having a clearly divine connection. In this respect, there is complete equivalence between prophet, lawgiver, and even military commander. If divine inspiration is reduced to the level of realpolitik, then, conversely, the latter is elevated to the level of divine inspiration. Even assuming that Machiavelli regarded the myth of the divine inspiration of the first founders as a kind of Platonic "noble lie"—a later invention of the statesman-fox intended to impart legitimation to his regime—he undeniably finds superhuman features in their actions.

The differences between the founder-leaders, each of whom had performed an act with an obviously divine connection, lay in the form and mode of divine inspiration. The association of the canonical prophet with the pagan lawgiver stems from this inspiration. For all the potential irony inherent in such an association, it is not at all illogical in Machiavelli's system. The problem of founding new states is so complex that although divine inspiration of the Mosaic type may offer one possible solution, and perhaps the preferable one, it is not the only option. Thus, when Machiavelli argues that the pagan lawgivers were no less successful than Moses, he is not expressing scorn for the divine source of the latter's mission. He is merely voicing the supposition that other ways, all with some form of divine significance, exist for achieving the goals of the initial lawgiver.[87]

Machiavelli's reservations about Moses as the prototype of the initial lawgiver do not weaken this status. In fact, they may even strengthen it. Moses is presented as the unique examplar of an initial lawgiver whose mission stems from direct divine inspiration. When Machiavelli remarks that the example of Moses is not relevant, he means that Moses was exceptional in being the only leader whose actions arose from divine inspiration of the monotheistic kind. This explains why ultimately Moses remains highly relevant for Machiavelli and consistently heads the list of initial lawgivers.

King David also appears on the list of the fifty-three possessors of *virtu*', but he is not among the select four. He is depicted as a king who possesses greater *virtu*' than the norm and who took power in an existing state. "David was beyond doubt a most extraordinary man in war, in learning, and in superior judgment" *(Davit, senza dubbio, fu un uomo, per dottrina, per arme, per guidizio, eccelentissimo, e fu tanta la sua virtu').*[88] True, the characterization "most excellent" is not juxtaposed with *virtu'*, as with Moses. It refers, instead, to a man of special political and military talents. His *virtu'*, while not *eccelente*, is nevertheless *fu tanta*, and this too is outstanding.

Machiavelli cites David as a model of right behavior in a new ruler, as described in *The Discourses* (I:6), in the chapter headed: "A new prince *[uno principe nuove]* in a city or province conquered by him should organize everything anew *[cosa nuova]*."[89] When a leader rises to power, the best way of establishing his rule is by destroying the old regime and creating completely new foundations. This means the formation of a new political, economic, and military establishment composed of men who were oppressed by the former regime and who have a personal interest in the rise and consolidation of the new government, on which they are absolutely dependent. Notice should be taken of the number of times the word "new" *(nuovo)* appears here, as in the text on Moses. This serves to emphasize the importance that Machiavelli assigns to the ruler's establishment of an entirely new order so as to entrench his rule:

> The best means for holding that principality *[a tenere quel principato]* is to organize the government entirely anew *[fare ogni cosa . . . di nuovo]* (he being himself a new prince *[nuovo principe]* [there]); that is, he should appoint new governors *[nuovi governi]* with new titles *[nuovi nomi]*, new powers *[nuove autoritā]*, and new men *[nuovi uomini]*, and he should make the poor rich, as David did when he became king *[quando e divento re]*, "who heaped riches upon the needy, and dismissed the wealthy empty-handed." Besides this, he should destroy the old cities and build new ones *[nuove cittā]*. . . . In short, he should leave nothing unchanged in the province, so that there is neither rank, nor grade, nor wealth that is not recognized as coming from him.[90]

Machiavelli, in elaborating the example of David, was probably referring to the description of David's supporters in his struggle against Saul: "every one that was in distress and every one that was in debt, and every one that was discontented . . ." (1 Sam. 22:2), as well as to the scriptural narrative of how, after his victory over Saul and after taking up the holy ark, David distributed bread and cake to the people (2 Sam. 6:19). His destruction of the economic regime that was dependent on the previous ruler is reflected in his conflict with Nabal the Carmelite (1 Sam. 25). David also wiped out Saul's political and military infrastructure and set up a new one based upon loyalty to, and dependence upon, him alone. Contrary to Machiavelli's assertion, however, many of these acts took place not after David became king but as part of his ongoing struggle with Saul.

Machiavelli's second example of right behavior by a leader is Philip of Macedon. David the Hebrew and Philip the Macedonian, then, are presented as the most successful examples in history of new rulers who used sophisticated political tactics.

One of Machiavelli's best known axioms appears in *The Prince:* "the chief foundations of all states . . . are good laws and good arms" *(le buone legge e le buone arme)*.[91] Without good laws, the existence of good defense is not possible; if the defense is good, the laws must necessarily be good. Machiavelli devotes a lengthy dissertation to the link between military and political affairs. As elsewhere, he distinguishes between troops belonging to the prince himself and mercenaries. In keeping with his well-known emphasis on the importance of the absolute independence of the prince, Machiavelli holds that a necessary condition for the success and survival of the prince is that he have a highly motivated private force, loyal to him alone. If he is dependent on mercenaries, who lack motivation and are out for gain, or on troops belonging to other men and therefore loyal to them, he has no chance of succeeding.

Typically, the chief examples that Machiavelli adduces are from Roman and Italian history. Toward the end of his discussion, however, he cites the biblical story of David and Goliath:

> I would also call to mind a symbolic tale from the Old Testament which will illustrate this point. When David made his offer to Saul to go and fight against the Philistine champion Goliath, Saul, to encourage him *[per dargli animo]*, armed him with his own arms, which when David had tried them on he refused, saying that with them he could not fight so well; he preferred, therefore, to face the enemy with his own sling and knife *[con la sua fromba e con il suo coltello]*.[92]

David exemplifies the principle of self-reliance on the part of the military leader. Machiavelli sums up the moral he draws from text thus: "In short, the arms of others either fail, overburden, or else impede you."[93] In the end, only the leader-commander's courage, resolution, and ability to maneuver will win the day. It was David's understanding of the basic principles of both the art of politics and the art of war that brought him success in his extended conflict with Saul.

The consequences of David's political and military wisdom were not only that he succeeded in making himself king of Judah, but also that he successfully invaded all the neighboring states and bequeathed a large kingdom to Solomon. Machiavelli applies these facts to support his argument that a weak ruler *(uno principe debole)* who succeeds an excellent ruler *(uno eccelente principe)* can retain power, but the state has no chance of survival if two weak rulers reign in succession. By contrast, the state will reach its peak if it has successive effective rulers:

If one king succeeds another of equally great abilities and courage *[sono di gran virtú]*, then it will often be seen that they achieve extraordinary greatness *[cose grandissime]* for their state, and that their fame *[fama]* will rise to the very heavens.[94]

Machiavelli offers the reigns of David and Solomon as the first non-Roman example of this happy circumstance:

David was beyond doubt a most extraordinary man in war, in learning, and in superior judgment; and such was his military ability that, having conquered and crushed his neighbors *[tutti i suoi vicini]*, he left a peaceful kingdom *[uno regno pacifico]* to his son Solomon, which he was able to maintain *[conservare]* by the art of peace *[con l'arte della pace]* and not by war *[e non con la guerra]* and could thus happily enjoy the results of his father's virtue and valor *[la virtu']*. But he could not thus transmit it to his son, Rehoboam, who had neither the merits of his grandfather *[non essendo per virtu' simile allo avolo]* nor the good fortune of his father *[ne per fortuna simile al padre]*; and it was with difficulty, therefore, that he remained heir to the sixth part of the kingdom.[95]

Moving to his second non-Roman historical example, the Turkish sultan Mahomet II and his son Bajazet, Machiavelli compares the Turkish case with the Hebrew prototype: "Mahomet, having, like David, crushed his neighbors, left his son a firmly established kingdom *[uno regno fermo]*, which he could easily preserve *[conservare]* with the arts of peace *[l'arte della pace]*."[96]

Solomon is portrayed in terms faithful to Scripture and to the medieval Judeo-Christian tradition as a ruler who maintained a peaceful, prosperous kingdom *(un regno pacifico)* as depicted in the verse, "And Judah and Israel dwelt secure, every man under his vine and under his fig-tree, from Dan even to Beer-Sheba, all the days of Solomon's reign" (1 Kings 5:5).[97] Here again, Machiavelli focuses exclusively on the narrow political aspect of Solomon's rule. He ignores the generalized Platonic characterization, common in medieval and Renaissance thought, of Solomon as the prototype of the philosopher king. This, of course, conforms with Machiavelli's basic thinking, which separates politics not only from religion but from philosophy as well. Solomon's wisdom, in his eyes, is political wisdom only. So the entire philosophical setting, in which Solomon is the wisest of men, is absent here.

David is depicted as a leader who assumed power in an existing state and stabilized it; Solomon, as a leader who successfully maintained it. Machiavelli states in several places in *The Prince* that his purpose was to study how it is possible "to obtain such a state and to maintain it" *(e mostro e modi con il quali molto hanno cerco di acquistarli e tenerli).*[98] David provides an outstanding example of how to seize a state, while Solomon provides the model of how to preserve it. David was a master of the art of war *(arte della guerra),* Solomon a master of the art of peace *(arte della pace).* David did not rely on luck but principally on his *gran virtu';* Solomon's success derived mainly from his good fortune *(fortuna).* Thus, for all his esteem for Solomon, Machiavelli did not include him in his list of possessors of *virtu'.* Solomon was not a lawgiver, a military commander, or the founder of a state by virtue of his own initiative, but a fortunate ruler who inherited a stable kingdom and successfully maintained it.

Since talent and good fortune are the only two roads to success, as Machiavelli states at the end of the first chapter of *The Prince* ("by good fortune or special ability" *[o per fortuna o per virtu']*),[99] both David and Solomon prospered. For each of them possessed at least one of these qualities. Rehoboam, who in Machiavelli's judgment possessed neither his grandfather's *virtu'* nor his father's *fortuna,* was destined to fail, and the decline of the ancient Hebrew state began with him.

Rome had great fortune *(una fortuna grandissima)* in its first three kings, Romulus, Numa, and Tullus. The first was a "courageous and warlike king" *(ferocissimo e bellicoso)* like David; the second was "peace-loving and religious" *(quieto e religioso)* like Solomon; and the third was "as courageous as Romulus, and preferred war to peace" *(simile di ferocita a Romolo, e piu amatore guerra che della pace),*[100] as Rehoboam should have been. The fortuitous combination made it possible for Rome to establish itself as a great power that lasted for a very long time. If Rehoboam had been capable of following his grandfather David's warlike ways, the Judean kingdom would have endured in all its glory. Since Rehoboam was a weak prince *(uno principe debole),* his kingdom did not fare well and was doomed to perish.

This description conforms only partially with the biblical narrative. Scripture gives two parallel explanations for Rehoboam's failure to hold Solomon's kingdom together. One is theological: divine punishment for the proliferation of idol worship in Solomon's time (1 Kings 11:31–37). The second reflects pure realpolitik: Rehoboam is presented as a ruler who chooses poor advisers, and therefore receives poor advice, leading to his downfall (ibid. 12:8–10). Machiavelli ignores the theological explanation. Having posited that history reflects a natural law and is therefore the product of human doings, he is unable to accept the medieval theological concept that sees the hand of God in historical events. Moreover, the theological explanation puts the blame on Solomon, not Rehoboam. Machiavelli portrays Solomon as an ideal ruler and places the entire blame on Rehoboam. He cannot accept the theological explanation from the outset.

Although Machiavelli prefers the realpolitik approach, he does not expand on the reasons for Rehoboam's failure. He is principally interested in the lessons to be learned from the achievements of David and Solomon, not the political shortcomings of Saul and Rehoboam. Machiavelli devotes an entire chapter to the question of the best advisers for a statesman, defining three kinds of ruler:

> The one understands things unassisted *[intende da se]*, the other understands things when shown by others *[discerne quello cho altri intende]*, the third understands neither alone nor with the explanations of others *[non intende ne se ne altri]*. The first kind is most excellent *[eccelentissimo]*, the second also excellent *[eccelente]*, but the third useless *[inutile]*."[101]

A prince's understanding is measured by the advisers he chooses. A ruler of the first kind *(primo grado)* does not need advisers at all. A ruler of the second kind *(secondo grado)* needs advisers but is capable of selecting them properly and of taking their advice critically:

> For every time the prince has the judgment to know *[iudicio di conoscere]*, the good and evil that any one does or says, even if he has no originality *[non abbia invenzione]*, he can recognize the bad and good works of his minister and correct the one and encourage the other; and the minister cannot hope to deceive him and therefore remains good *[mantiensi buono]*.[102]

But the third kind of ruler—the unsuccessful *(inutile)* ruler—not only lacks proper understanding of his own, but he is not even able to choose the right advisers; he is therefore doomed to fail.

Applying Machiavelli's analysis to the biblical text, we find that David, who is included in the list of possessors of *virtu'*, certainly belonged to the first class of ruler, those who are the most excellent *(eccelentissimo)*; Solomon belonged to the second class, the excellent *(eccelente)*; and Rehoboam, portrayed as a dismal failure *(inutile)*, belonged to the third class. Machiavelli showed interest in the ancient Hebrew state only so long as it provided him with examples of the art of politics: how to deliver a people from slavery and give it new laws and institutions (Moses); how to seize power in an existing kingdom and establish a stable regime (David); and how to preserve this regime successfully (Solomon). The moment the Hebrew state began to disintegrate (under Rehoboam), he lost interest in it. There is no mention in his discourse of the Hebrew state in the period of its subsequent decline.[103]

In several respects, perhaps more than is commonly realized, Machiavelli's *The Prince* continues the ancient tradition of the ideal ruler. His basic models are the mythological rulers of the remote past, not the real rulers of his own times. Moses, David, and Solomon, together with Solon, Lycurgus, and Romulus, still appear as the archetypes of the ideal ruler, with Moses, as in the medieval tradition, continuing to appear at the top of the list. In this respect we find a striking parallel between Machiavelli and Maimonides (*Guide* II:39). Despite Machiavelli's seemingly "pagan" tendency, he, like Maimonides, singles out Moses as a "public prophet." For all his outspoken censure of the dependence of politics on religion, Machiavelli still presents the ideal ruler as a kind of prophet who possesses unique faculties. Machiavelli has not really moved very far from the accepted medieval concept so well expressed in Maimonides, as well as in Dante, of the ideal leader as a reflection of God's rule on Earth. The theory of armed prophets, too, for all its modern tone, is by no means detached from medieval theology. As we have seen, Al-Farabi and many who came after him posit the talent for military leadership as one of the necessary characteristics of the ideal ruler. Like them, Machiavelli justifies coercive action when all other means of correcting the behavior of an errant people fail.[104]

Still, Machiavelli's *Prince* clearly deviates in one crucial respect from the medieval tradition of the ideal ruler. Machiavelli overturns the whole tradition of the *Speculum Principium*. The *virtu* of his ideal prince is far removed from the *virtus* of the philosopher king of the Platonic and Farabian versions or even of his contemporary, Erasmus. What we see here are no longer virtues in the classical sense but attributes of purposefulness and boldness possessed by the realistic statesman. The Hebrew patriarchs no longer appear as philosophical rulers who maintain the ideal state by means of their moral and intellectual perfection. Rather, they are presented as flesh and blood leaders who, by means of their *virtu*—arguably either good qualities or sheer nerve and force of will—cope with the state as it actually is.[105] The medieval king-Messiah, is transformed by Machiavelli, in the last chapter of *The Prince*, into a *principe* of the Italian Renaissance.

9

Rejection

Against the background of the transformation wrought by Machiavelli, let us now return to the arena of Jewish thought in the late Renaissance. Discussion of the ideal ruler, whether the Platonic philosopher king concept disseminated by Al-Farabi and Ibn Rushd, or the Latin Christian form of the *Speculum Principium,* gradually faded from Jewish thought in the sixteenth century, as it did from European philosophy generally. Machiavellian political ideas and the theory of *raison d'état* began to replace such medieval concepts.

No significant example of the treatment of the philosopher-king theory is to be found in sixteenth-century Jewish thought, while in the mid-seventeeth century it was explicitly rejected by the Venetian Jewish thinker Simone Luzzatto and later by Spinoza. Both these philosophers represent Jewish applications of the Machiavellian revolution. Both were seventeenth-century Jewish rationalists, reflecting the legacy of medieval philosophy and commentary side by side with the far-reaching effects of contemporary philosophical and political currents. Luzzatto remained true to his Judaism; Spinoza's radical rationalism, however, led him to cast off his religion.

Luzzatto's *Discorso* circulated in Amsterdam in the first half of the seventeenth century and was used, for example, by Menasseh ben Israel. Luzzatto's political positions show great similarity to Spinoza's. The two used many of the same sources. Spinoza, may well have read Luzzatto's work and been influenced by it.[1] However, Spinoza expresses a more radical rejection of the philosopher-king theory and a more Machiavellian-secular approach as to the development of the ancient Hebrew state and the image of Moses as political leader. A consideration of Luzzatto and Spinoza, then, constitutes a fitting ending to this study.

1

Luzzatto's two chief works are his apologetic *Discourse on the Jews of Venice (Discorso circa il stato degli Ebrei in Venezia)*, Venice, 1638, and the later, more generally philosophical *Socrates (Socrate—Overo dell'Humano Sapere)*, Venice, 1651—the latter completely neglected by scholars.[2] Both works, while they differ in scope, are solidly based on Machiavellian political theory and the tradition of *ragione di stato*. Both absorb mercantilist economic theory and are imbued with the implications of contemporary discoveries in the natural sciences, medicine, and astronomy.

In the *Discorso*, Luzzatto adopts a realist, utilitarian political position influenced by Aristotelian and Machiavellian ideas. He sharply criticizes Platonic political theory. Like many contemporary philosophers in Italy and throughout western Europe who accepted Machiavellian ideas and the theory of *raison d'état*, Luzzatto shuns Plato's idealism and the pronounced deductivism of his political thought.

Luzzatto sharply criticizes what he calls "artificial republics" *(machinate republiche)* such as those posited by Socrates, Plato, and Thomas More *(il moderno inventore della Utopia)*. He expressly prefers *The Republican* kind of solutions that Aristotle proposed for the problems of human society, praising Aristotle for "investing all his spirit" *(ogni suo spirito)* to reorganize and correct *(riordinare, e corregere)* the Platonic system.[3] Nevertheless, for all Luzzatto's esteem of the Venetian-type republican regime, the *Discorso* still contains obvious echoes of the old medieval philosopher-king theories. One example is his allegorical interpretation of Solomon's saying, "It is the glory of God to conceal a thing; but the glory of kings is to search out a matter" (Prov. 25:2). Luzzatto glosses:

> And this is the meaning of the saying: As it is appropriate that the hidden secrets of God and the true religion be obscure and hidden away from the ignorant multitude, as Virgil said, "fall back, unhallowed souls! the seer cried" (*Aen.* VI 2258–59), and as Solomon said in the consecration of the Temple: "The Lord hath said that He would dwell in the thick darkness" (1 Kings 8:12), so it is fitting for princes and the kings to penetrate into the innermost meaning of things, so they may be able, through their authority and the example they give, to lead the people to the true worship, and also so that they are not misled or trapped in the webs of lies of the superstitious and their illusions. Thus they will lie to themselves first, and then also to whoever follows them, since these opinions do not belong to the common people. A clear indication of this can be found in the holy books, concerning the giving of the Torah on Mount Sinai. As it is

said, "And the people stood afar off," as they were commanded previously, but about the legislator it was said, "But Moses drew near
unto the thick darkness where God was" (Exod. 20:13). This is the
way a ruler must behave.[4]

Here Luzzatto presents a medieval argument that is entirely Platonic,
revealing possible influences of Maimonides and Ibn Rushd. Luzzatto, in his
detailed discussion of the development of Jewish thought in the Middle Ages,
is generous in his praise of Maimonides and lauds the *Guide to the Perplexed*
as a book "full of sublime wisdom" that deeply influenced Christian thinkers
too. He makes a point of noting that Maimonides was "a contemporary of the
commentator Ibn Rushd."[5] Luzzatto amalgamates Jewish medieval theory
with the classical sources of humanism, drawing a parallel, for example,
between statements by Virgil and Moses that is characteristic of the tendency
to harmonize Judaism with contemporary cultural currents.

His exposition relies upon the medieval-Platonic distinction between
"true beliefs" and "necessary beliefs." The philosopher, as philosopher, must
strive to seek out the truth, but as ruler, he must hide this true thoughts from
the people, because of the danger latent in their distorted understanding, and
provide them instead with those truths—"noble lies," in Plato's terminology—
necessary for the maintenance of social order. In this way, Luzzatto rational-
izes the adherence of the ancient Israelites to superstitions, a trait singled out
by Tacitus in his acid criticism of the Jews. Luzzatto replies that as an intelligent political thinker *(statista che egli era),* Tacitus should have understood the
political need for superstition, to elicit obedience from the masses and to preserve the social order. The philosopher-rulers themselves, of course, must not
be affected by these superstitions.[6]

Thus, Luzzatto presents the ideal ruler in an Averroist image as a
philosopher-prophet-lawgiver: speaking of "the prophets who make law and
justice for future generations."[7] He compares this figure, in a pronounced
humanist spirit, with the first lawgivers of the pagan tradition, such as
Solon, Lycurgus, and Romulus: "If the lawgivers and the founders of civil
governments had not come and organized, with their wisdom and understanding, the human multitude into different levels and classes, its ugliness
would have been even greater than that of the famous ancient chaos."[8] Luzzatto superimposes on this characterization of the philosopher king the
medieval concept of the imitation of God. The ruler is presented as God's
representative on earth, or the "supreme lawgiver" *(principale instituitore):*
"As they are the representatives of God, it is appropriate for the rulers to
share in the actions of virtuousness and righteousness, since it is impossible
that the likeness of an image will be different from the image itself."[9] Luzzatto argues, in Maimonidean spirit, that the philosopher-prophet, who

knows the attributes manifested in God's acts—loving-kindness and charity—must imitate them in the way that he leads society.

In his clearly apologetic essay, Luzzatto uses the theory of the imitation of God to demonstrate that rulers are obliged to act fairly, in particular toward the Jews.[10] When the ruler acts justly toward his own people, or toward foreign residents, it may be assumed that he does so for utilitarian reasons only: to prevent rebellion among the former and an unfavorable reaction by the rulers of the latter. There can be no utilitarian motive for treating the Jews fairly, however, for they have no champion. This would be an act of justice for its own sake, a clear instance of the imitation of the moral perfection of God: "In this case, you can find the reason for it only in the heroic virtue of his noble spirit" *(una virtù eroica d'animo ingenuo).*[11] The source of this assertion is Plato's statement in the *Laws* that the ruler's ability to dispense justice for its own sake is reflected in his treatment of slaves.[12] Here, then, we witness how Luzzatto uses the medieval theory of the imitation of God to foster Jewish interests. Further on, however, we shall see him arguing that it is prudent for the prince to deal fairly with the Jews precisely for utilitarian reasons.

The medieval image of the philosopher king was thus transformed into *il principe* of the Italian Renaissance. Luzzatto uses Machiavelli's well-known analogy likening the active leader to a sculptor giving form to raw stone: "People are like a pile of stones, made of raw marble, which is used by a sculptor for many different purposes whenever he needs them. This is why he keeps them with him in large quantities."[13] This type of relationship between the active statesman and the passive masses recurs throughout the essay. The ruler cannot act without his raw material, just as the sculptor cannot work without his marble. The raw material by itself is meaningless; only the action of the ruler upon it gives it purpose, just as the block of marble has no meaning until the sculptor instills it with life. This concept of inert masses activated by the ruler is a logical consequence of Machiavelli's, and, following him, Luzzatto's[14] skeptical view of human nature. Only a wise and experienced ruler-initiator can motivate the masses to act in the desired way.

Excellence in two basic qualities mark the ruler as distinct from the masses: the ability to think instinctively according to the demands of expedience *(prudenza),* and initiative leading to action *(fortezza).* Only the right combination of these two abilities will lead to successful acts. The right decision without implementation is worthless, while action without proper reflection is likely to be disaster-laden. There must be *agere et intellegere.*

In the same vein, Luzzatto stresses the dangerous, potentially catastrophic consequences of superstition for rulers, as opposed to its essential character for the masses. In the Platonic medieval view, superstition was disastrous because it diverted the ruler from knowledge of the divine truth. In the Machiavellian Renaissance view, it was disastrous because it prevented thoughtful deliberation and led to passivity. Luzzatto produces a wealth of examples from Greek and Roman history. Even the Romans, who in his opinion were "very intelligent people," resorted to examining animals' innards and examined the movement of clouds in the sky in search of omens, instead of rationally weighing the practical alternatives before deciding on the most useful course and taking action accordingly.[15] Yet superstition was a useful tool for evoking obedience from the masses.

Like Machiavelli and Botero, Luzzatto emphasizes the necessity for the ruler to act vigorously and decisively without display of hesitancy lest signs of irresolution inspire the public to disobey and thus undermine social order: "A tyrannical government strives to oppress the people, while monarchic and aristocratic governments demand immediate obedience."[16] He, too, argues that the prince has the right to act cruelly, and even commit acts considered immoral when circumstances call for it. In typical Machiavellian spirit, Luzzatto portrays morals as irrelevant: "In this way also, rulers of people and military commanders acted when they committed atrocities against their enemies, in order to strengthen the spirit of their men and to acquire the loyalty of their people."[17]

Just as he utilized the imitation of God theory to promote Jewish interests, Luzzatto makes use of the reverse Machiavellian argument. Princes who succumb to the anti-Jewish tendencies of the mob have failed in their role as rulers, for protection of the Jews serves the interests of the state in two ways:[18] it obviates harm to the Jews; and, perhaps more importantly, it prevents the masses from imposing their will on the ruler. A situation in which the masses prevail is catastrophic both for the existence of the state and for the stability of the regime.

The transformed medieval philosopher king who has become the Machiavellian activist prince is found by Luzzatto in the figures of Moses and Solomon. They are cited as prototypes of the Maimonidean philosopher-prophet who employs rational perfection in the leadership of the people. Elsewhere, by contrast, and under the influence of humanist thought, Luzzatto portrays Moses as the prototype of the initial lawgiver, more elevated than the initial lawgivers of the pagan nations because of the divine source of his mission:

Those famous reformers who arose among the ancient nations of the world and gave them laws and commandments, were nothing but imperfect people, like the rest of humanity, and this is why their ideas and aims were also limited and restricted. Solon was satisfied with the fact that he educated the Athenians by his laws and justice. Lycurgus was satisfied by giving laws and justice to the people of Sparta, and Romulus did not give it but to his own narrow refuge. None of them cared for the rest of humanity. . . . Not so the Torah of

God, which Moses gave his people. The Torah endeavored to care for the best of the human race, since every man must consider himself as if he were a citizen of a single all-embracing republic.[19]

This last statement has a distinctly humanist, even Stoic flavor.[20] The Torah of Moses, on account of its divine source, is presented as a universal law, intended for all humankind, in contrast to the legislation of pagan lawgivers, who established a particular law for their nations alone; hence, its superiority. This is a proto-Enlightenment attempt to present Judaism as a universal religion.

Luzzatto's description of Moses' activity does not correspond to the Machiavellian image. Luzzatto is influenced here by other, neo-stoic currents of late Renaissance thought. Elsewhere in the *Discorso*, especially in his rebuttal of the charges against the Jews made by Tacitus, Luzzatto indeed depicts Moses as a Machiavellian prince. He presents the Torah of Moses, derided by Tacitus as a legitimation of superstition, carnal lust, sloth, and other evils, as the supreme expression of the wisdom of Moses' rule according to the best principles of reason of state. For example, the fallow year *(shemitah)*, which Tacitus cited as conclusive proof of the indolence of the Jews, is described by Luzzatto as an ingenious solution by Moses at once to social, political, and military problems.[21]

Other leaders of the ancient Hebrew state are also portrayed by him in conformity with the Machiavellian image of the prince. Luzzatto's commentary on Absalom's revolt—one of the major examples he adduced to refute Tacitus' contention that the Jews were debased by pleasures of the flesh—holds that Absalom committed adultery with his father's concubines not merely out of lust or even out of a wish to harm David's honor, but "from the desire to acquire political power" *(sopra la speme del'aquisto del regno)*. Following the advice of "the wise Ahitophel" *(sagace Achitofel)*, Absalom had to prove to his followers that he was determined to succeed David while the king was still alive. He therefore put an end to all chances of appeasement with his father, in order to allay his supporters' fear that "emotions of blood relationship would surpass the interests of the state" *(interesse di stato)*" and that he would eventually come to terms with his father after all and betray his adherents. Adultery with his father's concubines was intended to serve as conclusive proof to his adherents that they had nothing to fear. Only so would Absalom win their unhesitating support.[22]

This interpretation does in fact accord with the plain meaning of the biblical text, and with its accepted medieval interpretation, for example by Kimhi and Abravanel.[23] At the same time, though, it is invested with an unmistakable Machiavellian stamp—the house of Borgia in the land of Judah. Absalom appears as a true Machiavellian prince, a kind of Cesare Borgia, who can act vigorously, without wavering, prepared to commit cruel, immoral acts in order to further his goals. Ahitophel is depicted as the prince's clever adviser, the role Machiavelli aspired to fill for his own prince. Luzzatto describes the conduct of these players without criticism or reservation. The sphere of morals has become irrelevant in the political arena. The transformation from Platonic philosopher king to Machiavellian prince is complete.

This transformation reaches its final form in *Socrate*, a Platonic-style dialogue dealing with human knowledge and its moral implications. Luzzatto attempts to identify the mathematical and mechanical principles at work in the natural world and their implications for human behavior and the political structure of society. He derives four classes of regime from the four kinds of movement of heavenly bodies that he identifies, two positive (monarchy) and two negative (tyranny), thereby applying the ideas of modern science to the traditional division of regimes. The perfect regime, in his view, is one in which the prince elevates the general good over his personal good. It is the ideal monarchy.[24]

Luzzatto retains the medieval concept of monarchy as the ideal regime, along with the concept of the dichotomy between monarchy and tyranny. He attempts to explain these principles, however, in terms of the discoveries in natural science. Moreover, he is also undoubtedly affected by the monarchical currents in the political thought of his time. He discards the medieval Muslim and Jewish tradition of the philosopher king. The *Discorso* criticizes theoretical political thinkers *(politici teorici, li morali)* like Plato and More who developed idyllic theories that ignored political reality. Practical politicians *(li politici, statisti pratici)*, such as Aristotle, who dealt with political reality as it was are preferred. While echoes of the medieval philosopher king theory are still to be found in the *Discorso* Platonic theory is completely rejected in *Socrate*.

In the same vein, Luzzatto, an adherent of the mercantilist world view that characterized the Venetian republic, firmly dismissed what would later be termed communist theory—the affirmation of social and economic equality, the abolition of private property, and the delegitimation of luxuries, as put forward in the utopian works of Plato and Thomas More. Acceding to Aristotle's noted critique, Luzzatto regarded such a theory as unrealistic and contrary to human nature, and therefore necessarily doomed to failure.[25] Identifying the philosopher-king concept with these proto-communist theories, he rejected them out of hand. He dismisses Plato's renowned maxim, "Unless either philosophers become kings in their countries or those who are now called kings and rulers come to be sufficiently inspired with a genuine desire for wisdom . . . there can be no rest from troubles"[26]—in his words, *beato il genere homano divenirobbe se li filosofi regnassero, overo che il Re filosofassero,*[27]—as "an abhorrent saying, famous among the common people" *(reprobata quella sententia dali homini volgari celebrata)*. Should such a misadventure *(disaventura)* actually occur, the inevitable result, in his view, would be the destruction of ordered human society *(oppressa ogni cultura della vita civile)*.[28] Similarly, Luzzatto portrays Diogenes as an ascetic philosopher in the Ibn Bajja-style—a retiree from wordly life. If such a person were permitted to rule and to implement his austere theories, all humanity would revert to a bestial state. These philosophers were nothing less than enemies of human society *(nelli governi civili spenti che siano li nemici)*, and power must not be placed in their hands.[29] Bending Platonic theory toward Ibn Bajja's stance, with obvious exaggeration, Luzzatto totally rejects it.

If Erasmus of the *Speculum Principium* could still recount approvingly the meeting between Alexander the Great and Diogenes, and seek to arouse the young emperor's enthusiasm for the aged cynic whose "philosophic spirit [was] so proud, unbroken, unconquered, and superior to all things human" *(animam illum philosophicum, execelsum, infractum, inivictum e omnibus humanis rebus superiorem)*,[30] the Machiavellian Luzzatto, by contrast, portrayed Diogenes as a threat to the very existence of human civilization. The negation of Diogenes-style asceticism does not in itself constitute an automatic rejection of the philosopher-king theory,[31] but we must recall that the theory in its Platonic original was introduced in the context of the negation of luxury. Moreover, as has been noted, the medieval Muslim and Jewish commentators also emphasized these features of the ideal state. Thus, in rejecting the Platonic ideal, Luzzatto incorporates the mercantilist negation of self-denial.

Luzzatto sharply diverges from Platonic political theory in the *Discorso*, revealing the influence of the Machiavellian revolution regarding the image of the ideal ruler. Nevertheless, he still makes use of the Averroist philosopher-king theory in this work. In *Socrate*, however, the rejection of the philosopher-king theory is more explicit. Luzzatto is the first Jewish thinker to dismiss the theory so bluntly. He stands apart from the inherited theory of philosopher rulers as saviors of human society from the medieval tradition; and following the Machiavellian revolution, he presents them as its destroyers.

2

Luzzatto reflects the transition from the acceptance of the medieval philosopher-king theory to its rejection. Spinoza, taking this process one step further, calls for the separation of church and state. At the beginning of his final work, the unfinished *Political Treatise*, Spinoza unequivocally labels the Platonic wish to correct human society by means of the rule of the philosopher king absolute utopianism. In a Machiavellian vein, he denigrates philosophers because they:

> conceive of men not as they are *[ut sunt]* but as they themselves would like them to be *[ut eosdem esse vellent]*. Whence it has come to pass that instead of ethics they have generally written satire, and that

they have never conceived a theory of politics which could be turned to use *[ad usam]*, but such as might be taken for a chimera, or might have been formed in Utopia, or in that golden age *[aureo seculo]* of the poets when, to be sure, there was least need of it *[minime necesse erat]* ... no men are esteemed less fit to direct public affairs than theorists or philosophers *[Theoretici seu Philosophi]*.[32]

The revolution, then, is complete. If the medieval Jewish philosophers set the philosopher-prophet on a higher plane than mere mortals, Spinoza claims just the opposite. He regards the traditional philosopher, detached from empirical reality, as least capable. Whoever does not know human nature as it really is, is incapable of properly ruling human society.

In calling for the separation of religion and state, in viewing the sphere of belief and opinions as a private affair, Spinoza was obliged to reject any political system of the philosopher king type, since it conceives the supreme duty of rulers as directing the human multitude toward the one divine truth. The medieval philosopher strove to harmonize philosophy and theology. Spinoza sought their complete separation. He saw the state only as a means of protecting individual freedom and public order. A key to that goal was the utter exclusion of the sphere of belief and opinions from matters of state, and their relegation to the private domain. This situation, in which the right of the individual to maintain and express his views is recognized, so long as it does not undermine social order, forestalls conflicts over ideological differences. For the medieval thinker, governments were obliged to inculcate uniformity of opinion in order to protect the philosopher, preserve the social order, and promulgate correct opinions. For Spinoza, by contrast, a government that was constrained from interceding in ideological matters and that respected freedom of opinion within the framework of public order was likeliest to attain those very goals in the best possible manner.[33]

The common ground between the interests of the philosopher and those of the democratic state is thereby established. The existence of a democratic regime is in the interest of the philosopher who wishes to prevent the harmful effects of dogma and superstition. The essential interest of democracy is to support philosophical freedom; otherwise, a democratic regime would not be able to exist.

Thus, where the medieval conception identified the philosopher king with the prophet and stressed his political obligations, Spinoza assumed the contrary. He claimed that the prophets interfered in matters that did not concern them and, as a result, undermined social order, caused conflict, and even provoked civil wars. In his view, those able to better humankind were not the prophets, whose incessant carping only exasperated the people and worsened the situation, but the kings, who were properly equipped for the task. Furthermore, the liberty taken by the prophets to rebuke the kings, even those who did good in the eyes of God, was a flagrant abuse of their religious powers and ultimately harmed both religion and the state. Spinoza saw the prophets as "private men" *(viri privati)*, whose views should not have binding authority[34]—the complete antithesis of the medieval Platonic theory of the "public prophet."

Luzzatto supported a distinctly monarchical regime, albeit with Machiavellian elaboration. Spinoza, by contrast, was a pure republican. Luzzatto justified the use of superstition as a kind of "necessary belief" in the medieval manner intended to bring about obedience to the rulers. Spinoza, in the introduction to the *Theologico-Political Treatise,* views the encouragement of superstition in an almost Marxist fashion as a transparent trick meant to enslave the human spirit. Such enslavement is the hallmark of the monarchical regime in Spinoza's thinking. The Republican regime is its positive antithesis: it recognizes individual liberty and respects the right to independent thinking

> But if, in despotic statecraft *[regiminis monarchici],* the supreme and essential mystery be to hoodwink the subjects, and to mask the fear which keeps them down with the specious garb of religion, so that men may fight as bravely for slavery as for safety, and count it not shame but highest honor to risk their blood and their lives for the vainglory of a tyrant; in a free state *[libera republica]* no more mischievous expedient could be planned or attempted. Wholly repugnant to the general freedom are such devices as enthralling men's minds with prejudices, forcing their judgment, or employing any of the weapons of quasi-religious sedition.[35]

Nevertheless, in the body of his book Spinoza concedes that the masses, who are incapable of knowing rational truths, should have what he calls "salutary doctrines" *(salutabium opinionum)* forced on them "to impress obedience and devotion on their minds" *(ad obedientiam et devotionem eorum animis imprimendum).* This may be done through books, parables, and the recounting of miraculous acts such as those related in the Torah.[36] It would appear, therefore, that Spinoza's *libera republica* is just a remote ideal. Ultimately, the freedom of spirit that he discusses is no more than freedom for those who are capable of attaining it, that is, the philosophers. It is their freedom of opinion alone that he wishes to release from the yoke of the state, while he also desires to free them from direct political obligation.[37] As for the masses, Spinoza's attitude is still medieval, at once pessimistic and elitist. His democratic posture was in fact highly conservative.

Throughout the book Spinoza highlights the Republican regime as the preferred option *(optima respublica).* Monarchy is inferior, as its success depends on the extraordinary qualities of the ruler: "If power be in the hands of a few, or one man, that one man should be something above average humanity *[supra communem humanam naturam habere]* or should strive to have himself accepted as such."[38] Spinoza is doubtful about the likelihood of so superior a ruler coming to the fore. As is evident from the cynical Machiavellian thought at the end of the sentence, he counseled that the imperfect ruler at least convince the crowd of his rare talents so that they would obey his commands.

The same negative attitude towards monarchy is expressed in the *Political Treatise*. No single individual is able enough to rule alone and successfully manage the entire range of governmental tasks.[39] The natural course was for monarchy to sink into tyranny or, worse still, oligarchy, where power passes to advisers and relatives who abuse it. If there is no alternative but to establish the monarchical regime, Spinoza concludes, then it must be constitutional and limited.[40]

Spinoza identifies the Republic as the preferred regime, but he does not view the ancient Hebrew state as such a regime. The Hebrew nation was not yet ripe for a republican regime, which is suitable only for a populace able to sustain voluntary cooperation in a rational, egalitarian manner. The Hebrew nation received the regime that suited its needs at the time: a form of theocratic monarchy.

Spinoza offers a distinctly Machiavellian interpretation of the establishment of the ancient Hebrew state. Having left Egypt, the Israelites reverted to a natural state of detachment from any binding political framework. Thus, they were free to act in any way that could benefit them and supply their needs:

The Jews when they first came out of Egypt were not bound by any national laws and were therefore free to ratify any laws they liked, or to make new ones, and were at liberty to set up a government and occupy a territory wherever they chose.[41]

At this stage of their development they had no temporal government but maintained a semidemocratic theocratic framework:

Inasmuch as the Hebrews did not transfer their rights to any other person but, as in a democracy, all surrendered their rights equally *[omnes neque ut in Democratia jure cesserunt]*, and cried out with one voice, "Whatsoever God shall speak that will we do," it follows that all were equally bound by the covenant and that all had an equal right to consult the Deity, to accept and to interpret His laws, so that they all had an exactly equal share in the government. Thus at first they all approached God together, so that they might learn His commands.[42]

The Israelites, however, were not able to function equally and freely. The effect of their prolonged enslavement in Egypt was palpable: ". . . they were entirely unfit to frame a wise code of laws *[ad jura sapienter constituendum]* and to keep the sovereign power vested in the community *[collegialiter]*; they were uncultivated and sunk in a wretched slavery *[misera servitute]*."[43] Spinoza describes the Israelites' confused response to their first direct encounter with God in detail and with irony. He depicts Moses as a wily Machiviallian politician who had been waiting for this chance and now exploited it to the hilt. He manipulated the people to beg him to lead them and to transfer all their rights to him. He replaced the direct covenant with God, which the people were not able to cope with by themselves, with a social contract by which they vested all their rights and freedoms in him. Moses is portrayed by Spinoza as the prototype of Machiavelli's classic initial lawgiver.

The theory of the initial lawgiver provided a convenient and widely accepted solution to the problem of the passage of a people from their natural state to a political state. According to Spinoza, human beings in their natural state are controlled by passions and desires and are thus in a condition of perpetual mutual enmity. In such circumstances, a voluntary social contract was hardly conceivable. To solve this problem, the idea of the initial lawgiver evolved in classical and later in Machiavellian political thought. So well entrenched was this concept by Spinoza's time that he barely deals with the theoretical aspect of the subject and makes only the following comment at the beginning of the *Political Treatise:* "For men are so situated that they cannot live without some general law. But general laws and public affairs are ordained and managed by men of the utmost acuteness, or, if you like, of great cunning and craft."[44] Notably, he does not speak here of the wisdom of the initial lawgiver, but of "acuteness" and "cunning." The terminology reveals how far he has departed from the medieval theory of the philosopher king and toward Machiavelli.

The thrust of Spinoza's discussion of the initial lawgiver is made clear in its application to the figure of Moses and to the establishment of the ancient Hebrew regime. Moses is the prototype of leaders whom Spinoza defines, with a trace of irony, as being "of the utmost acuteness or, if you like, of great cunning and craft" *(viris acutissimis, sive astutis, sive callidis)*. With Moses, the anarchist-democratic theocracy of the natural state turns into a monarchist theocracy in a political state: "Moses, therefore, remained the sole promulgator and interpreter of the Divine laws *[solus legum divinarum lator et interpres mansit]* and consequently also the sovereign judge *[supremus judex]*, who could not be arraigned himself and who among the Hebrews acted the part of God *[vicem Dei]*."[45] Moses is depicted precisely as a Machiavellian prince, possessing divine virtue *[divina virtute]*. Taking charge of a people who are damaged and passive as a result of slavery and the tribulations of wandering in the wilderness, he forces them to function according to the laws that he himself issues in the guise of God: "Therefore the sovereignty *[imperium]* was bound to remain vested in the hands of one man who would rule the rest and keep them under constraint, make laws and interpret them. This sovereignty was easily retained by Moses because he surpassed the rest in God-given virtue" *[divina virtute]*.[46]

Like Machiavelli, Spinoza holds that obedience to the government is a necessary condition for the existence of an ordered state. Obedience in this instance is defined as the performance of acts that conform to the commands of the government. True obedience constitutes an inner act by the soul of whoever undertakes to obey the orders of another. Spinoza distinguishes between voluntary obedience and obedience out of fear and applies this distinction to the situation of the people of Israel in the desert, citing their famous obstinacy, which made it impossible to force them to obey through fear, and the need to wage war successfully, which required that the soldiers' spirits be uplifted rather than intimidated by punishment. All this necessitated voluntary obedience.[47] Religion, in Spinoza's view, is a clever means used by the initial lawgiver to induce the people to obey him voluntarily rather than through fear. For the masses in the chaotic primal condition, religious belief is a suitable substitute for superstition in terms of its political utility. The internalization of belief in the divine source of the law becomes a peerless tool in the hands of the subtle lawgiver to impel the people to obey willingly, "so that the people might do their duty from devotion rather than fear" *(ut populus non tam ex metu quam devotione suum officium faceret)*.[48] As with Luzzatto, and in direct adherence to Machiavelli, religion for Spinoza becomes a means of political legitimation.

The problem of motivating the populace to obey the government greatly exercised Spinoza. Without obedience, an orderly state could not function and improve the souls of its subjects. However, it is very difficult to win this obedience. Spinoza takes an extremely pessimistic, Machiavellian view of the fickle disposition of the multitude *(multitudinus ingenium)*—"for it is governed solely by emotions, not by reason" *(non rationis, sed solis affectibus gubernatur)*. Nevertheless, he looks at the situation rationally, arguing that the multitude have no reason to obey people not much worthier than themselves, and who even have the same flaws as they have: "All, both rulers and ruled, are men, and prone to follow after their lusts."[49]

The best way of solving this thorny problem is by exploiting popular superstitions, adapting them to serve the rulers' purposes, that is, disguising them as something they are not. Like Machiavelli, Spinoza views the myths of the divine origin of rulers and their laws as the best means available for attaining this goal:

For the sake of making themselves secure, kings who seized the throne in ancient times used to try to spread the idea that they were descended from the immortal gods, thinking that if their subjects and the rest of mankind did not look on them as equals but believed them to be gods, they would willingly submit to their rule and obey their commands.[50]

Historical examples given by Spinoza of users of this cunning political tactic are Augustus, Alexander of Macedon, and Moses himself.

The willingness of the people to submit to the absolute authority of Moses arose at a time of crisis, Spinoza points out. Afterwards, when the people were in a state of relative ease, their willingness to uphold the contract they had voluntarily undertaken dissipated. In as much as absolute readiness to obey stems from fear, once the initial fear has passed, the government is again at risk. Understandably, the sectors most harmed by the new order created by Moses—namely, the old aristocracy—began to organize against it. They accused him of arrogance, nepotism, and, still worse, duplicity, and they drew the crowd with them. The belief in the divine call of Moses began to crumble the moment that the immediate danger to the people's existence passed. This is how Spinoza analyzes the political rationale of the story of Korah (Num. 17):

As soon as the people in the wilderness began to live in ease *[otio]* and plenty, certain men of no mean birth began to rebel against the choice of the Levites and to make it a cause for believing that Moses had not acted by the commands of God but for his own good pleasure, inasmuch as he had chosen his own tribe before all the rest and had bestowed the high priesthood in perpetuity on his own brother. They therefore stirred up a tumult and came to him, crying out that all men were equally sacred and that he had exalted himself above his fellows wrongfully. Moses was not able to pacify them with reasons; but, by the intervention of a miracle in proof of the faith, they all perished. A fresh sedition then arose among the whole people, who believed that their champions had not been put to death by the judgment of God, but by the device of Moses *[Moisis arte]*.[51]

Moses succeeded in breaking the people's opposition with the artful Machiavellian blend of cleverness and cunning, which Spinoza regarded as essential in the founder of a state: "After a great slaughter, or pestilence, the rising subsided, from loss of vitality, but in such a manner that all preferred death to life under such conditions. We should rather say that sedition ceased than that harmony was re-established."[52] Even after smashing the people's opposition to his rule, Moses was forced to continue demonstrating his power, so as to show the might of God and his own status as God's representative on Earth. This was the only way to maintain the obedience of the people. These displays of force took various forms: military victories over the foes of Israel, the suppression of resistance by enemies within, recurrent manifestations of superior powers, and the general furtherance of the interests of the Israelite nation.

Like Machiavelli, Spinoza uses the Israelite example to show that the need to survive compels people to obey their rulers, but that the moment they become secure they tend to revert to rebelliousness. To prevent this regression, it is necessary precisely in times of calm both to maintain the powerful institution of superstition, which accustoms the people to obey the government, and to have a leader with a forceful personality. If these elements are missing, the social system will disintegrate. This applies both to established nations and to a nation in the state of initial development as the Israelite nation was in a wilderness: "In times of peace *[in otio]*, when striking miracles had ceased, and no men of paramount authority *[homines exquisitissimae authoritatis]* were forthcoming, the irritable and greedy temper of the people began to wax cold, and at length to fall away from worship."[53]

What Spinoza terms Moses' divine powers are in reality his natural leadership qualities.[54] As for Moses' alleged miracles, in light of Spinoza's explicit denial of the very possibility of miracles,[55] his Moses was simply acting in accord with Machiavelli's counsel that the ruler would do well to conjure up miracles to help him elicit total obedience.

Moses' first aim was to gain power and hold onto it. His second was to mold the character of the people. Having destroyed his enemies from within and discouraged their supporters, he then acted to shape their conduct in such a way that they would obey his orders without question. For this purpose, he established a complex system of laws and ceremonies which he obliged the people to execute meticulously, with no choice or personal reflection. As Machiavelli had observed, a populace used to a life of slavery would find it difficult to act out of thoughtful deliberation when they suddenly won freedom:

> He left nothing to the free choice of the individuals, long accustomed to servitude *[servituti assuetis]*; the people could do nothing but remember the law, and follow the ordinances laid down at the good pleasure of their rulers; they were not allowed to plow, to sow, to reap . . . or in fact to do anything whatever as they liked but were bound to follow the directions given in the law.[56]

From fearful obedience to the king of Egypt, the Israelites passed to willing obedience to the rule of Moses.

Thus, the people of Israel were forged by Moses' hand into a community possessing a regime, laws, and customs that highlighted the differences between them and other peoples, and holding beliefs that justified this state of affairs. Indeed, Spinoza sees laws and customs as the sole distinctiveness of each people:

> But nature forms individuals, not peoples; the latter are distinguishable only by the differences of their languages, their customs and their laws; while from the two last, i.e., customs and laws, it may arise that they have a peculiar disposition, a peculiar manner of life, and peculiar prejudices.[57]

Here lies the immense importance he ascribes to the processes of the molding of the people of Israel by the founder and initial lawgiver. For all his irony, directed at both the primitive level of the Israelites in the wilderness and Moses' allegedly divine power, Spinoza, like Machiavelli before him, indisputably considered this early stage of the process to be a positive and vital one in human history. The process, he believed, would attain full realization with the establishment of a rational, free republic. However, the Israelites in the desert, accustomed to a life of slavery, were certainly not yet ready. There are no shortcuts in history. Moses had to propel the people of Israel through the first, decisive stage in the long process of the development of a perfected human society.

In contrast to the medieval philosophers, who regarded the ancient Hebrew state as the ideal philosophical state, Spinoza saw it as an earthly state, created to meet the primitive needs of a nation of slaves. Moses is no longer presented as philosopher king and prophet whose purpose is to lead the people to a rational love of God. Instead, he is seen as a Machiavellian prince who establishes a state, fashions a people, and founds a regime in accordance with the highest principles of reason of state, all this by means of the cynical exploitation of the people's superstitions. In Moses' hands, religion becomes a sophisticated instrument for political legitimation. His "revelation" led not to philosophical knowledge of the divine but merely to laws and commandments having a limited, political application, intended to serve the specific needs of a particular people at a certain point in their development.

These laws have no necessary or immediate link with the realization of the supreme purpose of man as a rational being, which was well beyond the people's grasp at that stage of their development. Moreover, Spinoza was critical of the way in which the laws and customs enacted by Moses shaped the distinct national character of the Jews: "If, then, the Hebrews were harder of heart than other nations, the fault lay with their laws or customs."[58] He saw their obduracy as fraught with danger for the future of the Jewish state, observing that, indeed, it was this quality that ultimately sealed the fate of the state, causing it to disappear. In Spinoza's view, this proved the temporary nature of the laws promulgated by Moses, and hence the limits of the legislation itself: "If God had wished their dominion to be more lasting, He would have given them other rites and laws, and would have instituted a different form of government."[59]

The medieval philosophers viewed the ancient regime as the ideal one, destroyed through generations of corruption but destined to be renewed in the utopian, messianic future. Clearly, their historical vision was restorative. Spinoza, by contrast, put forward a modern, even radical version of the progressive theory, leading to diametrically opposite conclusions from those of the medievals. A free, rational community would arise when humankind finally attained its ultimate goal, which was based on reason. There would be no reconstruction of a primitive monarchy from the distant past; rather, a completely new phenomenon would emerge in human history.

So long as the Israelite monarchical theocratic regime lasted, from Moses until Samuel, the ancient Hebrew state existed in relative domestic peace, Spinoza pointed out. The moment it turned into a secular monarchy, with the anointing of Saul, civil war became routine. All the kings except Solomon, "whose virtue and wisdom [cuius virtus, sapientia scilicet] would be better displayed in peace than in war," saw it as their duty to fight not for peace and freedom, but for their own personal glory. This attitude necessarily led to perpetual warfare and, finally, to the destruction of the Temple.[60] Spinoza's description of events corresponds to his negative position regarding monarchy in general. Discounting the philosopher-king theory as utterly utopian, he also harbors many reservations about monarchy. The first secular Jew was a republican in every way.

Afterword

We have seen how the Platonic tradition of the philosopher king was introduced into medieval Jewish philosophy through Al-Farabi's and Ibn-Rushd's commentaries on Plato's political dialogues; how it was interpreted and adapted by Jewish thinkers; and how it was applied to the great leaders of the Hebrew people in antiquity: Abraham, Moses, David and Solomon. The "virtuous state" in its Farabian or Averroist Platonic version was identified with the ancient Hebrew state.

Reliance on Platonic theory disappeared from Jewish philosophy in the sixteenth century, as it disappeared generally from the philosophical thought of the time. While Alemanno and Abravanel still applied this theory in the late fifteenth and early sixteenth centuries, their Florentine contemporary, Machiavelli, substituted the image of his very unorthodox prince for the Neoplatonic philosopher king fostered by the Platonic Academy in Florence. Erasmus of Rotterdam fought a rearguard action, championing the philosopher king in the guidebook he wrote for the future Emperor Charles V, published the same year as Machiavelli's *The Prince* (1516). In Erasmus, Solomon appears as the prototype of the philosopher-king, just as he did in Aquinas, Alemanno, and Abravanel. The theory of the ideal ruler, however, whether in the Platonic version or in the Latin Christian version of the *Speculum Principium*, was fading from the political discourse of the period. Realist and utilitarian political concepts of the kind advanced by Machiavelli, Hobbes, and Spinoza gradually replaced idealistic medieval views, which, as Machiavelli observed in a much-quoted remark, did not deal with reality as it was *(come si vive)* but with reality as it was supposed to be *(come si doverrebbe vivere)*.[1]

Christian political thought became increasingly republican during the sixteenth century. No longer did it identify the ancient Jewish state and its great leaders as an embodiment of the philosopher-king principle, but rather as a mixed republican regime of the Aristotelian-Polybian kind. The political thinkers of the age, from Calvin and Althusius to Harrington, portray the regime established by Moses on Jethro's advice as the prototype of the perfect republic in the Venetian style.[2]

Similarly, Jewish thought in the sixteenth century no longer offered any real examples of the application of the philosopher-king theory,[3] and by the middle of the seventeenth century the theory was entirely cast aside by Luzzatto and Spinoza. Both of these thinkers represent the incorporation of the Machiavellian revolution into Jewish philosophy.

Quite a different mood, but ultimately with the same practical conclusions, is found in the eighteenth century, in Moses Mendelssohn's *Jerusalem*. Here we move from the spurning of the philosopher-king theory to a melancholy reconciliation with the contemporary state of affairs. Mendelssohn, as distinct from Spinoza, expressed a powerful yearning for the ideal condition of solitary rule by a statesman-prophet in the figure of Moses, the Hebrew equivalent of the philosopher king who combined spiritual and political authority—"earthly politics" *(irdische Politik)* with "heavenly politics" *(himmlische Politik):* "This constitution existed only once; call it the Mosaic constitution, by its proper name. It has disappeared, and only the Omniscient knows among what people and in what century something similar *(etwas ähnliches)* will be seen again."[4]

Where even Luzzatto, and certainly Spinoza, painted Moses' image in Machiavellian colors, Mendelssohn referred to "the simplicity and the moral grandeur of that original constitution" in idealistic medieval terms.[5] The apologetic introduction to his German translation of Menasseh ben Israel's *The Deliverance of Israel (Teshu'at Yisra'el)* contains a description of Moses, replete with medieval idealization, despite Machivellian-Spinozian overtones. Moses is presented as the sublime, divine lawgiver who established the ideal state:

> Moses, the legislator *[der Gesetzgeber Moses]*, discovered that it is possible to transform this vulgar mob *[diesen rohen Waufen]* into a decent, flourishing nation *[einer ordentlichen Nation]*, with superior laws and a perfect government, wise rulers and happy generals, judges and citizens.[6]

Luzzatto and Spinoza, depicting the image of the contemporary Machiavellian prince from a realist's perception, treated the rulers of the ancient Hebrew state accordingly. Mendelssohn, by contrast, influenced by Enlightenment deism, portrays the figure of the temporal, utilitarian, and arrogant ruler with sarcasm, reflecting a certain degree of nostalgia for the ideal that was presumed to have existed at the dawn of history.[7]

Like Spinoza, but for different reasons, Mendelssohn regards the kingdom of Saul, a flesh and blood king similar to those of all the other nations, as the great divide in Jewish history in particular and in the history of the world in general. His reign fractured the powerful unity of spirit and matter, of religion and state, of prophecy and kingdom. Mendelsohn interprets 1

Samuel 8 not in the context of a debate on the theory of regimes, but as the cataclysmic confrontation between temporal and spiritual power. In his view, unity between the two powers had been preserved until that period. The elevation of Saul by the wish of the people, who in their foolishness sought a flesh and blood king like all the nations, shattered this great unity irreparably.

Spinoza, advocating the division between religion and state, severely criticized the medieval, essentially Platonic view of the sphere of beliefs and opinions as being under the supreme jurisdiction of the ruler. He deemed this situation to be the root of all evil and injustice. Mendelssohn, by contrast, saw this arrangement as ideal in principle. Unity of matter and spirit, in his opinion, had existed until Saul ascended the throne. However, what was done could not be undone: "The unity of interests is now destroyed!" *(die Einheit des Interesse nun zerstort ist!)*.[8] Spinoza sought the separation of state and religion through the absolute rejection of the medieval world view. Mendelssohn accepted it as a regrettable, but inevitable practical result of the great fracture.

In any case, the separation between temporal and spiritual authority—between king and philosopher—ultimately became the theoretical foundation for the separation of religion and state in the modern era. As such, it also gave the Jew of the Emancipation the theological justification to be a Jew within and a man without. Nor is it a coincidence that the Platonic tradition disappeared from Jewish culture as we approach the period of the Enlightenment. Rather it is a direct result of its changing needs as the culture began to feel the influences of modernism and eventually went through a secularization process that, running its course, brought an end to the holistic framework of traditional Rabbinic Judaism.

Appendix:
The Hebrew Versions of the
Philosopher King's Virtues

This appendix assembles the Hebrew versions of the descriptions of the philosopher-king's virtues by the various philosophers we have considered. These passages are arranged in the order of their appearance in the book. Their English
translations (with the exception of B and M) are found in the body of the text.

A. Ibn Latif, *Sha'ar ha-Shamayim*, ms. Vatican 335.1 I, 20. fols. 32a–33a.
Based on Al-Farabi, *The Virtuous State*, 15, ed. R. Walzer, ibid., 247–49.
For the English translation, see ch. 5 nn. 7, 10, 11.

והנני מעמידך אתה המעיין אל תנאי האיש השלם בתכלית בשלימות הראויה להמצא באיש מאישי
המין האנושי הם י"ב מדות כמו שזכרם החכם הישמעאלי אבונצר ואכלול אני בעשר מדות. וצריך להיות
אלו המדות מטבעות מתחלת יצירתו. אחת שיהיה בנין גופו חזק ואיבריו שלמים וחזקים לעשות המעשים
שדרכם לבוא מן האיברים ההם. השני שיהיה גבור בנפשו לעשות המעשים הראויים בלי פחד ושיהיה
קשה לב לסלול לאנשי רשע. והשלישי שיהיה (בטבעו) ממהר בטבעו להבין הדברים שישמע על אמתת
מהותם ועל כונת האומר אותם. והרביעית שיהיה נח ללמוד וקשה לאבד ר"ל שיהיה זכרן ולא ישכח שום
דבר ממה שלמד או השיג או ששמע. והחמישי שיהיה זך ההבנה להבין הדברים העמוקים הנאמר ברמז
סתום וירגיש וישער עניניהם על אמתם מהותם. והששי שיהיה אוהב הלמוד ותהיה כונתו בו להבין
להועיל לנפשו ולזולתו ושיהיה טבעו נכון בענין שלא יחלישהו עת הלימוד. השביעית שתהיה לשונו צחה
מורגלת לבאר לזולתו מה שהוא מבין ביאור שלם. השמינית להיות טבעו עמו ושפל רוח עם היותו מכבד
ומוקיר נפשו מן הנבלות ומחברת הנבלים ושלא יתבזה ושלא יתבל בשביל שום תאוה מתאות העולם
אלא שמח בחלקו ובעל נפש נדיבה. והתשיעי להיות טבעו אוהב האמת ושונא הכזב. העשירית שיהיה
בטבעו אוהב היושר ובעלי היושר שונא החמס ובעלי החמס נושא ונותן באמונה ומקבל כל הבא עליו
בצדק ובסבר פנים יפות.

B. The anonymous Hebrew translation of Al-Farabi's *Fusul al-Madani*, ed.
J. Macy. ch. 51 in Najjar Arabic ed. ch. 58 in Dunlop's English translation, See ch. 5, n. 9.

אחד מהם הוא המלך באמת והוא הראשון והוא אשר יקבצו בו ששה תנאים:

1. החכמה,
2. וההשכל השלם,

189

3. וטוב ההלצה לישב דעת השומע בטענות מספיקות,
4. וטוב נתינת הדמיון,
5. והכח על ההשתדלות בגופו,
6. ושלא יהיה בגופו דבר מעיק אותו מהרגל הדברים הצריכים השתדלות וחריצות.   ומי שיתקבצו
בו אלו הדברים כלם הוא המסדר והראוי לסמוך עליו בהנהגתו ופעולותיו כלם ואשר יקובלו מאמריו
ומצוותיו. וזה האיש אשר ינהיג איך שיראה בעיניו ואיך שירצה.

C. Falaquera, *Reshit Hokhmah*, ibid., 70–71. Based on Al-Farabi, *Attainment of Happiness*, ed. M. Mahdi, 48–49. For the English translation, see ch. 5 nn. 23, 24.

והם הדרכים אשר זכרם אפלטון בספרו בהנהגה. והוא שיהיה טוב ההכנה והציור לדבר המקרי והעצמי. ושיהיה
סובל יגיעת הלימוד. ושיהיה בטבע אוהב היושר ובעליו. ואינו מתאוה אל המעדנים ותהיינה התאוות נקלות
בעיניו והעושר והדומה לזה. ושיהיה אוהב בטבע שיועיל ולומד בטבע גודל הנפש אצל מה שהוא בידי בני אדם.
ושיהיה קל להכניע לעשות הטוב וקשה להכניע לעשות הרע והחמס. ושיהיה אמיץ המחשבה על הדבר
האמיתי וחזק על הנימוסים והרגילים דומים למה שיעיין בו. ושיהיה מחזיק בשלימיות אשר הם מצד הפרסום
שלמיות ואינו סותר הפעלים הטובים אשר הם מצד הפרסום.

D. Falaquera, *Sefer ha-Ma'alot*, ibid., 16–17. Based on Al-Farabi, *The Virtuous State*, 15. ed. R. Walzer, 247–49. For the English translation, see. ch. 5 nn. 30–32.

ואמר אבונצר   וזה האדם שזכרנו הוא הראש הראשון למדינה החסידה והוא ראש האומה החסידה וראש
לכל הישוב. ולא יתכן שיגיע לזו המעלה אלא למי שנמצאו בו בטבע שתים עשרה מדות או רובם.
הראשונה שיהיה אבריו בריאים וחזקים ותהיה תנועתם קלה להניעם לכל מה שירצה. והשנית שיהיה
טוב הבנה לכל מה שיאמרו עליו וישכיל וישיג אמתת הדברים. השלישית שיזכור כל מה שיאמרו אליו וכל מה
שיראה וישמע ומה שישיג ולא ישכח אותו. הרביעית שיהיה זך המחשבה כשיראה על הדבר ראיה יבין
אותו על הדרך שתורה עליו הראיה. החמישית שיהיה צח ויכול לבאר כל מה שבלבו באור שלם. הששית
שיהיה אוהב תלמוד וממהר לשמוע ולא תכאיבהו יגיעת הלמוד והעמל אשר ישיגהו ממנו. השביעית
שיהיה אוהב בטבע הצדק ובעליו ושונא הכזב ובעליו.   השמינית שלא יתאוה תאוה רבה למאכלים
ומשקים והמשגל ויהיה פרוש מהצחוק ושונא התענוגות שהם מזה המין. התשיעית שיהיה גדול
הנפש תתגאה נפשו בטבע על כל דבר שהוא נקל ונבזה מהדברים ומתנשא נפשו בטבע אל המעולה
מהם. העשירית שיהיה הכסף והזהב ושאר מחמדי העולם קלים בעיניו. האחת עשרה שיהיה בטבע אוהב
היושר שונא העושק ובעליו ועושה דין מבני ביתו ומזולתם ויזהיר על היושר ונאות לכל שיראה וטוב
ונאה וקל וכשיקראוהו אל היושר קשה כשיקראהו אל החמס. השתים עשרה שיהיה אמיץ המחשבה על
כל דבר שהוא רואה שצריך שיפעלהו גבור ואינו מפחד.

E. Samuel ben Judah of Marseilles, The Hebrew Translation of *Ibn Rushd's Commentary on Plato's Republic*. II:ii ed. F. Rosenthal, 61–62. For the English translation, see ch. 5 n. 42.

והם התנאים הטבעיים למלך: אחד מהם והוא היותר מיוחד שיהיה מוכן בטבע ללמידת החכמות
העיוניות וזה בשהיה ביצירתו מכיר למה שבעצמתם ומבדיל אותו ממה ממנו שבמקרה. והשני, שיהיה שומר לא
ישכח כי מי שאינו בשני התארים הללו אי אפשר לו להתלמד דבר. וזה הוא שלא יסור מהיותו ביגיעה
תמיד עד שיעזוב הקריאה והלמידה. והשלישי, שיהיה אוהב הלמידה ואותה וכוסף להפליא להפליא כל חלקי

החכמה כי הכוסף מאד בדבר כמו שיאמר ירדה בכל מינין משל זה אוהב היין הנה הוא חושק בכל היינות
וכמו כן אוהב הנשים. והרביעי, שיהיה אוהב הצדק שונא הכזב. וזה שמי שיאהב ידיעת הנמצא על מה
שהוא עליו הוא אוהב הצדק, והאוהב הצדק בלתי אוהב הכזב ולזה לא יהיה מי שזה דרכו אוהב הכזב.
והחמישי, שיהיה מואס התאות המוחשות כי מי שתחזק תאותו בדבר מה תכלית הכח יטה נפשו משאר
התאות. וכמו כן העניין באלו. וזה שהם כבר נטו נפשותיהם אל הלמידה. והששישי שלא יהיה אוהב
הממון כי הממון תאוה והתאווה בלתי נאותות באלו האנשים. והשביעי, שיהיה גדול המחשבה כי החושק
לידיעת הכל וכלל הנמצאות. ומי שלא ירצה שיקצר מידיעת הדברים על מי שיחייבהו תחלת הדעת גדול
המחשבה מאד. ולכן אין מזאת הנפש המחשבת יחס כלל. והשמיני, שיהיה גבור כי מי שאין לו גבורה לא
יוכל למאוס מה שגדל עליו מן המאמרים הבלתי מופתיים ובפרט מי שגדל באלו המדינות. והתשיעי
שיהיה מוכן אל שיתנועע מפאת עצמו לכל מי שיראה אותו טוב ויפה מהשווי וזולת זה מן המעלות וזה
כשהתיה נפשו המתעוררת חזקה האמונה לסברה והמחשבה. וכבר יתווסף לאלו שיהיה טוב המליצה
יביאהו לשונו בהתחכמו אל כל מה שברעיוניו ושיהיה עם זה יכול על הגבול האמצעי במהירות.

F. Polkar, *Ezer ha-Dat,* 3. ed. J. Levinger, ibid., 41–42. Based on Al-Farabi,
   The Virtuous State, 15, ed. R. Walzer, 247–49. For the English translation,
   see ch. 6 nn. 4, 5, 6, 9.

כבר ביארו החכמים הפילוסופים כי האיש אשר ראוי למנותו שר ושלטון על האומה החסידה הנכבדת
צריך להמצאות בו שנים עשר תנאים. האחד שיהיה בריא בגופו שלם באבריו הראויות והמוצרכות
להיעשות אליו. והשני, שישכיל שיטבעו בכל אשר יפנה, שישיג את העניינים כאשר הם עצמם, גם כל
אשר ישמיע כפי כוונת הדובר בו. והשלישי, שיזכור תמיד כל אשר ידע וישכיל וישמע מבלי שישכח
דבר. והרביעי, שישכיל וישיג את הנעלמים מן הרמזים ומראשי הפרקים אשר ימסרו עד אשר יוציאם מן
המחבאים אשר יתחבאו שם, והוא המבין דבר מתוך דבר. והחמישי, שתהיה לו לשון למודים עד אשר
יוכל לשום פתרון נכון והתבוננות מבואר ומילים נכוחים לכל העניינים אשר בלבו, כדי להבין ולהורות
לאחרים. והששי, שיהיה חפץ ומרוצה ללמד ולהועיל בחכמתו לאחרים בלתי מתעצל ומקנא וכואב בעמל
הלימוד. והשביעי, שיהיה בטבעו אוהב את האמת ואת בעליה, שונא את השקר ואת המאמינים בו.
והשמיני, שלא יהיה שטוף במיני תענוגי הגוף אשר לא יועילו כזוללי בשר וסובאי יין והמנאפים
והשתעשע בראיית מיני השחוק ושמיעת הנגונים וספורי ההבלים. והתשיעי שיהיה מתגאה מתפאר
בנפשו בלתי מתג(א)\ל ומתנכל בדבר מכוער ונבזה, רק מתנשא בטבעו ומתעלה על זולתו. והעשירי,
שיהיה העושר וההון נבזה ונפחת בעיניו, וכן כל המקרים הגופיים בשררה והנקמה וזולתם. והאחד
עשרה, שיהיה בטבעו אוהב את הצדק ואת המשפט, שונא את העול ואת החמס ומתכון להציל את העני
מחזק ממנו באהבתו ותשוקתו אל המשפט לא בדרך זדון ואכזריות. והשנים עשר, שתהיין כל פעולותיו
בחוזק והבטחה לא בפחד ואימה רק בגובה לב וקשוי. ואני אומר, כי להשלים את האיש הזה כדי
שהגיעו עד התכלית האחרון ולהעלותו אל המדרגה אשר אין למעלה ממנה צריך להמצא בו מדה
אחרת לתשלום שלש עשרה מדות אשר בהן ידרוש האיש השלם והוא שתהין כל פעולותיו באות מצד
החלק האנושי אשר בו ולא מצד הבהמי.

G. Polkar, *Ezer ha-Dat* 3. ed. J. Levinger, ibid., 44–46. Based on Al-Farabi,
   The Virtuous State, 15, ed. R. Walzer, 247–49. For the English translation,
   see ch. 6 nn. 18, 19.

ואחרי אשר הגדתי אליך מדות האיש הלזה הראוי לשומו שר ושליט על האומה התמה והנכבדת ושעור
השגתו, אודיעך באמת כי משה אדונינו הוא היה בעל המדות האלו וגם הוא עלה אל האלוהים ר"ל אל

התכלית המדרגה העליונה. ואודיעך ראשונה כי בו נמצאו ונתראו השלש עשרה תנאים אשר זכרתי
בתכלית התיקון והיושר. ואמר בראשון, והוא שיהיה חזק ובריא בגופו, כי ידוע ענין חזקת בהריגת
המצרי המכה והושיעו את בנות יתרו מיד הרועים וגלילת האבן, ובהיותו בן מאה ועשרים שנה לא כהה
עינו ולא נס ליחה. וגם בתנאי השני גלוי וידוע אצל כל האומות גודל ידיעת משה ושלימות השגתו
והתורה העידה עליו, כי לא קם נביא עוד בישראל כמשה. ותנאי השלישי מפורסם בו כי בזוכרו להגיד
במשנה תורה כל הסיפורים והפרטים אשר לא אירעו לו לא שכח דבר עם כל התלאות אשר מצאוהו
בעסקי הקהל. והתנאי הרביעי נעלם בו ונדעהו בשני עדים כשרים: האחד כי בראותו את הסנה בוער
באש ואיננו אוכל דקדק והשכיל והשיג כי היה מלאך יי' בלבת האש מתוך הסנה. והשני כי כששאל מאת
האל ויאמר "הנה אנכי בא אל בני ישראל ואמרתי להם אלהי אבותיכם שלחני אליכם, ואמרו לי מה
שמו מה אומר אליהם" (שמ' ג, י"ג) והשיבו השם "כה תאמר אל בני ישראל אהיה שלחני אליכם" (שם,
שם. י"ד) והבין ממלה זו כבוד עצמיות האל בה' וידע כי הוא עצם ההויה, וסבת כל הוה, וגם שאין
מציאותו והויתו דבר נוסף על עצמו, ויתר העניינים הנשגבים והנוראים המובנים ממלה זאת, וכדי
להסתירם ולהעלימם ולהגניזם החליף והמיר אותיות אשר מנהגם להתחלף כפי הלשון והם אלף ביוד
ויוד בואו ונעשה השם המקודש. ובתנאי החמישי יראה לשונו הנמרצת ומליצותיו החמודות בשירת הים
ובפרשת האזינו ובשאר תוכחותיו ואזהרותיו. והתנאי הששי יודע בו ויוכר בבלתי קנאו באלדד ומידד
המתנבאים ואמרו "מי יתן כל עם ה' נביאים" (במד', י"א, כ"ט), ובלמדו אל הזקנים ואל יהושע והאצילו
מרוחו עליו וגם לאהרון וחור. והתנאי השביעי והאחד עשר ידועים ומפורסמים אצל המביט ביושר
משפטיו ותיקון חקותיו ותורותיו אף כי נאמר עליו "בכל ביתי נאמן הוא" (שם, י"ב, ז'). ותנאי השמיני
וגם העשירי ידועים בו בעזבו ומיאוסו בכל התענוגים הגשמים ובחר ברוחניים, כי גרש את אשתו
ושלחה משהתחיל להתנבא. וישב ברבעים יום מבלי אוכל וחי, מה שאין כן בכח התולדת. ואמנם התנאי
התשיעי ההוא מתעלה ומתפאר בעצמו קשה להמצאות במשה היות הכתוב מעיד עליו "והאיש משה ענו
מאד" (במד', י"ב, ג'), וידוע כי הענוה אמצעית בין הגאוה והשפלות, ושנטה משה במדותיו לצד
השפלות להיותו נבחר אצלו, כמו שאמרו חכמים ז"ל "מאד מאד הוי שפל רוח" (אב', ד', ד'). רק אי
אפשר לאיש כמוהו אשר הושם למלך ושלטון על עם רב ושלא תמצא בו לפעמים קצת מקושף לב וחמה
כדי להטיל אימה והפחיד אל הבועטים במוסר, ולזה יכנס במדותיו התנאי הששים השתים עשרה. והמדה השלוש
עשרה גם השלימות והתמימות והגעת התכלית האחרון הנזכרים ראוי עלינו ומחוייבים אנחנו להאמין
שנמצאו במשה, כי נפשו המתבודדת והמתפרדת מחמרה והמואסת בו שנתה מנהגי הטבע ועשתה הנסם
המפורסמים כמעשה צורות הנפרדות משנות החמרים ועושות בהן כל חפצן, ובהתנבאו בכל עת שיחפוץ
כמו שכתוב "עמדו ואשמעה מה יצווה יי' לכם" (במד', ט', ח'). וכל זה להתדבקו תמיד ברוחניים ושובו
אלהי שלם, כי לא היו מעכבים ודוחקים ומטרידים אותו המקרים הגשמיים, ולא היה פועל כח ההוגה
אז בשום כלי גופני, ואיך יחשב ותתיחס פעולת כח גופני למי שישב ארבעים יום וארבעים לילה מבלי
אכילה ושתיה?!?

H. Alemanno, *Hai ha-Olamim*. Ms Mantua, 21. fols. 351–52. Based on
Samuel ben Judah of Marseilles' Hebrew translation of *Ibn Rushd's Commentary on Plato's Republic*. II:ii ed. F. Rosenthal, 61–62. For the English
translation, see ch. 6 nn. 34–36.

ותאר אותו אפלטון בעשרה תארים הכוללים כל שלמיות העיון והמעשה, כי מתארי התורה לא ידע.
ואמר כי המלך צריך שיהיו לו אלו התנאים: הראשון הטבעי היותר מיוחד שיהיה מוכן בטבע החכמות
העיוניות, ר"ל שיהיה ביצירתו מכיר למה שבעצמו ומבדיל אותו ממה שבמקרה. השני, שיהיה שומר
לא שוכח. כי מי שאינו בשני התארים הללו אי אפשר לו להתלמד דבר, וזה שלא יסור מהיותו ביגיעה
תמיד עד שיעזוב הקריאה. השלישי, שיהיה אוהב הלמידה ובוחר אותה וכוסף להפליא כל חלקי החכמה,
כי הכוסף מאד בדבר ירצה בכל מיניו, משל זה אוהב היין הנה זה הוא חושק בכל היינות, וחושק הנשים,
בכל הנשים. הרביעיה, שיהיה אוהב הצדק, שונא הכזב, וזה מי שיאהב ידיעת הנמצא על מה שהוא עליו
הנה הוא הצדק. אלה השלמיות הד' הם לשכל העיוני, ואלה הן לשכל המעשי: החמישי, שיהיה
מואס התאוות המוחשות, כי מי שתחזק תאותו בדבר מה תכלית הכח יטה נפשו משאר התאוות, וכמו כן
הענין באלו. וזה שהם כבר נטו נטו בכל נפשותיהם אל הלמידה. הששי, שלא יהיה אוהב הממון, כי הממון

תאוה, ותאות בלתי נאותות באלו האנשים. השביעי, שיהיה גדול המחשבה, כי החושק לידיעת
הכל וכלל הנמצאות, ומי שלא יראה, שיקצר מידיעת הדברים על מה שיחייבהו תחלת הדעת הגדול
המעשה והמחשבה מאד, וכלן אין מזאת הנפש המחשבת יחס כלל. השמיני, שיהיה גבור, כי מי שאין לו
גבורה לא יוכל למאוס מה שגדל עליו מן המאמרים הבלתי מופתיים, ובפרט מי שגדל באלו המדינת.
התשיעי, שיהי' מוכן אל שיתנועע מפאת עצמו כל מה שיראה אותו טוב ויפה מהשווי, וזולת זה מהמעלות
וזה כשתהיה נפשו המתעוררת חזקת האמונה לסברא והמחשבה. העשירי, שיהיה טוב המליצה, יביאהו
לשונו בהתחברו אל כל מה שברעיוניו, ושיהיה עם זה מגיע אל הגבול האמצעי במהירות. ואולם מה
שבו שלמות וכח שאינו בטבע האדם, כי אם מצד מה שהוא מושפע ממנו, הם אלה: שיכתוב לו את משנה
התורה וקורא בה תמיד ונושא אותה על זרועו במקום תפילין של יד. שישמע אל דברי הכהן הרואה
באורים ותומים, כאמרו ולפני אלעזר הכהן יעמד. שכל עסק האומה ידוע למלך מכח מה שיגיד הכהן
השופט במשפט האורים והתומים. שיהיה נשמע אל דברי הנביא שבימיו, כי מפני זה לבד הוסר המלכות
משאול, מפני שסר מדברי שמואל הנביא. שיאהב העבודות האלהיות כמעשה הקרבנות והתפילות
ובנייני היכלות לה' אלהי ישראל, כמה שעשה דוד ושלמה והמלכים הצדיקים. וכאלה רבים כפי מה
שיבחין מצד החכמה המדינית והעיונית והנבואיית.

I. Abravanel, From the Commentary to Ex. 19. *Commentary on the Torah*, 161–64. For the English translation, see ch. 7 nn. 5, 7. Since Abravanel's discussion is very long, I cite here only the listing of the virtues itself. I have deleted his elaboration, which consists mainly of textual examples and proofs of the existence of these virtues in Moses.

הסבה הב' מפאת השליח והאמצעי שהיה ראוי שיהיה מוכתר בכל כתר המעלות והשלמיות כלם על כל
ילוד אשה וזה לא היה במין האנושי כמשה רבינו וזה לפי שכבר נמצאו במשה אדונינו עשר מעלות
ושלמיות שלא נמצאו באדם זולתו. הא' בגופו מזגו וטבעו אבריו... המעלה הב' היא היתה במידותיו אם
היותו מסתפק ומתרחק מהדברים הגשמיים... המעלה והשלמות הג' בידיעתו וחכמתו שהשיג בנבואתו
כי הוא השיג טבעי הדברים כלם עליונים ותחתונים הוא ראה וידע הבריאה הראשונה הכוללת... המעלה
והשלמות הד' כי הי היה מוכן לנבואה בכל עת ושאר הנביאים לא היו כן. המעלה והשלמות הה' שנמצא
במרע"ה הי היה שהוא היה מושיע ומציל ומוציא את ישראל מגלות מצרים ונוצח על מלחמותיהם מה שלא
נמצא בנביא אחר. המעלה והשלמות הו' היה שמרע"ה התחברו בו כל מדרגות מעלות האומה ומנהיגיה.
המעלה והשלמות הז' היא האמת והצדק שהיה בנבואת משה וכל חלקיה מה שלא היה כן בשאר הנביאים.
המעלה והשלמות הח' היא נבואתו של מש"ר שלא היה במשתמש בנבואתו בכחו הדמיוני וזה לא מעט ולא
הרבה כי היה הרוח והשפע הנבואיי המגיע אליו על שכלו בלבד במדרגה עליונה מבלי שתוף המדמה כמו
שהיה בשאר הנביאים ולכן לא באו בדבריו משלים וחידות כמו שבאו בדברי שאר הנביאים להשתמש
בכח המדמה. המעלה והשלמות הט' שמשה רבנו היה סבה מקור ומבוע שממנו נמשכה הנבואה אל כל
שאר הנביאים כי כמו שהעלול הראשון בשכלים הנבדלים הוא מקבל השפע מהסבה הראשונה יתברך
מבלי אמצעי והשכל העלול הב' נמשך מהעלול הראשון וכן כלם באותו השתלשלות מקבלים השפע
מהעלול הראשון ההוא וכל מה שיתרחקו העלולים מהראשון תתמעט מעלתם מכה היה בעין הנבואה
שמשה רבינו היה בה העלול הראשון במעלה וממנו קבלו כל שאר הנביאים כי עם היות ששפע האלהי היה
חל עליהם כפי הכנותיהם בעצמם הנה אותה הכנה ושלמות קנו הנביאים כלם ממשה כי הוא היה אביהם
שהולידם בה והרב שהדריכם בקבלתה ומיצוץ נבואתו העליונה הוכנה האומה כולה לחול באנשיה הרוח
הנבואיי משאר האומות. המעלה והשלמות הי' יהיו קדש לה' והוא שמשה רבינו היה מקבל נבואתו לא
מהשכלי הפועל ולא מאמצעי אחד מהנבדלים כמו שאר הנביאים אבל הפועל המשפיע הקרוב בנבואתו
היה הסבה הראשונה יתברך מבלי אמצעי אחר. הנה התבאר מזה כלו כמה מעלות טובות ושלמות נמצאו
במשה רבנו עד שמפני זה היה ראוי שתנתן התורה על ידו ואמצעותו ותקרא על שמו כמו כמו תורה צוה
לנו משה זכרנו תורת משה. והיא הסבה השנית שבעבורה נתנה התורה בזה הזמן.

J. Shalom, *Sefer Neveh Shalom*, vol. I:vii, 7. 105b. For the English translation, see ch. 7 n. 49.

וראוי שתדע שהתארים הראויים להמצא במלכי ישראל השלמים הם י"ב: הא' היותו זריז בדברים האלהיים וקיום הדת. הב' היותו אוהב צדקה ומשפט. הג' אוהב לחכמים. הד' היותו ענו לא גאה ויבעט מרוב טוב. הה' היותו חכם. הו' שיקבע עתים לתורה. הז' שיהיה רחמן לא אכזר. הח' היותו גומל ומעניש לאיש כדרכיו. הט' להיות גבור. הי' למאוס הקניינים המדומים והמותרות. הי"א לבער הרשע ואנשיו מקרבו ולשנוא אותם. הי"ב לקיים מצות התורה.

K. Shalom, *Sefer Neveh Shalom*, vol. I:vii, 7, 105b–106a. For the English translation, see. ch. 7 n. 54.

ואלה התארים רמוזים בפ' כי תשא וכו'. והתחיל בתאר הא' ואמר שום תשום עליך מלך אשר יבחר ה' בו והאיש שיבחר יי' הוא הקדוש והנזהר בדברים האלהיים שרשע ואוהב חמס שנאה נפשו. ואולם הב' רמז באו' למען ילמד ליראה את יי' שהיראה האמתית היא עשות משפט ואהבת חסד. הג' רמז עליו באומ' מלפני הכהנים הלויים שהזהירו שילמוד התורה ויכתבה לפניו' ועל פיהם לצוותו שיאהבתם ויראי יי' יכבד. הד' ברמזו באו' לבלתי רום לבבו מאחיו. הה' רמזו באו' והיתה עמו וקרא בו שהקריאה בתורה והעיון בה ישים האדם חכם. הו' רמז באו' והית' עמו כלומ' שיקבע עתים לתורה ובזה האופן יהיה עמו לא שישליך עיונה אחריו או יעין בה דרך עראי שאז לא תהיה עמו. הז' רמז באו' מקרב אחיך תשים עליך מלך וזה בסבת היות בני ישראל רחמנים כמשז"ל בג' הנמצאים בם ביישנים רחמנים גומלי חסדים. הח' רמזו באומר ולא יסור את לבבו שהמלך הבלתי גומל ומעניש לאיש בדרכיו נעשה כמי שסר לבבו ממנו נטה מני אורח דין המלוכה למה שאינו משגיח באנשים שתתחיין וזה סבה גדולה להפסד האישים ולעוו' המשפט מה שלא יעלם. הט' רמז באו' ולא ירבה לו סוסים וכו' שהגבור הוא ממוצע בין רך לב והמסתכן בנפשו ולז"א שאין ראוי שיבחר הקצוות והוא שישיב את העם מצרימה למען הרבות סוס שהוא מוזהר עליו מהתורה ע"ז אבל ראוי שיהיה גבור ויכבוש יצרו מזה וזה בשלא ירבה לו סוסים בשהרבוי בהם מביאו לסכנה והוא הפך הגבורה שהסתנז' בדבר שאין להסתכן עליו לא נתן לאנשי המעלה ובפרט למלך וזה שמצינו בדוד שהביאו לו ג' הגבורי' מים מבור בית לחם לא אבה לשתותם ואמר חלילה לי משתותי זאת הדם הדם האנשי' ההולכים בנפשותם ולא אבה לשתותם ואמנם עשה זה זה להורות שאין ראוי לשום אדם להסתכן במה שאין ראוי לכך ולא להיות מאותו הדבר הבא מהסכנה הנעשית ברוע סדו' כזה שממשחית נפשו הוא יעשנה ואמיץ לבו כגבורי' לא ישברחה ע"ז. הי' רמזו באומר לא ירבו לו נשי' שהמשגל אב הטומאה וכמש' ארסטו מחוש המשוש שחרפה היא לנו מאש' אנחנו אדם וכבר ידעת מאמר הנביא זנות ויין ותירוש יקח לב וע"כ סמך ולא יסור לבבו שהההליכה אחר הנאוף סבה בהסיר לב האדם ודעתו יסכל. הי"א הורה באומר וכסף וכו' כלומ' שיאהוב צדק וישנ' רשע ולא יפתה לרבוי כסף כמ"ש וכסף הרביתי להם וזהב עשו לבעל וידוע שמי שלבו הטהו לקבוץ הממון לא ינקה נלכ' בדרכי רשע כלו' אוהב שוחד וזה מגונה בחק כל שלם כ"ש בחק המלך שהמשפט בידו לעשוק אהב. הי"ב הורה באומר לשמור כל דברי התורה הזא' שהמלך השלם הוא המסבב שמירת התורה וממנו ויתד בקיום מצותיה להיות העם נשמעי' ונכנעים לעשותם.

L. Albo, *Sefer ha-Ikkarim*, IV, 26, ed. I. Husik, vol. IV: part 1, 245–48. For the English translation, see ch. 7 nn. 62–64.

ולפי הנראה שהמדות ההכרחיות למלך מצד המלכות הם ששה, וזה שהכוונה בהקמת המלך היא להלחם באויבים ולשפוט אם העם משפט צדק, אמרו ישראל כששאלו מלך ושפטנו מלכנו ויצא לפנינו ונלחם את מלחמותינו, ועל כן ראוי שימצאו בו המדות ההכרחיות לזה, אולם מדות השופטים כבר נתבארו בתורה שהם ארבע, אנשי חיל יראי אלהים אנשי אמת שונאי בצע, וכשנערב עם אלו התארים שהם הכרחיים מצד המלחמה, נמצאם בין כלם ששה. האחד שצריך שיהיה המלך אכזרי לזרים ורחמן לעמו ומוסר נפשו להצילם, כמו שמדרך הרועה לסכן נפשו להסיר המזיקין ולהלחם עם הארי והדוב

לשמור הצאן ולרחם עליהם בזרועו יקבץ טלאים ובחיקו ישא עלות ינהל. והשני שייטיב למטיבים
אליו ולעבדיו ולאנשי מלחמתו, שאם לא יעשה כן מי ימסור נפשו בעבור כבודו או מי יקנא בעדו אם
יבגדו בו. והשלישי שיהיה שונא בצע ולא יהיה חמדן, שהרועה שהושם לשמור הצאן אין ראוי לו לגזול
עורם מעליהם ושארם מעל עצמותם, שאז ישוב העניין בהפך, שיהיו הצאן לפרנס הרועה ולא הרועה
לשמור הצאן, ולזה אמר הכתוב וכסף וזהב לא ירבה לו מאד, שאם ישתדל לקבץ כסף וזהב אפילו מן
האויבים, כשלא ימצא בהם יקח מעמו. והרביעי שיהיה איש חיל חיל אמיץ כח לבו בגבורים לשבר מלתעות
עול ולא ישא פני דל ולא יהדר פני גדול ולא יירא מעשות משפט. והחמישי שיהיה אמת ולא ימצא עולה
בשפתיו וישפוט משפט צדק, שמי שהוא מכחש או דובר שקרים הנה הוא הא אם מפני הרואה או מפני שאינו
יכול להשיג רצונו בזולת זה, והשופט אין לו לירא משום אדם, אמר הכתוב לא תגורו מפני איש, וכל
שכן המלך שאין מי שיעכב על ידו מעשות רצונו, ועל כן אין ראוי לו שישקר, ועוד כי לא יבטח האדם
בדברי המלך אם תדברנה שפתיו עולה ולשונו תהגה רמיה. והששי שיהיה ירא שמים וחרד על דבריו
ויהיה נכנע לעובדי השם יתברך וישמור מצוותיו שנצטוותה עליהן מצד שהוא מלך או אחר שהוא מלך, ואף
בשאר המצות ראוי לו שלא יתגאה על אחיו לחשוב שהוא לב זן חורין מן המצות יותר מהם, אמר הכתוב
לבלתי רום לבבו מאחיו ולבלתי סור מן המצוה ימין ושמאל, וזה כמאמר החכם והדת אחים
נאמנים, ואם יראו העם את המלך מזלזל בתורה ובמלמדיה יבאו כל העם להקל בה ותפול התורה בכללה.

M. Ibn-Shemtov, From the Sermon to the Portion *Korah*, ms. Montefiori 61. Fols. 102a–103b. See ch. 3, n. 125.

וכאשר חקרתי עליהם מצאתים עשרה אשר אין גם אחד מהם נמצא במשה רבינו ע"ה אבל ימצאו
הפכיהם בו בתכלית השלמות והוא פלא עצום ר"ל המצא איש אחד מקבץ כל המעלות האנושיות
המיוחדות באדם המאושר מבלי שיחסר אליו דבר והוא באמת מלך במשפט אשר הוא יעמיד ארץ הפכי
לאיש תרומות ר"ל אשר הקימו אותו למלך מבלי שיהיה הוא ראוי אל המעלות לפי טבעו כי הוא יהרסנה.
ואיש אשר אלה לו הוציאו והשגחה האלהית להשלים המון האנושי ולחון אותו באופן יגיעו אישיו אל
התכלית אשר בעבורו נבראו וכמו שהאנשים אשר קבצו כל הפחתיות יצאו ממדרגת האנושות ורעתם הוא
מטבע הצבועים ואינו מתואר באנושות אבל שם השטן והשר יותר ראוי עליו מאיש רע ובליעל כן אשר
קבץ כל המעלות האנושיות יוצא מגדר האנושי ונכנס בגדר המלאכים ראוי לקרא לו אלהי וכמו שנאמר
בשביעי מספר המדות וכ"ש זה האיש העולה למעלה ראש קרוב אל ה' מאד ותמונת ה' יביט ששם איש
האלי"ם יותר נאות אליו מזולתו וכמו שאמר בסוף התורה.
ואלה העשרה דברים ראיתי להגיד למצא חשבון המעלות האנושיות מלבד
האלוהיות הנמצאות בזה האדון מלידה ומבטן קצתם בחיריות וקצתם אין לרצון מבוא בהם אבל בחמלת
ה' ימצאו בו אשר הן אלה.
המעלה הא' שכבר ימאסו האנשים במנהיג מצד שפלות משפחתו והיותו בן לאיש נורש, כ"ש
כאשר יהיו המונהגים רבי הכמות וגדולי המעלה, שהזרע הוא מיפה אותה בלי ספק. וביחוד בעיני ההמון
המביטים למקרי הדבר קודם הסתכלם במהותו... ותראה משה ע"ה בן לאיש נכבד משבט לוי שהיה
שלישי לבטן המוכן אל שיאמר בעבורו יורו משפטיך ליעקב, בן ליוכבד הצדקת המפורסמת בניסים
הגדולים נולד בחידושים גדולים ותרא אותו כי טוב הוא אשר בעבור מעלת אבותיו מוסף על עצמותו היה
ראוי לראשות ההנהגה .
השנית. העיון במה שהרגיל האדם מנעוריו והזכירה במה שגדל עליו מהשפלות וזה דבר גדול
בעיני ההמון אשר בעבור זה לא יוכלו לשאת עול איש רש ונקלה... וזה משה האיש אשר אנחנו בזכרון
קצת מעלותיו המדומות והאמיתיות גדל בשם טוב בין מלכים ויועצי ארץ אשר הערימה ההשגחה האלהית
לשים אותו לפניהם באופן יהיה מוכן אל ההנהגה ואל המעלה מנעוריו רב המחשבה וגדול העצה ... ואיש
אשר היתה זאת מדרגתו בגדול ובמוסר שאין מן הראוי שיהיה נמאס בעיני אנשי עמו.
השלישית. איכות מעלת האיש בעיני העמים כי זה ממה שישגיחו בו הפקחים השגחה נפלאה אתה
תראה שההוד וההו והיות האדם גדול בעיני רואיו מאת האלי"ם ינתן חן וכבוד יתן ה' ... ולזה הגדילה
התורה למשה אדוננו שהוא עם כל מה שקרב אל הש"י זה האופן מהקורבה מה שלא יעלם נתן כתר
מלכות בראשו ומהוד הכבוד והגדולה מה שהיה במקום חסרון לשונו אשר נשארה לסבה גדולה, וכמו
שאמר או מי ישום אלם הלא אנכי ה', שירצה, שכמו ששם פה לאדם לתכלית ידוע כי אין בדברים

הטבעיים דבר לבטלה כן ברא אותו בתכונה לא ישלם לו הדבור הצח והערב לתועלת עצום ולתכלית
גדולה בהשארות זאת התורה וקיום מאמריו באופן לא יחשב שערבות לשונו והפלגת מליצתו יביא
האנשים להמסר אליו ולזה היה גדול מאד בעיני אויביו ומלכים יראו וקמו מפניו וכמו שאמר גם האיש
משה גדול מאד בארץ מצרים וכו' אשר בעבור זה ראוי שיהיה גדול ליהודים ורצוי לרוב אחיו לא לבעט
בו ולבקש להסיר מלכותו.

הרביעית. גודל לב האיש וגבורתו כי זה ממה שיאות אל הגדולים בטבע שיהיו גדולי הלב רבי
המשרה כפני האריה פניהם לא ישובו מפני כל. אתה תמצא זאת המעלה בזה האדון על כל איש אשר
בעבורו לא ירא ולא יפחד והוא לבדו ומקלו בידו באמור אל מלך גדול וכסיל כה אמר ה' שלח את עמי
ויעבדוני ואם מאן אתה לשלוח וכו' ולכות אותו מכה אחר מכה עד יאמר אליו כן דברת לא אוסיף עוד
ראות פניך וכו' ויצא מעם פרעה בחרי אף שזה כלו להפלגת גבה לבו וגבורתו ביצירה וזאת המידה עם
שההרגל לדברים המהבילים והההמסר אליהם יעזרו אל הנפש אל קבולה אבל בלי ספק ביצירת האדם אם
בהרכבתא ומזגו ובפרט מזג הכח החיוני אשר בלב אם במצב שמימיי בעת ההולדה יש הכנה גדולה אליה
ועם שנתקבצו בזה האדון הדברים הטבעיים והאלהיים כלם כבר נעזר בזה במה שגדל בין השרים
והפרתמים גבורי כח אנשי מלך מצרים ולזה היתה זאת המעלה מחוייבה בנביאים שהיא מתאר הפרנס
וכמו שאמרו אין הב"ה משרה שכינתו אלא על חכם גבור עני ועשיר וכלם במשה אשר כלם כפשוטם
וכמשמעם בחלוף מה שפרשו בהם גדולי החכמים לבלתי עמדם על סודות ההנהגה ומה שצריך אליה
מהדברים אשר מחוץ. ובהיות זה כן הוא מבואר היות זה האדון מוכן בטבע ובהרגל אל מעלת הראשיות
בהיות אתו זה המעלה האנושית אשר היא עצמית מאד למנהיג מצד שהוא מנהיג וכ"ש שאין שיהיה ראוי
שיהיה נמאס בעיני בני עמו.

חמישית. כבר יברחו העם להמליך עליהם איש רודף אחר השררה מבקש הגגדלה ההמונית
ורוצה למלוך עליהם בחזקה וכל אדם בטבע יברח מאד מעלותיו האנושיות על דרך כלל שהוא בורח מן השררה
... ותמצא זה האדון אשר אנחנו מבקשים סיפור מעלותיו האנושיות על דרך כלל שהוא בורח מן השררה
הלא תראה אומרו לאל אשר שלחו מי אנכי כי אלך אל פרעה וכי אוציא את בני ישראל ממצרים וכאשר
אמר אליו כי אהיה עמך אמר לא איש דברים אנכי גם מתמול גם משלשום גם מאז דברך אל עבדך שירה
על ההפצר מלכת ולקחת השררה עד שאמר באחרונה אחר מה שעמד על סודות האלוהות וידע סתרי
מציאות ומה שירוה בו השם המפורש כי היתה תשוקתו לעניינים העיוניים עצומה, אמר שלח נא ביד
תשלח. וזה היה בקצה האחרון מהבריחה מהשררה עד שהרא אף ה' בו. הנמצא כזה איש גדול הנפש
מוכן אל המעלות בורח מהשררות ועם כל זה הגיע עניינו בין אלה האנשים הפושעים אל שישמע ומדוע
תתנשאו כי תשתרר עלינו גם השתרר אין זה כי אם רוע לב.

ששית. תשוקת הפרנס וחמדתו בהתפשטות היושר והצדק בין המדיניים כי זה ממה שהוא
התכלית האחרון ממלכת המלכות קיבוע היושר בין האנשים אשר לחלוף טבעיהם ורחב מזגם כל אחד
ידרוש לעצמו טוב מיוחד והוצרכו הפרנסים להמעיט כל דאלים גבר ... ולזה היתה זאת המעלה התכלית
האחרון למנהיגים והיא במדרגת הצורה להם ר"ל תשוקתם הטבעית אל היושר באופן לא יוכל סבול
העול כי המלכות איפשר שיתקיים עם הכפירה ואי איפשר שיתקיים עם החמס ולזה תמצא המלכים
העומדים על החמס שנואים מאד וסוף עניינם על הרוב שיהרגו העם אותם. ותמצא זה האדון מתואר בזאת
המעלה בהיותו בא בגדר אדם לא יוכל לסבול העול עם היותו איש בלתי בעל שרות ופרנסה אבל
לעוצם מעלתו משתדל בהסרת החמס וכמו שאמר ויפן כה וכה וירא כי אין איש ויך את המצרי ... שהוא
לנדיבות טבעו והיותו בטבע מוכן אל המעלות מאד מאד לא יכול להתאפק מנטוע היושר בין האנשים אשר
יתחבר אליהם וזה היה מעניינו טרם ידע את ה' וטרם נגלה אליו האלי"ם ויתן לו חקים ומשפטים ישרים ותורות
אמת וכמו שהעיד ע"ה וכי יש גוי גדול אשר לו חקים ומשפטים צדיקים וישרים ככל התורה הזאת. אבל
בצדק הטבעי והשכל אל היושר המעשי אשר אז היה אליו הקודם בטבע ובזמן לקבול הדת האלוהית היה זה
האופן מהתשוקה אל היושר המעשי ההוא כ"ש שיהיה אחרי ראותו את מעשה ה' כי נורא הוא ואת היושר
המתפשט בכל הנמצאות עם המצא עם כל אחד חלקו הראוי במיוחד והצריך אליו במציאותו והשארותו
בזמן האפשרי בחקו באופן מהחכמה מה שילאו רעיונותינו השגתו והיותו משיג יושר הפרנסה ביצירתו
של עולם אשר אמר בעבורו אל אמונה ואין עול שהוא עול יתחזק בזאת המדה מאד מאד וכמו שהזהיר אליה
במשנה תורה פעמים רבות צדק צדק תרדוף כי תועבת ה' אלוהיך כל עושה אלה כל עושה עול. שידיעה
הגדולה בנמצאות והעמידה על מעלות הש"י יעזור לאדם עזר גדול בקנין זאת המדה מבין שאר המעלות
האנושית. ואלה השנואים בקשו לפרוק מעל צואר בהמיותם הרע עול זה הפרנס הצדיק הישר.

שביעית. עזיבת השר משמוע זעקת עשוק ואשר הוא צריך אליו בהנהגה יביא את האנשים אל

הבעיטה ואל המרד. וזה דבר מחוייב בכח מנהיג. ... ולכן תאר זה האדון בזאת המעלה ההכרחית בהנהגת
עם רב ויעמוד העם על משה מן הבקר עד הערב. וכמו שאמר והיה כל מבקש ה', וכמו שצוה השופטים
ושפטו את העם בכל עת אשר רצה אל היותם מוכנים ומזומנים תמיד באופן ישמעו כל אשר יצטרך
אליהם וזאת ההנהגה דומה להנהגה האלוהית השומע תמיד זעקת דל והנה לא ינום ולא ישן בורא עולם
ומנהיגו ומשפיע בו תמיד מעשה בראשית באופן יעזור כל נברא על שלמותו... ולזה היה זה האדון מעותד
לראשית עם זאת המעלה המיוחדת אחר אשר תמצא רוב מלכי הארץ יברחו מהעמים ומליטפל לישא
טרחם וכמו שהתרעם הוא ע"ה איכה אשא לבדי טרחכם ומשאכם וריבכם ואלה הסכלים בקשו המרתו.
  שמינית. דרישת תועלת העם וההסתכן בעבורם עד שאתה תמצא רוב השרים והמלכים עם
שלהם תאוה טבעית בטוב עמם כמו הוא ראוי כי לכך נוצרו הם מתרפים מהבקשה רפיון גדול ולכן
בורחים מלהתחיל מלחמות ליראתם מהסכנה אשר תשיג בעבורם ויסבלו בעבור מה שישאו עול
וחרפה... אתה תמצא בחפוש מלכי הארץ מי שלהם זאת המדה הפחותה הפך מה שאמר יואב שר הצבא
חזק ונתחזק בעד עמינו ובעד ערי אלינו וה' הטוב בעיניו יעשה. ותמצא זה האדון עובר ומתעבר על איזה
דבר יגיע לעמו מהעמל וכמו שאמר אל הש"י בתחלת עניינו כי למה הרעותה לעם הזה למה זה שלחחתני
ומאז באתי אל פרעה לדבר בשמך הרע לעם הזה והצל לא הצלת את עמך ... ראה אהבת זה האדון אל עמו
ודרישתו אליהם כל טוב גשמי ורוחני ואיך שאל את נפשו למות אם ימותו ולא רצה לחיות אחריהם ואיש
אשר זאת היא הנהגתו הראוי שיאמר אליו העיני האנשים ההם תנקר לא נעלה .
  תשיעית. קושי עול השרים שהוא יעשה בעבורם בם ובבניהם... וזה האדון התפאר והעיד עליו
שמים וארץ שלא חמור אחד מהם נשא ולא הרע בדיבור ובמעשיו לאחד מהם. האפשר שתהיה ההנהגה
יותר מתוקה ועבדות יותר ערב מזה והארורים אמרו כי תשתרר עלינו.
  עשירית. והיא אחרונה עזיבת הגאוה אשר היא תועבת ה' ורבים מהפחותים הסכלים חושבים
כי מעלת גודל הלב סמוכה ומצורפת לגאוה אבל כל גדל הנפש עניו ושפל וכמו שאמר ית' לגדול
שבאנשים והוא המלך לבלתי רום לבבו מאחיו... והיה זה האדון מתואר בזאת המעלה על כל זולתו לא
מהמלכים ואנשי המשרה לבד אבל על כל אדם אשר היה על פני האדמה כמו שהעיד עליו בוראו ית' עד
שסבל מה שדברו עליו אהרן ומרים מהשתחות נבואתם המדומה לנבואתו האלוהית העולה על כל טבע
כמו שבאר להם ית' במאמר אם יהיה נביאכם ה' במראה אליו אתודע בחלום אדבר בו לא כן עביד משה
וכו'. ועם כל זה שתק ושמע חרפתו ואינו משיב ולא זעק אל ה' לשאול ממנו משפט וזהו וישמע ה' שהוא
לבדו ומעצמו נתקנה במשה בחירו לא למען מה שצעק אליו משה על זה כי האיש משה מטבעו להיות עניו
שפל אנשים בעיניו שומע חרפתו ואינו משיב ... התראה מנהיג זאת מלאכתו מהסכל ושמוע חרפה
ושותק שיקוצו עמו בני עמו ואלה המעלות הנפלאות העצומות אשר אתו. והם עם כל זה מבקשים
לפרוק מעליהם את עול הנהגתו.
  ואלה העשרה כולם מעלות אנושיות ראויות בכל מנהיג מצד שהוא מנהיג הנהגה אנושית.
וההנהגה האלוהית והנבואית יש לה מעלות אחרות נמצאות בתכלית השלמות במשה ע"ה אשר כבר
רמזתי אל מעלתו בנבואה הרמה בדרש עם נושא בה'. והארכתי בה לפי העיון התורי ואלה הארורים
קמו עליו ודברו בפניו דברים לא נתנו ליכתב וכמו שאמר ויקומו לפני משה. והוא עם זה סבל טרחם ולא
עזב הנהגתם אבל עמד בפרץ לפניו כאשר גזר עליהם. וכן ראוי לעשות לכל מנהיג אחריו.

Notes

ABBREVIATIONS

AJS Review	*The Journal of the Association for Jewish Studies*
APSR	*American Political Studies Review*
ASQ	*Arab Studies Quarterly*
BJRL	*Bulletin of the John Rylands Library*
HTR	*Harvard Theological Review*
HUCA	*Hebrew Union College Annual*
IOS	*Israel Oriental Studies*
JHI	*Journal of the History of Ideas*
JJOS	*Jewish Journal of Sociology*
JJS	*Journal of Jewish Studies*
JNES	*Journal of Near Eastern Studies*
JPSR	*Jewish Political Studies Review*
JQR	*Jewish Quarterly Review*
JSAI	*Jerusalem Studies in Arabic and Islam*
JSS	*Journal of Semitic Studies*
JWCI	*Journal of the Warburg and Courtland Institutes*
MGWS	*Monatsschrift für Geschichte und Wissenschaft des Judentums*
PAAJR	*Proceedings of the American Academy for Jewish Research*
REJ	*Revue des etudes Juives*

CHAPTER 1. PHILOSOPHER, KING, PROPHET

1. R. Walzer, ed., tr., and commentary, *Al-Farabi on the Perfect State* (Oxford, 1985), 430–31; "Platonism in Islamic Philosophy," in his *Greek into Arabic* (Oxford, 1963), 243–44; and "Arabic Transmission of Greek Thought to Medieval Europe," *BJRL* 29 (1945):164–83. Also S. Pines, "Aristotle's Politics in Arabic Philosophy," *IOS* 5 (1975):150–60; and "Le-heker torato ha-medinit shel Ibn Rushd," *Iyyun* 8 (1957):65–83; reprinted in his *Bein Mahshevet Israel le-Mahshevet ha-Amim* (Jerusalem, 1977), 84; R. Lerner and M. Mahdi, *Medieval Political Philosophy: A Sourcebook* (New York, 1967), introduction, 16; L. Strauss, *Philosophy and Law*, tr. F.

Baumann, foreword by R. Lerner (Philadelphia, 1987), 107–8; F. Rosenthal, *The Muslim Concept of Freedom* (Leiden, 1960), 31–32, n. 74; and *The Classical Heritage in Islam* (London, 1975), 109–16; M. E. Marmura, "The Philosopher and Society: Some Medieval Arabic Discussions," *ASQ* 1 (1979):309–23.

2. Walzer, "Platonism," 243; *Al-Farabi*, 11, 426–28; and "Aspects of Islamic Political Thought; Al-Farabi and Ibn Xaldun," *Oriens* 16 (1963):41–42.

3. See the studies listed above and also E. I. J. Rosenthal, *Political Thought in Medieval Islam* (Cambridge, 1968); "On the Knowledge of Plato's Philosophy in the Islamic World," *Islamic Culture* 14 (1940):387–422; and "Some Aspects of Islamic Political Thought," *Islamic Culture* 22 (1948):1–17, reprinted in his *Studia Islamica* (Cambridge, 1971), 17–33; L. Strauss, "On Abravanel's Philosophical Tendency and Political Teaching," in B. Trend and H. Loewe, eds., *Isaac Abravanel: Six Lectures* (Cambridge, 1937), 95–99; M. Mahdi, "The *Editio Princeps* of Farabi's '*Compendium Legum Platonis*,'" *JNES* 20 (1961):1–15; "Al-farabi et Averroes: Remarques sur le Commentaire d'Averroes sur la Republique de Platon," *Multiple Averroes* (Paris, 1978), 91–101; L.V. Berman, "Ibn Rushd's Middle Commentary on the Nicomachaean Ethics in Medieval Hebrew Literature," *Multiple Averroes* (Paris, 1978), 287–301; J. Macy, "The Rule of Law and the Rule of Wisdom in Plato, Al-Farabi, and Maimonides," in W. M. Brinner and S. D. Ricks, eds., *Studies in Islamic and Judaic Traditions* (Atlanta, 1986), 203–5; I. Rotter, "The Islamic Sources of Maimonides' Political Philosophy," *Gesher* 7 (1979):192; A. K. S. Lambton, "Al-Farabi: The Good City," in her *State and Government in Medieval Islam* (Oxford, 1981), 316–25.

4. E. I. J. Rosenthal, *Averroes Commentary on Plato's* Republic (Cambridge, 1969), 61. The expression *cohen*, priest, is the literal, but misleading, translation of the Muslim term *imam*; see Rosenthal, English translation, 177, note 2; and Lerner's translation, R. Lerner, *Averroes on Plato's* Republic (Ithaca, 1974), 72; and R. Walzer, *Al-Farabi*, 442, n. 664. See also J. L. Teicher's blunt review of Rosenthal's edition, *JSS* 5 (1960):176–95; Pines, "Le-heker torato ha-medinit shel ibn Rushd," *Iyy'un* 8 (1957):85. As for the passage of the expression *medina cohanit*, priestly state, from the Arabic sources to Hebrew, see the translation by Samuel ben Judah of Marseilles of Ibn Rushd's commentary to Plato's *Republic* in Rosenthal, 79; and in Lerner, 102; the Todorosi translation of Ibn Rushd's commentary to Aristotle's *Rhetoric*, J. Goldenthal ed. (Leipzig, 1843), 54; and after him, Judah Messer Leon, *Nofet Zufim* (Vienna, 1863), 106; I. Rabinowitz, ed. and tr., *The Book of the Honeycomb's Flow: Sepher Nopheth Suphim* by Judah Messer Leon (Ithaca and London, 1983), 306–7, n. 9; M. R. Hayoun, "Moses Narboni and ibn Bajja," *Da'at*, 18 (1987):35; the discussion in Rosenthal, *Political Thought in Medieval Islam*, 288, n. 32; 295, n. 52; and his edition of Ibn Rushd's commentary to Plato's *Republic*, 281. Cf. Falaquera's version based on Al-Farabi, *Reshit Hokmah* (Berlin, 1902), 77. For a comparison with his source, see M. Mahdi, *Al-Farabi's Philosophy of Plato and Aristotle* (Ithaca, 1969), 66–67; and Rosenthal, *Political Philosophy*, 131. Cf. *Al-Farabi philosophy*, 46–47; R. Lerner and M. Mahdi, *Medieval Political Philosophy*, 78–79; M. Mahdi, "Remarks on Alfarabi's Attainment of Happiness," in G. H. Hourani, ed., *Essays on Islamic Philosophy and Science* (Albany, 1975), 58, 61–62; J. L. Kraemer, "The Jihad of the Falasifa," *JSAI* 10 (1987):304–5. In contrast to Shmuel ben Judah of Marseilles, who translated Ibn

Rushd's commentary and turned *imam* into *cohen*, Falaquera was more cautious, preferring not to look for any Hebrew parallelism with the Muslim term but simply to ignore it (see below, ch. 5, n. 22). In Ibn Rushd's version, the prophet is deliberately omitted as a counterpart to all these figures; for the reasons, see below, ch. 2, n. 18. In Al-Farabi, this parallelism does not appear in all the sources (according to Rosenthal, perhaps partly because the reference is not to the initial lawgiver but to his descendents). Al-Farabi, however, unlike Ibn Rushd, expressly posits this parallelism, at least in regard to the highest stage of perfection: see below, ch. 2, n. 17; the same parallelism is found in Falaquera. See also the Hebrew translation by Samuel ibn Tibbon of *Sefer ha-Hathalot (The Book of Principles)*, in *Sefer ha-Asif,* Z. Filipowsky, ed. (Leipzig, 1849), 40–41. See M. Galston, "Philosopher King versus Prophet," *IOS* 8 (1978):205; and H. Kreisel, "Hakham ve-navi be-mishnat ha-Rambam u-benei hugo," in *Eshel Be'er Sheva* 3 (Be'ersheba, 1986), 151, and n. 10. For another example of this parallelism, see Alemanno's *Hai ha-Olamim* (below, ch. 6, n. 32). Alemanno follows Ibn Rushd's version; hence, the presence of the parallelism with the priest. Unlike Ibn Rushd, Alemanno later adds the power of prophecy; see below, ch. 6 (and cf. the discussion of Philo, ch. 3, n. 1, below).

    5. L. Strauss, "Farabi's Plato," in *Louis Ginzburg Jubilee Volume* (New York, 1945), 357–93, especially part II. L. V. Berman, "Maimonides on Political Leadership," in *Kinship and Consent,* D. J. Elazar, ed. (Ramat Gan, 1981), 13–25; see also Berman's "The Ideal State of the Philosophers and the Prophetic Laws," in *"A Straight Path: Studies in Medieval Philosophy and Culture: Essays in Honor of A. Hyman,* R. Link-Salinger et al., eds. (Washington, DC, 1987), 10–22. On politics as a supreme science, see Aristotle, *Nicomachaean Ethics* I:ii: "that study which has most authority and control over the rest." Cf. Falaquera, *Reshit Hokmah,* 57; and the distinction between the art of jurisprudence and the art of dialectical thought, 59. Cf. also Ibn Rushd's commentary to Plato's *Republic,* Rosenthal, ed., 71; Alemanno, *Hai Ha-Olamim* (Ms. Mantua, 108), fols. 350–351; and R. Jospe, *Torah and Sophia, The Life and Thought of Shem Tov Ibn Falaquera* (Cincinnati, 1988), 113, n. 165. For Ernest Barker's comment, see his *The Political Thought of Plato and Aristotle* (New York, 1959), 525.

    6. In contrast to Barker, see the position of R. Klibansky, *The Continuity of the Platonic Tradition During the Middle Ages* (London, 1981), emphasizing the continuity of the Platonic tradition not only in Judaism and Islam (14–18, 39–41), but also in medieval Christianity. Klibansky sees the Platonism of the Renaissance as the natural continuation of that of the Middle Ages, 35. Goitein claimed that Ibn Bajja's theory of the philosopher's seclusion was normative in both Islamic and Jewish philosophy. See S. D. Goitein, "Attitudes Towards Government in Islam and Judaism," in his *Studies in Islamic History and Institutions* (Leiden, 1968), 213; and Hebrew version, "Hayahas la-Shilton ba-Islamu-ba-Yanadut," *Tarbiz* 19–20 (1959):153–59. I do not agree with this conclusion, certainly not regarding the *falasifa* and the Jewish philosophers influenced by them. For a contrasting stand, see O. Leaman, "Ibn Bajja on Society and Philosophy," *Der Islam* 57 (1980):109–19. Leaman disagrees with Rosenthal's theory, which has been accepted by most scholars, that Ibn Bajja diverged from the Platonic tradition of the *falasifa* towards an "individualistic deviation." Leaman asserts that no proof can be found in Ibn Bajja's writings for such a deviation. My own findings tend

to support Rosenthal's position. See also L. E. Goodman, "Ibn Bajjah," in *History of Islamic Philosophy*, O. Leaman and S. H. Nasr, eds., vol. 1 (London, 1994), 294–312. For the establishment of the Islamic tradition on Plato, see Walzer, "Platonism."

7. Joseph Albo, *Book of Principles*, I:8. ed. and tr. I. Husik (Philadelphia, 1929), vol. I:32–33. On the Christian influence see A. Melamed, "Hok ha-teva ba-mahashavah ha-yehudit be-yemei ha-benayim ve-ha-renesans," *Da'at*, 17 (1986):49–50. Additional bibliography, ibid., nn. 1–3.

8. Leo Strauss, *Philosophy and Law*, tr. F. Bauman (Philadelphia, 1987), 100, 98, 54, 53, 51; Lerner and Mahdi, introduction, 11–18. The distinction between political theology and political philosophy is taken from this introduction, and it seems to me to be most useful. For Lerner and Mahdi's assertion on the existence of two branches of medieval Jewish political philosophy, with which I do not agree, see nn. 16, 17, below. See also in detail my "Abravanel ve-ha-*Politica* le-Aristo," *Da'at* 29 (1992):69–81, and the English version, *JPSR* 5 (1993):55–75; also "*Ha-Politica* le-Aristo ba-mahashava ha-yehudit be-yemei ha-benayim ve-ha-renesans," *Pe'amim* 51 (1992):27–69, which reinforces this conclusion.

9. Walzer, "Platonism," 246; "Al-Farabi," 425; Berman, "Maimonides, the Disciple of Al-Farabi," *IOS* 4 (1974):162; Lambton, 317; M. E. Marmura, "The Philosopher and Society: Some Medieval Arabic Discussions," *ASQ* 1 (1979):316. Kraemer emphasizes the Platonic foundation of Islamic political philosophy and states that such Islamic term, *jihad*, and *shari'a*, for example, were applied only for political reasons—for the sake of protecting the philosophers from accusations of heresy; see Kraemer, "Falasifa."

10. Falaquera, *Reshit Hokmah*, 70–71; cf. the source in M. Mahdi, ed., 48; Falaquera, *Sefer ha-Ma'alot, Ketavim* (Berlin, 1894), 13–19; and cf. Al-Farabi, *On the Perfect State*, ed. Walzer, ch. 15, 7–13, 239–53. See also Strauss, *Philosophy and Law*, 104, n. 107; B. Chiesa, "Note su Al-Farabi, Averroe, e Ibn Bagga (Avempace) in Traduzione Ebraica," *Henoch* 8 (1986):79–86.

11. See Rosenthal, ed., Hebrew 61–63, English 177–80; Lerner, ed., English 72–74.

12. M. Plessner, "Hashivuto shel R. Shem Tov Ibn Falaquera le-heker toledot ha-filosofia," *Homenaje A. Millas Villas Vallicorosa* (Barcelona, 1956), vol. II:161–84; Strauss, "Quelques Remarques sur la Science Politique de Maimonide et de Farabi," *REJ* 100 (1936):1–37.

13. See my *Aharonim mul ha-Rishonim: Toldot ha-Pulmus ba-Mahashavah ha-Yehudit shel Yemei ha-Benayim ve-ha-Renesans*, to be published by Bar Ilan University Press (forthcoming). See, for the time being, my "Le-makorotiv shel dimui ha-hagav ve-ha-anakim be'nedod hesir oni' le Abraham Ibn Ezra," *Mehkarei Yerushalayim be-Sifrut Ivrit* 13 (1992):95–102.

14. See my "Jethro's Advice in Medieval and Renaissance Jewish and Christian Political Thought," JPSR 2 (1990):3–41.

15. A. A. Halevi, "Mishpat ha-meleck (min ha-hagut ha-me'dinit ba-olam ha-atiq be-Israel u-va-amim)," *Tarbiz* 38 (1969):225–30; E. I. J. Rosenthal, "Some

Aspects of the Hebrew Monarchy," *JJS* 9 (1958):1–18, reprinted in his *Studia Islamica*, vol. 1 (Cambridge, 1971), 3–20; S. W. Baron, The Historical Outlook of Maimonides, *PAAJR* 6 (1935):5–113, reprinted in his *History and Jewish Historians* (Philadelphia, 1964), 131–35; G. J. Blidstein, "The Monarchic Imperative in Rabbinic Perspective," *AJS Review* 8–9 (1982–83):15–39; "On Political Structures," *JJOS* 22 (1980):47–58; *'Ekronot Medini'im be-Mishnat ha-Rambam* (Ramat Gan, 1983), ch. I. Also H. A. Wolfson, *Philo* (Cambridge, 1962), II:13; D. Polish, "Some Medieval Thinkers on the Jewish King," *Judaism* 20 (1971):323–29; "Rabbinic Views on Kingship—A Study in Jewish Sovereignty," *JPSR* 3 (1991):67–90; *Give Us a King: Legal-Religious Sources of Jewish Sovereignty* (Hoboken, New Jersey, 1989); F. Dvornik, *Early Christian and Byzantine Political Philosophy, Origins and Background*, vol. I (Washington, DC, 1966), ch. 6, 278–402; S. Federbush, *Mishpat ha-Melukha be-Israel* (Jerusalem, 1952), chaps. 4–6.

16. S. A. Cohen, "The Concept of the Three *Ketarim:* Its Place in Jewish Political Thought and Its Implications for a Study of Jewish Constitutional History," *AJS Review* 9 (1984):30–32. Also, *"Keter* as a Jewish Political Symbol: Origins and Implications," JPSR 1 (1989):39–62.

17. *Avot:* 6.5–6.

18. Blidstein, *'Ekronot medini'im*, 20–22. Notably, Saadia Gaon was indeed hesitant to establish monarchy as a halakhic norm, but he certainly regarded it as the preferred regime in principle: *The Book of Beliefs and Opinions*, 10, 12; Blidstein, *'Ekronot medini'im*, 1, n. 6.

19. Ibid., 21, n. 5. On Abravanel's position, see ch. 7, below. Abravanel was also pleased to assert that even Maimonides did not see monarchy as a halakhic obligation but only stated that if a king was crowned, he had to be Jewish, and so forth. See *Commentary to Deuteronomy*, ch. 17; and Blidstein, *Ekronot Medini'im*, 20–22.

20. *Duties of the Heart*, I:7, part one, ch. 7, end of chapter. Also see Abraham ibn Ezra, *Commentary to Ecclesiastes*, 9:14. Additional examples of the use of this verse as an argument for monarchy are found in A. Melamed, "Ha-diyyun ha-medini be-'Malmad ha-Talmidim' le-Ya'aqov Anatoli," *Da'at* 20 (1988):110, n. 60; and "Mishlei 28:2—Pirushim politiim le-text mikra'i," *Beit Mikra* 134 (1993):265–77.

CHAPTER 2. THE SOURCES

1. Plato, *The Republic* II:368. Translated with introduction and notes by F.M. Cornford (Oxford, 1967), 55.

2. *The Republic* IV:433:128.

3. Ibid., 427:121.

4. Ibid., 485:191.

5. Ibid., VI. 486:192.

6. Ibid., 487:193.

7. Ibid., 487:193.

8. Ibid., VII:511–18:227–35.

9. Ibid., V:473:178–79.

10. *Laws* IV:709. *The Dialogues of Plato.* Translated by B. Jowett with an introduction by R. Demos (New York, 1937), II:481; see also, in 482: "a tyrant who is young, temperate, quick at learning, having a good memory, courageous, and a noble nature."

11. E. Barker, *Greek Political Theory* (London, 1964), 385. On Al-Farabi's way of interpreting the *Laws*, see L. Strauss, "How Farabi Read Plato's *Laws*," in his *What Is Political Philosophy?* (New York, London, and Chicago, 1967 and 1969), 134–54.

12. *Theaetetus*, 176, Jowett, vol. 2:178. Also, *Laws* IV:716, 487–88; see Rosenthal, *Political Philosophy*, 122–23; and "The Concept of 'Eudaimonia' in Medieval Islamic and Jewish Philosophy," *Storia della Filosofia antica e medievale (atti del XII Congresso internazionale di filosofia, 1958)* (Firenze, 1960), 145–52; reprinted in his *Studia Islamica*, vol. 2 (Cambridge, 1971), 127–34. See, in contrast, Aristotle's assertion that the imitation of God can be achieved only in the intellectual sphere, *Ethics X*, 8.

13. See ch. 4, below.

14. See, e.g., Albo's criticism of the Platonic theory in this context, *Book of Principles*, ed., tr., Husik I:82: "Thus, Plato made a grievous mistake, advocating the unbecoming as though it were becoming. For his idea is that all the women of a given class should be held in common by the men of that class. Thus, the wives of the rulers should be common to all the rulers, the wives of the merchants common to all the merchants, and similarly the wives of the men of a given trade or occupation should be common to the men of that trade or occupation. This is a matter which the Torah forbids; even the Noachian law prohibits it." Albo presents this Platonic idea as one of the proofs of the superiority of divine law over human law, even that legislated by the perfected human understanding of the philosopher-king. See ch. 4, below. By contrast, Ibn Rushd, basing himself on Plato's egalitarian attitude to women, was critical of the accepted position in Islam in his time. See below. See also the critique, based on Aristotle's discussion in the second book of the *Politics*, of the Platonic ideal state in the anonymous fifteenth-century Hebrew translation of Aegidius Romanus' *De Regimine Principium, Sefer Hanhagat ha-Melakhim* Ms. Leiden Or 4749 (Warn. 11), Fols. 328–35. Also my "The Anonymous Hebrew Translation of Aegidius' *De Regimine Principum*: An Unknown Chapter in Medieval Jewish Political Philosophy," *Documenti e studi sulla traduzione Filosofica medievale* (1994):439–61.

15. *Laws*, 996. On this see, L. Strauss, "Plato," in Strauss and Cropsy, eds., *History of Political Philosophy* (Chicago, 1969), 59; T. A. Sinclair, *A History of Greek Political Thought* (London, 1967), 193–94; Barker, *Political Thought*, 405–10. As Barker states, "The end of the *Laws* is the beginning of the Middle Ages," 409.

16. Strauss, *Philosophy and Law*, 54.

17. This background discussion is largely based on Rosenthal, *Political Philosophy*, I:vi. Also M. Mahdi, "Al-Farabi," in *History of Political Philosophy*, 160–80; H. K. Sher-

vani, "Al-Farabi's Political Theories," *Islamic Culture* 12 (1938):288–305; F. A. Sankari, "Plato and Al-Farabi: A Comparison of Some Aspects of Their Political Philoso-phies," *The Muslim World* 60 (1970):218–225; Strauss, "Farabi's Plato." Rosenthal emphasizes Al-Farabi's Islamic starting point, and argues that "he was a Muslim first and a disciple of Plato, Aristotle, and their Hellenistic successors and commentators second." For a different opinion, see ch. 1, n. 9; see also below. Marmura aptly described Al-Farabi as "the architect of Islamic political Platonism," 316. See also M. Galston, "Realism and Idealism in Avicenna's Political Philosophy," *The Review of Pol-itics* 41 (1979):561–77; her *Politics and Excellence: The Political Philosophy of Alfarabi* (Princeton, 1990); H. Daiber, "The Ruler as Philosopher: A New Interpretation of Al-Farabi's Views," *Mededelingen der Koninklijke Nederlandse Akademie van Wetenschappen* (Amsterdam, 1986), 133–49.

18. The discussion here is based largely on E. I. J. Rosenthal, *Political Thought in Medieval Islam*, ch. 9, and Pines, "Le-heker torato ha-medinit shel Ibn Rushd." Also Teicher, "Review," and L. V. Berman's review of Rosenthal's *Averroes' Commentary on Plato's Republic* in *Oriens*, 21–22 (1968–89):426–39. Berman wholly accepts Pines' view. Also R. Lerner's introduction to his translation of Averroes' *Commentary on Plato's Republic;* Mahdi, "Alfarabi et Averroes"; C. E. Butterworth, "New Light on the Political Philosophy of Averroes," in *Essays on Islamic Philosophy and Science*, ed. G. F. Hourani (New York, 1975), 118–27; "Averroes: Politics and Opinions," *APSR* 66 (1972):894–901; "Ethics and Classical Islamic Philosophy: A Study of Averroes' Com-mentary on Plato's *Republic*," *Ethics in Islam*, R. G. Hovannisian ed. (Undena, 1985), 17–45; *Philosophy, Ethics and Virtuous Rule: A Study of Averroes' Commentary on Plato's 'Republic'*, Cairo Papers in Social Science, vol. 9, monograph 1 (Cairo, 1986); also, A. L. Motzkin, "Elia Del Medigo, Averroes and Averroism," *Italia* 6 (1987):11–13.

19. Pines, "Le-heker."

CHAPTER 3. FIRST INFLUENCES

1. Philo, *On the Life of Moses*, tr. F. H. Colson, vol. II:187. Loeb ed. (Cambridge, MA, 1957), vol. VI:542–43; also, II:292–595: "Moses, king, lawgiver, high priest, prophet." See also Strauss, *Philosophy and Law*, 56, 107; cf. the description of Moses in Josephus Flavius, *Contra Apion* II:16–19.

2. Wolfson, *Philo*, II, ch. 13; S. A. Cohen, "The Concept of the Three *Ketarim*." Since the discussion of the philosopher-king theory begins with Philo and ends with Spinoza, it would be appropriate here to note Wolfson's well-known theory that not only Jewish religious philosophy but Western philosophy generally was a structure originated by Philo and destroyed by Spinoza, both of them Jews. See *Philo, On the Life of Moses*, preface. Without entering into a discussion of this theory itself, it is worth noting that our discussion constitutes a sort of case study of it.

3. J. Weinberg, "The Quest for Philo in Sixteenth-Century Jewish Historiogra-phy," in *Jewish History, Essays in Honour of Chimen Abramski*, ed. A. Rapoport-Albert (London, 1988), 163–88.

4. Saadia Gaon, *The Book of Beliefs and Opinions*, tr. S. Rosenblatt (New Haven, 1967).

5. E. Schweid, "Omanut ha-dialoge be-*Sefer ha-Kuzari* u-mashma'utah ha-iyyunit," in *Ta'am ve-Hakasha* (Ramat Gan, 1970), 37–79. A. L. Motzkin, "On Halevi's Kuzari as a Platonic Dialogue," *Interpretation* 9 (1980/81):111–24.

6. On Muslim and Christian theories of the *Speculum Principium*, see below ch. 7, n. 31; and ch. 8, n. 11.

7. Judah Halevi, *Kuzari* III:1.

8. Judah Halevi, *Kitab al-Khazari*, tr. H. Hirschfeld, preface by M. M. Kaplan (New York, 1927), III:2–3, 137.

9. Judah Halevi, *Kuzari* III:5:137–40. Cf. Halevi's attitude to the theory of imitation, I:12. 45: "He pursues justice in order to resemble the Creator in His wisdom and justice."

10. *The Republic* IV:427–45.

11. For Ibn Pakuda, see ch. I, 20; for Ibn Ezra, *The Commentary on Ecclesiastes*, 9:14.

12. Judah Halevi, *Kuzari* III. 7; Halevi, *Kitab al-Khazari*, 141.

13. Moses Maimonides, *Iggerot ha-Rambam*, ed. I. Shilat (Jerusalem, 1987), II:553. On Maimonides' political philosophy in general, see also R. Lerner, "Maimonides," in *History of Political Philosophy*, 181–200.

14. See ch. 1, above.

15. L. V. Berman, "The Structure of Maimonides' Guide of the Perplexed," *Proceedings of the 6th World Congress of Jewish Studies* (Jerusalem, 1977), III:7–13.

16. S. Klein-Braslavy, "Perushei ha-Rambam le-halom ha-sulam shel Ya'akov," *Sefer Bar Ilan* 22–23 (1988):329–42. Regarding the motif of ascent and descent and the Platonic model, see L. V. Berman, *"Ibn Bajjah ve-ha-Rambam, and Maimonides: A Chapter in the History of Political Philosophy"* (Ph.D diss., Hebrew University, 1959), 10; also "The Structure"; A. Goldman, "Ha-avodah ha-meyuhedet shel-masigei ha-amitot," *Sefer Bar Ilan* 6 (1968):287–313; S. Pines, translator's introduction to *The Guide of the Perplexed* (Chicago, 1963), cxxi; D. H. Frank, "The End of the Guide: Maimonides on the Best Life for Man," *Judaism* 34 (1985):490. Also, D. Hartman, *Crisis and Leadership: Epistles of Maimonides* (Philadelphia, 1985), introduction and 151–52, 249, 280.

17. Moses Maimonides, *The Guide of the Perplexed*, I:15, tr., introduction and notes by S. Pines, introductory essay by L. Strauss (Chicago, 1963), 41.

18. *Guide* II:33, Pines, 364. Also D. Hartman, 151–52.

19. *Guide* III:11, Pines, 440–41. On the image of light and darkness, see Klibansky, *Continuity of the Platonic Tradition*, 17.

20. *Guide* III:54, Pines, 635.

21. *Guide* III:51, Pines, Ibid., 623.

22. *Guide* I:2, Pines, Ibid., 24–25.

23. See Berman, *Ibn Bajjah and Maimonides,* and his various other studies; ch. 1, above. Also see S. Pines, "Ha-mekorot ha-filosofiim shel *Moreh Nebukim,*" in his *Bein Mahshevet Israel le-Mahshevet ha-Amim* (Jerusalem, 1977), 103–73.

24. *Guide* III:51, Pines, 621.

25. Maimonides, *Millot ha-higayon* 14, 7; Maimonides, *Hilkhot De'ot,* I:6; Maimonides, *Hilkhot Teshuva,* 10, 6; Maimonides, *Hilkhot Melakhim,* 10, 12; *Guide* I:54, Pines, vol. I:127–28, (twice) I:69; I:170; III:27; II:510; III:51; II:621; III:54; II:638. Significantly, the statements appear in several of Maimonides' conclusions to his works, including the *Guide, The Book of Knowledge,* and the entire *Mishneh Torah.* For a discussion of the question of imitation, see *Eight Chapters* 7; *Hilkhot Yesodei ha-Torah* I:10; *Guide* I:54, and see S. Pines, "The Limitations of Human Knowledge According to Al-Farabi, Ibn Bajja, and Maimonides," *Studies in Medieval Jewish History and Literature,* ed. I. Twersky (Cambridge, MA, 1979), 82–109.

26. *Guide* III:51; Pines, 621. Cf. Moses Narboni's paraphrase of Ibn Bajja's *The Governance of the Solitary,* ed. Hayoun, 41.

27. *Guide* II:36, Pines, 371; I. Twersky, "Ha-Rambam ve-Eretz Yisrael," in *Tarbut ve-Hevra be-Toledot Yisrael be-Yemei ha-Benayim,* eds. R. Bonfil et al. (Jerusalem, 1989), 372–73.

28. *Guide* III:51, Pines, Ibid., 620.

29. *Guide* II:36, Pines, Ibid., 371.

30. Pines, Ibid., II:372.

31. *Eight Chapters* IV, trans. R. L. Weiss and C. E. Butterworth, *Ethical Writings of Maimonides* (New York, 1975), 69–70. Also *De'ot,* 3:1. On the therapeutic need for patients to exaggerate, see also *De'ot* 22:12. The literature on this subject is extensive. See, e.g. S. Ravidowicz, "Perek be-torat ha-musar le-Rambam," in *M. M. Kaplan Jubilee Volume* (New York, 1953), 205–35; E. Schweid, *Iyyunim be-'Shemonah Perakim' le-Rambam* (Jerusalem 1969), ch. 4; Y. Leibowitz, *Sihot al'Shemonah Perakim le-Rambam* (Jerusalem 1986), ch. 4; S. S. Schwarzschild, "Moral Radicalism and 'Middlingness' in the Ethics of Maimonides," *Studies in Medieval Culture* 11 (1977):65–94; M. Fox, "The Doctrine of the Mean in Aristotle and Maimonides: A Comparative Study," in *Studies in Jewish Religious and Intellectual History,* eds., S. Stein and R. Loewe (London, 1979), 93–120; R. Weiss, "The Adaptation of Philosophic Ethics to a Religious Community: Maimonides' 'Eight Chapters,'" *PAAJR* (1987):261–87; H. A. Davidson, "The Middle Way in Maimonides' Ethics," *PAAJR* 56 (1987):31–72. I do not agree with some of Davidson's conclusions on the differences between Maimonides' ethical approach in his earlier writings compared with the *Guide* and especially his views on the supreme perfection of man and the interpretation of the last chapter of the *Guide.* See D. H. Frank, "Humility as a Virtue: A Maimonidean Critique of Aristotle's Ethics," *Studies in Philosophy and History of Philosophy* 19 (1989):89–99; B. Safran, "Maimonides and Aristotle on Ethical Theory," in *Alei Shefer: Studies in the Literature of Jewish Thought,* ed. M. Hallamish (Ramat Gan, 1990), 75–93; L. V. Berman, "The Ethical Views of Maimonides within the Context of Islamicate Civilization," in *Perspectives on Maimonides,* ed., J. L. Kraemer (Oxford, 1991), 13–32.

32. Maimonides, *The Commentary to Mishnah Aboth*, tr. with an introduction and notes by A. David (New York, 1968), 31–32.

33. *De'ot*, 6:1. *The Book of Knowledge*, ed., introduction, notes and tr. by M. Hyamson (Jerusalem 1965), 54b. On the significance of the prophet Jeremiah's words, see below. Cf. Al-Farabi's similar statement in *Fusul Muntaza'a*, ed. F. M. Najjar (Beirut, 1971), 95. As translated by Marmura, 315: "A virtuous man ought not to live in corrupt political associations, and it is incumbent on him to emigrate to virtuous cities, if these exist in his time. If these do not exist, then the virtuous man is a stranger in the world, lives poorly in it, and death for him is better than life." Maimonides was obviously influenced by Al-Farabi here, except, of course, for the last comment.

34. Maimonides interprets the statement by Nittai the Arbelite in *Avot* I:7, "Remove [yourself] from an evil neighbor, do not befriend the wicked" as follows: "Do not befriend the wicked through any type of friendship or fellowship, lest you learn from his deeds. In the introductory chapters we have explained that a man will learn vices in the company of the wicked," *Commentary to Mishnah Aboth*, David, 10.

35. Maimonides, *Hilkhot Teshuva*, 3:1.

36. Ibid., 3:2. Cf. Falaquera's comparison between the righteous and the bestial state, ch.5, n.38, below.

37. On Maimonides' position on the decline of the generations in general and the serious condition of his period in particular, see the introduction to *The Book of Knowledge*, Hyamson, 46: "In our days, severe vicissitudes prevail, and all feel the pressure of hard times. The wisdom of our wise men has disappeared; the understanding of our prudent men is hidden." Also see *Guide* I:71, Pines, 175; *Iggeret Teman*, Shilat, ed., I. 156–7. See I. Twersky, "Sefer *Mishne Torah* le-Rambam: megamato ve-tafkido," *Diverei ha-Akademia ha-Israelit le-Madaim*, vol. 5 (Jerusalem 1962). See more recently, M. Kellner, *Maimonides on the 'Decline of the Generations' and the Nature of Rabbinic Authority* (Albany, 1996). And see ch. 1, n. 13, above.

38. Maimonides presents desert existence itself in a negative way, as a bestial form of existence, not fitting for a human being. See *Guide* III:47, 50, and so forth. Extensive discussion on this subject is found in my "Ha-Rambam al tiv'o ha-medini shel ha-adam: zerachim u-mehuyavuyot," *Tribute to Sara: Studies in Jewish Philosophy and Kabbalah presented to Professor Sara O. Heller Wilensky*, eds., M. Idel et al. (Jerusalem, 1994), 292–333.

39. *Maimonides' Commentary on the Mishnah*. Introduction to *Seder Zeraim*, tr. F. Rosner (New York, 1975), 130–31.

40. *Eight chapters*, ch. 4. *Ethical Writings*, 70. In this context, it is interesting to note that in his discussion of creation (*Guide* II:17), Maimonides relates a parable of a child being raised by a man (his father?) on an isolated island, that is highly reminiscent of Ibn Tufayl's idea of seclusion. See below, n. 116. The child, however, had difficulty in understanding true reality as a result of his secluded upbringing. In this, Maimonides again avoids identifying intellectual perfection with social isolation.

41. Maimonides, *Introduction to Seder Zeraim*, 127–31. For a detailed analysis of the text, see my article, *"Ha-Rambam al tiv'o ha-medini."*

42. See n. 16, above.

43. *Guide* II:36, Pines, 372; also *Guide* II:45, Pines, 398. On the second degree of prophecy, "so that he talks in wise sayings, in words of praise, in useful admonitory dicta, or concerning governmental or divine matters," see L. V. Berman, "Maimonides on Political Leadership," in *Kinship and Consent*, ed. D. J. Elazar (Ramat Gan, 1981), 13–25.

44. *Guide* II:37, Pines, 375. M. Galston, "Philosopher-King versus Prophet," 204–18. Also on this topic, see M. Kellner, *Maimonides on Human Perfection* (Atlanta, 1990).

45. *Guide* I:54, Pines, 124.

46. *Guide* I:54, Pines, Ibid., 126.

47. *Guide* I:54, Pines, Ibid., 124–25.

48. See also *Guide* III:54, and *De'ot*, I:6, *The Book of Knowledge*, 48a: "Thus, too, the prophets described the Almighty by all the various attributes 'long-suffering and abounding in kindness, righteous and upright, perfect, mighty and powerful' and so forth, to teach us that these qualities are good and right and that a human being should cultivate them, and thus imitate God, as far as he can." See Schwarzschild, "Moral Radicalism"; A. Melamed, "Al yithalal: Perushim filosofiim le-Yirmiyahu 9:22–23 ba-mahashavah ha-yehudit be-yemei ha-beinayim ve-ha-Renesans," *Jerusalem Studies in Jewish Thought* 4 (1985):55–56; Z. Harvey, "Bein filosofia medinit le-halakhah be-mishnat ha-Rambam," *Iyyun* 20 (1980):211–12. Berman, "Maimonides on Political Leadership"; "The Political Interpretation of the Maxim: The Purpose of Philosophy Is the Imitation of God," *Studia Islamica* 15 (1962):53–61.

49. *Eight Chapters*, 4; *Ethical Writings*, 73–74; and Maimonides, *Iggeret ha-She-mad*, Shilat ed., vol I:35. See, too, H. Kasher, "The Meaning of Moses' Sin in Maimonides' Doctrine," *PAAJR* 53 (1986):29–34; Also, *De'ot*, 2:3, *The Book of Knowledge*, 486: "He who is angry, it is the same as if he worshiped idols." See B. Safran, "Maimonides and Aristotle on Ethical Theory." In *Alei Shefer: Studies in the Literature of Jewish Thought*. Edited by M. Hallamish, 75–93. Ramat Gan, 1990. 151, n. 52; also D. H. Frank, "Anger as a Vice: A Maimonidean Critique of Aristotle's Ethics," *History of Philosophy Quarterly* 7 (1990):269–81. And see, more generally, Maimonides on the example that the Torah scholar must give the community through his behavior: *De'ot*, 5.

50. *Guide* III:51, Pines, 624; and *Hilkhot Avoda Zara*, 1:3. Twersky, "Ha-Rambam ve-Eretz Israel," 374.

51. *Guide* III:51, Pines, Ibid., 624.

52. *Guide* III:54, Pines, Ibid., 637–38; and n. 48 above. The source is Jeremiah 9:22–23. See my "Al yithalal"; Goldman, "Ha-avodah."

53. *Guide* I:15, Pines: "for the angels of God are the prophets"; also II:6:34. Klein-Braslavy, "Perushei ha-Rambam." Cf. *Kuzari* IV:1. Hirshfeld 198: "*Elohim* is a term signifying proprietor or governor of the world, if I allude to the possession of the whole of it, and of a portion, if I refer to the powers either of nature or the spheres, or of a

human judge," Also, Narboni's paraphrase of Ibn Bajja's *The Governance of the Solitary*, in M. R. Hayoun, "Moshe Narboni ve-Ibn Bajja," *Da'at* 18 (1989):35.

54. Plato, *Apology*, 31–32.

55. See nn. 31, 33, above. On the Islamic background of the obligation of the perfect man to separate himself from the evil state, see Kraemer, "Falasifa," 311, 314.

56. *Guide* II:37, Pines, 375.

57. *Guide* II:38, Pines, Ibid., 376–77. Thus, Maimonides includes courage among the virtues required by the philosopher-prophet to imitate God; see *De'ot*, 1.6 and n. 48, above. The intention here is, of course, spiritual courage, not physical courage. In this connection, the phrase, "a fortified city," acquires special significance in the setting of Proverbs 15:32: "He that ruleth his spirit (is better) than he that taketh a city." On the multiplicity of meanings of the term "courage" *(gevurah)*, see Melamed, "Al yithalal," nn. 11, 22–25.

58. *Guide* III:54, Pines, 637.

59. R. Lerner, "Maimonides' Governance of the Solitary," in *Perspectives on Maimonides*, ed., J. L. Kraemer (Oxford, 1991), 13–32. I do not agree with some of Lerner's conclusions. A very illuminating study is S. Harvey, "Maimonides in the Sultan's Palace," in *Perspectives on Maimonides*, ed. J. L. Kraemer (Oxford, 1991), 47–57. An obvious expression of this inner tension is to be found in Maimonides' Letters. See Hartman, *Crisis and Leadership* (Philadelphia, 1985). Maimonides' status not only as a communal leader and a teacher of halakhah, but also as a philosopher, undoubtedly influenced his emphasis on educational and political duty. This was in contrast to other philosophers who were not teachers of halakhah, and therefore tended to favor the elitist seclusion of the philosopher.

60. *Guide* III:11, Pines, 441. On Maimonides' messianic views, see A. Ravitzky, "Yemot ha-mashiah be-mishnat ha-Rambam," in *Meshihiyut ve-Eskatologia*, ed. Z. Baras (Jerusalem 1984), 191–200; G. J. Blidstein, "Al ha-Shilton ha-universali behazon ha-geulah shel ha-Rambam," in *Arakhim be-Mivhan Milhamah* (Jerusalem 1984), 155–72; *Ekronot Medini'im*, 108–13 and ch. 10; A. Funkenstein, "Maimonides: Political Theory and Realistic Messianism," *Miscellanea Medievalia* (Berlin and New York, 1977), 81–103; D. Hartman, "Maimonides' Approach to Messianism and Its Contemporary Implications," *Da'at*, 1(1978):5–33; *Crisis and Leadership*, 171–93. For particular emphasis on the Platonic nature of Maimonides' messianic outlook, see J. L. Kraemer, "On Maimonides' Messianic Posture," in *Studies in Medieval Jewish History and Literature*, ed. I. Twersky (Cambridge, MA, 1984), 2:109–42.

61. *Introduction to Perek Helek*, in *A Maimonidean Reader*, ed. I. Twersky (New York, 1972), 414: *Hilkhot Teshuva*, 9:2.

62. *Introduction to Perek Helek*, 414.

63. *Hilkhot Melakhim*, 12:4; *Introduction to Perek Helek*, 415. By contrast, Maimonides' declared position is that scholars must work for their living and not be dependent on the community, Commentary to *Avot*, 4:7; *Hilkhot Talmud Torah*, 3:10. See a discussion on this question, with additional bibliography, in my "Ha-Rambam al tiv'o ha-medini."

64. *Introduction to Perek Helek*, 416.

65. *Hilkhot Teshuva*, 9:2.

66. *Hilkhot Melakhim*, 12:5. Cf. *Introduction to Perek Helek*, 414: "However in those days it will be very easy for men to make a living. A minimum of labor will produce great benefits."

67. Rosenthal, *Political Philosophy*, 131, displays great discernment in identifying the philosopher/lawgiver/king/*imam* parallelism in connection with Al-Farabi. Maimonides himself speaks only of prophet/philosopher/lawgiver. The absence of king from this parallelism is not by chance. Still, it appears that Rosenthal assumes that Maimonides fully accepted Al-Farabi's stance on the question. See also his "Maimonides' Conception of State and Society," in *Moses Maimonides*, ed. I. Epstein (London, 1935), 198–99, reprinted in his *Studia Semitica* (Cambridge, 1971), I:280. Strauss, *Philosophy and Law*, 53, contends that "according to the teaching of the Islamic Aristotelians, which was transplanted by Maimonides in particular into Judaism, the prophet as philosopher and lawgiver is one . . . he is thus the founder of the ideal state. The classic model of the ideal state is the Platonic state. In fact, and even explicitly and programmatically, the Islamic Aristotelians understand the ideal state and the prophet according to the Platonic injunction. They understand the prophet as the founder of the Platonic state, as a Platonic philosopher king." See also, L. Strauss, "Quelques remarques," 2; and "On Abravanel," 105–6; L. V. Berman, "The Political Interpretation," 60: "The prophet [of Maimonides] is, therefore, equivalent to the Philosopher, imam, king and legislator of Al-Farabi"; S. S. Schwarzschild, "Moral Radicalism," 81: "The Platonic 'philosopher king' has been transmuted into the 'saint king.'" I. Rotter, "The Islamic Sources of Maimonides' Political Philosophy, *Gesher* 7 (1979):193–94; also R. Jospe, *What Is Jewish Philosophy?* (Tel Aviv, 1988), 13: "Al-Farabi's ingenious identification of the prophetic legislator of revealed religion with the Platonic philosopher king was to have a profound impact on Jewish political philosophy, most notably Rambam's *Moreh Nevukhim*." See also Jospe's *Torah and Sophia, The Life and Thought of Shem Tov Ibn Falaquera* (Cincinnati, 1988), 111–15. For a more qualified view, see Kraemer, "Maimonides' Messianic Posture," 129–30 and n. 71: "The correspondence . . . is never made explicit by Maimonides . . . but the various functions are severally assigned to him [Moses]." In contrast to Rosenthal, Strauss, and Berman, the position taken by Pines, Davidson, Galston, and Kreisel is closer to mine. Pines articulates it unequivocally in "Introduction to Guide," lxxxvi (also lxxxvi, n. 50): "He [Al-Farabi] declared that it was the philosopher's duty to engage in politics, that, in fact, the four terms philosopher, king, legislator and imam were synonyms. This is an extreme to which no counterpart can be found in the *Guide*, no political role being explicitly assigned in this work to the philosophers." See also M. Galston, "Philosopher King versus Prophet"; H. Davidson, "Maimonides' *Shemonah Peraqim* and Al-Farabi's *Fusul Al-Madani*," *PAAJR* 31 (1963):49: "Maimonides excludes the possibility of a 'philosopher-king,' except in so far as a prophet like Moses may have fulfilled that description"; H. Kreisel, *"Hakham ve-Navii,"* 153.

68. *Guide* III:54, Pines, 634: "A man's being a great king also belongs to this species of perfection. Between this perfection and the individual himself there is no

union whatever; there is only a certain relation, and most of the pleasure taken in the relation is purely imaginary. I refer to one's saying: This is my house, this is my slave, this money is mine, these are my soldiers. For if he considers his own individual self, he will find that all this is outside the self." Cf. *Guide* II:37, 376. See also Falaquera, *Sefer ha-Ma'alot*, 56.

69. *Guide* II. 40, Pines, Ibid., 382.

70. See ch. 4, n. 35, and ch. 7, n. 14, below.

71. Cohen, "The Three Crowns"; *Hilkhot Talmud Torah* 3:1.

72. *Hilkhot Melakhim*, 5:10. See the full discussion in Blidstein, *Ekronot Medini'im*.

73. On the special status of Moses, see *Guide* II:35; *Hilkhot Yesodei ha-Torah*, 7, 6. Also see J. Levinger, "Nevu'at Mosheh Rabenu," in his *Ha-Rambam ke-Filosof u-Posek* (Jerusalem 1989), 28–29. On his attribution of kingship to Moses in his halakhic writings, see *Hilkhot Beit ha-Behirah*, 6:11; discussion in Blidstein, 40, n. 97; S. W. Baron, "The Historical Outlook of Maimonides," *PAAJR* 6 (1935):121, 357, n. 43; Kraemer, "Messianic Posture," 130, n. 71.

74. Rosenthal, for some reason, asserts that there, too, we can find thirteen. See ch. 6, n. 32, below.

75. J. L. Kraemer, "Al-Farabi's 'Opinions of the Virtuous City' and Maimonides' Foundation of the Law," in *Studia Orientalia*, eds. J. Blau et al. (Jerusalem, 1979), 109, and n. 5

76. See n. 67, above.

77. See these distinctions in R. Jospe, "Shelilat ma'alot ha-middot ke-tahlit ha-adam," *Jerusalem Studies in Jewish Thought* 5 (1986):96–97. English version: "Rejecting Moral Virtues as the Ultimate End," in *Studies in Islamic and Judaic Traditions*, eds., W. Brinner et al. (Denver, 1986), 185–204.

78. See n. 77, above.

79. See ch. 5, below.

80. *Falaquera's Epistle of the Debate*, ed. S. Harvey (Cambridge, MA, 1987), 78; English text, 50; and S. Regev "Le-ba'ayat limud ha-filosofia be-hagut ha-me'ah ha-15," *Da'at* 16 (1986):67.

81. For a discussion of this matter, including additional examples from Falaquera's writings and a comparison with Ibn Bajja's text, see Jospe, "Rejecting Moral Virtues," 101–2; cf. Hayoun, ed., *The Governance of the Solitary*, 38.

82. Jospe, "Rejecting Moral Virtues," 102–4.

83. Jospe, Ibid., 104–8. Also see Jospe's *Torah and Sophia*, III:vii.

84. *Moreh ha-Moreh*, in *Sheloshah Kadmonei Mefarshei ha-Moreh* (Jerusalem, 1961), 138.

85. Falaquera's commentary, 136. Also see Jospe, "Rejecting Moral Virtues," 105; Maimonides, Commentary on *Avot*, 1:6. Significantly, each thinker is concerned with

a different problem of interpretation. Maimonides is occupied with why the term "acquire" *(keneh)* is used, and not "make a friend" *(aseh lekha haver)*. By contrast, Falaquera is exercised by the singular "a friend." In other words, Falaquera used the dicta of the sages to advance the theory of the governance of the solitary.

86. Falaquera, *Moreh ha-Moreh*, 136; Jospe, *Torah and Sophia*, 104.

87. Falaquera, Ibid., 136–37; Jospe, Ibid., 136; and see n. 121 below.

88. Jospe, "Rejection of Moral Virtues." Cf. Moses Narboni's translation of and commentary to *The Governance of the Solitary*, n. 121, below; and Y. Shifman, "Ibn Bajja ke-makor le-Perush shel rabbi Shem Tov Falaquera le-'Moreh Nevukim' III:51, 54," *Tarbiz*, 60 (1991):224–35.

89. Falaquera, *Moreh ha-Moreh*, 139. Falaquera frequently cites Ibn Bajja directly in *Moreh ha-Moreh*, especially in the commentary to *Guide* III:51, 54. In several places "Abu Nasr" (i.e., Al-Farabi) is quoted in the text where the reference should be "Abu Bakr" (i.e., Ibn Bajja). This seems to be a copyist's error. By contrast, Al-Farabi is mentioned quite a few times in other chapters of the commentary. See also Berman, *Ha-Rambam ve-Ibn Bajjah*, 5, n. 4, 32–33; Shifman, "Ibn Bajja he-makor."

90. H. Kasher, "Hitmakdut be-yahid o be-yahad, iyyun mashveh bein R. Yehuda ha-Levi u-bein ha-Rambam," *Iyyun* 37 (1988):238–46. On the differences between Ibn Rushd and Maimonides, see Pines, "Introduction," cviii–cxxiii. On the shift of philosophy to the defensive, see Regev, "Le-ba'ayat," with additional bibliography.

91. *Guide* II:40, Pines, ed., vol. III:27.

92. *Malmad ha-Talmidim* (Lyck, 1866), 121a. Also see my "Ha-diyyun ha-medini," 95–96.

93. *Malmad ha-Talmidim*, 122a–b; "Ha-diyyun ha-medini," 97–98.

94. *Malmad ha-Talmidim*, 143b. On the class theory in Anatoli, see ch. 4, below.

95. *Malmad ha-Talmidim*, 143a; "Ha-diyyun ha-medini," 97.

96. Isaak Polkar, *Ezer ha-Dat*, ed. Y. Levinger (Tel Aviv, 1984), 44. Cf. Ibn Bajja's position in *The Governance of the Solitary*, Hayoun ed., 41; and see ch. 6, below.

97. *Heshek Shelomoh*, ms. London 227, fol. 78, and ed. Halberstadt (1862):21a; A. Lesley, *The Song of Solomon's Ascents by Yohanan Alemanno; Love and Human Perfection According to a Jewish Colleague of Giovanni Pico della Mirandola* (Ph.D. diss., Berkeley, 1976), 2:480–81; compare his contrasting expressions, 323, and 393. Alemanno quotes directly from Moses Narboni's Hebrew translation of *The Governance of the Solitary* in his discourse on the material qualities of the Florentines. When he justifies concern with material possessions and tries to prove that this does not contradict a desire for intellectual perfection, he enlists the aid of Ibn Bajja, *Hai-ha-Olamim*, ms. Mantua, 21, fols. 107–8. See A. Melamed, "The Hebrew 'Laudatio' of Yohanan Alemanno, in Praise of Lorenzo il Magnifico and the Florentine Constitution," in *Jews in Italy. Studies Dedicated to the Memory of U. Cassuto*, ed. H. Beinart (Jerusalem, 1988), 23–27.

98. *Hai ha-Olamim*, fols. 344–45; see b. Shabbat, 33a–34b; E. Urbach, *The Sages* (Jerusalem 1975), 459. This reference to bar Yohai shows evidence not only of Ibn

Bajja's influence, but also of Alemanno's acceptance of the still more extreme position of Ibn Tufayl, author of *Hayy ibn Yaqzan* (see n. 117, below). Shem Tov before him identified bar Yohai with the figure of the ideal recluse of the Ibn Tufayl type (see n. 112, below). Alemanno's position is more critical. See, e.g., *Hai ha-Olamim*, fol. 109, and *"Shir ha-Ma'alot li-Shelomo,"* Lesley, *Song of Solomon's Ascents* II:528, 541 n. 216, 585, n. 260. We know that Alemanno possessed a copy of the ms. of the Hebrew translation of *Hayy Ibn Yaqzan* and that, at some stage, owing to penury, he pawned this document. See M. D. Cassuto, *Ha-Yehudim be-Firenzi be-Tekufat ha-Renesans*, tr. M. Artom (Jerusalem, 1967), 37, n. 127; 244, n. 147; 329–30. We also know from Alemanno's own account that not only was he aware of Ibn Tufayl's version in Narboni's commentary (see n. 97, above), but he also knew about Ibn Sina's version in Hebrew translation. The latter is mentioned in *Sha'ar ha-Heshek*. See Kaufmann's comments in the introduction to his edition (n. 117, below). Kaufmann himself relies on M. Steinschneider, *Al-Farabi* (St. Petersburg, 1896), 115, n. 49.

99. On Alemanno's portrayal of Solomon as the prototype of the philosopher king, see ch. 7, below. On the link with the theory of Platonic love, see my doctoral dissertation, "Ha-Mahshavah ha-Medinit," 147–48.

100. A. Ravitzky, "R. Shmuel Ibn Tibbon ve-sodo shel Moreh Nevukim," *Da'at* 10–11 (1983):45–46, n. 138; English version *AJS Review* 6 (1981):87–123; Kasher, "Hitmakdut," 246. See, too, *Ma'amar Yikkavu ha-Mayim* (Pressburg, 1837), 170. For another example, see M. Kellner, "Maimonides and Samuel ibn Tibbon on Jermiah 9:22–23 and Human Perfection," ed. M. Beer, *Studies in Halakhah and Jewish Thought Presented to M.E. Rackman* (Ramat Gan, 1994), 49–57.

101. *Moreh Nevukim*, with the commentaries of Efodi, Shem Tov, Crescas, and Abravanel (Jerusalem, 1960), I:15:33b.

102. Joseph Ibn Caspi, *Maskiyyot Kesef*, in *Sheloshah Kadmonei Mefarshei ha-Moreh* (Jerusalem, 1961), 31–2. Also Efodi and Abravanel's interpretations.

103. Joseph Ibn Caspi, *Mishneh Kesef. Ketavim* I (Pressburg, 1903), 60. On Caspi's discussion of the class theory, see ch. 4, n. 24, below. Elsewhere Caspi notes that the sole reason for the political intervention of the prophets was entirely selfish: the desire to prevent harm to themselves through the bad effects of a corrupt society. Otherwise, it would make no sense that people like them would be willing to suffer for the common good. See *Asarah Keley Kesef* (Pressburg, 1903), 38; and Kasher, "Hitmakdut," 246. Caspi took pains to prepare a summary of the Hebrew translation of Ibn Rushd's *Commentary to Plato's Republic*; see ch. 5, n. 39, below.

104. See n. 31, above.

105. See ch. 4 below, and n. 15 there.

106. See ch. 4 below, and nn. 22, 23, 25, 26.

107. See ch. 4, below, and nn. 32–34, 36.

108. See ch. 4, below, n. 51.

109. *The Guide* with commentaries III:51:64.

110. *The Guide* with commentaries III:54:71. Compare, however, the same Shem-tov's wedding sermon, which presents a debate between solitary and communal exis-tence and concludes, in an obviously Maimonidean fashion, that human perfection can be achieved only in society. Shemtov allows for solitary existence only in cases in which human society is completely corrupt. Among his arguments for solitary existence Shemtov presents the theory of the prophet-recluse as achieving ultimate human per-fection; see n. 112, below. Ultimately, however, his conclusion is pro-political. He does not deal with the theory of the philosopher-king or the public prophet. He relates to the human need for social existence in general, not to the political duties of the philosopher. This can be explained by the context, which is a wedding sermon and therefore relates to man's need for a social framework in general. See "Wedding Ser-mon," *Derashot al ha-Torah* (Venice, 1507; reprinted Jerusalem, 1974), n.p. I thank Prof. M. Saperstein for drawing my attention to this source.

111. Joseph ibn Shem Tov, *Kevod Elohim* (Ferarra, 1556). I also used H. Tirosh-Rothschild's, "Human Felicity, A Fifteenth-century Jewish Perspective," lecture deliv-ered at the Boston Colloquium in Medieval Philosophy (December 14, 1989). I am indebted to the author for sending me a copy of her lecture, which was of great assis-tance. The author accurately characterizes Shemtov's commentary to the *Ethics* as "a creative misreading."

112. *Kevod Elohim*, 12b. See also 19a.

113. *Kevod Elohim*, 12b. On the distinction between "the political man" and "the solitary man," see also 3a.

114. *Kevod Elohim* 15a; and see the Ibn Rushd source in Moses Narboni's Hebrew translation, in K. P. Bland (ed. and trans.), *The Epistle of the Possibility of Con-junction with the Active Intellect by Ibn Rushd with the Commentary of Moses Narboni* (New York, 1982); English section 7, 103, 108–10; Hebrew section 146, 149. By con-trast, in another composition, *Ma'aznei ha-Iyyun*, Shemtov, like Falaquera, stresses the duty of the philosopher to lead the masses; see Regev, "Le-Ba'ayat," 67.

115. Here I follow Tirosh-Rothschild, "Human Felicity."

116. E. I. J. Rosenthal, *Political Thought in Medieval Islam* (Cambridge, 1968), 168; R. Lerner and M. Mahdi, *Medieval Political Philosophy: A Sourcebook* (New York, 1967), 16. On Maimonides' use of such a theory, see n. 40, above.

117. Rosenthal, *Political Thought*, 157, 160, 168, 182, 272, 286, 289, 291; Lerner and Mahdi, *Medieval Political Philosophy*, 16. Marmura, "The Philosopher," 320; "*Iggeret Hay Mekiz* le-Ibn Sina," *Kovetz Al Yad*, ed. D. Kaufmann (Berlin, 1886), 1–29, 122–23, 134–62; *Hay Ben Yaqzan*, tr. by Abraham Ibn Ezra, ed. I. Levine (Tel Aviv, 1983); Ibn Bajja's *Governance of the Solitary, Kovetz al Yad*, ed. D. Herzog 6 (1986):3–33; E. I. J. Rosenthal, "Political Ideas in Moshe Narboni's Commentary on Ibn Tufail's *Hayy B. Yaqzan*," *Hommage a G. Vajda*, eds. G. Nahon and Ch. Touati (Louvain, 1980), 227–234; M. R. Hayoun, "Moses of Narboni and ibn Bajja"; and the English translation, *Ibn Tufayl's Hayy Ibn Yaqzan*, tr., introduction, and notes L. E. Goodman (1972; reprint, Los Angeles, 1984). See also Moses of Reiti's *Mikdash Me'at*, ed. J. Goldenthal (Vienna, 1851), 22b.

118. Rosenthal, "Political Ideas."

119. Hayoun, "Moses of Narboni," 34–35, and the summary of the translation, 44.

120. Rosenthal, "Political Ideas," 231.

121. Rosenthal, Ibid; *Political Thought in Medieval Islam*, 128; Lerner and Mahdi, *Medieval Political Philosophy*, 128; Marmura, "Philosopher and Society," 315–17; and n. 33, above; Jospe, *Torah and Sophia*, 136; Hayoun, "Moses of Narboni," 35; "Narboni and Ibn Bajja: *Iggeret ha-Petirah*," *Da'at*, 25 (1990):93–125. On the same idea in Augustine, where these people are called *"peregnini"* or *"viatores,"* see H. A. Deane, *The Political and Social Ideas of St. Augustine* (New York, 1966), 29–30; A. Funkenstein, "A Schedule for the End of the World," *Vision of Apocalypse, End or Rebirth*, eds. S. Friedlander et al. (New York, 1985), 55.

122. Psalms, 119; 18. Compare to Shemtov Ibn Joseph ibn Shemtov's wedding sermon (n. 110 above).

123. Hayoun, "Moses of Narboni," 43–44.

124. *The Guide* with commentaries; also Rosenthal, "Political Ideas."

125. Joseph Ibn Shemtov, sermon on the portion *Korah*, ms. Montefiori 61, fol. 102a–109b. See parts of the Hebrew text in the appendix. I would like to thank Dr. Shaul Regev, who kindly sent me a copy of the as yet unpublished text. For a discussion of this text see E. Gutwirth, "El Gobernador Judio Ideal: Acerna de un sermon Inedito de Yosef Ibn Shem Tob, in *"Congreso Internacional Encuentro Tres Culturas III* (Toledo, 1988), 67–75. This is a good description of the text and its background. I, however, would de-emphasize its connection to the Platonic tradition, even though Shemtov knew it well. The discussion of the ideal ruler's virtues, as indicated, belongs more to the traditional Jewish view, as found in other fifteenth-century thinkers in Spain, such as Albo and Shalom; see chaps. 5, 6, below. Shemtov's discussion was probably also influenced by his experience as an active courtier in the Castillian court and by the Christian tradition of the *Speculum Principium*. For specific references to Shemtov's discussion, see ch. 4, n. 17, and ch. 6, nn. 14, 20, below. There is no need to include a detailed discussion of Shemtov's version, since it is largely redundant and adds no new insights. Moreover, Gutwirth provides a good basic discussion of the text. For another late medieval example of the adoption of the theory of the "public prophet," see the Writings of Shemtov Ibn Shaprut, in N. E. Frimer and D. Schwartz, *Hagut be-Zel ha-Aimah* (Jerusalem, 1992), 95, 151, 153, 181.

CHAPTER 4. THE CLASS SYSTEM

1. *The Republic* II, and see ch. 2, above.

2. In *Fusul al-Madani* Al-Farabi differentiates five classes. See D. M. Dunlop, ed. and tr., *Aphorisms of the Statesman* (Cambridge, 1961), 50–51, 53–54. This class structure reflects Platonic, Hellenistic and various eastern influences. See also Krae-

mer, "The *Jihad* of the Falasifa," 297–98, nn. 15–18. The Hebrew translation of Ibn Rushd's commentary to *The Republic* contains a reference to three classes, corresponding to the Platonic structure; see E. I. J. Rosenthal ed., I–II. The Hebrew translations of these texts did not exist before the fourteenth century; but as Anatoli, Falaquera, and others used the class theory in the thirteenth century, it is clear that they were acquainted with these sources, directly or indirectly, from the Arabic texts themselves. Compare Aristotle's discussion, *Politics* VII:8.

3. E. Barker, *The Political Thought of Plato and Aristotle*, 526; Kraemer, "The *Jihad* of the Falasifa"; R. Mohl, *The Three Estates in Medieval and Renaissance Literature* (New York, 1933), 284–87.

4. *Introduction to Seder Zeraim*, 127–31.

5. See ch. 1, above.

6. E. I. J. Rosenthal ed., 28.

7. On commentaries in the military context, see my "Al yithalal."

8. See n. 7, above.

9. *Malmad ha-Talmidim*, 143–46. For Anatoli's political philosophy in general, with additional bibliography, see A. Melamed, "Ha-diyyun ha-medini be-'*Malmad ha-Talmidim*.'" For a discussion on this subject, see 104.

10. '*Malmad ha-Talmidim*,' 143b:

11. "Ha-diyyun ha-medini," 101–3; Proverbs 6:6.

12. '*Malmad ha-Talmidim*,' 143b.

13. '*Malmad ha-Talmidim*,' 143b.

14. '*Malmad ha-Talmidim*,' 143b.

15. "Ha-diyyun ha-medini," 102, 105.

16. '*Malmad ha-Talmidim*,' 143b.

17. '*Malmad ha-Talmidim*,' 144b. Cf. Plato, *The Republic* I:332, and for additional parallelisms, "Ha-diyyun ha-medini," 108, n. 55.

18. See the detailed discussion in "Ha-diyyun ha-medini," 108–9.

19. '*Malmad ha-Talmidim*,' 143b. For additional versions, see *Malmad*, 21b–22a, 113a–b, 152a.

20. For the history of these commentaries, see A. Melamed, "Motar ha-adam ba-mahashavah ha-yehudit be-Sefarad u-be-Italia be-yemei ha-beinayim ha-me'unarim u-ba-renesans," *Italia* 3 (1982):39–88.

21. Melamed, "Ha-diyyun ha-medini."

22. Falaquera, *Sefer ha-Ma'alot*, 43–44. By contrast, see *Sefer ha-Ma'alot*, 46. Here Falaquera refers to the original Platonic classification and, in fact, attributes it directly to Plato: ruler-philosophers, warriors, and craftsmen. Characteristically, when he interprets the story of the three sons of Adam, Falaquera distinguishes laborers, leaders, and

sages; just a few pages later, however, he presents the original Platonic classification with only a brief and incidental reference to the Platonic text. See also *Iggeret ha-Halom*, Malter, ed., *Ketavim* I:484. On Falaquera's discourse on the three parts of the soul and the parallel with the three kinds of men, see Jospe, *Torah and Sophia*, 125–27, 209–10. This discussion is useful, but it contains no reference to the link with the Platonic class system as reflected here.

23. Immanuel of Rome, *Commentary on Exodus*, Ms. Parma N. 3220 (404) fol. 58b. My article "Motar ha-adam," 50–51, 58, argues that Yehuda Romano and Immanuel of Rome are the first examples of this. Further research, however, shows that the thirteenth-century Anatoli and Falaquera preceded them. Furthermore, a comparison of the texts makes it clear that Immanuel actually copied Falaquera's version almost verbatim, as it appears in *Sefer ha-Ma'alot; cf. n. 22*, above. For yet another application by Immanuel of Plato's class system and the theory of the philosopher-king, see his commentary on *Proverbs* 28:2, *Book of Proverbs with the Commentary of Immanuel of Rome* (Naples, ca.1487, photo-reproduced, Jerusalem, 1981), introduction by D. Goldstein, 176.

24. Yosef Ibn Caspi, *Mishneh Kesef,* 58–60.

25. In *Sefer ha-Ikkarim* we find three references to the class theory. The first appears in a discussion of the political nature of man: I:6, Husik, I:75. Here the philosopher is presented not exactly as a king but as initial lawgiver. On the second occasion, the theory is mentioned as an exemplification of the argument that divine law is superior to human law, even the perfected law in the form of the Platonic republic. Albo refers here to Aristotle's criticism of the Platonic republic in the second book of *Politics*, I:8, Husik, I:82. See also ch. 2, n. 14. For Albo's source, see E. I. J. Rosenthal, ed., 40. The complete discussion of the subject refers, as was usual, to the commentary on the story of the sons of Adam, presented in the context of a consideration of the purpose of human existence: III:13, Husik, III:134–35. In this version, as was usual, the philosophers are quite detached from a life of action. On Albo's discussion, see my "Motar ha-adam," 54–58.

26. Abraham Bibago, *Derech Emunah* (Constantinople, 1521), 57b–c. Like Narboni, Crescas, Efodi, and Shemtov in their their commentaries to *Guide* II:30, Bibago attributes the discussion to Maimonides. In *Guide* II:30, though, Maimonides mentions the three sons of Adam only briefly and in a different context. See my "Motar ha-adam," 52–55. In contrast to the Platonic class system, which was largely static, Bibago describes a dynamic system, in which man passes from class to class in the stages of his development toward intellectual perfection. Later, Bibago applies this scheme to the three sons of Adam, as was common. See, too, the discussion in my aforementioned article, 59–61. A further variation on the subject is to be found in Alemanno's *Shir ha-Ma'alot li-Shelomo*, which describes the elevation of the soul above material life and the perfection of the intellect as an ascent from one class to the next. Class and functional differences are not entirely clear here. The philosopher class is not included in this version.(Lesley, ed., II:565).

27. This is first expressed in his use of the traditional commentary on the story of the three sons of Adam (n. 22, above). On his tendency toward the governance of the solitary, see ch. 3, above.

28. See ch. 3, n. 51, above.

29. *Commentary on Genesis* (Venice, 1575), 132. Indeed, in his commentary to the story of Noah and his sons, Abravanel returns to this subject: *Commentary on Genesis*, 10, 170; my article, "Motar ha-adam," 61–67. An additional version of this commentary on the nature of the three sons of Adam is found in Abravanel's later response to Shaul ha-Cohen Ashkenazi; see Abravanel *Opera Minora* (London, 1971), 15a.

30. *Commentary on Genesis*, 10, 171. See also Joseph ben Shemtov, *Kevod Elohim*, 15b. Shemtov's and Abravanel's attitude on this matter is based generally on Ibn Rushd's commentary, but is not copied directly from the Hebrew translation. Cf. Rosenthal, ed., Hebrew version I:Xxiii, 13; II.V:25.

31. *Pirkei Avot with Maimonides' commentary and Abravanel's commentary, Nahalat Avot* (New York, 1953), 142. Later in the same commentary, Abravanel applies this to the biblical text. Abravanel inconsistently included the magistrates *(shoterim)* in the class of wise men, probably a result of the biblical association, in which *shofetim*, and *shoterim* appear togther (Deut. 16:18). It should be noted that here Abravanel names the laborer class *am* (people). In the *Commentary on Genesis* 4, however, he gives this class the more usual name in medieval Hebrew literature, *am ha-aretz* (people of the land). (*Commentary on Genesis*, 132). We find the same in *Commentary on Ezekiel*, ch. 27 (see n. 33, below). Characteristically, when he presents the traditional version, Abravanel uses the traditional term *am ha-aretz* (cf. Maimonides, *Introduction to Seder Zeraim*, 127–31, and *Commentary on Avot*, II:6; V:6. Also see my "Ha-rambam al tiv'o ha-medini."). By contrast, when he presents the new version of the Platonic class theory, which by then conceivably incorporated the influence of Renaissance thought, Abravanel uses the term *am*, which is a Hebrew translation of the Italian *popolo* (or Latin *populus*) which had the identical sense. See D. Wilcox, *The Development of Florentine Humanist Historiography in the Fifteenth Century* (Cambridge, MA, 1969), appendix C, "Uses of the Word Populus": 211–12, and J. G. A. Pocock, *The Machiavellian Moment* (Princeton, 1975), which refers to this term in many places (index, 592). Pocock's definition of *popolo* as "the non-elite membership of the politically enfranchised classes" (105) is similar to what we find here in Abravanel. The same use of the term is made by Shlomo ibn Verga; see I. Baer, "He'arot hadashot le-sefer *Shevet Yehudah*," *Tarbiz*, 6 (1935):165, n. 12, who cites Francesco Guicciardini's use of this word, although it was already current before that. See also Luzzatto, *Discorso* 74: plebe, popolo minuto; and my "Al yithalal," 64–65, n. 75. In *Commentary on Jeremiah* 9, Abravanel uses the term *am* in the general sense of the entire community, not as its lowest class; see above and n. 33.

32. Abravanel, *Nahalat Avot*, 213.

33. *Commentary on the Later Prophets* (Jerusalem, 1957), 332.

34. *Commentary to the Torah* (Jerusalem, 1979), 24. Abravanel presents this version as an allegorical interpretation of the priestly blessing, and goes on to apply the class theory to the biblical text. Several other versions of the class theory appear in Abravanel, but they are mixed: they include elements from both the traditional and the new versions, and refer to more than three classes. In his allegorical commentary to the structure of the tabernacle and its vessels, *Commentary on the Torah*, Exodus 25:251–52,

Abravanel separates the warriors from the rulers, who in the tripartite versions always appear together. Another example is found in *Commentary on Ezekiel* 27, in *Commentary on the Later Prophets*, 541. Here Abravanel gives an allegorical interpretation, in the spirit of the class theory, to the prophet's description of the ship of the city of Tyre, which is reminiscent of Plato's famous parable of the sea captain (*The Republic* VI:488). Here, again, Abravanel distinguishes between rulers and philosophers. He also calls the laborers "*am ha-aretz*." See the discussion on this in n. 31, above. A further example is found in the allegorical interpretation that Abravanel gives to Isaiah 3:1–3 in *Nahalat Avot*, 14. Abravanel again includes warriors and rulers in the same group. He expressly links these matters to the allegorical class interpretation that he gave to the statement by Ben Zoma; see above and n. 32. Cf. Abravanel's commentary to Isaiah, ch. 3; *Commentary on the Later Prophets*, 33.

35. See E. I. J. Rosenthal, ed., *Averroe's Commentary on Plato's Republic*, 61, and see ch. 1, n. 4.

36. See n. 34, above. Cf. Caspi (n. 24, above) and later Azulay (n. 51, below).

37. B. Netanyahu, *Don Isaac Abravanel* (Philadelphia, 1972) [see "Renaissance" and "Humanism" in index]. See A. Melamed, "The Myth of Venice in Italian Renaissance Jewish Philosophy," *Italia Judaica* I (Rome, 1983), 301–13; also "Al-Yithalal," 66–70.

38. For an extensive discussion of these topics, with additional bibliography, see A. Melamed, "The Hebrew 'Laudatio' of Yohanan Alemanno." Del Medigo's Latin translation has been published in Averroe, *Parafrasi della "Repubblica" Nella Traduzione Latino di Elia del Medigo*. A Cura di A. Coviello e P. E. fornaciari (Florence, 1992). Also see my essay, "Eliyahu del Medigo ve-ha-masoret ha-polit ha-Aplatonit ba-renasans," *Italia* (1995):57–76.

39. Abravanel, *Nahalat Avot*, 313. "Al yithalal," 62.

40. For the various meanings of the term *gevurah* in medieval Jewish thought, see "Al-Yithalal," 42–43 and the notes there. On Falaquera's discourse, see ibid., 53–54.

41. H. Baron, "Cicero and the Roman Civil Spirit in the Middle Ages and the Renaissance," *BJRL* 22 (1938):72–97; Idem, *The Crisis of the Early Italian Renaissance* (Princeton, 1966); E. H. Kantorowicz, "'Pro Patria Mori,'" in *Medieval Political Thought," American Historical Review* 56 (1951):472–92; Pocock, *The Machiavellian Moment*, 58–60, and elsewhere (Index, p. 574); "Al yithalal," 66–7.

42. See the discussion in ch. 8, below.

43. See the full discussion on this in "Al yithalal," 67–68.

44. On the question of transliteration, see "Al Yithalal," 64, n. 75; 68–69, n. 86.

45. See n. 34, above.

46. See n. 31, above.

47. For a full discussion of this subject, with comprehensive bibliography, see my "Retorica u-filosofia be-Sefer Nofet Zufim le-R' Yehuda Messer Leon," *Italia* 1 (1978):7–37. For a consideration of humanist philosophy, see, e.g., J. E. Seigel, *Rhetoric*

and Philosophy in Renaissance Humanism (Princeton, 1968). For Messer Leon's rhetorical ideal, see Isaac Rabinowitz, ed. and tr., *The Book of the Honeycomb's Flow: Sefer Nophet Suphim* (Ithaca, 1983).

48. *Commentary to Jeremiah*, 332–33. parallel version in the commentary on Ben Zoma, *Nahalat Avot*, 3.

49. Cf. *Guide* II:39; Luzzatto, *Discorso* 13.

50. On the dating of Abravanel's various commentaries, see Netanyahu: on *Nahalat Avot*, 286, n. 52; on *Commentary on Jeremiah*, 289, n. 15; on *Commentary on Genesis*, 286, 289, n. 16; on *Commentary on Exodus*, 86, 289–90, n. 16; on *Commentary on Numbers*, 86; on the response to R. Shaul ha-Cohen Ashkenazi, 86–87.

51. For another example, see the encyclopaedia *Zel ha-Olam*, attributed to the Polish-born, Italian-educated, sixteenth-century Jewish Kabbalist and astronomer Mattathias Delacrut. *Zel ha-Olam* is a Hebrew paraphrase of a popular medieval French encyclopaedia. It uses a typical Platonic class division adapted to Jewish sources and historical examples. See *Zel ha-Olam* (1887, reprint, Jerusalem, 1968), 3. See also another sixteenth-century Hebrew encyclopaedia, *Kelal Kazar*, written by Judah Ibn Bulat, a Jewish emigré from Spain who settled in Turkey after the expulsion. The text was first published in Constantinople in 1532. In a section on political philosophy, Bulat follows the traditional pattern when presenting a detailed discussion of the class theory. He distinguishes among four classes. See *Kelal Kazar* (Jerusalem, 1936), 34. For the entire discussion, see 34–36. The last example I found for the use of the class theory is in the commentary by the seventeenth-century Abraham Azulai to *Avot* (Jerusalem, 1987), 26–27. Azulai presents the subject in connection with his interpretation of Shemaiah's terminology "love work," etc. (Avot I, 10). Azulai, reaching the same reclusive conclusion found in Caspi and Abravanel (nn. 24, 34, 36, above), removed the philosophers from the class structure entirely, thereby completely precluding the identification of king with philosopher. Clearly, Azulai bases himself here on the traditional class division version, which did not include the guardian class. Removal of the philosophers from the class division, and the need to adapt the topic to the mishnaic text, gave rise to a situation in which no qualitative difference exists between the second and third classes: the second includes the rulers, the third those close to them. See end of ch. 3, above.

CHAPTER 5. TRANSMISSION

1. S. O. Heller-Wilensky, "Isaac Ibn Latif, Philosopher or Kabbalist," in *Jewish Medieval and Renaissance Studies*, ed. A. Altmann (Cambridge, MA, 1967), 185–223; "Le-heker ha-mekorot shel Isaac ibn Latif," *Proceedings of the Fourth World Congress of Jewish Studies* (Jerusalem, 1965), 2:317–25; "Le-she'elot mehabro shel sefer *Sha'ar ha-Shamayim* ha-meyuhas le Abraham ibn Ezra," *Tarbiz 32* (1963):277–95, and see 293 for the date of the writing of *Sha'ar ha-Shamayim*.

2. Usually Ibn Latif uses the general expression: "What the Ishmaelite philosopher said," as in *Sha'ar ha-Shamayim*, ms. Vatican, 335.1, and No. 375 in the National

and University Library, Jerusalem, I:27, fol. 37a; or a more general form, "This philosopher" or "What this philosopher said" (ch. 28, fol. 37b). He mentions Al-Farabi by name in one place only, when discussing the virtues of the philosopher-king: "As the Ishmaelite philosopher Abu-Naser (i.e. Al-Farabi) said." (ch. 20, fol. 37b).

3. *Sha'ar ha-Shamayim*, ch. 28, fol. 37b. Also ch. 27, fol. 37a. Still, Ibn Latif subjects Al-Farabi to censorship, not for theoretical, but for political and educational reasons alone.

4. *Sha'ar ha-Shamayim*, ch. 28, fol. 37b.

5. Ms. Vatican, ch. 20, fol. 32a. Cf. Walzer, ed., *Al-Madina al-Fadilah*, ch. 15, 239–47.

6. *Sha'ar ha-Shamayim*, ch. 28, fol. 32a.

7. Ibid. Cf. Walzer, ed., 247.

8. See n. 24, below.

9. Lambton, "Al-Farabi," 321; Al-Farabi, *Fusul al-Madani*, Dunlop, I:54:50; Wilensky, "Ibn Latif," 197–98, n. 82. This composition was translated into Hebrew anonymously. Two mss. of this translation are extant: see Dunlop, *Aphorisms* 29:197–208. Ms. A (Dunlop, 29) contains the Hebrew translation of the six virtues noted by Al-Farabi in fol. 111b, ch. 52. The Hebrew translation is highly literal. In some places, the anonymous translator has added notes applying the statements to various Hebrew sources (e.g., Dunlop, 197), but not here. The six virtues appear just as presented by Al-Farabi. In contrast to the lists of the virtues present in other writings, which are of a Platonic philosophical nature, the list here lacks philosophical virtues entirely. Chiefly it contains the virtues of rulership, judgment, and warfare suitable for the Islamic ruler. Both Dunlop and E. I. J. Rosenthal ascribe this approach to the Muslim target audience of the composition. See Rosenthal, *Political Thought in Medieval Islam*, 132–34. On Ibn Rushd's use of this text, see Rosenthal, 202–3, and nn. 45–47, below. I was recently informed by Dr. J. Macy that he is preparing a critical edition of the Hebrew text. Dr. Macy kindly gave me the text of ch. 54 of the Hebrew version; see Appendix.

10. The ninth virtue is absent from Ms. Vatican. The text passes directly from the eighth virtue to the tenth. Presumably the copyist simply forgot to copy the ninth, which is understandable when one considers its brevity. I copied out the ninth virtue from Ms. London, 915, n. 5951, in the National and University Library, Jerusalem, fol. 44.

11. Ms. Vatican, fols. 32a–33a; see Hebrew text in the Appendix, below. Cf. Walzer, ed., *Al-Madina al-Fadilah*, 247–49.

12. Walzer, *Al-Madina al-Fadilah*, ch. 15, 247; "Aspects," 49. Rotter, 191–203; Mahdi, "Al-farabi's Enumeration of the Sciences," 132–33; Kraemer, "Maimonides' Messianic Posture," 130–36; "Falasifa," 293, n. 9; 303; E. I. J. Rosenthal, *Political Thought in Medieval Islam*, 173–78. Cf. Maimonides' position on the obligatory war as a duty of the king: *Hilkhot Melakhim* 5. For Falaquera's consideration of the question, see n. 33 below; for Polkar's, ch. 6, n. 5, below.

13. On the development of the meanings of *gevurah*, see my "Al yithalal"; also n. 34, below.

14. Walzer, ed., *Al-Madina al-Fadilah*, 249, 253.

15. Ms. Vatican, ch. 20, fol. 33a.

16. Ms. Vatican, ch. 20, fol. 33a.

17. See *Nedarim* 38a; *Shabbat* 92a.

18. Ms. Vatican, 28, fol. 37b. Cf. Al-Farabi, Walzer, ed., *Al-Madina al-Fadilah*.

19. *Reshit Hokmah*, 58. Cf. source in Al-Farabi in Lerner and Mahdi, *Medieval Political Philosophy*, 26. On Al-Farabi's division of the sciences and, following him, Falaquera's, see I. Efros, "Palquera's *'Reshit Hokhmah'* and Al-Farabi's *'Ihsa Al' Ulum*,'" *JQR* 25 (1934–35):227–35; L. Strauss, "Eine Vermisste Schrift Farabis," *MGWJ* 80 (1936):96–106; M. Mahdi, "Al-Farabi's Enumeration of the Sciences," in *The Cultural Context of Medieval Learning*, ed. J. Murdoch (Dordrecht, 1973), 113–47; "Remarks," 47–66; F. Rosenthal, *The Classical Heritage*, 54–55; G. Ben Ami Sarfatti, "Ha-targumim ha-ivri'im shel 'Minian ha-Madayim' le Al-Farabi," *Sefer Bar Ilan* I (1972):413–20. On Falaquera's philosophy in general, see M. Plessner, "Hashiuuto Shel R. Shem Tov Ibn Falaquera le-hekcr tobdot ha-filosofia," *Homenage a Milan Vallicorosa* (Barcelona, 1956), 2:161–84; and H. Malter, "Shem Tob ben Joseph Palquera," *JQR* 2 (n.s. 1910):151–81; Jospe, *Torah and Sophia*, 146–55.

20. *Reshit Hokhmah*, 76–77. Cf. Al-Farabi, Mahdi ed., 65. In *Sefer ha-Hathalot*, which is Samuel Ibn Tibbon's translation of Al-Farabi's *Siyasat al-Madaniyyah*, we find parallel statements, 41.

21. *Reshit Hokhmah*, 70–71. Cf. Al-Farabi, Mahdi ed., 47–48; and Lerner and Mahdi, *Medieval Political Philosophy*, 80. See the discussion on the problem of the mss. and the status of Falaquera's translation in Mahdi, 151–52. Falaquera evidently used an earlier ms. than those that have survived, so his translation may also help in reconstructing Al-Farabi's original version.

22. *Reshit Hokmah*, 70. Cf. Al-Farabi, Mahdi ed., 46–47. On the treatment of the term *imam*, see ch. 1, n. 4, and n. 25, below.

23. *Reshit Hokmah*, Mahdi, ed., Ibid., 48–49. Cf. the discussion on the conditions for attaining perfection of the intellect in Maimonides, *Guide* I:34.

24. *Reshit Hokmah*, 71; see Hebrew text, appendix, below. Cf. Mahdi ed., 48, n. 60. On the meaning of the phrase: "[He] should not forsake what are commonly recognized as noble deeds," see Mahdi's note, 137, n. 33(1), and E. I. J. Rosenthal, *Political Thought in Medieval Islam*, 132.

25. *Reshit Hokmah*, 71. Cf. Mahdi ed., 49, n. 62. Here, too, Falaquera ignores the term *imam*. See ch. 1, n. 4, above; and, by contrast, the position of Joseph Ibn Shem-tov, who places blame on the philosophers, not on the masses, in Regev, "Le-ba'ayat limud ha-filosofia," 67.

26. *Reshit Hokmah*, 71. See n. 72, below, for an additional example of the way in which Falaquera applied Al-Farabi's statements to the Hebrew sources. Also see my "Al yithalal," 55–56.

27. *Sefer ha-Ma'alot*, 13. Cf. Al-Farabi, *Al-Madina al-Fadilah*, Walzer, ed., ch. 15, 10–11:245–46. For Falaquera's discussion, see Jospe, *Torah and Sophia*, 44, n. 71; 111–15.

28. *Sefer ha-Ma'alot*, 13–14, 15. Cf. parallel discussions by Maimonides, Falaquera, and others on the virtues required of the prophet, based on the words of the sages: "Prophecy does not descend but on the wise, the mighty, and the rich." See n. 17, above.

29. See ch. 1, n. 4; ch. 5, n. 22, above. Also R. Walzer, "Aspects of Islamic Political Thought: Al-Farabi and Ibn Xaldun," *Oriens* 16 (1963):48; and his edition of *The Virtuous State*, 245.

30. *Sefer ha-Ma'alot*, 16. Cf. Al-Farabi, Walzer, ed., 247.

31. *Sefer ha-Ma'alot*,16.Cf. Walzer, ed., Ibid., 247. The term "degree" *(Ma'alah)*, as related here to the qualities of the king, is first referred to in *Avot* 6:5. In Al-Farabi's source, there is no mention at this point of the possibility that the philosopher king will possess most of the virtues. Falaquera makes this addition here based on what Al-Farabi said after listing the twelve qualities. See n. 34, below.

32. *Sefer ha-Ma'alot*, 16–17 See the Hebrew version in appendix, below. Cf. Al-Farabi, Walzer, ed., *Al-Madina al-Fadilah*, 247; "Aspects," 48. Later, Falaquera adds a short paraphrase on the subject, as if quoting Plato directly. *Sefer ha-Ma'alot*, 19. Cf. Walzer, ed., *Al-Madina al-Fadilah*, 245. Here, too, we find that Falaquera does not simply translate Al-Farabi but summarizes, edits, and arranges the material in a different order. Al-Farabi expressly notes twelve virtues (Walzer ed., 247), and, following him, so does Falaquera. For some reason, Rosenthal claims that in fact Al-Farabi lists thirteen virtues here; see E. I. J. Rosenthal, *Political Thought in Medieval Islam*, 276, n. 50, and also "Maimonides' Conception of the State," 198. Apparently he makes this assertion in order to be able to equate Al-Farabi's position with that of Maimonides regarding the thirteen virtues of God that the perfect man must imitate. See ch. 3, n. 67, above.

33. See n. 12, above. Also see *Reshit Hokmah*, 69. Cf. the source, *Attainment of Happiness*, ed. Mahdi, 37. Here, it appears, he was not troubled by the military purpose of the physical perfection of the philosopher-king, and he was quite capable of applying the Islamic idea to the Hebrew sources. See the military discussions in general in Falaquera and others in my "Al yithalal," and cf. "Averroes' Commentary," Rosenthal ed., 26; Kraemer, "Maimonides' Messianic Posture," 141; and G. J. Blidstein, "Holy War in Maimonidean Law," *Perspectives on Maimonides*, ed. J. L. Kraemer (Oxford, 1991), 209–20.

34. On the rhetorical capabilities of the philosopher-king, see Walzer, *Al-Madina al-Fadilah*, 438. Walzer assumes that Al-Farabi and the other Muslim philosophers based their view of the necessity for rhetoric on Plato's *Phaedrus* and Aristotle's *Rhetoric*. See W. F. Bogges, "Al-Farabi and the *Rhetoric:* The Cave Revisited," *Phronesis* 15 (1970):36–90; C. E. Butterworth, "Rhetoric and Islamic Political Philosophy," *International Journal of Middle East Studies*, 3 (1972):187–98. See the attribution of rhetorical perfection even to Moses, despite his speech impediment, in Polkar, *Ezer ha Dat*, ch. 6, n. 20, below.

35. *Sefer ha-Ma'alot*, 17. Cf. Letter to Hasdai halevi, attributed to Maimonides. Quoted by A. Halkin, "Classical and Arabic Material in Aknin's 'Hygiene of the Soul,'" *PAAJR*, 15 (1944):127, n. 165a; cf. the same claim by Ibn Aknin, citing Al-Farabi., 127, n. 240; and cf. Abravanel, ch. 7, n.14, below.

36. Walzer, *Al-Madina al-Fadilah*, 248–49; "Aspects," 49; Rosenthal, *Political Thought in Medieval Islam*, 133; J. Macy, "The Rule of Law and the Rule of Wisdom in Plato, Al-Farabi and Maimonides," eds., W. M. Brinner and S. D. Ricks, *Studies in Islamic and Judaic Traditions* (Denver, 1986), 133.

37. *Sefer ha-Ma'alot*, 17. Undoubtedly, the statement is based on Al-Farabi, but I have not found any direct source for this wording in *The Virtuous State*. A parallel exists between this and what we find in Al-Farabi's *Sefer ha-Hathalot* in Samuel ibn Tibbon's translation; see n. 20, above.

38. *Sefer ha-Ma'alot*, 17. Falaquera's discourse directly follows Al-Farabi in nn. 7–13 of ch. 15. After the discussion on the possibility that the philosopher will not possess all twelve virtues (n. 13), Al-Farabi moves on, as in *Sefer ha-Hathalot*, to a detailed consideration of the types of erring states. Falaquera, however, omits this topic. Although he (Falaquera) attributes the continuation of his discourse to *The Virtuous State*, 17, there is no direct parallel with that work, even though the content generally is in the spirit of Al-Farabi. This occurrence is characteristic of Falaquera, who used his sources freely, translating, summarizing, and interpreting them, but never slavishly adhering to them. See Plato, *Republic*, IV:404–5; and Ibn Rushd's commentary, E. I. J. Rosenthal ed., *Averroes' Commentary on Plato's Republic*, 37. Cf. Maimonides, *Eight Chapters*, I. Also see *Introduction to Seder Zeraim*, 100; Moses Narboni's paraphrase of Ibn Bajja's *The Governance of the Solitary*, 35; Polkar, *Ezer ha-Dat*, 33, ch. 6, nn. 13, 17, below; Alemanno, *Shir ha-Ma'alot li-Shlomo*, 504. In *Sefer ha-Mevakesh* (Vienna, 1875), Falaquera tells a story based on the philosopher-king theory and certainly taken from Arabic sources. It is about a king who rules the virtuous state and is perfect in all the virtues. Falaquera uses the usual medieval analogy of the rule of a king over his state to the rule of the sun over the stars. His son and heir apparent, however, does not meet the king's standards and disappoints him. It is clear to the king that the welfare of his people depends on the perfection of the qualities of their king. In a parallel organic analogy, Falaquera compares the role of the king to that of the heart among all the bodily organs. Falaquera paraphrases here Plato, *The Republic* V:473 (and see S. D. Goitein, "Attitudes Toward Government in Islam and Judaism"; Hebrew version in *Tarbiz* 19–20 (1959). Out of concern for the future of his people, the king sends for the philosophers to educate his intractable son and prepare him for kingship. But the youth is stubborn and incorrigible, and all the philosophers fail in their efforts. In desperation, the king casts his son out of his presence. Then one day a great poet comes to the court and undertakes to educate the rebellious son through the art of poetry. He succeeds in his task, turning the prince into a man perfect in all the virtues as well as a perfect poet who uses his eloquent tongue to lead the people properly. This story is influenced by the tradition of the philosopher as mentor to the ideal ruler; see ch. 8, below, in connection with the tradition of the *Speculum Principium*. Falaquera, however, substitutes the poet for the philosopher. See also English edition, M. H. Levine, tr. and ed., *The Book of the Seeker* (New York, 1976), 83–88, and nn. 100–3. A

further analogy compares the righteous state with the bestial state, *Sefer ha-Mevakesh*, 97–99. This, though, does not refer to the image of the philosopher king. Cf. the analogy given by Hillel of Verona, ch. 6, n. 23, below. For a further example of the education of the ideal ruler, this time by an "ascetic," see Abraham Halevi's paraphrase of the Arabic source, *Sefer ben ha-Melekh ve-ha-Nazir* (Warsaw, 1884).

39. See Rosenthal's and Lerner's introductions (above, ch. 1, n. 4); Pines, "Leheker torato ha-medinit shel ibn rushd," 84–102; L. V. Berman, "Greek into Hebrew, Samuel ben Judah of Marseilles, Fourteenth-Century Philosopher and Translator," *Jewish Medieval and Renaissance Studies*, ed. A. Altmann, (Cambridge, MA, 1967), 289–320, and ch. 2, n. 18. See also Joseph Ibn Caspi's summary of this translation, *Seder Hanhagah le-Aplaton*, which was included in his essay *Terumat ha-Kesef*. Caspi's summary does not change or add anything to the text; see B. Mesch, "Joseph Ibn Caspi. Fourteenth-Century Philosopher and Exegete" (Ph.D. diss., Brandeis University, 1972), 79, n. 112; 92; 108, n. 27; 112, n. 68.

40. Rosenthal ed., *Averroes' Commentary on Plato's Republic*, 61; the English translation, 177; and see ch. 1, n. 4, above.

41. On Rosenthal's and Pines' positions, see ch. 2 above, and Macy, "The Rule of the Law," 227, n. 50.

42. Rosenthal tr., *Averroes' Commentary on Plato's Republic*, 178–79; cf. Lerner tr., *Averroes' Commentary on Plato's Republic*, 72–74. See the Hebrew source in appendix, below.

43. See ch. 3, n. 13, above.

44. Rosenthal, *Averroes' Commentary on Plato's Republic*, 62; the English translation 179; also Kraemer, "Falasifa," 293, n. 9.

45. Rosenthal ed., *Averroes' Commentary on Plato's Republic*, 207–8, Hebrew source 80.

46. E. I. J. Rosenthal, *Political Thought in Medieval Islam*, 202–3.

47. On the Hebrew version of *Fusul al-Madani*, see n. 9, above. On physical perfection and its military context, see n. 12, above.

CHAPTER 6. ADAPTATION

1. Isaac Polkar, *Ezer ha-Dat*, ed. J. Levinger (Tel Aviv, 1984), introduction; G. Belasco, "Isaac Polgar's '*Support of Religion*,'" *JQR* O.S. 27 (1905):26–56. Also see S. Pines, "Al sugiyot ahadot ha-kellulot be-sefer '*Ezer ha-Dat*' le-Isaac Polker ve-tikbolot lahen ezel Spinoza," in *Mehkarim be-Kabbalah, be-Filosofia Yehudit u-be-Sifrut ha-Musar ve-ha-Hagut Mugashim Le-Y. Tishbi*, eds., Y. Dan et al. (Jerusalem, 1986), 405–44.

2. The first quotation is from *Ezer ha-Dat*, 40. the second, 33–34.

3. On the attitude to general ideas, see Ibid., e.g., 31 33; and, by contrast, e.g., 100–1. For a specific consideration of Muslim and Jewish philosophers, see Maimonides' introduction to *Eight Chapters*. Also Pines, 413, n. 82.

4. Polkar, *Ezer ha-Dat*, 3, 41.

5. Ibid., 41–42. The Hebrew original appears below in the appendix. Also see Belasco, "Isaac Polgar's," 34; Pines, 411–12.

6. Pokar, *Ezer ha-Dat*, 42.

7. On the theory of imitation in general, see M. Cordovero, *The Palm Tree of Deborah*, tr., introduction, and notes L. Jacobs (London, 1960), 18–20. D. S. Shapiro, "The Doctrine of the Image of God and Imitatio Dei," *Judaism* (1963):12, 57–77; and Maimonides, ch. 3, above.

8. Ch. 5, n. 32 above. Also *Ezer ha-Dat*, editor's note, p. 42, n. 4.

9. Polkar, *Ezer ha-Dat*, 42.

10. Ibid., 43–44.

11. Ibid., 44. Cf. Narboni's commentary to Ibn Bajja's *The Governance of the Solitary*, Hayoun ed., 41.

12. On Maimonides' position, see ch. 3, above.

13. Polkar, *Ezer ha-Dat*, 44.

14. Deuteronomy 1:12. Cf. Maimonides' use of this expression, n. 15, below.

15. See my "Motar ha-adam," and additional bibliography there; cf. Maimonides, *Hilkhot Melakhim* II,6.

16. For a further variation on the subject: *Ezer ha-Dat*, 33; and see ch. 5, n. 38.

17. Polkar, *Ezer ha-Dat*, 44.

18. Ibid., 44.

19. Ibid., 44–46. See Hebrew text in the appendix, below.

20. For Maimonides, see *Guide* III:51; *Hilkhot Talmud Torah* III:11–12; *Eight Chapters* IV; and *Commentary to Avot*, passim. Also see Schwarzschild, "Moral Radicalism."

21. On the king's need to act cruelly when the need arises, see C. Sirat, "Ra'ayonot politi'im shel Nessim ben Moshe me-Marsei," in *Sefer ha-Yovel le-Shlomo Pines*, eds. M. Idel et al. (Jerusalem 1990), 2:57–58. Also see Maimonides' position, ch. 3 and n. 49 there.

22. On Maimonides' concept of the miracle, see A. J. Reines, "Maimonides' Concept of Miracles," *HUCA* 14 (1975):43–87. M. Z. Nehorai, "Ba'ayat ha-nes ezel ha-Rambam," in *Sefer ha-Yovel le-Shlomo Pines*, eds. M. Idel et al. (Jerusalem, 1990), 2:1–18. On the description of the king-Messiah as one who does not perform miracles but operates only within the limits of natural law, see *Hilkhot Melakhim* XI:3. Maimonides reiterates this position in *Iggeret Tehiat ha-Metim*, Shilat ed., I:358. Also see Lerner, "Maimonides," 195.

23. Polkar, *Ezer ha-Dat*, 46. The parables of kings, which were as common in medieval Hebrew literature as in Muslim and Christian literature, convey clear intimations of the theory of the virtues of the philosopher-king in which the analogy is to

the question of the imitation of God (see, e.g., *Kuzari*, I:19–24, 109; *Guide* I:56, III:51, etc.). See, too, T. Blay Sneor, "Mishlei melech ba-hagut ha-yehudit bi-yemei ha-beinayim," Master's thesis, University of Haifa (1990). A striking example appears in the essay by Hillel ben Samuel of Verona, "Sefer tagmulei ha-nefesh," written in the second half of the thirteenth century. To exemplify his views of the theory of the soul, Hillel of Verona presents an original and detailed parable of a king that differs in many respects from the parables of the king that were current in Jewish philosophy before him. Our concern here is not with the analogy in the area of the theory of the soul, but with the political parable. The parable describes a minister sent by a great king to restore a "vicious state" to the right path. Because of the difficulties of the mission, it was necessary to choose a man possessing special qualities. The description of the qualities is clearly reminiscent of the Platonic enumeration of the virtues of the philosopher-king. *Sefer Tagmulei ha-Nefesh le-Hillel ben Shemuel Mi-Verona*, ed. J. B. Sermoneta (Jerusalem, 1981); the parable is on 170–75, the passage on 171. Therefore, a minister gifted with such qualities was chosen for the task. Although this minister had the necessary potential, he had not yet realized it. The challenge of correcting the wicked state would allow him to do so. Hillel of Verona chose to use the terms "attributes" *(te'arim)* when indicating the virtues of the perfect ruler. (Elsewhere [170], he defines the perfect man as possessing *middot* and *te'arim*), Sermoneta notes that the use of the terms *metoeret* and so forth, derives from the Latin or Italian. However, we have already seen that *te'arim* itself appears in the Hebrew translations of the Arabic sources. Sermoneta correctly observes that it is possible that Hillel of Verona found some inspiration in Maimonides' parable of the palace (*Guide* III:51), but there is no doubt that his central idea is quite different, being infused with a purely Platonic tone. Sermoneta refers to the theory of the soul as expressed in the analogy, but the text pertains equally to the political parable, which also shows a clearly Platonic influence (through Al-Farabi or Ibn Rushd), including references to the perfect virtues of the "great minister."

24. P. O. Kristeller, *Renaissance Thought and Its Sources* (New York, 1979); B. C. Novak, "Giovanni Pico della Mirandola and Jochanan Alemanno," *JWCI* 45 (1982):125–47.

25. Klibansky argued that the Platonic tradition continued in medieval Christian thought (above, ch. 1, n. 3), but clearly this does not relate to *The Republic*. For an early example of the influence of the Platonic theory of the philosopher king in the Renaissance, see E. Barker, *The Political Thought of Plato and Aristotle*, 525–30. Also see F. Gilbert, *Machiavelli and Guicciardini* (Princeton, 1965). I:iii; E. H. Gombrich, "Renaissance and Golden Age," in his *Norm and Form* (Phaidon, 1971), 29–34;. N. Rubinstein, "Political Theories of the Renaissance," in *The Renaissance—Essays in Interpretation*, ed. A. Chastel, ed. (London, New York, 1982), 174–75; H. Baron, *The Crisis of the Early Italian Renaissance* (Princeton, 1966), 425–27; Melamed, "The Hebrew *Laudatio*," J. Hankins, *Plato in the Italian Renaissance* (Leiden, 1991); A. Brown, "Platonism in Fifteenth-Century Florence and Its Contribution to Early Modern Political Thinking," *Journal of Modern History* 58 (1986):383–413.

26. See the introductions by Rosenthal and Lerner (ch.1, n. 4, above); E. I. J. Rosenthal, *Political Thought in Medieval Islam*, 302; Melamed, "The Hebrew *Lauda-*

tio," and "Elia del Medigo ve-ha-masoret ha-medimit ha-Aplatonit ba-renesans," *Italia* 11 (1995):57–76. Klibansky still assumes, as was usual in his day, that the del Medigo translation was lost; this was not corrected in the last edition of his book (1980), p. 18. See also above, ch. 4, n. 38.

27. *Hai ha-Olamim*, ms. Mantua, n. 21; see, e.g., fols. 291, 295, 304, 321, 327.

28. On *Hai ha-Olamim*, see, e.g., M. D. Casutto, *Ha-Yehudim be-Firenzi*, trans. M. Artom (Jerusalem, 1967), 235–46; A. Melamed, "Ha-mahashavah ha-Medinit," ch. 2; and *idem*, Italian Renaissance and Early Modern Encyclopedias," *Rivista di Storia della Filosofia* 40 (1985):91–112. On Alemanno's political philosophy, see Melamed, "Ha-mahashavah ha-medinit"; idem, "The Hebrew *Laudatio*"; idem, and "Yohanan Alemanno al hitpathut ha-hevrah ha-enoshit," *Proceedings of the Eighth World Congress of Jewish Studies* (Jerusalem, 1982), 3:85–93; E. I. J. Rosenthal, "Some Observations on Yohanan Alemanno's Political Ideas," in *Studies in Jewish Religious and Intellectual History*, eds. S. Stein and R. Loew (London, 1979), 247–61. The discussion of the virtues of the philosopher-king is found in ms. *Hai ha-Olamim*, fols. 351–52.

29. *Hai ha-Olamim*, fol. 351.

30. *Hai ha-Olamim*, fol. 351. Cf. Abravanel's expression, "The Divine Plato," *Commentary on Exodus* (Jerusalem 1964), 14. I thank M. Kellner for drawing my attention to Abravanel's use of this expression.

31. *Hai ha-Olamim*, fol. 351. Cf. Ibn Rushd, Rosenthal, ed., 6.

32. *Hai ha-Olamim*, fol. 351. Cf. ch. 1, n. 4, above. Alemanno presents these statements in other places in *Hai ha-Olamim* when discussing the seven good virtues of the Florentines. The sixth virtue relates to the perfection of wisdom. Ms. *Hai ha-Olamim*, fol. 109. Here, too, we observe how Alemanno ascribes these concepts directly to Plato, even though it is clear that they originated in Ibn Rushd's commentary. See Melamed, "The Hebrew *Laudatio*."

33. *Hai ha-Olamim*, fol. 351.

34. *Hai ha-Olamim*, fol. 351

35. *Hai ha-Olamim*, fol. 352. See the Hebrew version in the appendix, below; cf. Ibn Rushd's original, Rosenthal ed., 61–2.

36. *Hai ha-Olamim*, fol. 352. See the Hebrew version in the appendix, below.

37. On this episode, see S. A. Cohen, "The Concept of the Three Ketarim"; ch. 7, n. 4, below.

38. *Hai ha-Olamim*, fol. 351.

39. *Hai ha-Olamim*, fol. 351.

40. See Blidstein, "The Monarchic Imperative," 17, n. 8.

41. See Maimonides, *Hilkhot Avodah Zarah* I; *Guide* II:39; III:29; Albo, *Ikkarim* I:7; Abravanel, *Commentary on Exodus*, 19; idem, *Commentary on the Torah*, 161.

42. *Hai ha-Olamim*, fol. 351. Cf. Abravanel's comments on Nimrod. *Commentary on Genesis* (Jerusalem, 1964), 165. Cf. the attitude to Nimrod in Christian thought of

the time: J. G. A. Pocock, *The Machiavellian Moment*, 380–89. Also see in general Alemanno's detailed description of the good king versus the wicked king, ms. *Hai ha-
Olamim*, fols. 346–50; my Ph.D. diss., 154–57.

CHAPTER 7. APPLICATION

1. See the discussion of the entire question in Abravanel's *Commentary on Exodus*, 161–64.

2. On Abravanel's negative view of the monarchic regime and his "republican"
position, see I. Baer, "Don Isaac Abravanel al ba'ayot ha-historia ve-ha-medina," *Tarbiz* 8 (1937):241–58; L. Smoler and M. Auerbach, "Ha-melukha be-hashkafat olamo
shel Abravanel," *Hagut Ivrit be-Amerika* (Tel Aviv, 1973), 2:134–54; Strauss, "Abra-
vanel's Tendency"; Netanyahu, *Don Isaac Abravanel*, II:iii; A. Ravitzky, "Kings and
Laws in Late Medieval Jewish Thought (Nissim of Gerona vs. Isaac Abravanel)," in
Scholars and Scholarship: The Interaction Between Judaism and Other Cultures, ed. L.
Landman (New York, 1990). A Hebrew version of Ravitzky's paper was published in
R. Bonfil et al., eds., *Tarbut ve-Hevrah be-Toledot Israel be-Yemei ha-Beinayim*
(Jerusalem, 1989), 469–91.

3. On Abravanel's concept of prophecy, see Netanyahu, *Don Isaac Abravanel*,
121–23, 202–3; A. J. Reines, "Abravanel on Prophecy in the Moreh Nebukim," *HUCA*
31 (1960):107–35; 33 (1962):221–53, 37 (1966):147–74. Also see I. E. Barzilay,
Between Reason and Faith, Anti-Rationalism in Italian Jewish Thought, 1250–1650 (The
Hague and Paris, 1967), ch. VI.

4. See Cohen, "The Three Crowns," especially 29, 40. Moses appears as "king
and prophet" in the view of the Sages, e.g., *Shavuot* 15a. Rashi adheres to this position.
See Cohen, "Three Crowns," 29–30, n. 3, 40, n. 16. In philosophical thought, see, e.g.,
Philo's *On the Life of Moses* II:292: ". . . Moses, king, lawgiver, high priest, prophet."
Loeb ed., 595. Also see ch. 3, n. 1, above. Cf. the distinction made by Abravanel in
Commentary on Earlier Prophets, Commentary on II Samuel 7:334. By contrast, Abra-
vanel presents Moses elsewhere actually as king and primarily as supreme lawgiver,
215.

5. *Commentary on Exodus*, 161–64.

6. Cf. *Commentary on I Kings* 3, 490.

7. *Commentary on Exodus*, 164; and see the Hebrew version in the appendix,
below.

8. *Commentary to Earlier Prophets*, 466–79. Elsewhere, when he summarizes the
period of Solomon's rule, Abravanel notes three perfections: of wisdom, of courage and
government, and of riches (551–52). He also presents Solomon there as the greatest
king who ever existed both in Israel and in the nations of the world (552). This con-
trasts with what he states elsewhere, that both Moses and David were the finest of
kings (see n. 5, above). On Abravanel's discussion of the good virtues of King David,
see n. 66 below. Our discussion does not expand on Abravanel's treatment of the per-

fect virtues of David, first because in one case Abravanel simply cites Albo, whom we shall discuss separately below, and in the other cases his discussion is entirely stereotypical.

9. *Commentary to Earlier Prophets*, 473. Cf. Alemanno, *The Song of Solomon's Descents* (n. 2, above) II:334. See Melamed, "The Hebrew *Laudatio*"; idem, "Hebrew Encyclopedias," 105–7.

10. *Commentary to Earlier Prophets*, 466–67.

11. *Commentary to Earlier Prophets*, 467–70. Cf. Maimonides' discussion of the five factors preventing knowledge: Guide I:34.

12. *Commentary to Earlier Prophets*, 471. Cf. Shalom Alemanno's and Erasmus' interpretations of Solomon's dream.

13. *Commentary to Earlier Prophets*, 472.

14. *Commentary to Earlier Prophets*, 477. See n. 20, below. Cf. *Commentary to Exodus*, 18.

15. *Commentary to Earlier Prophets*, 476.

16. *Commentary to Earlier Prophets*, 476. Cf. Simone Luzzatto's interpretation of this verse, *Ma'amar al Yehudei Venezia* (Jerusalem, 1951), 97.

17. For the background to this activity by Abravanel, see Netanyahu, part I.

18. Ibid., 476. Cf. Abravanel's commentary on Isaiah 36 with that of his contemporary, Judah Messer Leon, *Nofet Zufin* (Vienna, 1863), IV:48.

19. *Commentary to Earlier Prophets*, 477.

20. *Commentary to Earlier Prophets*, 479.

21. *Commentary to Earlier Prophets*, 479.

22. *Commentary to Earlier Prophets*, 480. Cf. n. 7, above.

23. See n. 2, above, and also ch. 1, n. 14, above.

24. Cf. Al-Farabi in regard to the difficulty in finding a ruler perfect in all the virtues, and hence the possibility of joint rule by two or more rulers: Walzer, Al-Farabi, ch. 15, 13–14, and 449. See ch. 4, n. 31, above. Cf. one of Spinoza's reservations in respect to the monarchic regime: "And in fact they are much mistaken, who suppose that one man can by himself hold the supreme right of a commonwealth. . . . But the power of one man is very inadequate to support so great a load." See *A Political Treatise* VI:5, *The Chief Works of Spinoza*, tr. R. H. Elwes (New York, 1951), 317; and see ch. 9, below. Indeed, when in various places Abravanel presents the Platonic division into three classes of human society, he makes a sharp distinction between the philosophers, who belong to the first class, and the kings, who belong to the second. See ch. 4, above.

25. *The Song of Solomon's Ascents*, Lesely ed.

26. *The Song of Solomon's Ascents*, II:417. Also p. 335.

27. See ch. 6, nn. 24–25, above. On Lorenzo's image as philosopher-king in Alemanno himself, see *The Song of Solomon's Ascents*, II:329–30; also Melamed, "The Hebrew *Laudatio*."

28. *The Song of Solomon's Ascents*, 335.

29. *The Song*, 348.

30. *The Song*, 350.

31. *The Song*, 504. Also see 348–49. In the introduction, Lesley presents Solomon as the perfect man only in the philosophical-literary sense, certainly not as philosopher-king. He completely ignores the political context of the composition, and this omission, I feel, displays the work one-sidedly. He merely notes that Prof. A. Funkenstein remarked to him, rightly, that the composition seemed to be connected to the tradition of the *Speculum Principium*, but Lesley does nothing to develop this central feature of the work. See I, introduction, n. 4, and 294, n. 35. For literature on the *Speculum Principum* tradition, see L. K. Born, "The Perfect Prince According to Latin Panegyrists," *American Journal of Philology*, 55 (1934):20–35; "The Perfect Prince, a Study of 13th and 14th Century Ideals," *Speculum* 3 (1928):470–504; A. H. Gilbert, *Machiavelli's 'Prince' and Its Forerunners* (Durham, North Carolina, 1938). On this tradition in medieval Islamic literature, see *Ghazali's Book of Counsel for Kings*, tr. F. R. Bagley (Oxford, 1964); A. K. S. Lambton, "The Theory of Kingship in the 'Nasihat al-Muluk' of Ghazali," *Islamic Quarterly* (1954):47–55; E. I. J. Rosenthal, *Political Thought in Medieval Islam*, 67–77, 256–57. For a medieval Hebrew translation of a typical Christian *Speculum Principum*, see above, ch. 2, n. 14.

32. *The Song*, 521.

33. See Al-Farabi, *Al-Madina*, Walzer ed., 51–52; Kraemer, "Falasifa," 308–10. Of relevance to this question is Alemanno's discussion of the need of the philosopher king to be perfect in two kinds of legal teaching, in which he follows Falaquera's translation of Al-Farabi's division of sciences (418–36). Cf. ms. *Hai ha-Olamim*, fol. 392.

34. See Lesely's introduction, I:57, and, e.g., Alemanno, 335.

35. Lesely, introduction, 55; and D. A. Rees, "The Classification of Goods in Plato and Aristotle," in *Islamic Philosophy and the Classical Tradition*, eds., S. M. Stern et al. (Columbia, SC, 1972), 327–36.

36. Alemanno frequently cites Al-Farabi. Sometimes he refers to him generally, and at other times he notes the particular essay which he is quoting, usually from the *Division of Sciences*. See, e.g., *The Song of Solomon's Ascents*, II:42, 429, 436–37, 447. He almost certainly was acquainted with Al-Farabi's *Division of Sciences* through Falaquera's Hebrew translation, which appears in *Reshit Hokhmah*. In one place, he quotes directly from Falaquera's discussion of Plato's philosophy (529), which is essentially translation-summary of Al-Farabi. In another place (447), he cites Al-Farabi to the effect that he who is perfect in wisdom and also in the ability to educate others is preferable to one who is perfect in wisdom alone. The requirement that the philosopher-king be perfect in both these virtues appears in Al-Farabi's discussion of the virtues of the philosopher-king and, following him, in Falaquera (ch. 5, nn. 32, 33, above). On Falaquera's influence on Alemanno, who regarded him as a mystic, see Jospe, *Torah and Sophia*, 2, 43, 44, 67, 143.

37. Lesley, introduction, 56.

38. *The Songs*, 536.

39. Abraham Shalom, *Sefer Neveh Shalom* (Venice, 1575), II vols. On Shalom, see H. Davidson, *The Philosophy of Abraham Shalom* (Berkeley and Los Angeles, 1964); H. Tirosh-Rothschild, "Filosofia medinit be-mishnat Avraham Shalom: ha-masoret ha-Aplatonit," in *Sefer ha-Yovel le-Shlomo Pines*, M. Idel et al., eds. (Jerusalem, 1990), 2:409–40. The last also includes a short discussion of the attributes of the perfect king in Shalom.

40. *Neveh Shalom*, I. vii, 7:105a–106b. The source is *Berachot* 9b.

41. Davidson, introduction.

42. *Neveh Shalom*, 105a. See, also, V. 7:72b. Cf. *Guide* II:40. 43.*Neveh Shalom*, 105a.43. *Neveh Shalom*, 105a.

44. *Neveh Shalom*, 105a

45. *Neveh Shalom*, 105a.

46. *Neveh Shalom*, 105a. Also II. ix, 1:153b

47. *Neveh Shalom*, 105a. See Shalom's discussion of Saul's sin of holding back from destroying all of Amalek: V:6:71a; Davidson, introduction, 6; cf. Albo's consideration of the subject, below.

48. See the discussion of the theory of imitation, II:IX. 8, 166a–b. See Davidson's discussion of Shalom's theory of imitation, ch. 3.

49. *Neveh Shalom*, 105b. See the Hebrew version in appendix, below. See Tirosh Rothschild, "Filosofia medinit," 437–38.

50. *Neveh Shalom*, 106a. And see 108a.

51. *Neveh Shalom*, 106a. The source is 1 Kings 12:8.

52. This assumption stems from the similarity between the content and structure of Shalom's text and these elements in the classic medieval discourses on the king's attributes. The sources used by Shalom, however, do not support this assumption, and therefore I have preferred to use the cautious formulation "some notion." Among the mediating Islamic sources, Shalom chiefly cites from Ibn Rushd's commentaries to the Aristotelian corpus (Davidson, 13–14). Of these, only the commentary to the *Ethics* is connected with the political discussion, and it contains no reference to our subject. Shalom quotes only once from Al-Farabi's works—namely, from *Sefer he-Hathalot* (VIII:8:141a; Davidson, 14), and not in a political context. Moreover, *Sefer he-Hathalot* makes only a passing reference to the philosopher-king. Al-Farabi's and Ibn Rushd's commentaries to Plato's *Republic* are not mentioned by Shalom at all, nor does he refer to even one of the classic texts in the Hebrew tradition of the philosopher-king. Additionally, the structure of the discussion, which is based on two methods of narration of the virtues of the perfect king in Israel, does not necessarily derive from the classic tradition. Shalom frequently—obsessively, in fact—cites reasons or virtues in the form of a numbered list. Yet, there is still considerable similarity between his discussion of the virtues of the perfect king and the philosophical discourse on the subject, and this fact speaks for itself. As for the possible influence of Albo, Shalom was familiar with *Sefer ha-Ikkarim*, and quotes from it twice: I:15a and 25b; see Davidson, introduction, 8, n. 74; 15, 17, n.16; 23, 57.

53. *Neveh Shalom*, I:105b. For some reason, the text relates these matters to the biblical portion *Ki Tisa*. Clearly, the discussion is based on Deuteronomy 17, that is, the portion *Shoftim*.

54. *Neveh Shalom*, 105a–106a; Hebrew version, appendix below.

55. On the use of the theory of the middle way, see *Eight Chapters*, 5. On the discussion of the sense of touch, see *Guide* III:8, 49.

56. *Neveh Shalom*, 106a.

57. *Neveh Shalom*, 106. See n. 51, above. Cf. the attitude to Ahab in Aquinas, and to Reheboam in Machiavelli, ch. 8, below.

58. *Neveh Shalom*, II. IX:9:168b–169a.

59. *Neveh Shalom*, 168b; also V:13. For the entire subject, see my "Eretz Israel ve-ha-teoria ha-aklimit ba-mahashavah ha-yehudit," *Eretz Israel ba-Hagut ha-Yehudit bi-Yemei ha-Beinayim*, eds., M. Halamish and A. Ravitzky (Jerusalem 1991), 52–78; and Tirosh-Rothschild, "Filosofina medinit," 436.

60. *Book of Principles*, IV:26. Husik, ed., IV:1:235–57.

61. *Book of Principles*, 242–43; see S. A. Cohen, "The Bible and Intra-Jewish Politics: Early Rabbinic Portraits of King David," *JPSR* 3 (1991):49–65. Machiavelli made the same distinction between the sinful David as a private individual and the virtuous and courageous David as a political and military leader; see S. de Grazia, *Machiavelli in Hell* (Princeton, 1988), III:12; and ch. 8, below.

62. *Book of Principles*, 245.

63. *Book of Principles*, 245–46.

64. *Book of Principles*, 246–48; see the Hebrew text in the appendix, below.

65. *Book of Principles*, 248.

66. *Book of Principles*, 248–51. Abravanel quotes this discussion extensively and concludes as did Albo. *Commentary on the Earlier Prophets, Commentary on 1 Samuel* 9:249–50. Elsewhere he sets out different variations of the discussion of David's kingly perfection; see *Commentary to 1 Samuel*, 17:254–55, and *Commentary to 2 Samuel*, 22:394. In both cases, he notes six virtues of King David, which are very different in detail from the virtues listed by Albo and only generally parallel the classification of the philosopher king according to the Platonic tradition. In one place (396), he notes ten virtues that helped David defeat his enemies.

67. *Book of Principles*, 250–51.

CHAPTER 8. CHRISTIAN APPLICATIONS AND THE MACHIAVELLIAN REVOLUTION

1. See ch. 7, n. 9, above.

2. *The Republic*, V:473.

3. See ch. 7, n. 31, above.

4. Aquinas, *Selected Political Writings*, ed. and introduction A. P. D'Entreves, tr. J. G. Dawson (Oxford, 1970), introduction.

5. *Political Writings*, 5, 9, 17, 19, 31, 33, 57, 61, 95, 101.

6. *The Politics*, I:5.

7. *Political Writings*, 100–1.

8. *Political Writings*, 52–53.

9. *Political Writings*, 148–49. Also see A. Melamed, "Jethro's Advice in Medieval and Early Modern Jewish and Christian Political Thought," *Jewish Political Studies Review* 2 (1990):3–41.

10. *Political Writings*, 47.

11. Erasmus, *The Education of a Christian Prince*, tr., and introduction L. K. Born (New York, 1968), introduction, I, II; Latin version, Desiderii Erasmi Roterdami, *Opera Omnia*, cura et impensis P. Vander (MDCCIII), tomus quartus, 559–612. For a discussion of *imitatio Dei*, see Latin version 584; Born ed., 191.

12. Born, introduction, IV.

13. *The Education*, introduction, 34; text, 200.

14. *The Education*, 34, 133, 168, 200.

15. *Opera Omnia*, 588, 202.

16. *Opera Omnia*, 588, 203.

17. See ch. 5, above.

18. Ch. 5, above. Cf. also Luzzatto's commentary: "and Solomon himself, who was a man of action no less than he was a man of contemplation, asked God to give him wisdom after he made up his mind to become King of Israel. And with it he later acquired whatever can be acquired." *Discorso*, ch. 15; Hebrew ed., 132. Also see Septimus, 430 (ch. 9, n. 2, below).

19. *Opera Omnia*, 559; Born ed., 133–34 (and see his definition of the term "philosophy" there); *Opera Omnia* (559) states: "Philosophiam, inquam, non istam, quae de principiis, de prima materia, ed motu aut infinito disputat, sed quae falsis vulgi opinionibus, ac vitiosis offectibus animum liberans, ad aeterni numinis exemplar recte gubernandi rationem commonsirat." The formulation is clearly Platonic, almost "Maimonidean" in essence.

20. *The Education*, 133; *Opera Omnia*, 599. Immediately thereafter, Erasmus actually attributes this perfection of wisdom to Avishag the Shunamite, who succeeded in finding favor in the eyes of King David by means of her embraces alone!

21. *The Education*, 133. The editor mistakenly relates the text to v. 16; it actually appears in v. 15. *Opera Omnia*, 559.

22. *The Education*, 133; *Opera Omnia*, 581.

23. *The Education*, 185; *Opera Omnia*, 581.

24. *The Education*, 96.

25. *The Education,* 185–86; *Opera Omnia,* 581.

26. This is evident in various essays, especially his chief composition on the subject, *Querela Pacis (The Complaint of Peace).* See Born, introduction, 15–19; ch. 11 in the text. ·

27. *The Education,* 255–56; *Opera Omnia,* 610.

28. See ch. 7, above.

29. *The Education,* 185; *Opera Omnia,* 581.

30. See the discussion on this subject, *The Education,* 166–67; in Abravanel, ch. 5, n. 2, above.

31. *The Education,* 166–67; *Opera Omnia,* 573.

32. *The Education,* 167–68; Plato, *The Republic,* I:345, III:416, IX:588.

33. *The Education,* 167.

34. *Il Principe,* 6. I used Martelli's Italian edition, N. Machiavelli, *Tutte Le Opere.* A cura di M. Martelli (Florence, 1971); English edition, *The Prince and the Discourses by Niccolo Machiavelli,* with an introduction by M. Lerner (New York, 1950). For a short preliminary discussion of the subject, see S. B. Robinson, "Medinat Israel ha-tanachit be-torat medinah le-dugmah be-kitveihem shel hogei de'ot politi'im ba-me'ot ha-16–18," in his *Hinuch bein Hemshekhyut le-Petihut* (Jerusalem, 1975), 21–22. Also A. Melamed, "Machiavelli al avot ha-ummah ha-Ivrit: degem le-manhigut politit," *Proceedings of the Eleventh World Congress of Jewish Studies* (Jerusalem, 1990), 2:338–44. The influence of Hebrew sources on Christian political thinkers at the beginning of modern times merits investigation in depth.

35. *Discorsi* I:1.

36. *Discorsi* III:30; Italian edition, 237. Also see on this Robinson, "Medinat Israel," 22; and W. Winiarski, "Machiavelli," in *History of Political Philosophy,* eds., L. Strauss and J. Cropsey (Chicago, 1969), 264; S. de Grazia, *Machiavelli in Hell,* 54. De Grazia translates this: "whoever reads the Bible sensibly."

37. Moses is discussed in *Discorsi* I:1, 9; II:8; III:30; *Il Principe* 6, 26. David is discussed in *Discorsi* I:19, 26; *Il Principe,* 13. Solomon and Rehoboam are discussed in *Discorsi* I:19. Winiarski (265) asserts that Machiavelli also refers to Joshua. I have not found this reference in his writings.

38. N. Wood, "Machiavelli's Concept of *Virtu'* Reconsidered," *Political Studies* 15 (1967):159–72. See also Q. Skinner, *Machiavelli* (Oxford, 1981), ch. 2. The literature offers extensive discussion of Machiavelli's *virtu',* with reference to the term found in almost every study on him. For specific consideration of this concept, see the discussion between F. Gilbert and L. C. Mackinney elicited by the publication of Gilbert's "On Machiavelli's Idea of Virtu'," *Renaissance News* 4 (1951):53–55. This was followed by Mackinney's response, 5 (1952):22, and Gilbert's counter position in the same issue, 70–71. Wood's article also elicited responses. See R. Price, "The Senses of Virtu' in Machiavelli," *European Studies Review* 3 (1973):315–45. Price, criticizing Wood's analysis, contends that Wood based himself only on *Il Principe* and the *Discorsi,* ignor-

ing the wide use of this term in Machiavelli's many other political, historical, and literary works. In his view, Wood's conclusions about the roster of leaders possessing *virtu'* are mistaken. Price asserts that according to Machiavelli's other writings, a substantial number of the possessors of *virtu'* are medieval as well as from Machiavelli's own times, contrary to Wood's argument. This reservation is irrelevant from our viewpoint, because Machiavelli cites the leaders of the Hebrew nation only in *Il Principe* and in the *Discorsi;* in terms of a comparison with them, therefore, the content of his other texts changes nothing. For us, Wood's analysis is still very useful. Also see I. Hannaford, "Machiavelli's Concept of Virtu' in 'The Prince' and 'The Discourses' Reconsidered," *Political Studies,* 22 (1972):185–89. J. Plamenaz, "In Search of Machiavellian Virtu'," in *The Political Calculus, Essays on Machiavelli's Philosophy,* ed., A. Parel (Toronto and Buffalo, 1972), 157–78 (the example of Moses is mentioned on 159).

39. *Il Principe,* 6; English ed., 20; Italian ed., 264; see Winiarski, "Machiavelli," 268; J. Plamenatz, *Man and Society* (London, 1972), I:6–7.

40. *Il Principe* ch.6,

41. Wood, "Machiavelli's Concept," 162.

42. English ed., 21; Italian ed., 265.

43. *Il Principe,* 26; English ed., 95; Italian ed., 297. Also see de Grazia, *Machiavelli in Hell,* 197.

44. *Il Principe,* 26; English ed., 20–21; Italian ed., 264–65.

45. *Il Principe;* English ed., 22; Italian ed., 265.

46. *Il Principe,* 26; English ed., 95; Italian ed., 297.

47. *Discorsi* I:9; English ed., 40; Italian ed., 91. Also see, Skinner, *Machiavelli,* and de Grazia, *Machiavelli in Hell,* 31, 53, 69, 175, 206, 234, 275. And n.b.: "the first and greatest of Niccolo's trio of heroes," 358.

48. *Il Principe,* 6; English ed., 20; Italian ed., 264.

49. *Discorsi* I:1; English ed., 107; Italian ed., 77; Wood, "Machiavelli," 162. On Romulus, see I:19.

50. *Il Principe,* 1–3.

51. *Discorsi* I:1; English ed., 107; Italian ed., 77.

52. *Discorsi* II:8; English ed., 304. Italian ed., 175. See n. 38, below. See also P. S. Donaldson, *Machiavelli and the Mystery of State* (New York, 1988), 141; H. C. Mansfield, Jr., "Necessity in the Beginnings of Cities," *The Political Calculus,* 101–25 (Moses is referred on 109, 111).

53. *Discorsi* I:1; English ed., 107: "And as men work either from necessity *[per necessita]* or from choice *[per elezione]* as it has been observed that virtue *[maggior virtu']* has more sway where labor is the result of necessity rather than choice"; Italian ed., 77. Also *Il Principe,* 23; Italian ed., 294; English ed., 89: "For men will always be false to you unless they are compelled by necessity *[necessitá]* to be true."

54. *Il Principe,* 6; English ed., 21; Italian ed., 264.

55. *Il Principe*, 26; English ed., 95; Italian ed., 297.

56. *Il Principe*, 6; English ed., 20; Italian ed., 264: "And in examining their life and deeds it will be seen that they owed nothing to fortune *[fortuna]* but the opportunity *[occasione]* which gave them matter *[materia]* to be shaped into what form *[forma]* they thought fit; and without that opportunity *[occasione]* their powers *[la virtú dello animo loro]* would have been wasted, and without their powers *[virtu']* the opportunity *[occasione]* would have come in vain." Also see ch. 26, English ed., 94: "Whether at present the time was not propitious in Italy for a new prince *[nuovo principe]* and if there was not a state of things *[materia]* which offered an opportunity *[occasione]* to a prudent and capable man *[uno prudente e virtuoso]* to introduce a new system *[forma]* that would do honour to himself and good to the mass of the people." Also *Arte della Guerra*, Italian ed., 388.

57. Machiavelli, *The Prince*, English ed., 138; Italian ed., 90. And see J. G. A. Pocock, *The Machiavellian Moment*, 170–71.

58. *Il Principe*, 112–13; *Arte della Guerra*, passim.

59. *Discorso*, III:6; *Il Principe*, 19.

60. *Discorso*, I:1, 49.

61. *Il Principe*, 12–13; *Arte della Guerra* I.

62. This subject is discussed by many scholars. See, e.g., I. Berlin, "The Originality of Machiavelli," *Studies on Machiavelli*, ed. M. P. Gilmore, (Florence, 1972), 147–206; F. Chabod, *Machiavelli and the Renaissance* (New York, 1965), 69, n. 2; R. M. Adams, tr., and ed., *The Prince* (New York, 1977), 16; J. H. Whitfield, "Machiavelli's Use of 'Ordini,'" in Adams, *The Prince*, 203–4; Pocock, *The Machiavellian Moment*, 168; F. Gilbert, "Mechiavelli's 'Discorsi,'" in his *History, Choice and Commitment* (Cambridge, MA, 1977), 126.

63. *Discorsi*, I:10. The entire subject of initial lawgivers is discussed extensively by H. F. Pitkin, *Fortune is a Woman, Gender and Politics in the Thought of N. Machiavelli* (Berkeley, 1984), 20–21 and ch. 3.

64. *Il Principe*, 6. See Price, "The Senses of Virtu'," 329. For the theory of *occasione*, see De Grazia, *Machiavelli in Hell*, 206. On Machiavelli's *theory of fortuna*, see T. Flanagen, "The Concept of Fortuna in Machiavelli," *The Political Calculus*, 127–56.

65. *Il Principe*; English ed., 21; Italian ed., 264.

66. *Discorsi*, I:1; F. Gilbert, *Machiavelli and Guicciardini*, 102.

67. *Il Principe*, 26; English ed., 95; Italian ed., 297. This is partially quoted in n. 22, above.

68. "La Vita di Castruccio Castracani da Lucca," *Tutte le Opere*, 615. Pitkin, 57; A. Kontos, "Success and Knowledge in Machiavelli," in *The Political Calculus*, 56–57; T. A. Sunberg, "Castruccio Castracani," *Interpretation* 16 (1988–89):285–93.

69. See *Discorsi*, I:11; Italian ed., 94; English ed., 147: "In truth, there never was any remarkable lawgiver amongst any people who did not resort to divine authority, as otherwise his laws would not have been accepted by the people; for there are many

good laws, the importance of which is known to the sagacious lawgiver, but the reasons for which are not sufficiently evident to enble him to persuade others to submit to them; and therefore do wise men, for the purpose of removing this difficulty, resort to divine authority. This did Lycurgus and Solon, and many others who aimed at the same thing." Although Machiavelli presents Lycurgus and Solon, but not Moses, as examples here, he expressly states that others also did the same thing, meaning Moses, too. See Robinson, "Medinat Israel," 22; Donaldson, *Machiavelli and Mystery*, 171–75. Cf. Halevi's *Kuzari*, I:80: "The first element of religion appeared no doubt among single individuals, who supported one another in upholding the faith which it pleased God should be promulgated. Their number increases continually, they grow more powerful, or a king arises and assists them, also compels his subjects to adopt the same creed." For Machiavelli's claim about the usage of myths as a means for political legitimation, see B. Lewis, *History Remembered, Recorded, Invented* (Princeton, 1975), 59–64.

70. *Il Principe;* English ed., 64: "A prince being thus obliged to know well how to act as a beast must imitate the fox and the lion."

71. *Discorsi* II:8; English ed., 304; Italian ed., 157. Also see Pitkin, *Fortune Is A Woman*, 99–100, 102–3.

72. *Discorsi* II:8.

73. See n. 19, above.

74. *Discorsi* I:9; English ed., 140; Italian ed., 91. On the legitimacy of violent action, see also Berlin, "The Originality."

75. *Discorsi* III:30; English ed., 498; Italian ed., 237. The source is Exodus 32:19–20. On this, see Adams, *The Prince*, 18; Pocock, *The Machiavellian Moment*, 172; Winiarski, "Machiavelli," 264; Donaldson, *Machiavelli and Mystery*, 193–94; De Grazia, *Machiavelli in Hell*, 82, 275. For Machiavelli's justification of the use of violence in politics in general, see N. Wood, "Machiavelli's Humanism of Action," *The Political Calculus*, 33–54.

76. On the history of the interpretation of these verses, see M. Walzer, "Exodus 32 and the Theory of Holy War, The History of a Citation," *HTR* 61 (1968):1–14. Machiavelli's example is not mentioned in this article. For Machiavelli's interpretation, see also Donaldson, *Machiavelli and Mystery*, 22; de Grazia, *Machiavelli in Hell*, 54, 275.

77. *Discorsi* III:30; English ed., 498; Italian ed., 237. Also see D. Weinstein, "Machiavelli and Savonarola," in *Studies on Machiavelli*, ed. M. P. Gilmore (Florence, 1972), 225.

78. Walzer notes (9) that Augustine overlooked the role of the Levites in this story, while Aquinas preferred to ignore the role of Moses. In this respect, Machiavelli follows Augustine.

79. *Il Principe*, 6; English ed., 22; Italian ed., 265. See *Il Principe*, 10; English ed., 39: "I consider those capable of maintaining themselves alone who can, through abundance of men and money, put together a sufficient army." This subject, too, is given a

great deal of consideration in the literature on Machiavelli; see, e.g., Whitfield, "Machiavelli's Use of 'Ordini,'" 200–10; Weinstein, *Machiavelli and Savonarola*, 263; Pocock, *Machiavellian Moment*, 170–72.

80. *Il Principe*, 6; English ed., 20; Italian ed., 264. See Winiarski, "Machiavelli," 264–65.

81. Exactly the same circumstance occurs when Machiavelli deals with church principalities. He states that he cannot consider them because he does not understand theological matters, yet immediately embarks on a detailed discourse with an obviously political connection: "But as they are upheld by higher causes, which the human mind cannot attain to, I will abstain from speaking of them; for being exalted and maintained by God, it would be the work of a presumptuous and foolish man to discuss them. However, I might be asked. . . ." *Il Principe*, 11; English ed., 42; and Winiarski, "Machiavelli," 265. Also see what he says about Savanarola, *Discorsi* I:11; English ed., 149.

82. A. Polvare, *Il Principe e Altri Scritti, con introduzione e commento* (Turin, 1944), ch. 6.

83. See, e.g., his scorn for church states in the opening segment of *Il Principe*, 11.

84. *Discorsi* II:2; English ed., 285; Italian ed., 149. Also I:11–12. See Berlin, "The Originality." On the subject in general, see J. S. Preus, "Machiavelli's Functional Analysis of Religion: Context and Object," *JHI* 61 (1979):171–90.

85. See n. 47, above. In fact, Frederick II of Prussia, author of the classic "anti-Machiavel," responded to Machiavelli's "complication" with the problem of Moses' divine mission in these forceful terms: "It seems to me, in addition, that Machiavelli classes Moses rather haphazardly with Romulus, Cyrus, and Theseus. Either Moses was inspired or he was not. If he was not, he can only be regarded as an archscoundrel, a trickster and an imposter, who used God as poets use the deus ex machina to bring a play to a conclusion when they are in a bind. Moses was, besides, so inept that he led the Jewish people for forty years over a distance that they could have very conveniently covered in six weeks. He profited very little from the lights of the Egyptians, and he was in that sense much inferior to Romulus, Theseus, and the other heroes. If Moses was inspired by God, he can only be regarded as the blind organ of divine omnipotence; and the leader of the Jews was greatly inferior to the founder of the Roman Empire, to the Persian monarch, and to the Greek heroes who performed greater actions by their own valor and and strength than he ever performed with the immediate asistance of God." Frederick of Prussia, *Anti-Machiavel*. Introduction, tr. and notes, P. Sonnino (Athens, Ohio, 1981), 55.

86. *Il Principe*, 26; English ed., 96; Italian ed., 297. See Adams, *The Prince*, 73, n. 8; Donaldson, *Machiavelli and Mystery*, 22–23, n. 44.

87. On the entire subject, see Pitkin, *Fortune Is A Woman*, 102–3; Pocock, *Machiavellian Moment*, 170–75, 190. Donaldson tends to ignore the whole issue. For him: ". . . Machiavelli mentions Moses' divine call in *Il Principe*, only to ignore it, placing the Exodus in the context of pagan and purely human achievements," 181. In his opinion, Machiavelli did not distinguish at all between Moses and pagan legislators, 202. I disagree.

88. *Discorsi* I:19; English ed., 172; Italian ed., 104. Also see Price, "The Senses of Virtu'," 327; de Grazia, *Machiavelli in Hell*, 111–12, 358. For the distinction between the private and the public David, see de Grazia, Ibid., 111–12, and ch. 7, n. 61, above.

89. *Discorsi* I:26; English ed., 193; Italian ed., 109.

90. *Discorsi* I:26; Italian ed., 109; English ed., 184.

91. *Il Principe*, 12; English ed., 44; Italian ed., 275. Also *Discorsi* III:31.

92. *Il Principe*, 13; English ed., 51; Italian ed., 278. See the biblical source, 1 Samuel 17:38–41. By adding a knife to David's armor, Machiavelli evinces a lack of precision and expertise in the Bible. For the expression "to encourage him" *(per dargli animo)* and its parallelisms, see A. Melamed, "Simone Luzzatto on Tacitus: Apologetica and Ragione di Stato," *Studies in Medieval Jewish History and Literature*, ed., I. Twersky, (Cambridge, MA, 1984), 164, and nn. 91–93.

93. *Il Principe*, 13; Italian ed., 51. On the citizens' army, see also Pitkin, *Fortune Is A Woman*, 21.

94. *Discorsi* I:19; English ed., 172; Italian ed., 104.

95. *Discorsi* I:19; English ed., 172–73; Italian ed., 104; and see Price, "The Senses of Virtu'," 327. The English translator erred by translating "con l'arte della pace" as "peace and war." I have made the appropriate correction.

96. English ed., 173. For the Turkish example, see Mansfield, "Necessity in the Beginnings," 119.

97. Compare his Jewish contemporaries, Alemanno and Abravanel, ch. 7, above.

98. *Il Principe*, 12; English ed., 44. The English translation does not exactly accord with the original, and I have emended it as necessary. Italian ed., 275. Also ch. 2, English ed., 5: "How the various kinds described above can be governed and maintained"; and the Italian original, 258: "e disputero come questi principi si possino governare e mantenere."

99. *Il Principe*, 22; English ed., 86; Italian ed., 258.

100. *Discorsi* I:19; English ed., 172; Italian ed., 104. See Price, "The Senses of Virtu'," 327

101. *Il Principe*, 22; English ed., 86; Italian ed., 293.

102. *Il Principe*, 22; English ed., 86; Italian ed., 293. See Melamed, "Simone Luzzatto on Tacitus," 162–63.

103. There is no mention of the Hebrew state in the Second Temple period, either, though Machiavelli could have made much of the Hasmonean rebellion, for example. He probably was not acquainted with the sources on that era.

104. On the sources for the writing of *Il Principe* see A. H. Gilbert, *Machiavelli's "Prince" and its Forerunners;* F. Gilbert, "The Humanist Concept of the Prince and the Prince of Machiavelli," in his *History, Choice and Commitment* (Cambridge, MA), 91–114; Skinner, *Machiavelli*, 42–44. For Dante, see *De Monarchia* (Florence, 1965), I:8–9.

105. *Il Principe*, 15; English ed., 56: "And many have imagined republics and principalities which have never been seen or known to exist in reality; for how we live is so far removed from how we ought to live, that he who abandons what is done for what ought to be done, will rather learn to bring about his own ruin than his preservation." Italian ed., 280.

CHAPTER 9. REJECTION

1. On Luzzatto and Ben Israel, see B. Septimus, "Biblical Religion and Political Rationality in Simone Luzzzatto, Maimonides and Spinoza," *Jewish Thought in the Seventeenth Century*, ed. I. Twersky (Cambridge, MA, 1987), 416 and n. 78, with additional bibliography. On the possible influence of Luzzatto on Spinoza and parallelisms between them, see Melamed, "Luzzatto on Tacitus," 136, n. 90, and in greater detail, Septimus, 416ff.

2. For a discussion of Luzzatto and his public life and philosophical works, see the introductions by R. Bacci and M. A. Shulvass to the Hebrew edition, *Ma'amar al Yehudei Venezia*, ed. A. Z. Aescoly (Jerusalem, 1950). Bacci's essay also appeared in Italian in the compilation of his articles, *Israele Disperso e Riconstruito* (Rome, 1952). His analysis of Luzzatto's political philosophy errs on many points. A more accurate presentation is to be found in his article, "La Dottrina sulla Dinamica delle Citta: secondo G. Botero e secondo S. Luzzatto," *Atti della Accademia Nazionale dei Lincei. 8sr.* (1946):369–78, which was reprinted as the introduction to the facsimile rendition of the original Italian edition (Bologna, 1976). See also B. C. I. Ravid, *Economics and Toleration in Seventeenth Century Venice: The Background and Context of the Discorso of Simone Luzzatto* (Jerusalem, 1978); A. Melamed, "Luzzatto on Tacitus," and *"Ha-Mahashavah ha-Medinit,"* ch. 4. Also see Septimus, "Biblical Religion," 399–435. There is hardly any discussion of *Socrates* in the scholarly literature. On its political contexts, see Melamed, *"Ha-Mahashavah ha-Medinit,"* ch. 4.

3. *Ma'amar*, 6th Discourse; Hebrew ed., 93; Italian source, 23–23a.

4. *Ma'amar*, 15th Discourse; Hebrew ed., 145; Italian source, 82. See also the application of the ideas to the proper attitude towards the Jews, 12th Discourse, Hebrew ed., 110–11. On the mob's opposition to the Jews settling in the city: "They even discredit the careful perception of their ruler, since they boast to be exalted in their bat's eyes over the vision of the ruler who has the eyes of a leopard, and is never deterred from investigating and interrogating and contemplating the most hidden and obscure doings of his subjects." Italian source, 44.

5. *Ma'amar*, 16th Discourse; Hebrew ed., 142. Later he notes that he is in possession of some of Gersonides' translations of Ibn Rushd's commentaries to Aristotle. Ibn Rushd's commentary to Plato's *Republic* is, of course, not included here. However, Jacob Maninus' Latin translation had been published in the mid-sixteenth century as part of the Venice edition of Aristotles' *Opera Omnia*, which contained Ibn Rushd's commentaries, including those on *The Republic*. This edition was widespread in the second half of the sixteenth and early-seventeenth century, and Luzzatto was likely to

be acquainted with it. It is not at all accidental that he does not refer to Al-Farabi, for the latter's influence on Latin Christian culture was less by far than that of Ibn Rushd. Cf. Alemanno, ch. 6.

6. *Ma'amar*, 15th Discourse; Hebrew ed., 133–34; Italian original, 69a–70. On Luzzatto's response to Tacitus' accusations, see Melamed, "Luzzatto on Tacitus."

7. *Ma'amar*, 10th Discourse; Hebrew ed., 103; Italian original, 34a–35.

8. *Ma'amar*, 6th Discourse; Hebrew ed., 93; Italian original, 22. Also: "The Lacedaemonians who received their laws from Lycurgus, who was admired by the oracle of Apollo as one of the Gods . . ." *Ma'amar*, 15th Discourse; Hebrew ed., 125; Italian original, 60a–61.

9. *Ma'amar*, 10th Discourse; Hebrew ed., 103; Italian original, 34a–35. Cf. *Guide* I:54; III:54.

10. *Discorso*, 34–34a.

11. *Ma'amar*, 10th Discourse; Hebrew ed., 103; Italian original, 35a.

12. *The Laws* 6:777.

13. *Ma'amar*, 8th Discourse; Hebrew ed., 97; Italian original, 27a. Cf. Machiavelli, *Discorsi* I:11.

14. *Ma'amar*, 11th Discourse; cf. Machiavelli, *Discorsi* I:3; and see ch. 8, above.

15. *Ma'amar*, 15th Discourse.

16. *Ma'amar*, 5th Discourse; Hebrew ed., 92; Italian original, 21a.

17. *Ma'amar*, 15th Discourse; Hebrew ed., 127; Italian original, 62. On the meaning and the Machiavellian source of the phrase "to strengthen their spirit," see Melamed, "Luzzatto on Tacitus," 164; and see n. 44, below.

18. *Ma'amar*, 17th Discourse; Hebrew ed., 149; Italian original, 86a.

19. *Ma'amar*, 13th Discourse; Hebrew ed., 113; Italian original, 46–46a.

20. It is not accidental that Luzzatto cites Grotius here, *Ma'amar*, 13th Discourse; Hebrew ed., 115; also 162, n. 81. Also see Lipsius, 15th Discourse, 147, 215, n. 174; see G. Oestreich, *Neo-Stoicism and the Early Modern State* (Cambridge, 1982).

21. *Máamar*, 15th Discourse. See a detailed discussion on this in Melamed, "Luzzatto on Tacitus."

22. *Máamar*, 15th Discourse; Hebrew ed., 127. Italian original, 62. See Melamed, "Luzzatto on Tacitus."

23. David Kimhi, *Commentary on II Samuel* (Lemberg, 1878), 35. Abravanel, *Commentary to the Earlier Prophets* (Jerusalem, 1956). And cf. Isaac Arama, *Commentary to Proverbs*, 11; Spinoza, *Political Treatise* 7, 14; idem, *Theological-Political Treatise*, 5, 78. See on Efodi's discussion of the subject, in E. Gutwirth, "Duran on Ahitophel: The Practice of Jewish History in Late Medieval Spain," *Jewish History* 4 (1989):59–74.

24. *Socrate-overo del humano sapere* (Venice, 1681), 260–61.

25. *Ma'amar,* 6th and 7th Discourses; Aristotle, *Politics* II.

26. *The Republic* V:473.

27. *Socrate,* 304.

28. Ibid.

29. *Socrate, 304–5.* For a medieval Hebrew version, see Goitein, "Attitude towards Government," 159.

30. Erasmus, *Opera Omnia,* 559; idem, *The Education,* 134. Further on Diognes, 193.

31. Septimus, "Biblical Religion," 411, n. 56.

32. *The Chief Works of Benedict de Spinoza: A Theological-Political Treatise and A Political Treatise,* tr. from the Latin with an introduction by R. H. M. Elwes (New York, 1951); *Political Treatise* I:1, 287; Latin ed., *Opera,* Recognoverunt J. Van Vloten et J.P.N. Land, Tomus secundus (Hague, MCMXIV), 3; English ed., 288: "Yet there can be no doubt that statesmen have written about politics far more happily than philosophers. For, as they had experience with their mistress, they taught nothing that was inconsistent with practice." Our discussion will treat only this particular aspect of Spinoza's political thought. For his political thought in general, see R. J. McShea, *The Political Philosophy of Spinoza* (New York, 1968); S. Rosen, "Spinoza," *History of Political Philosophy,* eds. L. Strauss and J. Cropsey, 413–32. McShea's book, for all its usefulness, is flawed in its neglect of the Jewish background generally, and the medieval background particularly, in Spinoza's political philosophy. This creates an imbalance in his presentation. On Spinoza's rejection of the philosopher-king theory, see Rosen, "Spinoza," 413; and M. Brinkner, "Ha-medinah ha-tovah ve-utopia lefi Torat ha Middot ve-Ha Masechet ha-Medinit," in *Baruch Spinoza,* eds. M. Brinkner et al. (Tel Aviv, 1979), 94–105.

33. Rosen, "Spinoza," 417.

34. *Theological-Political Treatise* 18:223. Also see Z. Harvey, "Spinoza mul ha-nevi'im be-she'elat bikoret ha-shilton," *Kivunim* 12 (1981):83–90.

35. *Theological-Political Treatise,* introduction, 7.

36. *Theological-Political Treatise* 5:78.

37. Rosen, "Spinoza," 425–26; Harvey, ibid.

38. *Theological-Political Treatise* 5:74.

39. *Political Treatise* 6, 5:317; and see Rosen, "Spinoza," 423.

40. *Political Treatise* 7.

41. *Theological-Political Treatise* 5:74–75. See, generally McShea, ch. 6. On the Machiavellian influence on Spinoza, see in McShea; A. Rava, "Spinoza e Machiavelli," *Studi Filosofico-giuridici* (Modena, 1931), 2, 299–313.

42. *Theological-Political Treatise* 17:206.

43. *Theological-Political Treatise* 5:75. Cf. Machiavelli, *Discorsi* I:11.

44. McShea, 95; *Political Treatise* 1:3.

45. *Theological-Political Treatise* 17:207.

46. *Theological-Political Treatise* 5:75. Cf. Machiavelli, *Discorsi* I:1, and see ch. 8, above; McShea, ibid; N.C. Brown, "Philosophy and Prophecy," *Political Theory* (1986):14, 195–213.

47. For a discussion on the question of obedience, see *Theological-Political Treatise* 5. On the expression "to encourage the soldiers" *(virtute et magnanimitate animi clarere),* see n. 17, above.

48. *Theological-Political Treatise* 5:75. Cf. Machiavelli, *Discorsi* I:11; and ch. 8, above.

49. Ibid., 17:216.

50. Ibid., 217.

51. Ibid., 234.

52. Ibid., 234.

53. Ibid., 233.

54. Ibid., 3. Note the natural meaning he ascribes to the terms, "The help of God" *(Rei auxilium)* and "The guidance of God" *(Dei directio).*

55. Ibid., 6.

56. Ibid., 5:75.

57. Ibid., 17:232.

58. Ibid., 7:232.

59. Ibid., 17:232.

60. Ibid., 17, 18.

AFTERWORD

1. On Machiavelli, see ch. 8, above, and n. 105 there. On Spinoza, see ch. 9, above, and n. 32 there.

2 .See Melamed, "Jethro's Advice."

3. A marginal expression of the idea of the philosopher king is still found in Joseph Del Medigo (Yashar of Kandia) in his *Sefer Elim* (Odessa 1864–67), 82.

4. Moses Mendelssohn, *Schriften zur Philosophie Aesthetik und Apologetik* (Hildesheim, 1968), 2, 463. See the English translation of *Jerusalem* by A. Arkush, with an introduction and commentary by A. Altmann (Hanover and London, 1983), 131. Also, J. Guttmann, "*Yerushalayim Le-Mendelssohn ve-ha-Masecet ha-Teologit-Medinit le-Spinoza,*" in his *Dat U-Madah,* translated by S. Ash (Jerusalem, 1969), 192–217; A. Berney, "Tefisato ha-historit ve-ha-medinit shel Mosheh Mendelson,"

Ziyyon (1950):5, 99–111, 248–70. N. Rotenstreich, "Mendelsson ve-ha-ra'ayon ha-medini," *M. M. Kaplan Jubilee Volume* (New York, 1953), 237–47. See also Rotenstreich's introduction to the Hebrew edition of *Jerusalem* (Ramat Gan, 1977), 7–32.

5. Mendelsson *Jerusalem*, English translation 131; German ed., 484.

6. Translated from the German ed., 484; Hebrew translation, 155.

7. *Jerusalem*, English translation, 131: "Just as little that a politician a la mode will understand you if you speak to him of the simplicity and moral grandeur of that original constitution. As the former knows nothing of love but the satisfaction of base lasciviousness, the latter speaks, when statesmanship is the subject, only of power, the circulation of money, commerce, the balance of power and population; and religion is to him a means which the lawgiver uses to keep the unruly man in check, and the priest to suck him dry and consume his marrow." In the German edition, 463–64.

8. German ed., 465; English translation, 133.

Bibliography

A. PRIMARY SOURCES

MANUSCRIPTS

Alemanno, Yohanan. *Hai ha-Olamim.* ms. Mantua. 21.

————. *Heshek Shelomo.* ms. London-Montefiori. 227.

Ibn Latif, Isaac. *Sha'ar ha-Shamayim.* ms. Vatican.335. 1

————. *Sha'ar Ha-Shamayim.* ms. London. 915.

Immanuel of Rome, Perush le-Bereshit. ms. Parma. 3220.

Romanus Aegidius, *De Regimine Principium*—An anonymous Hebrew translation—*Sefer Hanhagat ha-Melakhim.* Ms. Leiden. Or 4749 (Warn. 11).

Shemtov, Joseph Ibn Shemtov, *Sermons.* ms. London-Montefiori 61.

BOOKS

Abravanel, Isaac. *Perush al-ha-Torah.* 3 Vols. Jerusalem, 1979.

————. *Perush al Nevi'im Aharonim.* Jerusalem, 1957.

————. *Perush al "Moreh Nevukhim."* In *Sefer Moreh Nevukhim be Ha'atakat Rabbi Shemuel Ibn Tibbon im Arba'ah Perushim.* Jerusalem, 1960.

————. *Pirkei Avot im Perush ha-Rambam u-Perush Abravanel: "Nahalat Avot."* New York, 1953.

————. *Opera Minora.* London, 1972.

Albo, Joseph. *Sefer ha-Ikkarim (Book of Principles).* Edited, translation, and notes by I. Husik. Hebrew text and English translation. 5 Vols. Philadelphia, 1929.

Alemanno, Yohanan. "Shir ha-Ma'alot li-Shelomo: The Song of Solomon's Ascents by Yohanan Alemanno: Love and Human Perfection According to a Jewish Collegue of Giovanni Pico della Mirandola." Edited, introduction, translation, and notes by

A. M. Lesley. Hebrew text and English translation. 2 Vols. Ph.D. diss., University of California, Berkeley, 1976.

Al-Farabi. *Al-Madina al-Fadilah (On the Perfect State)*. Edited, translation, and commentary by R. Walzer. Arabic text and English translation. Oxford, 1985.

———. *Fusul Muntaza'a*. Edited by F. M. Najjar. Beirut, 1971.

———. *Alfarabi's Philosophy of Plato and Aristotle*. Edited, translation, and notes by M. Mahdi. Ithaca, 1969.

———. *Fusul al Madani (Aphorisms of the Statesman)*. Edited, translation, and notes by D. M. Dunlop. Arabic text and English translation. Cambridge, 1961.

———. *Sefer ha-Hathalot*. Translated by Samuel Ibn Tibbon. In *Sefer ha-Asif*. Edited by Z. Filipowsky, 1–64. Leipzig, 1849.

Al-Ghazali. *Ghazali's Book of Counsel for Kings*. Edited, translation, and notes by F. R. C. Bagley. Oxford, 1964.

Anatoli, Jacob. *Malmad ha-Talmidim*. Lyck, 1866.

Aquinas. *Selected Political Writings*. Edited and Introduction by A. P. D'Entreves. Translated by J. G. Dawson. Latin text and English translation. Oxford, 1970.

Aristotle. *Nicomachaean Ethics*. Introduction, translation, and commentary by J. A. K. Thomson. Baltimore, 1969.

———. *The Politics*. Translation, introduction and commentary by T. A. Sinclair. Bungay, 1967.

Azulay, Abraham. *Perush le-Masekhet Avot*. Jerusalem, 1987.

Bibago, Abraham. *Derekh Emunah*. 1521. Reprint, Jerusalem, 1969.

Dante, Alighieri. *De Monarchia*. A cura di P. G. Ricci. Florence, 1965.

Delacrut, Mattathias. *Zel ha-Olam*. 1887. Reprint, Jerusalem, 1968.

Del Medigo, Joseph. *Sefer Elim*. Odessa, 1864–67.

Erasmus of Rotterdam. *The Education of a Christian Prince*. Translation, and Introduction by L. K. Born. New York, 1968.

———. *Opera Omnia*. Cura et impensis P. Vander. Tomus Quaetus. 1703. Reprint, London, 1962.

Efodi. *Perush al "Moreh Nevukhim."* In *Sefer Moreh Nevukhim be Ha'atakat Rabbi Shemuel Ibn Tibbon im Arba'ah Perushim*. Jerusalem, 1960.

Frederick of Prussia. *Anti-Machiavel*. Introduction, translation, and notes by P. Sonnino. Athens, Ohio, 1981.

Flavius Josephus. *Against Apion. Works*. Vol. 1. Translated by H. St. J. Thackeray. London, 1961.

Halevi, Abraham. *Sefer Ben ha-Melekh ve-ha-Nazir*. 1884. Reprint, Jerusalem, 1962.

Halevi, Judah. *Kitab al Khazari*. Translated by H. Hirshfeld. Preface by M. M. Kaplan. New York, 1927.

Hillel of Verona. *Sefer Tagmulei ha-Nefesh*. Edited by J. B. Sermoneta. Jerusalem, 1981.

Ibn Bajja. *Beur Kavanat le-Abu Baker Alzaig be-Hanhagat ha Mitboded*. Edited by D. Herzog. *Kovetz Al Yad* 6 (1896):3–33.

Ibn Caspi, Joseph. *Maskiyyoth Kesef. Sheloshah Kadmonei Mefarshei Ha-Moreh*. Jerusalem, 1961.

———. *Mishneh Kesef. Ketavim*. Vol. 1. Pressburg, 1903.

———. *Asarah Keley Kesef. Ketavim*. Vol. 1. Pressburg, 1903.

Ibn Ezra, Abraham. *Hayy ben Yaqzan*. Edited by I. Levine. Tel Aviv, 1983.

Ibn Falaquera, Shem Tov. *Reshit Hokhmah. Ketavim*. Vol. 2. 1902. Reprint, Jerusalem, 1970.

———. *Sefer ha-Ma'alot. Ketavim*. Vol. 1. 1894. Reprint, Jerusalem, 1970.

———. *Epistle of the Debate*. Edited and translated by S. Harvey. Hebrew text and English translation. Cambridge, MA, 1987.

———. *Moreh ha-Moreh*. 1837. Reprint, *Sheloshah Kadmonei Mefarshei ha-Moreh*, Jerusalem, 1961.

———. *Iggeret ha-Halom*. Edited by H. Malter. *Ketavim*. Vol. 1. 1881. Reprint, Jerusalem, 1970.

———. *Sefer ha-Mevakesh*. 1875. Reprint, Jerusalem, 1960.

———. *The Book of the Seeker*. Edited and translated by M. H. Levine. New York, 1976.

Ibn Pakuda, Bahya Ben Joseph. *The Book of Direction to the Duties of the Heart*. Introduction, translation, and notes by M. Mansoor. London, 1973.

Ibn Rushd. *Averroes' Commentary on Plato's Republic*. Edited, introduction, translation, and notes by E. I. J. Rosenthal. Hebrew text and English translation. Cambridge, 1969.

———. *Averroes on Plato's Republic*. Edited, introduction, translation, and notes by R. Lerner. Ithaca, 1974.

———. *Parafrasi della "Repubblica" nella traduzione Latina di Elia del Medigo*. A cura di A. Coviello e P. Fornaciari. Florence, 1992.

———. *The Epistle of the Possibility of Conjunction with the Active Intellect by Ibn Rushd with the Commentary of Moses Narboni*. A critical edition and annotated translation by K. P. Bland. Hebrew text and English translation. New York, 1982.

———. *Biur Sefer ha-Halazah le-Aristo be-Ha'atakat Todros Todrosi*. Edited by J. Goldenthal. Leipzig, 1842.

Ibn Sina. *Iggeret Haj Ben Mekiz le-Ibn Sina*. Edited by D. Kaufman. *Kovetz Al Yad*. 2:1–25. Berlin, 1886.

Ibn Tibbon, Samuel. *Ma'amar Yikkavu ha-Mayyim*. Pressburg, 1837.

Ibn Tufayl. *Hayy Ibn Yaqzan*. Translation, introduction, and notes by L. E. Goodman. New York, 1972.

Immanuel of Rome. *Commentary on the Book of Proverbs*. Introduction by D. Goldstein. Naples, ca.1487; photo-reproduced, Jerusalem, 1981.

Lerner, R., and M. Mahdi, eds. *Medieval Political Philosophy: A Sourcebook*. New York, 1967.

Luzzatto, Simone. *Discorso circa il stato degli Ebrei in Venezia*. Venice, 1638.

――――. *Ma'amar al Yehudei Venezia*. Translated from the Italian by D. Lates with introductions by R. Bacci and M. A. Shulvass. Jerusalem, 1951.

――――. *Socrate overo dell humano sapere*. Venice, 1651.

Maimonides Moses. *Iggrot ha-Rambam*. Edited by I. Shilat. 2 Vols. Jerusalem, 1987.

――――. *The Guide of the Perplexed*. Edited, translated, introduction, and notes by S. Pines. Introductory essay by L. Strauss. Chicago, 1963.

――――. *Ethical Works of Maimonides*. Edited by R. L. Weiss and C. E. Butterworth. New York, 1975.

――――. *The Commentary to Mishnah Aboth*. Translated, introduction, and notes by A. David. New York, 1968.

――――. *The Book of Knowledge*. Introduction, notes, and translation by M. Hyamson. Hebrew text and English translation. Jerusalem, 1965.

――――. *Commentary to the Mishnah: Introduction to Seder Zeraim*. Translated by F. Rosner. New York, 1975.

――――. *The Code of Maimonides. Book 14. The Book of Judges*. Translated by A. M. Hershman. New Haven and London, 1963.

――――. *A Maimonidean Reader*. Edited by I. Twersky. New York, 1970.

――――. *Rambam. Readings in the Philosophy of Moses Maimonides*. Selected, translated, introduction, and commentary by L. E. Goodman. New York, 1970.

Machiavelli, Niccolo. *Tutte le Opere*. A cura di M. Martelli. Florence, 1971.

――――. *The Prince and the Discourses by Niccolo Machiavelli*. Translated and introduction by M. Lerner. New York, 1930.

Mendelsshon, Moses. *Schriften zur Philosophie Aestetik und Apologetik*. Vol. 2. Hildesheim, 1968.

――――. *Jerusalem*. Translated by A. Arkush. Introduction and commentary by A. Altmann. Hanover and London, 1983.

Messer Leon, Judah. *The Book of the Honeycomb's Flow. Sepher Nofeth Suphim* by Judah Messer Leon. Introduction, translation, and notes by I. Rabinowitz. Hebrew text and English translation. Ithaca and London, 1983.

Nissim of Gerona. *Shneim Asar Derashot le-ha-Ran*. Edited by A. I. Feldman. Jerusalem, 1974.

Plato. *The Republic*. Translated, introduction, and notes by F. M. Corenford. Oxford, 1967.

———. *The Dialogues of Plato*. Translated by B. Jowett with an introduction by R. Demos. New York, 1937.

Polkar, Isaac. *Ezer ha-Dat*. Edited by Y. Levinger. Tel Aviv, 1984.

Philo. *On the Life of Moses*. Translated by F. H. Colson. Cambridge, MA, 1957.

Rieti, Moses. *Mikdash Me'at*. Edited by J. Goldenthal. Vienna, 1851.

Romanus Aegidius. *De Regimine Principum*. 1556. Reprint, Frankfurt, 1968.

Rosenthal, F., ed. *The Classical Heritage in Islam*. Translated by E. and J. Marmorstein. London, 1975.

Saadia Gaon. *The Book of Beliefs and Opinions*. Translated by S. Rosenblatt. New Haven, 1967.

Shalom, Abraham. *Sefer Neveh Shalom*. 2 Vols. 1575. Reprint, Jerusalem, 1967.

Shemtov, Joseph Ibn Shemtov. *Kevod Elohim*. Ferarra, 1556.

Shemtov, ben Joseph Ibn Shemtov. *Perush al "Moreh Nevukhim."* In *Sefer Moreh Nevukhim be-ha'atakat Rabbi Shemuel Ibn Tibbon im Arba'ah Perushim*. Jerusalem, 1960.

———. *Derashot al ha-Torah*. 1507. Reprint, Jerusalem, 1974.

Spinoza, Benedict. *The Chief Works of Spinoza*. Translated by R. H. Elwes. New York, 1951.

———. *Benedicti de Spinoza Opera quotquat reperta sunt*. Recognoverunt J. Van Volten and J. P. N. Land. Editio tertio, Tomus primus. The Hague, 1914.

SECONDARY SOURCES

Bacci, R. "La dottrina sulla dinamica della citta—secondo Giovanni Betero e secondo Simone Luzzatto." *Atti della accademia nazionale dei lincei* 8 ser. (1946):369–78.

Baer, I. "He'arot hadashot le-sefer *Shevet Yehudah*." *Tarbiz* 6 (1935):152–79.

———. "Don Isaac Abravanel al ba'ayot ha-historia ve-ha-medinah." *Tarbiz* 8 (1937):241–58.

Barker, Ernest. *The Political Thought of Plato and Aristotle*. New York, 1959.

———. *Greek Political Theory*. London, 1964.

Baron, H. "Cicero and the Roman Civil Spirit in the Middle Ages and the Renaissance," *Bulletin of the John Rylands Library* 22 (1938):72–97

———. *The Crisis of the Early Italian Renaissance*. Princeton, 1966.

Baron, S. W. "The Historical Outlook of Maimonides." In *Proceedings of the American Academy for Jewish Research* 6 (1935):5–113. Reprinted in his *History and Jewish Historians*. 109–63, 348–404. Philadelphia, 1964.

Barzilay, I. E. *Between Faith and Reason: Anti-Rationalism in Italian Jewish Thought, 1250–1650*. The Hague and Paris, 1967.

Belasco, G. "Isaac Polgar's 'Support of Religion.'" *Jewish Quarterly Review O.S.* 27 (1905):26–56.

Berlin, I. "The Originality of Machiavelli." In *Studies on Machiavelli.* Edited by M. P. Gilmore, 147–206. Florence, 1972.

Berman, L. V. "Ibn Bajja ve-ha-Rambam." Ph.D. diss., Hebrew University of Jerusalem, 1959.

――――. "The Political Interpretation of the Maxim: The Purpose of Philosophy is the Imitation of God." *Studia Islamica* 15 (1961):53–61.

――――. "Greek into Hebrew: Samuel ben Judah of Marseilles, Fourteenth-Century Philosopher and Translator." In *Jewish Medieval and Renaissance Studies.* Edited by A. Altmann, 289–320. Cambridge, MA, 1967.

――――. Review of Rosenthal's "Averroes' Commentary on Plato's Republic." *Oriens* 21–22 (1967–69):426–39.

――――. "Maimonides, the Disciple of Alfarabi." *Israel Oriental Studies* 4 (1974):154–78. Reprinted in J. A. Buijs, ed. *Maimonides: A Collection of Critical Essays,* 195–214. South Bend, Indiana, 1988.

――――. "The Structure of Maimonides' Guide of the Perplexed." *Proceedings of the Sixth World Congress of Jewish Studies.* Vol. 3:7–17. Jerusalem, 1977.

――――. "Ibn Rushd's Middle Commentary on the Nicomachaean Ethics in Medieval Hebrew Literature." *Multiple Averroes,* 287–301. Paris, 1978.

――――. "Maimonides on Political Leadership." in D. J. Elazar, ed., *Kinship and Consent.* Edited by D. J. Elazar, 13–25. Ramat Gan, 1981. Hebrew version: "Ha-Rambam al manhigut medinit." In *Am ve-Edah.* Edited by D. J. Elazar. Jerusalem, 1990.

――――. "The Ideal State of the Philosophers and the Prophetic Laws." In *A Straight Path: Studies in Medieval Philosophy and Culture. Essays in Honor of A. Hyman.* Edited by R. Link-Salinger et al., 10–22. Washington, DC, 1987.

――――. "The Ethical Views of Maimonides within the Context of Islamicate Civilization." In *Perspectives on Maimonides.* Edited by J. L. Kraemer, 13–32. Oxford, 1991.

Berney, A. "Tefisato ha-historit ve-ha-medinit shel Mosheh Mendelson." *Ziyyon* 5 (1950):99–111, 248–70.

Bildstein, G. J. "On Political Structure." *Jewish Journal of Sociology* 22 (1980):47–58.

――――. "The Monarchic Imperative in Rabbinic Perspective." *AJS Review* 8–9 (1982–83):15–39.

――――. *Ekronot Medini'im be-Mishnat ha-Rambam.* Ramat Gan, 1983.

――――. "Al ha-Shilton ha-universali be-hazon ha-geulah shel ha-Rambam." In *Arakhim be-Mivhan Milhamah,* 155–72. Jerusalem, 1984.

――――. "Holy War in Maimonidean Law." In *Perspectives on Maimonides.* Edited by J. L. Kraemer, 209–20. Oxford, 1991.

Blay, Sneor T. "Mishlei Melekh ba-hagut ha-yehudit be-yemei ha-beinayim." Masters' thesis, University of Haifa, 1990.

Blumberg, Z. "Al-Farabi, ibn Bajjah ve-ha-Rambam al hanhagat ha-mitboded." *Sinai* 78 (1976):35–45.

Bogges, W. F. "Al-Farabi and the *'Rhetoric':* The Cave Revisited." *Phronesis* 15 (1970):36–90.

Born, L. K. "The Perfect Prince, a Study of the 13th and 14th Century Ideals." *Speculum* 3 (1928):470–504.

———. "The Perfect Prince According to Latin Panegyrists." *American Journal of Philology* 55 (1934):26–35.

Brinker, M. "Ha-medinah ha-tovah ve-utopia lefi Torat ha Middot ve-Ha-Masekhet ha-Medinit." In *Barukh Spinoza.* Edited by M. Brinker et al., 94–105. Tel Aviv, 1979.

Brown, A. "Platonism in Fifteenth-Century Florence and Its Contribution to Early Modern Political Thinking." *Journal of Modern History* 58 (1986):383–413.

Brown, N. C. "Philosophy and Prophecy: Spinoza's Hermeneutics." *Political Theory* 14 (1986):195–213.

Butterworth, C. E. "Averroes: Politics and Opinions." *American Political Science Review* 66 (1972):894–901.

———. "Rhetoric and Islamic Political Philosophy." *International Journal of Middle East Studies* 3 (1972):187–98.

———. "New Light on the Political Philosophy of Averroes." In *Essays on Islamic Philosophy and Science.* Edited by G. F. Hourani, 118–27. New York, 1975.

———. "Ethics and Classical Islamic Philosophy: A Study of *Averroes' Commentary on Plato's Republic.*" In *Ethics in Islam.* Edited by R. G. Hovannisian, 17–45. Undena, 1985.

———. *Philosophy, Ethics and Virtuous Rule: A Study of Averroes' Commentary on Plato's Republic.* Cairo Papers in Social Science. Vol. 9. Monograph 1. Cairo, 1986.

Carlyle, R. W., and A. J. *A History of Medieval Political Theory in the West.* 6 vols. Edinburgh, 1903–36.

Cassuto, U. *Gli ebrei a firenze nell'eta del rinascimento.* Florence, 1918. Hebrew edition: Cassuto, M. D. *Ha-Yehudim be-Firenzi be-Tekufat ha-Renesans.* Translated by M. Artom. Jerusalem, 1967.

Chabod, F. *Machiavelli and the Renaissance.* Translated from the Italian by D. Moore with an introduction by A. P. D'Entreves. New York, 1965.

Chiesa, B. "Note su Al-Farabi, averroe e Ibn Bagga (Avempace) in Traduzione Ebraica." *Henoch* 8 (1986):79–86.

Cohen, S. A. "The Concept of the Three Ketarim: Its Place in Jewish Political Thought and its Implication for a Study of Jewish Constitutional History." *AJS Review* 9 (1984):27–54.

————. "Keter as a Jewish Political Symbol: Origins and Implications." *Jewish Political Studies Review* 1 (1989):39–62.

————. "The Bible and Intra-Jewish Politics: Early Rabbinic Portraits of King David." *Jewish Political Studies Review* 3 (1991):49–65.

Daiber, H. "The Ruler as Philosopher: A New Interpretation of Al-Farabi's View." *Mededelingen der Koninklijke Nederlandre Akademie van Wetenschappen*, 133–49. Amsterdam, 1986.

Davidson, H. A. "Maimonides' 'Shemonah Perakim' and Al-Farabi's 'Fusul Al-Madani.'" *Proceedings of the American Academy for Jewish Research* 31 (1963):33–50.

————. *The Philosophy of Abraham Shalom.* Berkeley and Los Angeles, 1964.

————. "The Middle Way in Maimonides' Ethics." *Proceedings of American Academy for Jewish Research* 54 (1987):31–72.

Deane, H. A. *The Political and Social Ideas of St. Augustine.* New York, 1966.

DeGrazia, S. *Machiavelli in Hell.* Princeton, 1988.

Donaldson, P. S. *Machiavelli and Mystery of State.* New York, 1988.

Dvornik, F. *Early Christian and Byzantine Political Philosophy—Origins and Background.* Vol. 1. Washington, DC, 1966.

Efros, I. "Palquera's 'Reshit Hokhmah' and Al-Farabi's 'Ihsa al-Ulum.'" *Jewish Quarterly Review* 25 (1934–35):227–35.

Federbush, S. *Mishpat ha-Melukhah be-Israel.* Jerusalem, 1952.

Fox, M. "The Doctrine of the Mean in Aristotle and Maimonides: A Comparative Study." In *Studies in Jewish Religious and Intellectual History.* Edited by S. Stern and R. Loewe, 93–120. London, 1979. Reprinted in J. A. Buijs, ed., *Maimonides—A Collection of Critical Essays*, 234–66. South Bend, Indiana, 1988.

Frank, D. H. "The End of the Guide: Maimonides on the Best Life for Man." *Judaism* 34 (1985):485–95.

————. "Humility as a Virtue: A Maimonidean Critique of Aristotle's Ethics." *Studies in Philosophy and History of Philosophy* 19 (1989):89–99.

————. "Anger as a Vice: A Maimonidean Critique of Aristotle's Ethics." *History of Philosophy Quarterly* 7 (1990):269–81.

Frimer, N. E., and D. Schwartz. *Hagut be-Zel ha-Aimah.* Jerusalem, 1992.

Funkenstein, A. "A Schedule for the End of the World." In *Vision of Apocalypse, End or Rebirth.* Edited by S. Friedlander et al. New York, 1985.

————. "Maimonides: Political Theory and Realistic Messianism." *Miscellanea Medievalia*, 81–103. Berlin and New York, 1977.

————. "Demut ha-shalit be-hagut ha-yehudit be-shalhei yemei ha-beinayim." In his *Tadmit ve-Toda'ah Historit be-Yahadut u-be-Sevivata ha-Tarbutit*, 182–87. Tel Aviv, 1991.

Galston, M. "Philosopher King Versus Prophet." *Israel Oriental Studies* 8 (1978):204–18.

———. "Realism and Idealism in Avicenna's Political Philosophy." *The Review of Politics* 41 (1979):561–77.

———. *Politics and Excellence: The Political Philosophy of Alfarabi.* Princeton, 1990.

Gilbert, A. H. *Machiavelli's 'Prince' and Its Forerunners.* Durham, 1938.

Gilbert, F. "On Machiavelli's Idea of Virtu'." *Renaissance News* 4 (1951):53–55.

———. *Machiavelli and Guicciardiai.* Princeton, 1965.

———. "Machiavelli's 'Discorsi.'" In his *History, Choice and Commitment,* 115–33. Cambridge, MA, 1977.

———. "The Humanist Concept of the Prince and 'The Prince' of Machiavelli." In his *History, Choice and Commitment,* 91–114. Cambridge, MA, 1977.

Goitein, S. D. "Attitudes Towards Government in Islam and Judaism." In his *Studies in Islamic History and Institutions,* 197–213. Leiden, 1968. Hebrew version: "Hayahas la-shilton ba-Islam u-ba-Yahadut." *Tarbiz* 19–20 (1959):153–59.

Goldman, E. "Ha-avodah ha-meyuhedet shel massigei ha-amitot." *Sefer Bar-Ilan* 6 (1968):287–313.

Gombrich, E. H. "Renaissance and Golden Age." In his *Norm and Form: Studies in the Art of the Renaissance,* 29–34. London and New York.

Goodman, L. E. "Ibn Bajjah." In *History of Islamic Philosophy.* Edited by O. Leaman and S. H. Nasr, 1:294–312. London, 1993.

Guttman, J. "'Yerushalayim' le-Mendelson ve 'Ha-Masekhet ha-teologit-medinit' le-Spinoza." In his *Dat u-Madah.* Translated by S. Ash, 192–217. Jerusalem, 1969.

Gutwirth, E. "Duran on Ahitophel: The Practice of Jewish History in Late Medieval Spain." *Jewish History* 4 (1989):59–74.

———. "El Gobernador Judio Ideal: Acerca de un sermon Inedito de Yosef Ibn Shem Tob." *Congreso Internacional Encuentro Tres Culturas.* Vol. 3:67–75. Toledo, 1988.

Hale, J. R. *Machiavelli and Renaissance Italy.* London, 1961.

Halevi, A. A. "Mishpat ha-melekh (min ha-hagut ha-medinit ba-olam ha-atik be-Israel u-ba-amim)." *Tarbiz* 38 (1969):225–30.

Halkin, A. "Classical and Arabic Material in Aknin's 'Hygiene of the Soul.'" *Proceedings of the American Academy for Jewish Research* 15 (1944):25–147.

Hankins, J. *Plato in the Italian Renaissance.* Leiden, 1991.

Hannaford, I. "Machiavelli's Concept of Virtu' in 'The Prince' and 'The Discourses' Reconsidered." *Political Studies* 22 (1972):185–89.

Hartman, D. "Maimonides' Approach to Messianism and its Contemporary Implications." *Da'at* 1 (1978):5–33.

———. *Crisis and Leadership: Epistles of Maimonides.* Philadelphia, 1985.

Harvey, S. "Maimonides in the Sultan's Palace." In *Perspectives on Maimonides*. Edited by J. L. Kraemer, 47–75. Oxford, 1991.

Harvey, Z. "Bein filosofia medinit le-halakhah be-mishnat ha-Rambam." *Iyyun* 29 (1980):198–212.

———. "Spinoza mul ha-nevi'im be-she'elat bikoret ha-shilton." *Kivunim* 12 (1981):83–90.

Hayoun, M. R. "Moshe Narboni ve-Ibn Bajja." *Da'at* 18 (1989):27–44.

———. "Ibn Bajja u-Moshe Narboni: 'Iggeret ha-Petirah.'" *Da'at* 25 (1990):93–125. French version: "Ibn Bajja et Moise de Narbonne: 'Iggeret ha-Petirah.'" In *Alei Shefer: Studies in the Literature of Jewish Thought*. Edited by M. Hallamish, 75–93. Ramat Gan, 1990.

Heller-Wilensky, S. O. "'Le she'elat mehabro shel sefer 'Sha'ar ha-Shamayim' ha-meyuhas le-Ibn Ezra." *Tarbiz* 32 (1963):277–95.

———. "Le-heker ha-mekorot shel Ibn Latif." *Proceedings of the Fourth World Congress of Jewish Studies*. Vol. 2:317–25. Jerusalem, 1965.

———. "Isaac Ibn Latif: Philosopher or Kabbalist?" In *Jewish Medieval and Renaissance Studies*. Edited by A. Altmann, 185–223. Harvard, 1967.

Jospe, R. *Torah and Sophia: The Life and Thought of Shem Tov Ibn Falaquera*. Cincinnati, 1988.

———. "Rejecting Moral Virtues as the Ultimate End." In *Studies in Islamic and Judaic Traditions*. Edited by W. Brinner and S. D. Ricks, 185–204. Denver, 1986. Hebrew version: "Shelilat ma'alot ha-middot ke-takhlit ha-adam." *Jerusalem Studies in Jewish Thought* 5 (1986):93–113.

———. *What Is Jewish Philosophy?* Tel Aviv, 1988.

Kasher, H. "Mashma'o shel heth Mosheh be-mishnat ha-Rambam." *Proceedings of the American Academy for Jewish Research* 53 (1986):29–34.

———. "Hitmakdut be-yahid o be-yahad iyyun mashveh hein R. Yehuda ha-Levi u-bein ha-Rambam." *Iyyun* 37 (1988):238–46.

———. "The Meaning of Moses' Sin in Maimonides' Doctrine." PAAJR 53 (1986):29–34.

Kantorowicz, E. H. "'Pro Patria Mori' in Medieval Political Thought," *American Historical Review* 56 (1951):472–92.

Kellner, M. *Maimonides on Human Perfection*. Atlanta, 1990.

———. "Maimonides and Samuel ibn Tibbon on Jeremiah 9:22–23 and Human Perfection." In *Studies in Halakhah and Jewish Thought Presented to M. E. Rackman*. Edited by M. Beer, 49–57. Ramat Gan, 1994.

———. *Maimonides on the 'Decline of the Generations' and the Nature of Rabbinic Authority*. Albany, 1996.

Klein-Braslavy, S. "Perushei ha-Rambam le-halom ha-sulam shel Ya'akov." *Sefer Bar Ilan* 22–23 (1988):329–49.

Klibansky, R. *The Continuity of the Platonic Tradition During the Middle Ages.* London, 1981.

Kontos, A. "Success and Knowledge in Machiavelli." In *The Political Calculus: Essays on Machiavelli's Philosophy.* Edited by A. Paul. Toronto and Buffalo, 1972.

Kraemer, J. "Al-Farabi's 'Opinions of the Virtuous City' and Maimonides' 'Foundation of the Law.'" In *Studia Orientalia, Memoriae D. H. Baneth Dedicata.* Edited by J. Blau et al., 107–53. Jerusalem, 1979.

———. "On Maimonides' Messianic Posture." In *Studies in Medieval Jewish History and Literature.* Edited by I. Twersky, 109–42. Vol. 2. Cambridge, MA, 1984.

———. "'Namus' ve-'sharia' be-mishnat ha-Rambam." *Teudah 4* (1986):183–202.

———. "The *Jihad* of the Falasifa." *Jerusalem Studies in Arabic and Islam* 10 (1987):289–324.

Kreisel, H. "Hakham ve-Navi be-mishnat ha-Rambam u-benei hugo." *Eshel Beer Sheva* 3 (1986):149–69.

———. *Maimonides' Political Thought.* Albany, 1999.

Kristeller, P. O. *Renaissance Thought and Its Sources.* New York, 1979.

Lambton, A. K. S. "The Theory of Kingship in the 'Nasihat al-Muluk' of Ghazali." *Islamic Quarterly* 1 (1954):47–55.

———. "Al-Farabi: The Good City." In *State and Government in Medieval Islam.* Oxford, 1981.

———. *State and Government in Medieval Islam.* Oxford, 1981.

Leibowitz, Y. Sihot al 'Shemonah Perakim' le-Rambam. Jerusalem, 1986.

Leaman, O. "Ibn Bajja on Society and Philosophy." *Der Islam* 57 (1980):109–19.

Lerner, R. "Maimonides." In *History of Political Philosophy.* Edited by L. Strauss and J. Cropsey, 181–200. Chicago, 1969.

———. "Maimonides' Governance of the Solitary." In *Perspectives on Maimonides.* Edited by J. L. Kraemer, 33–46. Oxford, 1991.

Levinger, J. "Nevuat Mosheh Rabenu." In his *Ha-Rambam ke-Filosof u-Posek,* 29–38. Jerusalem, 1989.

Lewis, B. *History: Remembered, Recovered, Invented.* Princeton, 1975.

Macy, J. "The Rule of Law and the Rule of Wisdom in Plato, Al-Farabi and Maimonides." *Studies in Islamic and Judaic Traditions.* Edited by W. M. Brinner and S. D. Ricks, 205–21. Denver, 1986.

Mahdi, M. "The *Editio Princeps* of Farabi's '*Compedium Legum Platonis.*'" *Journal of Near Eastern Studies* 20 (1961):1–15.

———. "Al-Farabi's Enumeration of the Sciences." In *The Cultural Context of Medieval Learning.* Edited by J. Murdoch, 113–47. Dordrecht, 1973.

———. "Remarks on Al-Farabi's Attainment of Happiness." In *Essays in Islamic Philosophy and Science.* Edited by G. H. Hourani, 47–66. Albany, 1975.

———. "Al-Farabi." In *History of Political Philosophy*. Edited by L. Strauss and J. Cropsey, 160–80. Chicago, 1969.

———. "Al-Farabi et Averroes: Remarque sur le Commentaire d'Averroes sur la 'Republique' de Platon." *Multiple Averroes*. Paris, 1978):91–101.

Malter, H. "Shem Tov ben Joseph Palquera." *Jewish Quarterly Review*, n. s. 2 (1910):151–81.

Marmura, M. E. "The Philosopher and Society: Some Medieval Arabic Discussions." *Arab Studies Quarterly* 1(1979):309–23.

McShea, R. J. *The Political Philosophy of Spinoza*. New York, 1968.

Melamed, A. "Ha-mahashavah ha-Medinit ba-filosofia ha-yehudit ba-renesans ha-italki." 2 Vols. Ph.D. diss., Tel Aviv University, 1976.

———. "Retorica ve-filosofia be sefer 'Nofet Zufim' le-Rabbi Yehudah Messer Leon." *Italia* 1 (1978):7–38.

———. "Motar ha-adam ba-mahashavah ha-yehudit be-Sefarad u-be-Italia be-yemei ha-beinayim ha-me'uharim u-ba-renesans." *Italia* 3 (1982):39–88.

———. "Yohanan Alemanno al hitpathut ha-hevrah ha-enoshit. " *Proceedings of the Eighth World Congress of Jewish Studies*. Vol. 3:85–93. Jerusalem, 1982.

———. "The Myth of Venice in Italian Renaissance Jewish Thought." *Italia Judaica* I. Rome (1983):401–13.

———. "Al yithalal: Perushim filosofiim le-Yirmiahu 9:22–23 ba-mahashavah ha-yehudit be-yemei ha-beinayim ve-ha-Renesans." *Jerusalem Studies in Jewish Thought* 4 (1985):31–82.

———. "Hebrew Medieval and Early Modern Encyclopedias." *Rivista di storia della filosofia* 40 (1985):91–112. Revised and Reprinted in *The Hebrew Encyclopedias of Science and Philosophy*. Edited by S. Harvey, 441–64. Dordrecht, 2000.

———. "Hok ha-teva ba-mashavah ha-yehudit be-yemei ha-beinayim ve-ha-rene-sans." *Da'at* 17 (1986):49–66.

———. "Ha-diyyun ha-medini be-'Malmad ha-Talmidim' le-Ya'acov Anatoli." *Da'at* 20 (1988):91–115.

———. "Simone Luzzatto on Tacitus: Apologetica and Ragione di Stato." In *Studies in Medieval Jewish History and Literature*. Vol. 2. Edited by I. Twersky, 143–70. Cambridge, MA, 1984.

———. "The Hebrew 'Laudatio' of Yohanan Alemanno—In Praise of Lorenzo il Magnifico and the Florentine Constitution." In *Jews in Italy: Studies Dedicated to the Memory of U. Cassuto*. Edited by H. Beinart, 1–34. Jerusalem, 1988.

———. "Jethro's Advice in Medieval and Early Modern Jewish and Christian Political Thought." *Jewish Political Studies Review* 2 (1990):3–41.

———. "Machiavelli al avot ha-ummah ha-Ivrit: degem le-manhigut politit." *Proceedings of the Eleventh World Congress of Jewish Studies*. Vol. 2:338–44. Jerusalem, 1990.

———. "Ha-Rambam al tiv'o ha-medini shel ha-adam: zerahim u-mehuyaviot." In *Minha Le-Sara: Studies Dedicated to S. O. Heller-Wilensky*. Edited by M. Idel et al., 292–333. Jerusalem, 1994.

———. "Eretz Israel ve-ha-teoria ha-aklimit ba-mahashavah ha-Yehudit." *Eretz Israel ba-Hagut ha-Yehudit b-Yemei ha-Beinayim*. Edited by M. Halamish and A. Ravitzky, 52–78. Jerusalem, 1991.

———. "Abravanel ve-ha-'Politikah' Le-Aristo." *Da'at*, 29 (1992):69–81. The English version: Isaac Abravanel and Aristotle's Politics: A Drama of Errors." *Jewish Political Studies Review* 5 (1993):55–75.

———. "Ha-'Politikah' le-Aristo ba-mahashavah ha-Yehudit be-yemei ha-beinayim ve-ha-renesans." *Pe'amim* 5 (1993):55–75.

———. "Elia del Medigo ve-ha-masoret ha-medinit ha-Aplatonit ba-renesans." *Italia* 11 (1995):57–76.

———. "Medieval and Renaissance Jewish Political Philosophy." In *History of Jewish Philosophy*. Edited by D. Frank and O. Leaman, 415–49. London and New York, 1998.

Mesch, B. "Joseph Ibn Caspi, Fourteenth-Century Philosopher and Exegete." Ph.D. diss., Brandeis University, 1972.

Mohl, R. *The Three Estates in Medieval and Renaissance Literature*. New York, 1933.

Motzkin, A. L. "On Halevi's 'Kuzari' as a Platonic Dialogue." *Interpretation* 9 (1980–81):111–24.

———. "Elia del Madigo, Averroes, and Averroism." *Italia* 6 (1987):7–19.

Nehorai, M. Z. "Ba'ayat ha-nes ezel ha-Rambam." In *Sefer ha-Yovel le-Shlomo Pines*. Vol. 2. Edited by M. Idel et al., 1–18. Jerusalem, 1990.

Netanyahu, B. *Don Isaac Abravanel: Statesman and Philosopher*. Philadelphia, 1972.

Novak, B. C. "Giovanni Pico della Mirandola and Jochanan Alemanno." *Journal of the Warburg and Courtauld Institutes* 45 (1982):125–47.

Osterich, G. *Neo-Stoicism and the Early Modern State*. Cambridge, 1982.

Parel, A., ed. *The Political Calculus: Essays on Machiavelli's Philosophy*. Toronto and Buffalo, 1972.

Pines, S. "Le-heker torato ha-medinit shel Ibn Rushd." *IYYUN* 8 (1957):65–83. Reprinted in his *Bein Mahashevet Yisrael le-Mahashevet ha-Amim*, 84–102. Jerusalem, 1977.

———. "The Philosophic Sources of the 'Guide of the Perplexed.'" *Moses Maimonides, The Guide of the Perplexed*. Edited, translated, introduction, and notes by S. Pines, introductory essay by L. Strauss. Vol. 1:lvii–cxxxiv. Chicago, 1963. Hebrew version: "Ha-mekorot ha-filosofi'im shel 'Moreh Nevukhim.'" In his *Bein Mahashevet Yisrael le-Mahashevet ha-Amim*, 103–73. Jerusalem, 1977.

———. "Aristotle's Politics in Arabic Philosophy." *Israel Oriental Studies* 5 (1975):150–60. Reprinted in his *The Collected Works of Sh. Pines Vol. II—Studies in Arabic Versions of Greek Texts and Medieval Science*, 146–56. Leiden, 1986.

――――. "The Limitations of Human Knowledge According to Al-Farabi, Ibn Bajja and Maimonides." In *Studies in Medieval Jewish History and Literature*. Edited by I. Twersky. Vol. 1:82–109. Cambridge, MA, 1979. Reprinted in J. A. Buijs, ed. *Maimonides: A Collection of Critical Essays*, 91–121. South Bend, IN, 1988.

――――. "Al sugiyot ahadot ha-kellulot be-sefer 'Ezer ha-Dat' le-Isaac Polkar ve-tikbolot lahen ezel Spinoza." In *Mehkarim be-Kabbalah, be-Filosofia Yehudit u-be-Sifrut ha-Musar ve-ha-Hagut Mugashim le-Y. Tishbi*. Edited by Y. Dan et al., 405–44. Jerusalem, 1986.

Pitkin, H. F. *Fortune Is a Woman, Gender and Politics in the Thought of Machiavelli*. Berkeley, 1984.

Plamenatz, J. *Man and Society*. London, 1972.

――――. "In Search of Machiavellian *Virtu*'." In *The Political Calculus, Essays on Machiavelli's Philosophy*. Edited by A. Paul. Toronto and Buffalo, 1972.

Plessner, M. "Hashivuto shel R. Shem Tov Ibn Falaquera le-heker toledot ha-filosofia." *Homenage a Millas Vallicorosa*. Vol. 2:161–84. Barcelona, 1956.

Pocock, J. G. A. *The Machiavellian Moment*. Princeton, 1975.

Polish, D. "Some Medieval Thinkers on the Jewish King." *Judaism* 20 (1971):323–29.

――――. "Rabbinic Views on Kingship—A Study in Jewish Sovereignty." *Jewish Political Studies Review* 3 (1991):67–90.

――――. *Give Us a King: Legal-Religious Sources of Jewish Sovereignty*. Hoboken, New Jersey, 1989.

Preus, J. S. "Machiavelli's Functional Analysis of Religion: Context and Object." *Journal of the History of Ideas* 61 (1979):171–90.

Price, R. "The Senses of Virtu' in Machiavelli." *European Studies Review* 3 (1973):315–45.

Rava, A. "Spinoza e Machiavelli." *Studi filosofico—giuridici*. 2:299–313. Modena, 1931.

Ravid, B. C. I. *Economics and Toleration in Seventeenth-Century Venice: The Background and Context of the 'Discorso' of Simone Luzzatto*. Jerusalem, 1978.

Ravidowitz, S. "Perek be-torat ha-musar le-Rambam." In *M. M. Kaplan Jubilee Vol:* 205–35. New York, 1953.

Ravitzky, A. "R. Shmuel Ibn Tibbon and the Esoteric Character of the 'Guide of the Perplexed.'" *AJS Review* 6 (1981):87–123. Hebrew version: "R. Shemuel Ibn Tibbon ve-sodo shel 'Moreh Nevukhim.'" *Da'at* 10–11 (1983):19–45.

――――. "Yemot ha-mashiah be-mishnat ha-Rambam." In *Meshihiyut ve-Escatologia*. Edited by Z. Baras, 191–220. Jerusalem, 1984. English version: "To the Utmost of Human Capacity: Maimonides on the Days of the Messiah." In *Perspectives on Maimonides*. Edited by J. L. Kraemer, 221–56. Oxford, 1991.

――――. "Kings and Laws in Late Medieval Jewish Thought (Nissim of Gerona vs. Isaac Abravanel)." In *Scholars and Scholarship: The Interaction between Judaism and Other Cultures*. Edited by L. Landman. New York, 1990. Hebrew version: "Al

Melakhim u-mishpatim be-hagut ha-yehudit be-yemei ha-beinayim." In *Tarbut ve-Hevrah be-Toledot Israel be-Yemei ha-Beinayim.* Edited by R. Bonfil et al., 469–91. Jerusalem, 1989.

Regev, S. "Le-ba'ayat limud ha-filosofia be-hagut ha-me'ah ha-15." *Da'at* 16 (1986):57–85.

Rees, D. A. "The Classification of Goods in Plato and Aristotle." In *Islamic Philosophy and the Classical Tradition.* Edited by S. M. Stern et al., 327–36. Columbia, SC, 1972.

Reines, A. J. "Abravanel on Prophecy in the 'Moreh Nebukhim,'" *Hebrew Union College Annual* 31 (1960):107–35.

———. "Maimonides' Concept of Miracles." *Hebrew Union College Annual* 46 (1975):243–87.

Robinson, S. B. "Medinat Israel ha-tanakhit be-torat medinah le-dugmah be-kitveihem shel hogei de'ot politi'im ba-me'ot ha-16–18." In his *Hinuch bein Hemshekhyut le-Petihut,* 13–69. Jerusalem, 1975.

Rosen, S. "Spinoza." In *History of Political Philosophy.* Edited by L. Strauss and J. Cropsey, 413–32. Chicago, 1969.

Rosenthal, E. I. J. "Maimonides' Conception of State and Society." In *Moses Maimonides.* Edited by I. Epstein, 191–206. London, 1935. Reprinted in his *Studia Semitica* 1. Cambridge, 1971):275–89.

———. "On the Knowledge of Plato's Philosophy in the Islamic World," *Islamic Culture* 14 (1940):387–422.

———. "Some Aspects of the Hebrew Monarchy." *Journal of Jewish Studies* 9 (1958):1–18. Reprinted in his *Studia Islamica.* Vol. 1:3–20. Cambridge, 1971.

———. "Some Aspects of Islamic Political Thought." *Islamic Culture* 22 (1948):1–17. Reprinted in his: *Studia Islamica.* Vol. 2:17–33. Cambridge, 1971.

———. "The Concept of 'Eudaimonia' in Medieval Islamic and Jewish Philosophy." *Studia della Filosofia antica e Medievale (atti del XII Congresso di Filosofia, 1958).* 145–52. Florence, 1960. Reprinted in his: *Studia Islamica.* Vol. 2:127–34. Cambridge, 1971.

———. "Some Observations on the Philosophical Theory of Prophecy in Islam." In *Melanges Henri Masse.* Edited by A. Akar Siassi, 343–53. Teheran, 1963. Reprinted in his *Studia Islamica.* Vol. 2:135–44. Cambridge, 1971.

———. *Political Thought in Medieval Islam.* Cambridge, 1968.

———. "Some Observations on Yohanan Alemanno's Political Ideas." In *Studies in Jewish Religious and Intellectual History.* Edited by S. Stern and R. Loewe, 247–61. London, 1979.

———. "Political Ideas in Moshe Narboni's Commentary on Ibn Tufail's 'Hayy Ben Yaqzan.'" In *Hommage a G. Vajda.* Edited by G. Nahon and Ch. Touati, 227–34. Louvain, 1980.

Rosenthal, F. *The Muslim Concept of Freedom*. Leiden, 1960.

———. *The Classical Heritage in Islam*. 109–16. London, 1973.

Rotenstreich, N. "Mendelson ve-ha-ra'ayon ha-medini." In *M. M. Kaplan Jubilee Volume*. 237–47. New York, 1953.

Rotter, I. "The Islamic Sources of Maimonides' Political Philosophy." *Gesher* 7 (1979):182–204.

Rubinstein, N. "Political Theories of the Renaissance." In *The Renaissance—Essays in Interpretation*. Edited by A. Chastel, 153–200. London and New York, 1982.

Safran, B. "Maimonides and Aristotle on Ethical Theory." In *Alei Shefer: Studies in the Literature of Jewish Thought*. Edited by M. Hallamish, 75–93. Ramat Gan, 1990.

Sankari, F. A. "Plato and Al-Farabi: A Comparison of Some of Their Political Philosophies." *The Muslim World* 60 (1970):218–25.

Sarfatti, G. "Ha-targumim ha-ivri'im shel 'Minian ha-Madayim' le Al-Farabi." *Sefer Bar Ilan* 1 (1972):413–20.

Schwarzschild, S. S. "Moral Radicalism and 'Middlingness' in the Ethics of Maimonides." *Studies in Medieval Culture* 11 (1977):65–94.

Schweid, E. *Iyyunim be-'Shemoneh Perakim' le-Rambam*. Jerusalem, 1968.

———. "Omanut ha-dialoge he-Sefer ha-Kuzari u-mashma'uta ha-iyyunit. In *Ta'am ve-Hakashah*. Ramat Gan, 1970.

Seigel, J. E. *Rhetoric and Philosophy in Renaissance Humanism*. Princeton, 1968.

Septimus, B. "Biblical Religion and Political Rationality in Simone Luzzatto, Maimonides and Spinoza." In *Jewish Thought in the Seventeenth Century*. Edited by I. Twersky, 399–435. Cambridge, MA, 1987.

Shapiro, D. S. "The Doctrine of the Image of God and Imitatio Dei." *Judaism* 12 (1963):57–77.

Shervani, H. K. "Al-Farabi's Political Theories." *Islamic Culture* 12 (1938):288–305.

Shifman, Y. "Ibn Bajja ke-makor le-Perush shel Falaquera le-'Moreh Nevukim.' III:51, 54." *Tarbiz* 60(1991):224–35.

Sinclair, T. A. *A History of Greek Political Thought*. London, 1967.

Sirat, C. "Ra'ayonot polit'im shel Nissim ben Moshe me-Marsei." In *Sefer ha-Yovel le Shlomo Pines*. Edited by M. Idel et al., 2:53–76. Jerusalem, 1990.

Skinner, G. *Machiavelli*. Oxford, 1981.

Smoler, L., and M. Auerbach. "Ha-melukhah be-hashkafat olamo shel Abravanel," *Hagut Ivrit be-America*. Vol. 2:134–57. Tel Aviv, 1972.

Sneor, T. Blay. "Mishlei Melech ha-hagut ha-yehudit bi-yemei ha-beinayim." Master's thesis, University of Haifa, 1990.

Steinschneider, M. *Al-Farabi*. St. Petersburg, 1869.

Strauss, Leo. *Philosophy and Law.* Translated by F. Bauman. Forward by R. Lerner. Philadelphia, 1987.

———. "Quelques Remarques sur la Science Politique de Maimonide et de Farabi." *Revue des Études Juives* 100 (1936):1–37.

———. "On Abravanel's Philosophical Tendency and Political Teaching." In *Isaac Abravanel, Six Lectures.* Edited by B. Trend and H. Loewe, 95–129. Cambridge, 1937.

———. "Farabi's Plato." In *Louis Ginsburg Jubilee Volume.* 357–93. New York, 1945. Reprinted in *Essays in Medieval Jewish and Islamic Philosophy.* Edited by A. Hyman, 391–427. New York, 1977.

———. "How Farabi Read Plato's *Laws.*" In his *What is Political Philosophy?* 7–63. Chicago, 1969.

———. "Eine Vermisste Schrift Farabis." *MGWJ* 80 (1936):96–106.

Sunberg, T. A. "Castruccio Castracani." *Interpretation* 16 (1988–89):285–93.

Teicher, J. L. Review of Rosenthal's "Averroes on Plato's Republic." *Journal of Semitic Studies* V (1960):176–95.

Tirosh-Rothschild, H. "Filosofia medinit be-mishnat Avraham Shalom: ha-masoret ha-Aplatonit." In *Sefer ha-Yovel le-Shlomo Pines.* Edited by M. Idel et al. Jerusalem, 1990.

Twersky, I. "Ha-Rambam ve-Eretz Israel," In *Tarbut ve-Hevrah be-Toledot Yisrael be-Yemei ha-Beinayim.* Edited by R. Bonfil et al., 353–81. Jerusalem, 1989. English version: "Maimonides and Eretz Israel: Halakhic, Philosophic and Historical Perspectives." In *Perspectives on Maimonides.* Edited by J. L. Kraemer, 256–94. Oxford, 1991.

———. "Sefer 'Mishneh Torah' le-Rambam: megamato ve-tafkido." *Divrei ha-Accademiah ha-Israelit le-Mada'im* 5. Jerusalem, 1962.

Urbach, E. *The Sages.* Jerusalem, 1975.

Walzer, M. "Exodus 32 and the Theory of Holy War: The History of a Citation." *Harvard Theological Review* 61 (1968):1–14.

———. "Exodus 32 and the Theory of Holy War, The History of a Citation." *HTR* 61 (1968):1–14.

Walzer, R. "Arabic Transmission of Greek Thought to Medieval Europe." *Bulletin of the John Rylands Library* 29 (1945):164–83.

———. "Aspects of Islamic Political Thought: Al-Farabi and Ibn Xaldun." *Oriens* 16 (1963):40–60.

———. *Greek into Arabic.* Oxford, 1963.

Weinberg, J. "The Quest for Philo in Sixteenth-Century Jewish Historiography." In *Jewish History: Essays in Honour of Chimen Abramskyi.* Edited by A. Rapoport-Albert and S. J. Zipperstein, 163–87. London, 1988.

Weinstein, D. "Machiavelli and Savonarola," In *Studies on Machiavelli*. Edited by M. P. Gilmore, 251–64. Florence, 1972.

Weiss, R. L. "The Adaptation of Philosophic Ethics to a Religious Community: Maimonides' 'Eight Chapters.'" *Proceedings of the American Academy of Jewish Research* 54 (1987):261–87.

Whitfield, J. H. "Machiavelli's Use of 'Ordini.'" In *The Prince*. Edited by R. M. Adams, 194–206. New York, 1977.

Wilcox, D. *The Development of Florentine Humanist Historiography in the Fifteenth Century*. Cambridge, MA, 1969.

Winiarski, W. "Machiavelli." In *History of Political Philosophy*. Edited by L. Strauss and J. Cropsey, 247–76. Chicago, 1969.

Wolfson, H. A. *Philo*. Cambridge, Mass., 1962.

Wood, Neal. "Machiavelli's Concept of Virtu' Reconsidered." *Political Studies* 15 (1967):159–72.

———. "Machiavelli's Humanism of Action." In *The Political Calculus: Essays on Machiavelli's Philosophy*. Edited by A. Paul. Toronto and Buffalo, 1972.

Index

Abel, 65–66
Abraham, 6, 108–109, 139
Abravanel Isaac, xv, 6, 9, 10, 48, 49,
   55–56, 60, 62–63, 67–74, 101,
   108, 111, 113–122, 130, 134, 137,
   145, 147, 148, 172, 185, 193,
   219n.31, 219–220n.34
Absalom, 172
Active intellect, 18, 77, 96, 117
Adam, 29, 48, 67, 113
Adams' three sons, 62, 63, 65–66, 73,
   74, 217–218n.22, 218n.26, 219n.29
Aegidius Romanus, 204n.14
Ahab, 133, 142
Ahitophel, 172–173
Albertus Magnus, 3
Albo, Joseph, 2, 6, 56, 66, 111, 125,
   134–139, 194–195, 204n.14,
   218n.25
   Sefer ha-Ikkarim (Book of Principles), 2,
      134–139, 194–195, 204n.14
Alemmano, Yohanan, xiv, xv, 6, 10, 48,
   49, 53–54, 58, 60, 62, 66, 70, 93,
   101–109, 111, 113, 122–125, 130,
   132, 134, 137, 145, 147, 185,
   201n.4, 213n.97, 213–214n.98,
   218n.26
   Hai ha-Olamim (Eternal Life), xiv, xv,
      101–109, 123, 137, 201n.5
   *Heshek Shelomo (The Passion of
      Solomon)*, 122–123
   *Shir ha-Ma'alot li-Shelomo (The
      Song of Solomon's Ascents)*, 122–125
Alexander the Great, 24, 174, 180

Al-Farabi, 2, 4–7, 10, 16–19, 26, 38, 40,
   44–45, 46, 47, 48, 49, 51, 69,
   75–87, 90–91, 93–96, 102, 106,
   111, 113–114, 116, 119, 120, 124,
   129, 133, 166, 167, 185, 189–191
   Aphorisms of the Statesman, 77, 90–91,
      189–190, 222n.9
   Civil Government, 17, 26
   On Attaining Happiness, 17, 18, 81
   The Philosophy of Plato and Aristotle, 5,
      77, 82, 86
   The Virtuous State, 5, 6, 17–18, 26, 48,
      75–81, 84, 94–96, 189–192
Althusius, 185
Amalek, 46, 135, 138
Amsterdam, 167
Anarchy, 8
Anatoli, Jacob, 48, 51–52, 56, 62, 63–66,
   218n.23
   Malmad ha-Talmidim (Student's Goad),
      51–52, 63–66
Anger, 101
Apologetics, 6, 111
Aquinas, Thomas, 141–143, 144, 146,
   149, 185
Aristocracy, 7, 142
Aristotle, Aristotelianism, xii, 1, 2, 4, 7,
   9–10, 17, 19, 24, 26, 38, 42, 48,
   51, 62, 63, 66, 67, 69, 100, 102,
   119, 133, 142, 144, 146, 147, 168,
   173, 185, 204n.14
   Metaphysics, 4
   Nicomachaean Ethics, 1, 4, 17, 19, 48,
      51, 58, 62, 66, 67, 142, 201n.5

Aristotle, Aristotelianism *(continued)*
The Politics, xii, 1, 2–3, 4, 17, 66, 102,
    142, 144, 147, 204n.14
Armed prophets, 157–158, 160, 166. *See
    also* Military functions (of the
    king), Holy War
Ascent and descent, 27–28, 34, 54–55
Ashkenazi Shaul ha-Cohen, 73
Athens, 13, 15, 72, 171
Augustine, 4, 157
Azulai, Abraham, 56, 62, 66, 67,
    221n.51

Balaam, 121
Barbaro, Ermalao, 71
Barker, E., xiii, 2, 61, 71
Barzillai the Gileadite, 138
Bath Sheba, 107, 135, 138
Ben Asher, Bahya, 9
Ben Israel, Menasseh, 167, 186
Ben Zeruiah, Yoav, 70–71
Berman, L.V., xiv, 27
Bibago, Abraham, 56, 62, 66, 218n.26
Bible, 7–8, 27, 46, 60, 61, 62, 71, 107,
    122, 132, 144, 147, 149, 152, 157,
    165. *See also* Torah
Borgia, Cesare, 172
Botero, Giovanni, 171
Bruni, Leonardo, 71
Byzantium, xiii

Cain, 65–66, 157
Calvin, 185
Canaan, 67
Carlyle, R. W., xiv
Castracani Castruccio, 155
Charles V, 143, 185
Christian political philosophy, xiv, 2,
    3–4, 9, 66, 71, 102, 141–149, 185
Christianity, xi–xii, 9, 51, 71, 112, 118
Cicero, 71, 144
Class System, 13–15, 16, 42, 51–52, 56,
    61–74
Commandments, 47, 138–139
Common people (common men, multi-
    tude, masses), 13–14, 28, 29, 33,

34, 35, 38, 43, 61–74, 83–84, 86,
    169, 170
Communalism, 16, 42, 61
Courage (might), 14, 41, 47, 66, 70–71,
    72, 74, 79, 95, 105, 210n.57
Cyrus, 150, 151, 155, 158

Daniel, 121
Dante, 166
David, 6, 8, 44, 47, 59, 106, 107, 108,
    111–112, 113, 121, 127–128, 129,
    131, 133, 135, 137–139, 142–143,
    144–145, 147, 149–150, 151,
    160–166, 172, 185
Defoe, Daniel, 58
Del Medigo, Eliah, 102
Delacrut, Mattathias, 221.n.51
Della Mirandola, Pico, 102
Democracy, 7, 13, 142, 176
Despotism, 8, 139, 147. *See also* Tyranny
Di Medici, Lorenzo, 102, 123
Diaspora, 6, 79, 111
Diogenes, 24, 173–174
Dionysius of Syracuse, 15, 24, 25, 141
Divine attributes (divine actions, thir-
    teen attributes), 6, 24, 27, 38–39,
    42, 96, 101, , 47–48, 54, 93, 104,
    109, 128, 170
Divine will, 60, 80, 85
Dogma, 3
Dukes, L., 7
Dunlop, D. M., 91, 222n.9

Economics, 120, 168
Efodi, 5, 55, 56
Egypt, 98, 115, 131, 152–155, 177–178,
    181
Eldad and Medad, 99, 115
Elijah, 25, 57
Elisha, 121
Emanation, 34–35, 40–41, 45, 77, 96,
    117, 121–122, 128
Emancipation, 187
Enlightenment, xi, xii, 6, 172,
    186–187
Enoch, 25

Erasmus of Rotterdam, 130, 142–149,
166, 174, 185
Exilarchs, 8–9
Exodus, 153

Falasifa, 20, 201n.6
Ficino, 70, 102, 123
Florence, 101–102, 185
Frederick II, 240n.85

Generally accepted opinions, 83–84, 86
Geonim, 8–9
Gerondi, Nissim, 100
Gibeon, dream at, 112, 118, 122,
123–124, 130, 144–146
Gideon, 8
Goitein, S. D., 201n.6
Goliath, 138, 162
Good, 124–125
Governance of the solitary (solitary life,
solitude, seclusion, isolation), 5,
28–34, 38, 42, 48–60, 67, 97,
213n.85
Greece, 6, 150–151, 171
Guardians, 13–14, 62–63, 66, 68, 69,
70–71

Halakhah, 6, 7–11, 24, 26, 39, 42, 46,
63, 93, 107, 108, 116, 130, 132,
135, 136, 138, 210n.59
Halevi, Judah, 5, 24–26, 28
Hameiri, Menahem, 9, 62
Hankins, J., xii
Hannibal, 71, 150
Harrington James, 185
Hellenistic philosophy, xi–xiii, 1, 16–17
Hierarchy, 63–65, 116
Hillel ben Samuel of Verona, 228n.23
Hobbes, Thomas, 185
Holy War (Jihad, Milhemet mitzvah),
79, 86, 90, 91
Humanism, 71, 102, 123, 169, 171

Ibn Bajja (Avempace), 1, 5, 19, 24, 29,
40, 48, 49, 50, 53, 56, 57, 58–60,
69, 97, 174, 201n.6, 213n.97

Ibn Bulat, Judah, 221n.51
Ibn Caspi, Joseph, 5, 9, 49, 55–56, 60,
62, 66, 214n.103
Ibn Ezra, Abraham, 9, 26, 58
Ibn Falaquera, Shemtov, 2, 5, 6, 48–50,
56, 59, 60, 63, 66, 75, 78, 81–87,
88, 89, 90, 91, 93, 95, 96, 102,
119, 120, 135, 190, 201n.4,
213n.85, 217–218n.22, 218n.23,
224n.32, 225–226n.38
Iggeret ha-Vikkuha (The Epistle of
the Debate), 49
Moreh ha-Moreh (Guide of the
Guite), 49
Reshit Hokhmah (beginning of
Wisdom), 2, 5, 49, 81–84, 85, 86,
119, 190, 223n.21
Sefer ha-Ma'alot (Book of Degrees) 5,
6, 49, 84–87, 91, 94, 96, 190
Ibn Latif, Isaac, xiv, 5, 7, 48, 75–81, 84,
85, 86, 87, 88, 89, 90, 91, 94, 95,
96, 189
Sha'ar ha-Shamayim (Gate of Heaven),
xiv, 5, 75–81, 189
Ibn Pakuda, Bahya, 9, 26
Ibn Rushd (Averroes), Averroism,
xii–xiii, xv, 2, 4–7, 10, 19–21, 42,
48, 51, 57, 60, 63, 69, 70, 72, 77,
82, 87–91, 93, 102–106, 111, 113,
123, 130, 167, 169, 174, 185, 190,
192–193, 201n.4, 204n.14
Commentary on Plato's Republic, xii–xiii,
2, 19–21, 60, 63, 70, 77, 82,
87–91, 93, 102–106
Epistle of Conjunction, 57
K. Fasl al-Maqal, 20–21
Ibn Shemtov, Joseph, 56–58, 60
Ibn Shemtov, Shemtov ben Joseph, 5,
49, 54–55, 56–57, 195–197,
215n.110, 216n.125
Ibn Sina, 58
Ibn Tibbon, Samuel, 5, 26, 49, 51,
53–54, 59
Ma'amar Yikkavu ha-Mayyim, 54
Ibn Tufayl, 53, 57, 58–60, 214n.98
Hayy Ibn Yaqzan, 58–60

Imagination. *See* Soul, Imaginative
Imam. *See* Priest
Imitation of God *(Imitatio Dei)*, 10, 16,
  27, 35–36, 38, 39, 40, 45, 48, 49,
  53, 65, 101, 104, 109, 127, 135,
  169–170, 171
Immanuel of Rome, 56, 62, 66,
  218n.23
Isaac, 121
Isaiah, 28, 44
Islam, Muslim culture, xi–xiii, xiv, 1,
  2–6, 9, 11, 16–21, 24, 26, 48, 66,
  75, 79, 91, 102, 107, 112, 118,
  141, 142, 173, 174

Jacob's dream, 27–28, 54–55, 56, 66
Jeremiah, 38, 40–42, 43, 54, 57, 59, 63,
  68, 72, 73, 74, 121, 127–128
Jerusalem, 133–134
Jesus, 4, 147, 149
Jethro, 7, 99, 113, 115, 142, 185
Joash, 133
Joshua, 108
Josiah, 133
Judea, kingdom of, 72, 107, 112, 162
Justice, 13–14, 65, 83, 86, 95, 149, 170,
  171

Kabbalah, 51, 57, 125
Khazar king, 23–25
Kimhi, David, 172
King of Israel, 6, 7–11, 93, 98–101,
  103–104, 105–109, 111–113,
  118–139, 141
Klibansky, R., 2, 201n.6
Knowledge (Classification of), 119–122
Korah, 60, 180

Law, 3, 18, 21, 28, 46, 69, 93–94, 98, 99,
  124, 126, 138, 162, 171–172,
  181–183
  Human law *(nomos)*, 18, 20, 46,
    204n.14
  Ideal (Perfect) law, 18, 20, 123, 133,
    134
  Natural law (Law of nature), 94

Revealed law (Divine law), 3, 18, 20,
  26, 28, 46, 93–94, 99, 117,
  126–127, 204n.14
Lawgiver (legislator), 2, 3, 16, 18, 19, 23,
  34, 40, 45, 48, 63, 69, 72, 73, 82,
  84, 88, 94, 102–103, 107, 111,
  133, 150, 153, 157, 158, 160, 169,
  171–172, 178, 182
Leaman, O., 201n.6
Lerner, R., xiv, 4, 202n.8
Lewis, E., xiv
Livy, 71, 144, 149
Luther, 143
Luzzatto, Simone, xv, 6, 149, 167–174,
  179, 186
  *Discorso (Discourse on the Jews in
    Venice)*, 167–174
  Socrate, 168, 173–174
Lycurgus, 156, 166, 169, 171

Machiavelli, Machiavellism, 6, 70, 112,
  135, 142, 144, 147, 149–166, 167,
  168, 170–171, 172, 174, 177–179,
  180, 181, 182, 185–186
  Discorsi (The discourses), 150–154,
    156–157, 158, 161
  Fortune *(Fortuna)*, 154, 159, 164
  Il Principe (The Prince), 149–166,
    185
  Necessity *(Necessità)*, 152–153
  Opportunity *(Occasione)*, 153–155
  virtù, 150–158, 161, 163, 164, 166
Mahdi, M., 3, 202n.8
Maimonides, Maimonidean, 5, 8, 10, 19,
  21, 26–60, 61, 62, 66, 79, 80, 81,
  83, 84, 88, 93, 94, 96–97, 98, 100,
  101, 106, 108–109, 112–113, 114,
  121, 126, 128, 129, 133, 136, 137,
  139, 166, 169, 171
  Book of Judges, 39
  Book of Knowledge, 30
  Commentary on the Mishnah (Avot),
    208n.34, 210n.63, 212–213n.85
  *Commentary on the Mishnah
    (Introduction to Perek Helek)*, 42,
    43, 112

Commentary on the Mishnah (Zera'im),
    33, 61
Eight Chapters, 30–31, 101, 108, 112
Guide to the Perplexed, 5, 21, 26–60, 81,
    84, 93–94, 97, 101, 112–113, 121,
    129, 166, 169
Hilkhot De'ot, 30, 31–32, 57
Hilkhot Melakhim, 8, 46, 79, 98, 106,
    112, 136, 137, 227n.22
Hilkhot Talmud Torah, 46, 210n.63
Hilkhot Teshuvah, 32, 33, 43, 44
Hilkhot Yesodei ha-Torah, 34, 39, 48
Mishneh Torah, 39, 42, 43, 48
Parable of the Blind Man, 27–28
Parable of the King's Palace, 28–29,
    38, 39, 46, 56
Mantinus, Jacob, 102
Memory, 14, 85, 88
Mendelssohn, Moses, 6, 186–187
Meribah, water of, 101, 107, 112
Messer, Leon Judah, 71
Messiah, Messianism, 4, 16, 27, 28, 42,
    43–44, 47, 79, 101, 112, 166, 183
Midas, 147
Middle way (middle course, path, road),
    49, 100–101
Middot, 77, 85, 94, 96, 135
Military functions (of the king), 46–47,
    86, 95, 117, 136–137, 153–154,
    157–158, 162, 166. *See also* Holy
    War, Armed prophets
Miracles, 60, 101, 181
Mirror of princes *(speculum principium)*,
    24, 25, 141, 166, 167, 174, 185,
    216n.125, 225n.38
Moab, 138
Monarchy, Monarchism, 7–11, 24, 46,
    107, 111, 114, 122, 132, 139, 142,
    148, 173, 176–177, 183
More, Thomas, 143, 149, 168, 173
Moses, xi, 4, 5, 6, 7, 8, 10, 23, 25, 27–28,
    29, 34, 36–38, 42, 44, 45, 46, 47,
    54, 60, 73, 93, 94, 95, 97–109,
    111–113, 113–118, 121, 124, 142,
    144, 147, 149, 150–161, 169,
    171–172, 178–183, 185, 186

Moses of Coucy, 9
Moses of Rieti, xii
Mount Sinai, 25, 28, 34, 114, 157, 158,
    168
Muhammad, 4, 5, 20
Multitude. *See* Common people

Nabal the Carmelite, 161
Nahmanides, 9
Narboni Moses, 58–60, 213n.97
Nathan, 138–139
Neoplatonism, 1, 16, 63, 185
Nero, 148
Nimrod, 109, 139
Noah, 67, 73, 74, 113
Nostalgia, 6

Paganism, 3, 107, 143, 151, 159, 160,
    166, 172
Patriarchs, 6, 37, 50, 59, 113, 121, 149,
    166
Peace, 120, 146–147, 163–134, 184, 183
Perfection, 29–30, 34–35, 38, 39, 40,
    41, 42, 44, 48, 49, 51, 58, 59, 61,
    66, 78–80, 83, 84–85, 93, 94–95,
    87, 96–97, 98–100, 102–106,
    113–118, 122, 124, 126, 128,
    134
  intellectual (rational, theoretical) 4, 14,
    16, 18, 26, 28, 38, 39, 40, 41, 42,
    43, 47, 48, 49, 51, 64, 76–77,
    78–80, 81, 82–84, 86, 88, 89, 90,
    91, 94–95, 96, 99–100, 113, 114,
    115, 117, 118–119, 122, 123, 128,
    134, 137, 166
  moral (ethical), 15–16, 28, 47, 49,
    78–80, 83–84, 86, 88, 89–90, 89,
    90, 91, 95, 99–100, 112, 113,
    114–115, 117, 120, 122, 128, 137,
    166
  physical, 47, 51, 78–79, 86, 91, 94–95,
    98–99, 102, 113–114, 117, 128
  rhetorical, 71, 78–79, 86, 89, 90, 91,
    95, 99, 100, 105
Philip of Macedon, 162
Philo of Alexandria, xi, 23, 66, 205n.2

Physician (of body and soul), 42, 97, 98, 120

Pines S., xiv, 20–21, 88

Plato, xi–xii, xiv, xv, 1, 2, 4, 5, 6, 7, 9–11, 13–21, 23, 24, 25, 26, 27, 33, 40, 42, 43, 44, 47, 48, 49, 51, 56, 57, 58, 60, 61–74, 75, 77, 79, 81, 83, 84, 86, 89–90, 91, 93, 94, 98, 102, 103–104, 106, 107, 109, 112, 120, 122, 123, 125, 127, 129, 132, 134–135, 137, 141, 142, 144, 145–146, 148, 153, 160, 163, 166, 167, 168, 169, 170, 173, 174, 185, 187, 204n.14

Apology, 15, 40

Laws, 1, 15, 102

Myth of the cave, 15, 27–28, 34, 53, 54

Noble lies, 160

Parmenides, 1, 2

Platonic love, 53

The Republic, xii, 1, 2, 5, 13–16, 18, 19, 48, 57, 90, 93, 58, 70, 73, 75, 77, 81, 83, 84, 102, 144, 145–146, 148

Theaetetus, 1, 16

Timaeus, 2

Plotinus, 17

Plutarch, 144

Political nature (of man), 29–34, 53, 93–94, 126

Political theology, xii, 3–4, 202n.8

Polkar Isaac, 5, 6, 10, 49, 52–53, 60, 93–101, 106, 108, 113, 114, 127, 132, 137, 138, 191–192

Ezer ha-Dat (Defence of the Law), 93–101, 191–192

Polybius, 7, 185

Portugal, 120

Powers of the Soul. See also Soul

growing power, 63–64

irascible power, 66

rational power, 63–64, 66

vital power, 63–64

Practical Intellect, (knowledge, wisdom), 103, 104–105, 119, 124, 129–130, 134

Priest (Cohen, Imam), 2, 19, 23, 45, 46, 69, 72, 82, 88, 103, 107, 116, 132, 200–201n.4

Proclus, 1

Public prophet, 34, 40, 48, 79, 109, 166, 176, 216n.125

Qur'an, 5

Reason of state, 167, 168, 172

Rehoboam, 122, 130, 133, 163–165

Renaissance, xi–xiii, xv, 6, 7, 23, 53, 61, 63, 70–71, 102, 143–166, 167, 170

Republic, Republicanism, 122, 168, 172, 176–177, 182, 183, 185

Revelation, 3, 18, 28, 182

Rhetoric, 71–72, 86, 89–90, 91, 95, 99, 100, 105, 224n.34

Robinson Crusoe, 58

Rome, 6, 150–151, 162, 163, 171

Romulus, 150, 151, 155, 156, 157, 158, 166, 169, 171

Rosenthal, E. I. J., xiv, 1, 19–20, 44–45, 48, 88, 91, 201–202n.6, 211n.67, 224n.32

Saadya Gaon, 5, 8, 10, 24

Sages, 8, 23, 61, 62, 63, 80, 84, 100, 112, 126

Amoraim, 8

Avot, 31, 32, 67–68, 70, 84, 100, 126

Ben Zoma, 69, 70, 74

Nittai the Arbelite, 208n.34

R. Judah, 8

R. Nehora'i, 8

R. Shemaya, 126

R. Simeon bar Yohai, 53, 57, 213–214n.98

Tanaim, 8

R. Yohanan, 126

Samuel, 7–8, 59, 112, 116, 122, 136, 138–139, 148, 149, 183, 187

Samuel ben Ali, 9

Samuel ben Hofni, 9

Samuel ben Judah of Marseilles, 2, 5, 63, 75, 82, 87–91, 102, 105, 106, 190–191, 200–201n.4

Sanhedrin, 116
Saul, 6, 8, 106, 107, 108, 128, 133, 135,
    137–139, 161, 183, 186–187
Savonarola, 157
Seneca, 144
Seth, 65, 66
Shalom, Abraham, 111, 125–134, 194
Sharia, 20
Sheba, queen of, 112
Shemita (fallow year), 172
Socrates, 15, 25, 40, 109, 168
Solomon, 6, 8, 10, 24, 26, 44, 53, 106,
    107, 111–113, 118–125, 133,
    142–143, 144–147, 150, 151,
    163–166, 168, 171, 183, 185
Solon, 156, 166, 169, 171
Sophists, 13, 71, 79
Soul, 13–14, 62, 63–66, 81
    Imaginative soul, 18, 34–35, 45, 84, 90,
        91, 117
    Practical soul, 4, 48
    Rational (intellectual, theoretical
        philosophical) soul, 4, 14, 18, 39, 45,
        48, 76–77, 96, 117, 119
Spain, 51, 120, 125
Sparta, 171
Spinoza, 6, 149, 167, 174–183, 185–186,
    187, 205n.2
    Political Treatise, 174–175, 177
    Theologico-Political Treatise, 174–183
State
    Ignorant state, 17, 76, 81, 83
    Islamic (Muslim) state, 20
    Platonic state, 4, 13–15, 61, 123

Righteous (ideal, perfect, virtuous)
    state, 13–15, 32, 57, 58, 61, 66, 76–77,
    81, 84, 87, 94, 111, 112, 185, 186
Wicked (evil) state, 32, 76
Strangers (gerim), 50, 59
Strauss, L., xii, 3, 7
Superstitions, 169, 171, 172

Tacitus, 169, 172
Temporal authority, 3, 65, 187
Theocracy, 7, 122, 177, 183
Theology. See also Political theology
Theseus, 150, 151, 155, 158
Three Crowns (ketarim), 8, 10, 23, 46,
    63, 116
Three Estates theory, 61
Torah, xi, 5, 7–8, 23, 26, 47, 51, 53, 65,
    72, 73, 86, 94, 98–101, 103–104,
    105–106, 113, 114, 116, 117, 118,
    119, 120, 127, 130–131, 134, 136,
    138, 139, 168, 171–172, 176,
    204n.14
Tyranny (despotism), 103, 109, 122,
    133, 142, 147–148, 171, 173

Ullmann, W., xiv
Utopia, 16, 42, 143, 149, 168, 173,
    174–175, 183

Venice, 168–169, 173, 185
Virgil, 168–169

Walzer, R., 1, 224n.34
Wolfson, H. O., 205n.2